A Student's Guide to 50 American Novels has been edited by Abraham H. Lass, a well-known teacher, school administrator, and writer. Mr. Lass is Principal of Abraham Lincoln High School in Brooklyn, New York, and the author of **How to Prepare for College, The College Student's Handbook, The Way to Write,** and many other works.

Equally well-known in the field of college counseling, Mr. Lass has for a number of years written a popular weekly column, "College and You," which has appeared in the *New York Herald Tribune, New York Post, Boston Traveler, The Detroit Free Press, The Philadelphia Inquirer,* and other newspapers.

The plot summaries, critical essays, and character analyses collected in this volume and its companion work, **A Student's Guide to 50 British Novels,** are designed to enrich the reader's understanding and appreciation of the great and famous books that are a vital part of our literary heritage. A special section, "How to Read a Novel," provides the reader with the basic skills and insights that will give his reading new and more meaningful dimensions.

A Student's Guide to
50 American Novels
edited by Abraham H. Lass
Principal, Abraham Lincoln High School, Brooklyn, New York

WSP

WASHINGTON SQUARE PRESS, INC. • NEW YORK

A STUDENT'S GUIDE TO 50 AMERICAN NOVELS

A *Washington Square Press* edition

1st printing.......................February, 1966
3rd printing.....................September, 1966

Published by
Washington Square Press, Inc., 630 Fifth Avenue, New York, N.Y.

L

WASHINGTON SQUARE PRESS editions are distributed in
the U.S. by Simon & Schuster, Inc., 630 Fifth Avenue,
New York, N.Y. 10020 and in Canada by Pocket Books
of Canada, Ltd., Richmond Hill, Ontario, Canada.

To Betty and Janet

Preface

Preface

"Of making many books there is no end," goes the complaint in *Ecclesiastes;* and the modern reader is tempted to add, "and much study of books-about-books is a weariness of the flesh."

What purposes, then, are to be served by this book?

We hope to reach two kinds of readers. First, the reader who is not yet the reader he wishes to be—who knows there is much in store for him, who has not tasted more than a portion of the feast, and who is grateful for a bill of fare. To him we offer an overview so that he may fall to with a whetted appetite. He will *know about* these novels (characters, plots, themes, styles) before he goes on to *know* them. Second, the reader who has sampled many of these novels and needs little more than a review of what he has already enjoyed or a reference guide as an ever-ready help for study.

For each novel we present:

1) an annotated list of the main characters
2) a full, clear, comprehensible summary of the significant incidents and themes
3) a biographical sketch of the author
4) a digest of present-day critical opinion of the novel, placing it in its proper context in the development of the novel and indicating how contemporary readers and critics evaluate it

While no selection of titles could please everyone, we believe that the novels chosen for this book will challenge the intelligent person to make his own rich and varied reading program. Here are the masterpieces and the milestones, the "classics and commercials," the great books and the near-great. Here are the seed books, the novels from which have sprung new novels and new ideas. All of them are still widely read and discussed. They are part of every reader's heritage.

If these novels have one thing in common despite differences in age and manners, it is that they have all (in Wordsworth's phrase) "kept watch o'er man's mortality." They have something everlasting to report to us about ourselves, and they report it in the syllables of art.

To read or to reread these novels—and this book will have achieved its purpose if it sends you back to the originals—is to take part in a magnificent adventure of the spirit: to understand what made D. H. Lawrence say, with an artist's pardonable license, "Being a novelist, I consider myself superior to the saint, the scientist, the philosopher, and the poet. The novel is the one bright book of life."

February 1966   A. H. L.

Contents

How To Read a Novel

Why do we pick up a novel? For the moment, the world we know is too much for us—or it is not enough. We seek surcease or discovery. And so we turn a page and step into another man's world.

In one novel we may find what Graham Greene calls "an entertainment," a tale unfolded for our enjoyment; we shall not even mind a few tears in the telling of it. In another novel perhaps we find a few of the answers. What we have only half suspected of human experience is blindingly clear in the author's searchlight; a facet of man has been illuminated.

Often a novel offers us both adventure and insight. Herman Melville in *Moby Dick* takes us on a heroic whaling voyage; from the moment we ship out of Nantucket with Ishmael and Queequeg and the harpooners, we are exploring strange waters on a mad quest. Yet it is a means to exploring ourselves. When we are home again we are richer for understanding certain profound ambiguities in Captain Ahab's, in all men's, nature.

Whatever the novel, it is well to look sharp in the writer's world. For each novel is the individual vision of an artist, his direct impression of reality. To share his discoveries we must look at the view he sees from his personal porthole. If every prospect immediately displeases and every man seems vile, we may be allowing our prejudices to come between us and the writer's sights. (Tom Sawyer so troubled the good ladies of nineteenth-century Brooklyn that they had him banished from the public library; Huckleberry Finn was condemned as subversive of the morals of youth, as indeed he is, if youth are bound to such widely accepted principles as the sanctity of law, property, and public opinion over the sanctity of man.) Before we complain to the novelist that we find his country uninhabitable, we should be humble and permit him to show us its "manners, climates, councils, governments."

The Novelist's View of Reality

Very well, says the reader with humility to the novelist, show me a slice of life.

Novelist *A* may choose to cut his slice horizontally; Novelist *B*, vertically. The method calls for close attention.

A, following a straight chronological line, begins at the beginning of his hero's story, goes on through the middle until he comes to the end, and stops. Pete Prentiss is born, attends school, falls in love with Lucille Lambent, serves in the army, and (after a suitable number of interesting complications linked by character and motive) marries or dies.

B, on the other hand, is going to ignore chronology and cut Pete down the middle for our examination; like Macbeth, he'll "unseam" him from the nave to the chaps. He will disclose his memories, joys, agonies, reveries—with no respect to time. There will be a flashback to Kitten Huxley's cocktail party, when Lucille first met that awful Mike Ebsen, and Pete had the strange talk with the Swami Vitrananda. If Novelist *B* is quite modern, he will not end his novel, but will leave his hero (who is not a hero at all) in the middle of a moment of consciousness which can be traced backward or forward in time, as the reader wishes.

The meaning of reality, the nature of the real, has been a point of dispute among novelists, as between philosophers and physicists, for more than half a century. One of the most illuminating quarrels was carried on between Virginia Woolf and a group of novelists—Arnold Bennett, H. G. Wells, John Galsworthy—whose "materialism" seemed to Mrs. Woolf to be the negation of life. In *Mr. Bennett and Mrs. Brown*, she pointed out how these novelists had crowded out reality with the furniture of their novels; they had laid so much dull stress on environment, social setting, the fabric instead of the substance, that the essence of being had escaped them.

In a famous statement in her essay "Modern Fiction" in *The Common Reader*, Mrs. Woolf puts the case for all the novelists of sensibility, the "stream of consciousness" stylists, who were to follow. "Life is not a series of gig-lamps symmetrically arranged," said Mrs. Woolf (demolishing Novelist *A*); life is "*a luminous halo, a semi-transparent envelope*" which surrounds man from the beginning of consciousness to the end.

Mrs. Woolf developed her own luminous style—a delicate and subtle handling of those currents of consciousness where she believed the truth of "reality" lay—in her novels *Mrs. Dalloway, To the Lighthouse,* and *The Waves.* In the work of many of our contemporaries, as in Mrs. Woolf's and in Joyce's work, the stream of consciousness has become an almost lyrical flow.

For one of Mrs. Woolf's characters, Mrs. Ramsay in *To the Lighthouse,* when life sinks down for a moment and there is no need to act, the range of implicit experience seems limitless. In the depth of being herself, "a wedge-shaped core of darkness," she triumphs over life; things come together in "this peace, this rest, this eternity."

This is a very different kind of reality, of course, from that in many novels, or for that matter in many people's experience. Meeting it in prose fiction today, the reader does well to approach it as he approaches the reality of a poem: with a response to its rhythms, its imagery, its timeless flow of memories and impressions.

Character in the Novel

Mr. Bennett and Mrs. Woolf were agreed on one point at least: The essential concern of the novelist is with "character in itself"; only if the characters are real has the novel any chance of surviving. "The only classification of the novel that I can understand," wrote Henry James in *The Art of Fiction,* "is into that which has life and that which has it not."

The characters above all in a novel can *solace* us, in E. M. Forster's words. We who can hardly understand ourselves, much less one another, in our imperfect world, meet in the novelist's world "a more comprehensible and thus a more manageable human race" and we have the enormously comforting illusion of understanding, at last, the secret, invisible truth of people.

When the reader puts together all the clues to character that the novelist has included in his book, when he perceives the truth of Ahab or Mr. Dimmesdale or Martin Eden or Isabel Archer, even though none of these may know it of himself, he is almost like the Creator in all-knowing wisdom.

Yet, according to Elizabeth Bowen, a sensitive novelist and, in her "Notes on Writing a Novel," a most illuminating critic, characters are not *created* by the novelist at all. They are *found;* they pre-exist in his consciousness and reveal themselves slowly to his perception as he is writing, as might "fellow-travellers seated opposite one in a dimly lit railway carriage."

What the novelist is inviting the reader to do, then, is to *recognize* the people of the novel as they play their roles in the story.

We use the word *play* advisedly: The people of the novelist's world are very busy every moment. They are making choices of alternative behavior; they are speaking or not speaking in a certain way; when they are not around, they are being discussed by other characters.

To recognize Sister Carrie, the reader of Dreiser's pages might well imagine that he is watching her in a drama literally played upon a stage. He may ask himself the same questions about the people in a novel that he subconsciously asks about the figures in grease paint who move before footlights:

What is the effect on these people of the *setting* they are in?

What do I know of the *antecedent action?*

What signs of *motive* do I perceive?

Where are the evidences of *conflict* (within and without)?

How does this person see himself? How does he wish others to see him? How is he seen by others?

How does he give himself away—in gesture, inflection, choice of words?

Where is the *climax* of this person's conflict? Is it inevitable in terms of what has gone before?

And so on. It is a game only a little different from the one the reader plays every day. Listening to his neighbor protest, "I am the last person in the world to gossip," he knows her for a talebearer; trying to solve the riddle of the face opposite him in the subway (eyes full of pain, slack mouth, shaving-cut on chin), he wonders what the combination of all these features means. In novels, however, the characters are explicable; the writer has willed it so. If the reader is perceptive enough, he can pluck out the heart of each man's mystery.

Sometimes the clues are tiny. Every reader understands the significant event, the major decision. But it is also a revealing incident, says Henry James, when a woman stands up with her hand resting on a table and looks at you in a certain way. A chance word or sigh, Forster reminds us, is just as much evidence of character as a speech or a murder.

The playwright, of course, has always understood this, and that is why we urge the reader of novels to behave as if he were watching a play.

Chekhov, in whose dramas there is no melodrama, only the reverberation of the thousand small shocks that make life palpable, said in one of his letters that the things that happen onstage should be as complex and yet as simple as they are in daily life. "For instance, people are having a meal at a table, just having a meal, but at the same time their happiness is being created, or their lives are being smashed up."

How many meals are eaten in novels! And every one of them is "evidence." Ethan Frome, having supper alone with Mattie Silver after his wife, Zeena, has gone to Bettsbridge, inarticulately expresses his love in a dozen ways. Wang Lung, because it is the morning of his wedding day, sprinkles a dozen curled dried leaves of tea into the boiling water in his father's breakfast bowl; the old man protests that it is like eating silver, but drinks greedily, and we understand the poverty of the good earth and the hunger of age, so like a child's eagerness for its feeding. Little Pip, in Dicken's *Great Expectations*, is judged "naterally wicious" by all the company at Mrs. Joe Gargery's Christmas dinner, but we know that he is eating his heart out, along with his dinner.

(In Dickens, by the way, there are few characters, and many caricatures: The people are the same each time they appear. They never surprise us. They are readily identifiable by tag lines and stock reactions. Mr. Micawber is predictably optimistic; Uriah Heep consistently 'umble. According to E. M. Forster's terminology, useful in modern fiction also, such "flat" characters, or static figures, are in contrast to "round" characters, who develop and behave unpredictably, though always inevitably. Elizabeth Bowen believes that ideal novels should contain only "round" characters—yet what a pity to lose Dickens's people on a literary technicality! Genius, having created and populated a world, can also animate it with "flats.")

Living characters in novels, once fully perceived, are life-stretchers for us all. We love, hate, suffer, comprehend with them vicariously. They satisfy our hunger to share the news about the human condition. Real people have a way of keeping themselves to themselves; characters in books open their hearts. We know what Huck Finn went through trying to decide what to do with the runaway slave he loved. We share every moment of Henry Fleming's first experience of battle.

Sharing is a two-way journey. What is the reader's part? Empathy, imaginative sympathy, understanding of human values. As the characters grow larger in our imagination and in our sympathy, they take on meanings larger than themselves, possibly larger than life. Ahab is no longer the captain of the *Pequod,* but the symbol of all obsessive pursuit of the unattainable.

At the very least, the reader of novels will have, as Thoreau did at Walden, a great deal of company in his house, especially in the morning, when nobody calls.

The Novelist at Work

"Why should a story not be told in the most irregular fashion that the author's idiosyncrasy may prompt, provided that he gives us what we can enjoy?" asked George Eliot, in her *Leaves from a Notebook.* "The dear public would do well to reflect that they are often bored from the want of flexibility in their own minds. They are like the topers of 'one liquor.' "

No two novelists are alike; there are as many kinds of novel today—there have always been as many kinds of novel—as there are readers to discover them. Without too much literary analysis, it is possible to satisfy one's curiosity about the way in which a novelist has set about making us enjoy his book.

Here is a brief list of checkpoints. Each novelist will have approached a checkpoint in his own way.

Description of the Characters

The story-teller is no painter, but he must leave images in the reader's mind.

Here is Billy Budd as Melville first pictures him for us:

> He was young; and despite his all but fully developed frame, in aspect looked even younger than he really was. This was owing to a lingering adolescent expression in the as yet smooth face, all but feminine in purity of natural complexion, but where, thanks to his seagoing, the lily was quite suppressed and the rose had some ado visibly to flush through the tan.

Obvious? But more will be demanded from the reader before he will be able to see Billy. The young foretopman, says the novelist,

> showed in face that humane look of reposeful good nature which the Greek sculptor in some instances gave to his heroic strong man, Hercules.

That sentence calls for background. Melville will set his picture up for you only if you will collaborate with him.

In *The Old Man and the Sea*, Hemingway recreates reality —his reality—with such precision of vivid detail that the whole world seems to be his own invention. For example, here is his description of the old man catching a dolphin:

> Just before it was dark, as they passed a great island of Sargasso weed that heaved and swung in the light sea as though the ocean were making love with something under a yellow blanket, his small line was taken by a dolphin. He saw it first when it jumped in the air, true gold in the last of the sun and bending and flapping wildly in the air. It jumped again and again in the acrobatics of its fear and he worked his way back to the stern and crouching and holding the big line with his right hand and arm, he pulled the dolphin in with his left hand, stepping on the gained line each time with his bare left foot. When

the fish was at the stern, plunging and cutting from side
to side in desperation, the old man leaned over the stern
and lifted the burnished gold fish with its purple spots
over the stern. Its jaws were working convulsively in
quick bites against the hook and it pounded the bottom of
the skiff with its long flat body, its tail and its head until
he clubbed it across the shining golden head until it
shivered and was still.

To experience this passage is to know not only fish and man
but the novelist as well. Who else could have written this?

Point of View

"The whole intricate question of method, in the craft of fiction, I take to be governed by the question of the *point of
view*—the question of the relation in which the narrator
stands to the story." And Percy Lubbock goes on to say (in
The Craft of Fiction) that the novelist can describe his characters from the outside, as an impartial or partial observer; or
from the inside, as a presumably omniscient force. He can also
take the viewpoint of one character who does not know the
motives of the others.

Although Henry James felt that the novelist should stick to
one point of view in a story and not shift arbitrarily, E. M.
Forster has been able to cite a number of instances where a
novelist has been able to manage more than one shift rather
well. For our part it matters very little how the novelist manages his camera-eye just so he puts in focus for us a world that
is both plausible and lasting. What he shows us will depend
on his *moral* lens.

Stendhal, writing to Balzac says: "I see but one rule, *to be
clear*. If I am not clear, all my world crumbles to nothing."

Plot, Story, Theme

These are words to play with. When they are well handled
by a writer, the reader does not have to notice them at all. But

if you lift an eyebrow at such cavalier treatment of textbook terms, here are some definitions:

> The *story* is the answer to "And then what happened?"
> The *plot* tells us why it happened just so.
> The *theme* explains why the writer had to tell this particular story.

Or, in the delightful simplicity of *Aspects of a Novel*: "The King died and then the Queen died" is a story. "The King died and then the Queen died of grief" is a plot. (We do not have a theme for this yet.)

Causality is everything. Well, nearly everything. In his introduction to Henry James's *The Princess Casamassima*, Lionel Trilling outlines a story which has run through a number of nineteenth-century English, continental, and American novels, the story of The Young Man from the Provinces. Of humble and often mysterious birth, intelligent and proud, he moves into society, making great demands on life.

In one way or another, this is the skeleton of *The Red and the Black, Great Expectations,* and the later *The Great Gatsby.* Yet plot, story, theme are nothing without the essence of all, which is the novelist's personal idiom, his statement outside logic or causality, a statement poetic in that it is always its own excuse for being.

And that brings us to the question of style.

Style

In Leo Tolstoi's *Talks with Tolstoi,* we have the following description of a writer's approach to his art:

> Sophia Andreevna said: 'It was the last time Turgenev stayed at Yasnaya, not long before his death. I asked him: 'Ivan Sergeevich, why don't you write now?' He answered: 'In order to write I had always to be a little in love. Now I am old I can't fall in love any more, and that is why I have stopped writing.'

And Tolstoi himself, speaking in exasperation:

One ought only to write when one leaves a piece of one's flesh in the ink-pot each time one dips one's pen.

Lest you think, "Ah well, the Russians—!" here is another novelist's statement of what it means to write. Arnold Bennett, in his *Journals*:

The novelist should cherish and burnish this faculty of seeing crudely, simply, artlessly, ignorantly; of seeing like a baby or a lunatic, who lives each moment by itself and tarnishes by the present no remembrance of the past.

There we have it: On every page of his novel, the writer has left his signature for us to read. The oldest quotation of all, Buffon's "The style is the man," is still the most accurate.

And now we come back to the question of how to read a novel. Why, by sitting down in an armchair, seeing that there is a good light over our left shoulder, and turning the page.

Here we are in another man's world.

February 1966   A. H. L.

The Nineteenth
Century

The Last of the Mohicans

by

JAMES FENIMORE COOPER (1789–1851)

Main Characters

Natty Bumppo—(known, too, as Leatherstocking, "La Longue Carabine" or Long Rifle, Hawkeye, and at other times in his career, as Deerslayer and Pathfinder): Tall, lean, hard, a supreme woodsman and a natural moralist. Proud and loyal, he speaks sometimes like a backwoodsman and sometimes like a philosopher.

Chingachgook—The "noble savage"—a Mohican of the Delaware family, silent, a fierce enemy and devoted friend, the soul of honor and a master of woodsman's lore.

Uncas—His son, an even nobler savage, the "last of the Mohicans," an Indian Adonis, without fear and without deceit.

Magua—The wicked Indian, handsome, eloquent, but treacherous. The inheritor of the most fearsome qualities of the Hurons (or Mingoes, in the language of the Delawares), he has also developed the most reprehensible characteristics of the whites.

Colonel Munro—Commander of the besieged Fort William Henry, an affectionate father, a resolute soldier, now a gallant old man despite military and personal misfortunes.

Cora—His eldest daughter, beautiful, high-spirited, indomitable, in her early twenties. Her "charged color" betokens the "dark" half of her origin.

3

Alice—Cora's blonde half sister, four or five years younger
than Cora, dazzling to look at, but timid and easily overwhelmed by circumstances.

Major Duncan Heyward—A colonial officer, brave, honorable,
forthright, a bit pompous, ignorant of Indian ways and war-
fare. He loves Alice Munro.

David Gamut—The lank, awkward, ingenious psalmodist
whose main ambition is to sing and teach the songs of
David (in very poor translations) and who is capable of
remarkable fortitude.

The Story

The year is 1757. Fort William Henry, near Lake Cham-
plain in upper New York, commanded by Colonel Munro, is
under siege by the French and by the Huron Indians (Mingoes). Cora and Alice Munro set out from Fort Edward along
the Hudson to join their father. In their party are an ungainly
and eccentric teacher of psalmody, David Gamut; a gallant
young officer, Major Duncan Heyward; and a fierce, cunning
Indian guide, Magua. Magua misleads them. Pretending to
have lost the way, he takes them into Huron territory. Luckily
their path crosses that of Natty Bumppo, the intrepid scout,
and his two Indian companions, Chingachgook and his brave
son Uncas, the "last of the Mohicans." Quickly they agree to
seize Magua. But before they can act, Magua escapes into the
forest.

Realizing that the hostile Mingoes surround the party, the
scout makes the party wait till dark. Then, while his Indian
companions hide the horses, he leads the others to a canoe
that he has hidden among the bushes, and ferries them to an
island. Here there is a cavern where they can rest in relative
safety. But the horses, set upon by wolves, scream in terror,
and the Mingoes discover and attack their enemies. The scout,
an infallible shot (nicknamed "La Longue Carabine"), picks
off the boldest Mingoes on the opposite shore.

Natty and his friends have run out of ammunition. Resolutely the fugitives wait, determined to meet death bravely. Cora,
the elder and more spirited of the sisters, urges them to escape.
Somewhat unwillingly, the scout, Uncas, and Chingachgook

cast themselves into the current to emerge at a distant point in the forest opposite. Major Heyward, David Gamut, and the ladies are captured and hurried along a trail by the Hurons. Cora breaks branches to mark their path till one of the Indian rear guard stops her, pointing significantly to his tomahawk. During a pause in the march, Magua offers to release Alice if Cora will come to his wigwam as his wife. Cora rejects him. Maddened, Magua hurls his tomahawk at Alice. It misses and quivers above her head. Heyward bursts his bonds, hurling himself at one of the savages. The savage slips from his grasp, raises his knife—when suddenly a rifle cracks and the Indian falls dead.

Natty, Chingachgook, and Uncas have come to the rescue. A fierce battle follows, in which the captors are overcome but Magua escapes. Natty then explains that he and his Indian comrades have been following their trail all along.

Once again the party sets out for Fort Henry which is surrounded by Montcalm's forces. Luckily a dense fog has settled over the Fort, obscuring them from the enemy, but causing them to lose their way. The keen-eyed Uncas, however, lights upon the furrow of a cannon ball fired from the Fort and gives them their bearings.

The reunion between Colonel Munro and his daughters is affecting. Nevertheless, since the Fort is threatened, Natty and Heyward must go about their separate duties. Natty, back from a mission to Fort Edward to deliver the Colonel's plea to Webb, the British commander, is captured. General Montcalm releases him, after taking from him the letter from Webb, and invites Munro to a personal interview. In his place, Munro sends Heyward, who cannot get any relevant information from Montcalm. Upon Heyward's return, Munro insists that he disclose his feelings before reporting on his mission. Heyward then confesses his love for Alice—much to Munro's disapproval, since he thinks that Cora, the daughter of his mulatto first wife, has been rejected because of her mixed blood. After Heyward, with less than complete candor, reassures him, the Colonel listens to Heyward's report and decides to go with him to Montcalm.

Montcalm shows them the letter from Webb who declares that he cannot send reinforcements to the Fort and counsels surrender. Shattered, the Colonel determines to resist despite

the odds. He is dissuaded by Montcalm, who offers him honorable terms of surrender. Munro accepts.

But Montcalm cannot control the savagery of his Indian followers. They attack a party of women and children leaving
the Fort and slaughter them without mercy. Magua, their
leader, again captures Cora and Alice, along with Gamut, who
does his futile best to protect them. Magua leads his prisoners
to the camp of the Hurons, among whom he is a chief (though
in disgrace for his addiction to firewater). He gives Alice into
their custody, leading Cora to the camp of the nearby Delaware tribe.

But Natty and his Indian friends are on the trail, with
Munro and Heyward. They arrive at the Huron camp where
they see Gamut who has escaped confinement because the
Hurons think he is mad. Heyward decides to enter the Huron
camp, disguised as a healer. He is tentatively accepted by the
Indians, and one even requests his services for his stricken
daughter-in-law. But before Heyward can oblige, Uncas is
captured and the Hurons hold a council to decide his fate.

On the way to the sick woman, Heyward and the Huron are
followed by a bear. The Huron knows that the bear is a local
magician, but Heyward does not and is understandably nervous. Left alone to perform his ministrations, Heyward sees the
bear remove his head: Natty Bumppo is revealed! The two
now make their way to the chamber of the cave where Alice is
imprisoned. Magua surprises them but is subdued by Natty.
Heyward and Natty escape, carrying Alice to the Delaware
camp. Natty then returns to the Hurons and in his bear outfit
rescues Uncas.

The party reach the Delaware camp again, but Magua follows them, demanding the sisters and denouncing Natty.
When Heyward pretends to be "La Longue Carabine," Natty
displays his unbelievable prowess as a marksman to establish
his identity. The ancient Delaware chief Tamemund comes
forward to listen to Magua's argument that he be given all the
English prisoners. Tamemund agrees, but Cora pleads that
Uncas be allowed to speak. Uncas's brave demeanor impresses
the Delawares, but Tamemund nevertheless pronounces his
doom. One of the Delawares rips Uncas's hunting shirt and
leaps back astonished, for beautifully tattooed on Uncas's

breast is the figure of a small tortoise, the totem of the Mohicans, the race from which the Delawares spring.

Tamemund welcomes Uncas as the chief who will succeed him. Magua, however, demands Cora, since she is his hostage according to Delaware law. Though Hawkeye offers to take her place, Magua's demand is granted. Uncas warns Magua that he will pursue him as soon as sundown arrives. Magua laughs scornfully and leaves.

At sundown the Delawares pursue, aided by Heyward and Natty. There is a devastating fire fight. The battle seems to be going against the Delawares when the Colonel and Chingachgook, who have remained hidden in a nearby beaver dam, appear and turn the tide. The Hurons are destroyed or scattered—all except Magua, who with two of his men seizes Cora and escapes. But Uncas follows—to his doom. Magua buries his knife in the Mohican, while another Indian kills Cora. Magua bounds over the rocks and almost eludes his pursuers—but Natty's rifle finds its mark and Magua falls from a precipice to his death.

At the Delaware camp there is deep mourning. Chingachgook laments the death of his noble son, the Colonel his courageous daughter. After solemn burial ceremonies, the whites return to their civilization—all except Natty, who remains with Chingachgook.

Critical Opinion

Cooper's *Leatherstocking Tales* have firmly imprinted on the minds of Americans and Europeans an image of the Indian and the frontiersman. That the image is violently distorted may be regrettable. It is apparently ineradicable as well. The novels, published at different times in Cooper's long career, create a powerful myth of early America—its brave and incredibly capable frontiersmen, its wicked and noble savages, its wide, beautiful virgin forests, its gradual and reluctant acceptance of civilization. Listed according to *Leatherstocking's* chronology, they are *The Deerslayer* (1841), in which Natty is a young man; *The Last of the Mohicans* (1826) and *The Pathfinder* (1840), Natty from age thirty-five to thirty-nine;

The Pioneers (1823), which finds Natty in his seventies; and
The Prairie (1827), in which Natty is an old man past eighty.

Of all the novels, *The Last of the Mohicans* is the most attractive. Here we find the noble Chingachgook and his nobler son Uncas, the exciting chases, pursuits, and rescues, the splendid panorama of the fresh and vital American land. The novel is marked by Cooper's faults, too: the wooden speech of the characters, the incidents that exceed not only belief but possibility, the plot endlessly coiling back upon itself. Mark Twain has summarized all the negative criticisms in his hilarious attempt to prove that Cooper simply could not manage to tell a story.

Yet Cooper still holds his readers. The breathless action of *The Last of the Mohicans,* the continuous excitement it generates, the animated pictures it paints of woods, camps, and settlements ("some of the loveliest, most glamorous pictures in all literature," D. H. Lawrence says), its poetic, pastoral vision of a frontier life, justify its great and continuing popularity. It is one of the supreme narratives of adventure in American literature.

The Author

James Fenimore Cooper was born in 1789 in Burlington, New Jersey. When Cooper was a year old, his father settled in Lake Otsego, in southern New York, where he owned a vast tract of land (now Cooperstown). In this semi-frontier area (from which the Indians had departed much earlier), Cooper was brought up to be an active country gentleman. After being tutored privately, he entered Yale College, from which he was expelled for setting off a small explosion in another student's room. In 1806, at his father's suggestion, Cooper shipped to England as a common sailor on a merchant vessel; later, however, he was commissioned and served three years in the U.S. Navy, resigning after his father's death to take over the management of the family estate. In 1811, he married Susan Augusta DeLancey, daughter of a wealthy Westchester landowner whose family had been staunchly Tory during the Revolution.

It seemed hardly likely that Cooper would become an

author. He hated even to write a letter. But in 1819, he boasted to his unbelieving wife that he could write a better novel than the one they were reading together. She challenged him. The result was *Precaution* (1820), a polite and moralistic tale laid in England. *The Spy* (1821) was a far more significant work, employing American backgrounds and characters and enjoying an enormous success.

From the age of thirty-one to his death, Cooper wrote thirty-three novels, besides a number of volumes of travel, social commentary, and naval history. The most important are of course the *Leatherstocking Tales*, the saga of Natty Bumppo and America's receding frontier: *The Pioneers* (1823), *The Last of the Mohicans* (1826), *The Prairie* (1827), *The Pathfinder* (1840), and *The Deerslayer* (1841). Cooper's sea stories, too, especially *The Pilot* (1823), *The Red Rover* (1828), and *The Two Admirals* (1842), are brisk and vigorous fiction, and nautically authentic besides.

For seven years (from 1826 to 1833), Cooper lived in Europe both to improve his health and to protect the European rights to his books. While he was there, Cooper's ardent patriotism was aroused by unfair British attacks on America, and he attempted to answer them in *Notions of the Americans* (1828). However, when he returned to America he was severely critical of the changes effected by Jacksonian democracy in the years he had been abroad. In *The American Democrat* (1838), he incorporated his objections which were considered thoroughly objectionable by the majority of his countrymen.

The last seventeen years of Cooper's life were spent in a series of battles for aristocratic social principles coupled (as his enemies generally failed to observe) with democratic political principles. The lawsuits—for libelous assaults upon him, and for infringements on his property—to which he devoted his energies (successfully, as a rule) made his final years troubled ones. He died at Cooperstown in 1851, recognized throughout the world as America's first great novelist.

Billy Budd—Foretopman

by

HERMAN MELVILLE (1819–1891)

Main Characters

Billy Budd—Foretopman of the *Indomitable*, a handsome, innocent, cheerful sailor who generates good will and who is falsely accused by Claggart.

Claggart—Master-at-arms on the *Indomitable*, an intelligent, smooth-spoken, malignant petty officer.

Captain Vere—Captain of the *Indomitable*, a stern but fair intellectual for whom the good of the British Navy takes precedence over all other considerations.

The Story

Billy Budd, foretopman of the H.M.S. *Indomitable* in the year 1797, is extraordinarily genial and good-looking. But more, he generates the kind of amiability and good will that turns even a surly and disgruntled crew into a cheerful and united one. Admired by officers and men alike, Billy is the model of "the handsome sailor." He has been impressed from an English merchantman, *Rights-of-Man*, aboard the *Indomitable*, and he accepts his new status gracefully.

Billy, however, incurs the enmity of Claggart, the master-at-arms, a petty officer who functions as a sort of police chief. Claggart, a spare, apparently balanced man of superior intelligence, hates Billy for reasons that may not be easily fathomed —perhaps simply the natural antagonism that evil feels for innocence. He torments Billy in a number of underhanded ways that Billy does not at all suspect. Even when he is told by a grizzled old seaman that Claggart is down on him, that Claggart has been disarranging his gear and is thus responsible for the dressing down that Billy has been receiving from other petty officers—even then Billy can scarcely believe that Claggart could be so hostile to him.

Soon Claggart attempts a more vicious tactic. He directs one of his minions to approach Billy and offer him a bribe if he will join in a plot against the ship's officers. Billy rejects the tempter, but he does not divulge the offer to anyone.

Claggart, progressively maddened by Billy's innocence and goodness, finally takes overt action. He approaches the commanding officer of the *Indomitable*, Captain Vere. Vere has proved his value to the Navy more than once. An intrepid officer, strict but fair, dedicated to his task and remarkably efficient, Vere is subject to criticism only on the grounds of his intellectual, almost scholarly temperament. To him, Claggart makes an astonishing accusation: that Billy Budd has been fomenting disaffection aboard the *Indomitable*, very likely mustering the men for mutiny. Despite his dislike of Claggart and his doubts about the truth of the accusation, Vere has Billy summoned.

Billy has one flaw. Under emotional stress, he stammers and gurgles, and can speak only with the greatest difficulty. This proves to be tragic. For when Claggart repeats his accusation before Billy, the latter is stricken dumb. Urged by Vere to speak, Billy strikes out instead. His right arm shoots forward, and Claggart, who receives the blow full upon the forehead, falls to the deck. Though Vere, Billy, and then the ship's surgeon try to revive him, their efforts are fruitless. Claggart is dead.

The Captain calls a drumhead court composed of three officers. He will not wait till the ship reaches shore because the late mutinies make immediate disciplinary action imperative. Billy testifies that he had not intended to kill Claggart—that could he have spoken he would not have struck the blow. The court believes him and seems inclined to leniency. But Captain Vere insists that the court has one matter to consider and only one: not the motives or the provocation but simply the consequences of the blow, the deed itself. It is to be concerned not with speculative natural justice but with rigorous martial law. Billy may be acquitted by God, not by the court-martial proceeding under the law of the Mutiny Act. There is no arguing against the Captain's brief. Billy is sentenced to be hanged at the yardarm next morning.

Billy spends the night in an agony proceeding less from fear than from realization of the diabolical in some men. Captain Vere visits him, but what passes between them remains unknown. Next morning, after a brief session with the Chaplain, Billy speaks his last sentence, "God bless Captain Vere!"

A singular event occurs when Billy's body reaches the end of the yardarm. No muscular spasm is discerned, a singularity that the officers discuss without arriving at an explanation. The sailors' reaction to Billy's death is evidenced by the legends and stories and ballads that soon spring up. Billy becomes a kind of folk hero to them. As for Captain Vere, not long after, he falls in battle when the *Indomitable* engages the *Atheiste*. His last words are "Billy Budd, Billy Budd."

Critical Opinion

Billy Budd—Foretopman, written in the last decade of Melville's life, was not published until 1924, thirty years after the author's death. It is now generally considered one of his major works, his final statement about man's condition on earth. What the statement means, however, has been argued vigorously. Most critics regard it as Melville's "testament of acceptance." Billy Budd, symbol of innocence, of natural virtue, is disgraced. Following a natural impulse, he strikes and accidentally kills his false accuser. As a result, he is condemned to be hanged.

And rightly, for this world is a battleship of sorts. A battleship has one reason for being: to fulfill a mission—the destruction of an enemy. But to accomplish the mission, it must be rigorously governed—by martial rules, by discipline, by rank. Billy breaks the chain of command and so must be punished. However, it is only in this battleship world—where right and wrong are pragmatic by necessity, where justice is keyed to mission—that Billy's sentence is "right" and "just." Before God's great judgment seat—where absolute right prevails, where justice is keyed to motive and intent—Billy will be rewarded. Billy, who at times resembles Adam in his innocence and Christ in his agony, perhaps represents virtuous man, whose purposes a diabolical force (Claggart) distorts, while God (Vere) looks unhappily on—bound by His own laws.

On the other hand, a few critics regard *Billy Budd* as another chapter in Melville's long pessimistic commentary on man, God, and destiny. They insist that it is not different from *Moby Dick* or *Pierre* in essence, that it extends Melville's rejection of the world as it is. Thus the short novel must be read with a continuous awareness of its ironies, and Billy's final cry, "God bless Captain Verel," masks Melville's real meaning. In any event, *Billy Budd* has a fascinating surface. Its subsurface interpretation will continue to excite critics for a long time to come.

Moby Dick

by

HERMAN MELVILLE

Main Characters

Ishmael—The narrator, a young man who goes to sea whenever life on land makes him feel desperate.

Queequeg—A tattooed cannibal, Starbuck's harpooner, who is a brave and generous comrade to Ishmael.

Ahab—Captain of the *Pequod*, a blighted man whose relentless pursuit of the great white whale, Moby Dick, strips him of human sympathies.

Starbuck—First mate of the *Pequod*, a courageous and rational man who tries ineffectively to turn Ahab from his obsession.

Stubb—Second mate of the *Pequod*, a man whose function in
    life is killing whales and who consequently has become
    more of an instrument than a human being.
Flask—Third mate of the *Pequod*, careless, mindless, fearless.
Tashtego—A Gay Head Indian, harpooner for Stubb.
Daggoo—A gigantic Negro savage, harpooner for Flask.
Fedallah—A mysterious Parsee, Ahab's harpooner, possessed
    of occult powers and, it may be, in league with diabolical
    ones.
Father Mapple—The eloquent preacher of the Whaleman's
    Chapel at New Bedford.

The Story

Ishmael, the narrator, having little money and finding
life on shore grim, decides to go to sea. Quitting Manhattan,
he journeys to New Bedford and puts up at the Spouter Inn.
To his consternation, he discovers that his roommate is a
tattooed cannibal named Queequeg who prays to a Congo
idol and is armed with a tomahawk that does double duty as
a pipe. Queequeg, however, proves to be a really amiable
young man. After sharing the same bed for a night, he and
Ishmael become firm friends. Next morning being Sunday,
Ishmael goes to the Whaleman's Chapel where he hears an
eloquent sermon preached by Father Mapple, once a whaler
himself. His subject is Jonah; his theme (of central importance): "If we obey God, we must disobey ourselves."

Ishmael joins forces with Queequeg whose essential nobility he comes to realize. They take passage to Nantucket
where they hope to sign aboard a whaling ship. On the way
Queequeg first chastens a bumpkin who mimics him, then
rescues him when he falls overboard. At Nantucket, the pair
find the *Pequod* and Queequeg's remarkable skill with the
harpoon quickly gets them berths aboard her. The Quaker
owners, however, promise Ishmael a very small portion of the
proceeds to accrue from the voyage. Though Ishmael and
Queequeg are warned by a ragged old sailor named Elijah not
to sail on the *Pequod*, they disregard his dire prophecies.

Not till the *Pequod* is well under way does Ahab, captain
of the vessel, appear. A tall, broad man seemingly made of

bronze, Ahab is blighted. A livid white scar, superstitiously attributed to his strife with the elements, threads its way down from his gray hair. He has a white leg, made from the jaw of a sperm whale. His own leg was snapped off by Moby Dick, a huge white whale, the source of terrifying stories. Before long, Ahab's relentless mission becomes clear: he is determined to pursue Moby Dick and kill him.

Ahab soon summons the entire ship's company and nailing a Spanish gold coin to the mainmast, promises that it shall belong to the man who first raises the white whale. Then, his passionate eloquence overriding all resistance, he pledges the crew to his purpose in flagons of rum. By force of his will, he compels the mates to cross their lances while he grasps them at their center—a kind of diabolical communion. Finally he fills the hollow sockets of the harpooners' harpoons with rum and bids them drink to the death of Moby Dick.

The three mates provide intriguing contrasts. Starbuck, the first mate, is a brave but rational man who hunts whales simply to make his living. Only he opposes Ahab's monomaniacal drive, albeit futilely, since he does not have Ahab's intensity or power. Stubb, the second mate, is a human instrument for the destruction of whales. Flask, the third mate, is careless, mindless, fearless. For the whaleboat he commands, each mate has the harpooner corresponding to his temperament—Starbuck has Queequeg; Stubb has Tashtego, a Gay Head Indian; Flask has Daggoo, a gigantic Negro savage.

As the *Pequod* cruises, she encounters other ships and stops for gams (gossip). There is the *Bachelor,* homeward bound, laden with whale oil, manned by a crew pleasantly occupied with the Polynesian girls who have eloped with them. There is the *Jeroboam,* which has suffered from closing with Moby Dick and which carries a mad prophet, Gabriel, who warns that the white whale is God. And most disheartening, there is the *Rachel,* which has lost a whaleboat among whose crew was the Captain's twelve-year-old son. Though the Captain has long been a comrade of Ahab's, Ahab will not join in the search for the missing boy.

Ahab alienates himself more and more from the human condition. He throws his pipe overboard, an act that points up his rejection of such homely pleasures as might be afforded by his home, his young wife, his child. He broods, curses, despairs—but he persists in his quest for Moby Dick. Starbuck attempts to bring him back to some consideration for his men, but he rejects the mate's persuasions. Only to Pip, the small Negro boy, half-crazed from narrowly escaping death by water, does Ahab show even the remotest kindliness.

A symbol of Ahab's progressive dehumanization is Fedallah, the leader of the group of Parsees (Persian fire-worshipers) whom Ahab has smuggled on board. Fedallah serves as Ahab's harpooner, perhaps his evil spirit as well, for he is almost always present when Ahab performs any of his defiant, diabolical acts. Ahab baptizes the lance fashioned by the ship's blacksmith, using the blood of the three pagan harpooners as the baptismal fluid, not in the name of the Father but in the name of the devil. With the Parsee watching, Ahab destroys the ship's quadrant. Again, during a great storm in which corposants (glowing balls of flame) tip all the yardarms, Ahab places his foot on the Parsee, grasps the mainmast links, and defies the lightning. After the thunder reverses the compasses, Ahab constructs others with the sailmaker's needles.

It is Fedallah, too, who issues the strange prophecy that heartens Ahab because he misconstrues it. Fedallah declares that Ahab can have neither hearse nor coffin; before he dies he must see two hearses at sea, the first not made by mortal hands, the wood of the second grown in America. Moreover, Ahab can be killed only by hemp and, at the last, Fedallah will precede him—be his pilot.

After wearying months of pursuit, the crew sight Moby Dick, his dazzling hump high above his slightly projecting head. He is surrounded by hundreds of sea fowl. Tall broken spears are embedded in his huge back. The whaleboats are lowered for the encounter. Moby Dick eludes his pursuers, dives deep, then surfaces and snaps Ahab's boat, hurling Ahab and his Parsee crew into the water. Aboard the *Pequod* once more, Ahab scornfully rejects Starbuck's interpretation that the wrecked boat constitutes an omen.

The next day, Moby Dick is again sighted and again the chase is on. The monstrous whale wreaks more havoc this time, swamping all three whaleboats, tangling all the harpoon lines, and breaking Captain Ahab's ivory leg. In the melee,

Fedallah is drowned. For the second time, Ahab turns a deaf ear to Starbuck's plea that he abandon his pursuit of the white whale.

On the third day, the spout that signals the white whale's presence is seen for the third time. Ahab again leads the chase. Maddened by the harpoon wounds inflicted on the two previous days, Moby Dick flails the mates' boats apart, churns the water, and swims away—revealing as he does the body of Fedallah, lashed to the white whale by the lines of the irons that had pierced him on the preceding day. Part of the Parsee's prediction is fulfilled: Fedallah has gone before Ahab to be his pilot. Suddenly the enraged white whale sees the black hull of the *Pequod* and, turning, bears down upon it and strikes it with monstrous force. The ship reels, settles, and begins to sink. The second part of the prophecy comes to pass: The *Pequod* is the second hearse, its wood grown in America. Ahab's boat comes alongside the white whale, and he hurls his harpoon into Moby Dick. The line, however, runs foul and, as Ahab stoops to clear it, the flying turn catches him round the neck, and he is shot out of the boat and instantly strangled. The Parsee's prophecy is now fully realized: Ahab is killed by hemp.

Only Ishmael escapes. He crawls atop a coffin built by Queequeg. The coffin had been shot from the *Pequod*. On the closed coffin Ishmael floats till the *Rachel*, still in search of her Captain's son, finds him.

Throughout Ishmael's story, from the sailing of the *Pequod* on, are interspersed chapters on whaling. While they do not further the story, they comment upon it obliquely, supplying the background and pointing up the symbolism. The ubiquity of whales, whaling as a pattern of life, the kinds of whales, the parts of the whale, the habits of whales—these matters continually interrupt and simultaneously deepen the narrative.

Critical Opinion

Moby Dick is a towering book—and a profound one. The narrative has a surging movement, exciting episodes, and dramatic confrontations. The style is by turns poetic, humor-

ous, romantic, and factual. But *Moby Dick* has depths that
"make a man swim for his life."

Melville wrote *Moby Dick* at the height of his powers.
"Until I was twenty-five," he wrote Hawthorne, "I had no
development at all. From my twenty-fifth year I date my life.
Three weeks have scarcely passed at any time between then
and now that I have not unfolded within myself. But I feel
that I am now come to the inmost leaf of the bulb, and that
shortly the flower must fall to the mould." He derided the
novels he had published because they did not "dive," because
they were not charged with "the powers of darkness," because
they did not draw to exhaustion on his creative potential.

He apparently began *Moby Dick* as another realistic,
broadly comic whaling adventure, but after the twenty-second
chapter revised his purpose. The *Pequod* became more than
a whaling vessel; it became a small, contained world. The
monomaniacal captain and the huge whale he pursued, though
they remained realistic beings, became symbolic figures as
well—great and complex creations that each reader must
interpret for himself. Is Ahab evil man trying to destroy good,
hurling himself futilely against God or attempting to become
God? Is Ahab heroic man striving to wrest the secret of creation, or protesting against the evil of the universe or against
evil fate? Is Ahab simply mad, or irresponsible, or mistaken
in his quest? These are only a few of the innumerable questions that have been asked and "answered." But, as one critic
points out, "To set down an 'approved' answer, as to a
problem in algebra, would be presumptuous—and besides,
some problems have no approved answer."

But if *Moby Dick* is a challenging book, if it forces its
reader to "depth-dive," it is also, as more than one critic has
affirmed, "the best sea story ever written," at once "the epic
and the encyclopedia of whaling." And it is as well the epic of
man refusing against all reason to submit to things as they are.

The Author

Herman Melville was born in 1819 in New York City, of
Scotch-English and Dutch ancestry. When he was eleven, his
family moved to Albany, where he attended the Albany

Academy for two years. Then, after his father died deep in debt, the thirteen-year-old boy embarked on a variety of occupations. For five years he worked as a clerk, a farm hand, even a teacher, despite his own scanty schooling.

At eighteen, perhaps because no better alternatives offered themselves, Melville became a sailor, signing aboard as a cabin boy on a trading vessel bound for Liverpool. The brutalities he witnessed on ship and on shore in the Liverpool slums destroyed his romantic notions of a sailor's life. Four years after his return, however, finding nothing to keep him on land, he sailed again, this time on the *Acushnet,* a whaler bound for the South Seas. Conditions aboard were intolerable. With a companion Melville jumped ship at one of the Marquesas Islands, where for a month he was a guest of the Typees, a cannibal tribe. Though he enjoyed the experience for the most part, he was glad to accept a berth aboard the Australian whaler that rescued him. But once again, after participating in a mutiny and being jailed briefly, he deserted at Eimeo, near Tahiti, and wandered among the natives, vastly preferring them to the missionaries. He made his way to Hawaii aboard a whaling ship cruising the South Pacific, worked for fourteen weeks in Honolulu spotting pins in a bowling alley, and then enlisted in the U.S. Navy for a homeward cruise. He landed in Boston nearly three years after his departure on the *Acushnet,* his sailing career ended.

No other career beckoning him, Melville began to write, drawing freely on his seagoing experiences for his first four novels: *Typee* (1846) describes his cannibal experiences; *Omoo* (1847), his wanderings in Tahiti; *Redburn* (1849), his maiden voyage to Liverpool; and *White-Jacket* (1850), his last voyage on a United States warship. *Mardi* (1849) is an allegory rather than a novel, confused but intermittently fascinating in its satiric comments. Unlike his autobiographical novels, it failed disastrously.

Melville's great novel, *Moby Dick,* was (like *Mardi*) an attempt to break away from the romantic semi-autobiographical narratives which pleased the public but not the author. Its critical reception was mixed and it sold badly. *Pierre* (1852), subtitled *The Ambiguities,* a tortured, perverse, deeply pessimistic book, was greeted with unmixed and uncomprehending attacks. From this point on Melville's productivity declined. *Israel Potter* (1855), *The Piazza Tales* (1856), *The Confidence Man* (1857), a volume of poems, *Battle Pieces and Aspects of the War* (1866), a long narrative poem, *Clarel* (1876), and the posthumously published *Billy Budd* (1924) did not increase his contemporary reputation.

Melville had married in 1847, and the need to support his family forced him to try magazine writing and lecturing. In 1866 he became an inspector in the New York Customs House, a position he retained until 1886. He died, almost forgotten, in 1891.

Since then his fame has skyrocketed. He is one of the two most widely read and written-about authors of nineteenth-century America. Mark Twain is the other. Melville's poems, stories, and novels, long out of print, have been republished in a variety of editions. Once virtually ignored, he is today almost universally hailed as America's greatest novelist.

The Scarlet Letter

by

NATHANIEL HAWTHORNE (1804–1864)

Main Characters

Hester Prynne—The adulterous wife of an elderly English scholar, beautiful, passionate, loyal, and noble in enduring her penance—the embroidered scarlet "A" (for "Adultery") that she is condemned to wear.

Roger Chillingworth—The name assumed by Hester's husband to conceal his identity so that he may more easily discover the partner of her sin. Short, thin, pale, dim-eyed from poring over books, he becomes progressively more distorted in his relentless pursuit of the wrongdoer.

Arthur Dimmesdale—The minister who is Hester's "fellow sinner and fellow sufferer." Deeply religious, eloquent, intellectually gifted, he suffers because of his inability to confess his sin.

Pearl—The illegitimate daughter of Hester and the minister, radiantly lovely, yet perverse and defiant.

The Story

The introductory essay describes the author's term as Surveyor of the Salem Custom House, his antiquated colleagues and subordinates, and his politically motivated "decapitation," or discharge. Examining old records one day,

21

he comes across a faded, gold-embroidered "A" and a small roll of dingy paper. Recorded there by an ancient predecessor is the dark, dramatic tale that, suitably edited, Hawthorne pretends to give us in *The Scarlet Letter*.

The narrative opens with the chorus-like denunciation by the women of Boston—the Puritan Boston of the mid-seventeenth century. Their anger is directed against Hester Prynne who leaves the jail carrying her three-month-old baby and is guided to the platform of the pillory. Hester, whose husband has not been heard from for two years, has borne an illegitimate child and refuses to divulge the identity of the father. For her crime she has been sentenced to stand for three hours on the platform of the pillory and for the rest of her life to wear the mark of shame on her bosom—the scarlet "A." An aged clergyman exhorts her to reveal the identity of the father. She refuses, even when the Reverend Arthur Dimmesdale adds his heartfelt, compassionate plea.

In the crowd, watching curiously, is a small, slightly deformed man whom Hester recognizes with dread. After returning to prison, Hester and the child need a physician and are visited by the observer, who has learned the arts of medicine from books and from the Indians among whom he has sojourned. He calls himself Roger Chillingworth; he is in reality Hester's husband. Having administered a soothing medication to his patients, he declares that by a kind of intuitive, sympathetic penetration, he will discover Hester's fellow sinner. Before leaving, he makes Hester promise to keep his own secret as she has her lover's.

Hester leaves prison and establishes herself in an abandoned cottage on the outskirts of the town, earning her scant livelihood by the expert work of her needle—the same needle that embroidered the beautiful and baleful scarlet "A" which she must always wear. Her daughter, Pearl, grows into an exquisite, elfin child. Not the least of Hester's tortures are Pearl's frequent questions as to where she came from and her refusal to accept the answer that her Heavenly Father sent her.

The minister, Arthur Dimmesdale, has meanwhile been declining. He grows daily paler and thinner, and often suffers heart pains. He accepts the proffered medical aid of Roger Chillingworth who becomes his regular companion. Chillingworth has another purpose besides curing the minister. He

penetrates deeply beneath the surface spirituality of the
minister and detects a secret sin working there. In the process
of searching, Chillingworth becomes more evil and ugly.
Indeed, many people in Boston whisper that Arthur Dimmesdale is haunted by Satan or Satan's emissary.

One day, when the minister has fallen into a deep sleep,
Roger Chillingworth enters, lays aside the vestment that
covers his patient's bosom, and sees—what? We are not told,
but the sight seems to please him immensely.

On an obscure night in May, the minister, as if in the
shadow of a dream, walks to the scaffold where Hester under-
went her public shame. Sunk in misery, he stands in her place.
Hester, who has been watching at the bed of the dying
Governor Winthrop, comes to the scaffold, accompanied by
Pearl, and stands beside the minister. Pearl asks him if he will
stand with her mother and her at noon tomorrow. Not tomorrow, he replies, but at the final judgment. Pearl's laugh is
interrupted by an immense "A" which seems to flare across
the sky. Or perhaps it is merely a meteor that the guilty imagination of the Reverend Dimmesdale construes as an "A,"
the symbol of Hester's sin. At the same moment Pearl points
to the dim figure of Roger Chillingworth who has suddenly
appeared and who with apparent concern leads the minister
home.

The minister's illness continues—and his physician seems
to grow more devilish. Hester, however, develops the hidden
resources of good within her. She cannot achieve peace,
though, because of her anxiety about Pearl and the minister.
On a chill afternoon, she meets her pastor in the forest. She
is again filled with tenderness for him as she sees him ill and
suffering. He tells her of Chillingworth's probing. His own
sin, grave as it is, nevertheless is not so black as that of the
physician who has violated the sanctity of a human heart.
Hester insists that their deed of passion had a consecration of
its own. Though he does not accept her justification, neither
does he repudiate it. And soon they determine (at her strong
suggestion) to escape together to another place where his
talents can be fulfilled. She discards her scarlet "A"—but
Pearl, who has been playing elsewhere during the passionate
interlude, refuses to rejoin her mother till Hester replaces it.

The third great scene of the novel also unfolds on the

scaffold. The minister has delivered the election sermon for the new governor. It is an eloquent and moving address. The minister's suffering, though stemming from sin, appears now to make him spiritual. Ironically, as his spirit clouds through concealment, his power as minister increases.

But his sermon seems to have deprived him of vital force. Leaving the church, he almost falls, yet refuses support. He sees Pearl and Hester in the audience, calls them to him, and embraces them—in spite of the protests of Roger Chillingworth who thrusts himself forward. With Hester's help, Dimmesdale ascends the platform to declare that he is a polluted priest who has compounded his sin of adultery by hiding it cunningly, hypocritically. He bares his breast to reveal what has been engraved upon it. As he does, Roger Chillingworth mutters, "Thou hast escaped me!" The minister acknowledges Pearl as well as Hester, then expires.

What was the revelation? Most spectators testified that it was a scarlet letter like Hester's but imprinted in flesh. Some contended that Chillingworth's magic had produced it, others that it had been the operation of spiritual guilt upon the flesh. Certain of the witnesses, nevertheless, maintained that the minister's breast had borne no mark whatever.

Deprived of the object of his revenge, Roger Chillingworth dies within a year. It is believed that Pearl, redeemed by the minister's confession, grew into a softened and subdued woman who married well and happy. As for Hester, after some absence, she returns to Boston to live out her life comforting and counseling the sorrowful and erring. At her death she is buried near the minister, one tombstone serving both and bearing the legend: "On a Field, Sable, the Letter A, Gules."

Critical Opinion

Almost unanimously, critics agree that *The Scarlet Letter* is Hawthorne's one faultless book. Elsewhere, Hawthorne's symbolism and allegory may be intrusive, his intensity too great for the story, his characters bloodless, his humor forced. But in *The Scarlet Letter* the "representation is as imaginatively real as its meaning." Hawthorne's characters fully embody the dark drama that he conceived.

From Hawthorne's day, when Melville (who learned much from him) praised "the great power of blackness in him" and his deep tragic sense, to the present, when Harry Levin notes the "vivid particularity" with which Hawthorne projects his "general vision of evil," commentators have focused on his brooding moral insight. Hawthorne felt in every fiber of his being that current notions of "the perfectibility of man" were illusory; worse, they were comfortable lies. He believed that the imaginings of man's heart were wicked and that original sin was a reality. Thus he could perceive psychological depths where other novelists merely skimmed surfaces.

The "moral" of *The Scarlet Letter* is that adultery is sinful and that those who sin must suffer. But penance is not enough; it must be fused with penitence. Dimmesdale's pride, his egotism, his fear of social ostracism render his suffering fruitless because he conceals his sin, shrinks from joining Hester in her disgrace. Hester grows spiritually as the minister declines.

Yet the sin of Hester and Dimmesdale is not the most dehumanizing one: it is a sin of passion, of the heart. Chillingworth, however, has sinned through calculation, through the deliberate misuse of intelligence. "He has violated, in cold blood, the sanctity of the human heart."

Pearl, who has been called the scarlet letter endowed with life, is perhaps the only character in the book who deserves (and has received) adverse criticism. She never is more than an allegorical figure, never is assimilated into the story itself. Hawthorne needed her as the emblem of the sin that the romance analyzes. But readers wish they could accept her as real. She is the only imperfection in a tale that powerfully and poetically exploits the discordant motives and destructive passions deep within us.

The House of the Seven Gables

by

NATHANIEL HAWTHORNE

Main Characters

Colonel Pyncheon—The ruthless Puritan who seizes Matthew Maule's land.

Matthew Maule—The "Wizard" condemned for witchcraft through Colonel Pyncheon's zeal.

Thomas Maule—Matthew's son, who builds the "House of the Seven Gables."

Hepzibah Pyncheon—The sweet-natured but sour-faced maiden lady who in 1850 inhabits the house.

Clifford Pyncheon—Hepzibah's beloved brother, a handsome and sensitive man, intellectually torpid from his long imprisonment.

Phoebe Pyncheon—The pretty, sprightly niece of Hepzibah and Clifford, who brings some cheerfulness into the gloomy old house.

Holgrave—The young daguerreotypist, a reformer who lives in one of the gables and who falls in love with Phoebe.

Uncle Venner—The aged odd-job man of the town, a homely philosopher who helps cheer Hepzibah and Clifford.

Judge Jaffrey Pyncheon—The cousin of Hepzibah and Clifford, an apparently benevolent man, rich and respected, but really a vicious hypocrite.

The Story

Almost two centuries before the story opens, Matthew Maule built a small thatched house in one of the pleasantest locations of old Salem. With the growth of the town during the next thiry or forty years, the site became very desirable to Colonel Pyncheon, a strong-willed Puritan who put forward a substantial legal claim to it. Maule, however, was obstinate in defending his rights and the Colonel's claim was unsuccessful.

Those were the days when even the soberest men and women believed in witchcraft, and Maule was accused of its practice. No one was more zealous in bringing about his condemnation than Colonel Pyncheon. At the moment of execution, Maule cursed his enemy. Pointing to the Colonel, grimly watching, he said, "God will give him blood to drink."

The Colonel paid no attention to the curse. After Maule's death, he took over his land and on the very place where Maule's small house had stood built a mansion with seven peaked gables. Strangely, the Colonel offered the job of architect to Thomas Maule, the son of the man he had helped hound to death; and strangely, too, Thomas Maule accepted the job and performed it faithfully.

But "Wizard" Maule's curse proved effective. The Colonel, like more than one of his descendants, died of apoplexy, choking on his own blood. Though he left his son a large fortune, the deeds or other documents supporting his son's claim to a great tract of land in Maine could not be found.

In the middle of the nineteenth century, the time of our story, the "House of the Seven Gables" on Pyncheon Street (once Maule's Lane) is occupied by Hepzibah Pyncheon, a descendant of the Puritan Colonel. She is a kind-hearted woman, but so cross-looking that she either frightens children or excites them to mockery. She decides to eke out her income by opening a penny-shop and selling soap, candles, brown sugar, etc. Unfortunately, her vinegary looks discourage customers and her business seems likely to fail.

Quite unexpectedly, Hepzibah receives a visit from a country cousin, Phoebe Pyncheon, a pretty, cheerful young woman. Her visit is to be short or long, depending on how she and Hepzibah suit each other. Hepzibah welcomes Phoebe reluctantly, for her brother Clifford is to come home soon and Hepzibah is uncertain how he will accept Phoebe. Clifford has been in prison for thirty years, convicted, on the basis of a long chain of circumstantial evidence, of having killed his uncle, old Jaffrey Pyncheon.

Phoebe soon proves that she suits Hepzibah very well indeed. She takes over the penny-shop, and her energy and her bright personality make it a profitable enterprise. More-

over, she pleases Clifford immensely. His loving but forbid-
ding-looking sister oppresses him. Hepzibah bravely turns to
Phoebe, and she agrees to take care of Clifford. It is no easy
task. An extraordinarily handsome and sensitive man, Clifford
has been blighted by his prison years and is now lacking in
physical or mental energy. Nevertheless, Phoebe's attentive-
ness as well as her gaiety and youthful beauty rouse Clifford
and frequently lift the wretchedness that has descended on
him.

Phoebe also charms another resident of the old house, a
young daguerreotypist named Holgrave who inhabits one of
the gables. In spite of Holgrave's tendency to join a variety
of reform movements, Hepzibah has grown rather fond of him.
And Phoebe, who often works with him in the little garden
kept for Clifford's pleasure, also begins to trust and rely on
him.

With the occasional exception of Uncle Venner, who lives
at the farm maintained for old folk by the town and who does
odd jobs for the townspeople, Clifford, Phoebe, and Hepzibah
are the only people who ever enter the parlor of the house,
a forbidding room dominated by the green portrait of Colonel
Pyncheon. Once, Judge Jaffrey Pyncheon, the cousin of
Hepzibah and Clifford, tries to force his way into it to speak
to Clifford, but Hepzibah's agitation and Clifford's wails of
alarm—perhaps, too, the presence of Phoebe—cause the
Judge to abandon his attempt. The Judge is the great man of
the town, rich and respected, though not very much liked
despite his studied benevolence and ingratiating manners.
Clifford obviously is terrified of him, and Hepzibah despises
and fears him.

After staying with the brother and sister a number of weeks,
Phoebe decides to go home for a few days to make arrangements for moving permanently to the house of the seven
gables. She says an affectionate goodbye to Clifford and
Hepzibah, and a cordial one to Holgrave whose statements
and, even more, reticences puzzle and disquiet her. She is
not gone very long when Judge Pyncheon arrives at the
house determined to speak to Clifford about his happiness
and well-being. Hepzibah resists the Judge firmly but tremu-
lously.

The Judge abandons all pretense, threatening to have Clifford committed to an asylum for the insane if Hepzibah continues her resistance. Boldly Jaffrey Pyncheon puts forth his reason: he is convinced that the uncle whose fortune he inherited—the uncle whom Clifford is alleged to have murdered —left an estate two or three times as large as appeared after his death and that Clifford can give him a clue to the recovery of the remainder. Hepzibah knows that the Judge means to carry out his threat. She has no choice except to summon her brother. Judge Pyncheon enters the parlor and sits beneath Colonel Pyncheon's portrait, on the very chair in which the old Puritan was found dead more than a century and a half earlier. Hepzibah goes in search of Clifford. He is nowhere to be found. Frantically Hepzibah returns to the parlor to ask the Judge's help. The Judge is sitting motionless. Just then Clifford appears, laughing wildly. He points to the Judge. He is dead! Clifford insists that they leave the house at once. He and Hepzibah take a train ride during which Clifford talks freely and even fearlessly to complete strangers. Formerly he shunned everyone except the inmates of the house of the seven gables.

Meanwhile Phoebe has returned from her visit home. She is admitted by Holgrave who tells her that the Judge is dead. He has suffered a stroke of apoplexy just as his ancestor, the Colonel, had. The uncle whom Clifford was accused of killing undoubtedly suffered the same fate. Phoebe wishes to throw open the doors and make the secret known, but Holgrave prevents her. He tells her that he loves her, that she is his only hope for happiness. She protests that it seems wrong to speak of love at such a time, but nevertheless confesses that she loves him, too.

In the midst of Phoebe and Holgrave's avowals, Clifford and Hepzibah return. The Judge is declared by the authorities to have died from natural causes, the hereditary illness of his family. It is clear as well that the uncle, allegedly murdered, must have died in the same manner and that Jaffrey Pyncheon, to gain the inheritance, planted the fraudulent evidence that convicted Clifford.

Clifford, his mind far less troubled now, recalls that as a boy he discovered a secret spring that caused the portrait of Colonel Pyncheon to swing forward and reveal a compartment in which important documents were hidden, but he has forgotten the location of the spring. Holgrave, though, says he can find it. He presses the spring, the portrait falls to the floor, and behind it is a recess holding the deeds to a vast tract of land—Colonel Pyncheon's missing property. The Judge supposed, erroneously, that Clifford knew of lands belonging to their uncle, not of these lands, which are worthless after the lapse of so many years.

Phoebe asks Holgrave how he came to know about the secret spring, and Holgrave reveals his identity. He is a descendant of "Wizard" Matthew Maule and of Thomas Maule who had built the house of the seven gables. The secret of the spring and the documents had been passed from father to son through the Maule generations. The marriage of a Maule and a Pyncheon—which shortly takes place—at last dissipates the curse.

Clifford and Hepzibah inherit the Judge's estate and, with Holgrave, Phoebe, and Uncle Venner leave the house of the seven gables to live in the Judge's mansion.

Critical Opinion

The House of the Seven Gables appeared in 1851 when Hawthorne was living near Lenox in the Berkshire Hills of Massachusetts. It was written when Hawthorne's "situation was as close to ideal as it gets for a writer." He liked his new home; the success of *The Scarlet Letter,* published a year earlier, had brought him fame and relieved him of financial worries; his family was flourishing. Consequently *The House of the Seven Gables,* though it traces the same pattern of guilt and expiation as *The Scarlet Letter* and points up as grim a moral—that "the wrongdoing of one generation lives into the successive ones"—is a less intense and far less gloomy book.

Hawthorne, indeed, believed that it was "a more natural book for him to write" and preferred it to *The Scarlet Letter.* Most of his contemporaries agreed; few modern readers do. *The House of the Seven Gables* is light, charming, and fanciful, but it lacks the dark power of the earlier tale. It is more relaxed, more diffuse, more digressive. Some episodes—the frantic train trip of Hepzibah and Clifford, for example—seem irrelevant to the plot. Moreover, Hawthorne hurries the events of his story and resolves too many of its complications too easily.

The House of the Seven Gables, Hawthorne insisted, was not a novel but a romance. Fidelity to the truth—except "the truth of the human heart"—was not a requirement for the romance: the author could alter and arrange facts, even introduce the marvelous if he chose to. The figures of the romance, too, need not be real; and Hawthorne's, as Henry James comments, are "figures rather than characters, . . . pictures rather than people." Yet they are perfectly in harmony with the story, perfectly capable of carrying its weight, perfectly at home among its lights and shadows. If *The House of the Seven Gables* is not Hawthorne's most moving work, it is his most graceful and most pictorial.

The Author

Born in Salem of a distinguished Puritan family, *Nathaniel Hawthorne* seems early to have been destined for suffering. His father, a sea captain, died of yellow fever in Guiana when Nathaniel was four. His mother entered upon a long period of mourning, secluding herself in her home, even taking her meals alone. Between the ages of nine and twelve, Hawthorne was invalided by a leg injury sustained while playing ball. A three-year stay in the Maine woods, which he thoroughly enjoyed, helped his recovery.

Hawthorne enrolled in Bowdoin College and graduated in 1825. Then he, too, embraced solitude, spending the next twelve years in his mother's house, reading, writing, and thinking. A juvenile novel and some excellent short stories and sketches are the products of these lonely years.

Partly with the help of Sophia Peabody, whom he married in 1842, he escaped from his self-imprisonment. During the next eight years, he wrote much, became Measurer at the Boston Customs House (1839-40), joined the Utopian Community of Brook Farm for six months (1840-41), and accepted the position of surveyor of the Salem Customs House (1846-49). Discharged from the last position when the Democrats fell from power, he again devoted himself to writing. During the early 1840s he had composed his first distinctive tales which were distinguished by a heightened Puritan conscious-ness of sin and suffering. Now, freed from his Surveyorship, Hawthorne experienced a release of creative energy. In 1850 he wrote his greatest study of Puritan sensibility, *The Scarlet Letter.* The next year saw the publication of *The House of the Seven Gables,* a novel of ancestral guilt, and the year follow-ing, the story of his disillusionment with the Brook Farm adventure, *The Blithedale Romance.*

As a reward for a presidential campaign biography he wrote for his Bowdoin classmate Franklin Pierce, Hawthorne was appointed consul at Liverpool and later Manchester (1853–56). He stayed abroad for seven years in England and in Italy, where he began *The Marble Faun* (1860). He returned to America in 1860, settling in Concord.

In spite of such diversions as politics, consular service, and travel, Hawthorne dedicated his life to writing the tales and novels that make him the first American who truly merits a place in world literature.

Uncle Tom's Cabin

by

HARRIET BEECHER STOWE (1811–1896)

Main Characters

Uncle Tom—A Negro slave, gentle, devout, humble, but resolute in cleaving to the good.

Aunt Chloe—A famous cook, a devoted servant, Tom's self-sacrificing wife.

Arthur Shelby—Tom's master in Kentucky, a "fair average kind of man," good-natured and self-indulgent.

Emily Shelby—His wife, an excellent mistress but powerless to aid Tom when he needs her most.

George Shelby—Their son, high-spirited, generous, deeply loyal.

Dan Haley—A slave trader immune to human decency.

Tom Loker—A slave hunter, but potentially redeemable.

Marks—His shrewd, self-serving ally.

Eliza Harris—A sweet, brave, loving slave.

George Harris—Her proud and intelligent husband.

Harry—Their captivating child.

Senator John Bird—An essentially good man whose human sympathies are briefly obscured by false principles and opportunistic politics.

Rachel Halliday—A kindly, sweet-tempered Quaker lady, who serves the cause of anti-slavery.

Simeon Halliday—Her husband.

Phineas Fletcher—A fighting Quaker.

33

Aunt Dorcas—Tom Loker's Quaker nurse who helps restore him to health and to humanity.

Augustine St. Clare—Tom's New Orleans master; on the surface, clever, cynical; at heart, idealistic, tormented.

Marie St. Clare—His selfish, egotistic wife.

Ophelia St. Clare—His Vermont cousin, an epitome of New England merits and faults, strait-laced, honest, conscientious, truly religious.

Evangeline (Eva)—St. Clare's saintly young daughter, moved by more than human love, faith, goodness.

Topsy—The mischievous black sprite who disorders the St. Clare household until Eva's love reforms her.

Simon Legree—Tom's last master, sadistic and bestial.

Cassy—The unhappy quadroon whom Legree forces to serve his base requirements but who nevertheless retains compassion and dignity.

Quimbo and *Sambo*—Two Negro slaves whom Legree has debased but who are saved by Tom's heroic example.

Emmeline—The lovely hopeless and terror-stricken girl whom Legree purchases to replace Cassy.

The Story

During the years before the Civil War, the Shelby plantation in Kentucky seems a happy place. Its master, Arthur Shelby, is open-handed and good-natured; his wife, Emily, benevolent and sincerely religious; their young son George, warm and affectionate—the plantation favorite. The slaves are treated kindly—almost like human beings instead of property. Uncle Tom, a devout and devoted Negro, is Mr. Shelby's trusted agent. His wife, Aunt Chloe, is regarded as more than a superb cook; she is practically one of the Shelby family. And their children give promise of walking in the upright ways of their parents.

But Mr. Shelby is improvident, and his debts force him to sell Uncle Tom to a gross slave trader, Dan Haley. With Tom, he must also sell Harry, the five-year-old son of Eliza and George Harris, the former a beautiful young quadroon whom he owns, the latter an intelligent and manly mulatto who is the chattel of an unfeeling slaveholder. Fearing to be sold down the Mississippi River and unable to endure his master any longer, George determines to escape to Canada and freedom. He takes sorrowful leave of his son and wife. Soon after his departure, she discovers that Shelby has agreed to sell Harry and, unable to endure that prospect, she too plans to escape.

Carrying the child, Eliza trudges wearily to a village on the banks of the Ohio River. Here she finds refuge at an inn and waits for a boat that will carry her across the ice-caked river. The abysmal Haley, however, has followed her though he has been delayed by the false directions of the Shelby slaves who accompany him. Eliza sees him and fears capture. Frantically she vaults from the bank of the river to a cake of ice, then to another, and still another. Leaping, slipping, bleeding, she somehow miraculously reaches the Ohio side.

There she is directed to the house of Senator Bird, a good man imprisoned by his "principles." He has voted for the law forbidding shelter or aid to escaped slaves. But when he sees poor Eliza and Harry, pity stirs in him and he takes them to the farm house of a Southerner who, convinced that slavery is sin, has freed his own slaves and aids others to escape. He conducts Eliza and Harry to the home of Rachel and Simeon Halliday, members of a Quaker settlement. They both hate slavery. There Eliza finds warmth and hope. The Hallidays make possible a reunion between her and her husband George who, fierce for freedom, has armed himself and has passed as a Spaniard.

Meanwhile Haley has enlisted the services of two slave hunters, the brutal Loker and his vicious assistant Marks, who follow the trail of the refugees. Accompanied by Phineas Fletcher, another valiant Quaker, George, Eliza, and Harry flee once again. They are overtaken at a narrow pass, but George puts up a spirited defense and Phineas hurls Tom Loker into a chasm. The fugitives proceed by boat to Canada, a free country.

Uncle Tom's progress is not so happy. His departure from the Shelby plantation is dismal: Aunt Chloe despairs, the children sob, George Shelby rages, vowing that he will have Tom back when he is a man. Haley takes Tom on a steamboat down the Mississippi to New Orleans. Along the way he sees the dreadful sights of slavery—the suffering in squalid quarters, families torn apart, a woman ending her miseries in the river when separated from her child. Tom reads his Bible and sings his hymns, but is nonetheless forlorn. He makes friends with a lovely golden-haired girl, little Evangeline (Eva) who is traveling with her father. When she falls overboard, Tom jumps in to rescue her. After this, Eva easily prevails upon her father, Augustine St. Clare, to buy Tom.

St. Clare is returning from Vermont where he has recruited his spinster cousin, Ophelia St. Clare, to act as his housekeeper and to keep the St. Clare household in order. Its master is indolent, its mistress lost in hypochondria, self-pity, and selfishness. Tom's existence there, however, is relatively pleasant. He idolizes Eva, and she responds lovingly. Love is her central quality—one she lavishes on all, even on Topsy, the mischievous little black sprite whose training has made lying and stealing as familiar to her as being whipped. She can remember nothing of her family or origins. "I spect I grow'd. Don't think nobody never made me," she says. Topsy is redeemed, finally, but far more by Eva's love than by Miss Ophelia's severities and moralities.

Eva is doomed. She grows paler and more languid each day, though her bright spiritual light does not fade. Tom, whom St. Clare at Eva's urging has promised to free, feels that her end is near. Even Marie emerges from the miasma of self-pity. Eva's dying is an ascent to glory, to the Christ whom she adores.

After Eva's death, the household is desolate. St. Clare, deeply skeptical, struggles for a faith in the divine purpose, a faith that eludes him. He puts off giving Tom his freedom, though he firmly intends to. Then one day at a café he tries to separate two brawling men and is fatally wounded. He dies, not before he, too, is vouchsafed a vision of infinite pity.

Disregarding her husband's wish, Marie decides to sell her slaves, Tom among them. Auctioned at a slave warehouse, he is purchased, along with Emmeline, a beautiful fifteen-year-old girl, by Simon Legree, a bestial plantation owner. Legree hates Tom, piles the cruelest labors on him. Emmeline he reserves for his own pleasures, displacing for her his handsome quadroon mistress, Cassy. Tom suffers but his Bible and his faith help him to endure—even when, because he will not whip a sick woman, Legree has him whipped by his two

religious tracts and religious schools. Had she been born a boy, she would certainly have become a preacher, like six of her brothers—one of them the renowned Henry Ward Beecher. But since that career was closed to her, she did the next best thing. She became a teacher when she was fourteen.

When she was twenty-one, she moved with her family to Cincinnati, and taught for a time in the Lane Theological Seminary, of which her father was president. At twenty-four, she married a fellow teacher, Professor Calvin E. Stowe, already a distinguished Biblical scholar.

In 1850, Harriet moved East again with her husband and seven children. Calvin Stowe had been called to a professorship at Bowdoin, then at Andover. In spite of her family and religious duties, Harriet started to write, releasing the imagination that since childhood had been directed into other channels.

She began writing *Uncle Tom's Cabin* in 1851 for serial publication in an abolitionist journal, *The National Era,* of Washington, D.C. The phenomenal success of the novel has obscured the worth of her other writings, which many scholars regard as superior to *Uncle Tom's Cabin*: *The Minister's Wooing* (1859), *Oldtown Folks* (1869), *Sam Lawson's Fireside Stories* (1871), *Poganuc People* (1878). This group of New England fiction—set between Maine and Connecticut— is, despite didacticism, an important and influential contribution to regional literature.

Harriet Beecher Stowe's novels and stories, which she continued to write for fifty years till her death in 1896, run to sixteen volumes. Some of the "yarns" are dated, but more than a handful, "in addition to being authentic, . . . are charming and comic—the mature creations of a great writer."

Tom Sawyer

by

SAMUEL LANGHORNE CLEMENS (1835–1910)

(MARK TWAIN)

Main Characters

Tom Sawyer—A twelve-year-old boy, endowed with a wildly romantic imagination and an inordinate love of mischief.

Sid—Tom's priggish, tattling brother.

Aunt Polly—Tom's kind-hearted, devout, and fussy aunt and guardian.

Becky Thatcher—The lovely blonde, blue-eyed girl whom Tom chooses for his sweetheart.

Joe Harper—Tom's bosom friend.

Huck Finn—The homeless, ragged, but self-sufficient son of the town drunkard.

Injun Joe—The vicious halfbreed who terrorizes Tom and Huck.

Muff Potter—The town drunk and scapegoat.

The Story

Tom Sawyer of St. Petersburg, Missouri, has a talent for mischief and none at all for school. He plays hooky one day and his righteous brother Sid tells their Aunt Polly. Tom is sentenced to whitewash the fence, an unpleasant chore, but he pretends to be fascinated by it. Shortly, several of his cronies offer to relieve him. Tom allows them to whitewash—at a price, and thus becomes possessor of the richest boys' treasure in town.

Tom manages to get into all kinds of trouble. He accumulates yellow tickets by trade, not by memorizing the Bible verses for which they are awarded. When he is asked, as an informal test of his knowledge, who were the first two apostles, he replies, "David and Goliath." In church he finds the sermon much less intriguing than watching the pinch bug he has released fasten onto a dog which runs howling out of church. He challenges the overdressed, sissified new boy in town to combat and defeats him.

Another newcomer, Becky Thatcher, captures Tom's youthful fancy with her blue eyes and blonde hair. At the cost of a whipping from the schoolmaster, Tom contrives to sit next to her in class. Working very rapidly, he declares his love for her, forces a similar declaration from her, and becomes her accepted fiancé. But when he inadvertently lets slip that he has been engaged at least once before, Becky spurns him and Tom leaves full of self-pity and anger.

Playing Robin Hood with his friends, racing ticks, fighting mock battles, planning a career as a pirate, and taking part in whatever adventures come along are far more attractive to Tom than going to school. One adventure has dire consequences. Eluding the vigilance of Aunt Polly and Sid, Tom sneaks out with Huck Finn, the town ragamuffin, to make a midnight visit to the graveyard. They plan to visit the grave of someone wicked, wait for a devil to emerge, then swing a dead cat (Huck has procured one) after them, saying, "Devil follow corpse, cat follow devil, wart follow cat, I'm done with ye!" Instead of the devil, though, the boys come upon three grave robbers: young Dr. Robinson, Injun Joe, a malevolent halfbreed, and Muff Potter, the local drunk. Out of sight, they hear Injun Joe demand more money, Muff Potter second the demand, and Dr. Robinson refuse. The doctor strikes Muff, knocking him out. Injun Joe, furious, drives his knife into the doctor. Then he puts the knife into the hand of the still-unconscious Muff, and when Muff awakens, convinces him that he jumped the doctor and knifed him. But Injun Joe magnanimously promises to be silent. Frightened, the boys run off and take a bloody oath never to tell what they have seen. They are sure that if they do, Injun Joe will exact some kind of dreadful revenge.

Tom and Huck try their best to forget, even when Muff Potter is arrested for murder. In this they are aided by a pirate interlude. Feeling much put upon by Aunt Polly, who makes him swallow evil-tasting medicine, Tom escapes to nearby Jackson's Island in the company of Huck and Joe Harper. The boys have a glorious time fishing, swimming, and learning to smoke a pipe. Meanwhile they see boats go by searching for their bodies, and they finally realize that their folks must be worried. Besides, the boys are getting bored. Tom swims back to town at night to discover what he can. He finds his Aunt Polly and Mrs. Harper and their neighbors dissolved in tears. Everyone is recalling Tom and Joe fondly. Tom is tempted to show himself when he hears about the funeral service being planned for him and his companions on Sunday. He sneaks out of the house and returns to the island. On Sunday, just at the height of the congregation's wailing and in the midst of the preacher's eulogy, Tom, Joe, and Huck walk down the aisle. Joy, tears, and thanksgiving are their reward.

Tom and Becky make up. The normal round of St. Petersburg life proceeds until the trial of Muff Potter. Evidence against him is overwhelming; conviction seems sure. Then Tom is called to the witness stand. He bravely tells how Injun Joe killed the doctor and framed Muff. Injun Joe jumps out the window and escapes. Muff goes free, and Tom is the hero.

But time again weighs heavily on Tom. With Huck he decides to dig for treasure. (Robber bands had frequented the area near St. Petersburg not long before.) After some fruitless digging, the boys take pick and shovel to a haunted house. While they explore the upper story of the house, they hear voices, and peering through knotholes, see a ragged creature and a Spaniard. The Spaniard turns out to be Injun Joe, come to bury $650. While digging, Injun Joe strikes a box filled with a few thousand dollars in gold coins—presumably robbers' treasure. But Joe has grown suspicious. He decides to remove the treasure, he tells his crony, to "Number Two—under the cross."

The boys decide to watch for the false Spaniard and his friend, and to trail them if they appear. They finally locate Injun Joe, drunk at a tavern. Since Tom is to go on a picnic given by Becky for her friends, Huck agrees to stand guard and see if he can follow the Indian to the treasure hoard. One night he and his partner emerge, and Huck pursues. Hidden, he overhears their plan to rob the Widow Douglas and to mark her up with a knife. Injun Joe still bears a grudge against her late husband. Though terrified, Huck summons aid. The villains are routed but escape.

Meanwhile, at the picnic, Becky and Tom have entered a cave and become separated from the other picnickers. For three terrible days they are imprisoned in the cave without food or light. One day Tom sees a hand holding a lighted candle! It is Injun Joe hiding out! Luckily Injun Joe does not recognize Tom, and flees. At last Tom sees a gleam of light. With Becky he follows it to an opening in the cave, and together they return to their rejoicing families. Becky's father closes up the cave to prevent further accidents. Injun Joe is trapped inside. Tom tells Huck he is convinced the treasure must be in the cave. He and Huck enter the cave through the opening Tom and Becky used, and in one of the chambers find a cross made with candle smoke, and under it the treasure!

Tom and Huck transfer the gold coins to small bags and carry them to St. Petersburg. They are stopped at the Widow Douglas's and invited in. There Huck's heroism in rescuing the widow is revealed, and Tom tops the revelation by displaying the treasure. The boys are wealthy now with an income of a dollar a day. But Huck, who has been taken in by the widow and made to dress in civilized fashion and even to attend school and church, is not happy. He leaves the widow. Only Tom's inducement, that he will form a robber band and Huck will be a member, moves Huck, reluctantly, to give the thing another chance.

Critical Opinion

If the reader chooses not to commit himself to *The Adventures of Tom Sawyer,* he can advance reasons enough for his restraint. The plot is as melodramatic as a dime novel's. The sequence of events is casual, even wayward—or, as Howells puts it, Mark Twain "sets down the thing that comes into his mind without fear or favor of the thing that went before or the thing that may be about to follow." The adult characters are sticklike figures, conventionally conceived supernumeraries. The sentimentality engendered by nostalgia sometimes overflows to drown out the reality.

Such reasons, nevertheless, miss their mark. *Tom Sawyer* is American myth, not realistic record—despite its "acute minor realisms." To read it otherwise is to misread it and so to miss the magical experience that several generations of boys—and their fathers—have found it.

For if the reader gives himself to it, *Tom Sawyer* is a steady delight. The book has been called an "American idyl," "a romantic remembrance of things past," and by the author, "simply a hymn, put into prose form to give it a worldly air." Mark Twain said that he recalled, not invented it. "Most of the adventures recorded in the book really occurred," he wrote in the preface.

Tom Sawyer is rich in pastoral scenes that have become American classics: Tom's whitewashing of the fence (with collaboration), his releasing of the pinch bug in church, his gallant blame-taking for Becky's misdemeanor in school. And darker scenes, too: Tom's frightened glimpse of Injun Joe in the cave, his graveyard visit with Huck, his testimony for Muff Potter.

Moreover, the talk in the book—its idiom and syntax—is a triumphant achievement (as well as a model for the writers who followed Twain). The boys whose conversation we overhear are sometimes "splashed by caricature," but their actions "turn on the hard hinges of true boy-psychology." Finally the lines of the plot, though far-flung, all converge satisfyingly at the climax. Had Mark Twain not written *The Adventures of Huckleberry Finn,* says Dixon Wecter, this would be his finest novel.

The Adventures of Huckleberry Finn

by

SAMUEL LANGHORNE CLEMENS

(MARK TWAIN)

Main Characters

Huckleberry Finn—The narrator, a thirteen-year-old boy who
hates all the restraints of "civilization."

Tom Sawyer—Huck's bosom companion, a highly imaginative
and romantic boy.

"Pap" Finn—Huck's disreputable father, a drunken bully.

Widow Douglas—The kind, well-meaning lady who attempts
to "civilize" Huck.

Miss Watson—Her spinster sister.

Judge Thatcher—Guardian of Huck's fortune.

Jim—A Negro slave, illiterate and superstitious but brave,
generous, and good.

Colonel Grangerford—The head of an aristocratic family engaged in a blood feud with the neighbors, the Shepherdsons.

Buck—His good-natured son, about Huck's age.

The King—A confidence man befriended by Huck and Jim.

The Duke—Another confidence man, who proves as untrustworthy as his companion, the king.

Mary Jane—The innocent and very gullible niece of the dead
Peter Wilks, an easy prey for the confidence men.

Sally Phelps—Tom Sawyer's good-hearted aunt.

Silas Phelps—Tom Sawyer's equally good-hearted uncle.

The Story

Huckleberry Finn, a thirteen-year-old boy living in St.
Petersburg, Missouri, has been taken in hand by the Widow
Douglas, who with the overzealous help of her spinster sister,

Miss Watson, undertakes to civilize him. Huck is chided when he attempts to smoke or even fidget. He is introduced to spelling and compelled to say his prayers—projects he wholeheartedly opposes. Only his adventures with Tom Sawyer, his bosom friend and a complete romantic, make his captivity bearable. Huck and Tom have discovered a buried treasure,* and Huck fears that his blackguard father will take the money from him. Consequently he "sells" his fortune—$6,000—to Judge Thatcher, a fiction that will prevent the senior Finn from getting his hands on it.

"Pap" Finn, a dirty, fish-belly-white, regularly drunk villain, catches Huck and keeps him prisoner in an abandoned cabin on the Illinois side of the Mississippi. Although Huck enjoys fishing and hunting, he is periodically terrified by his father's drunken, maniacal rages—often accompanied by beatings. So he decides to escape. Once, when Finn (old at fifty) goes to town for whiskey, Huck tunnels his way out and shoots a pig. Then he smashes the door, hacks the pig's throat, bloodies the ax and the cabin generally—all to make it appear that he has been murdered by a burglar or other intruder. After this fevered activity, he puts some provisions into a canoe and makes for Jackson's Island near Hannibal.

There, when he hears the boom of cannon, he knows that his strategy has been successful, that a searching party on a ferryboat is firing cannon to make his body surface. Having had a smoke, he proceeds to explore the island. He comes upon a campfire and recognizes Miss Watson's Negro slave Jim sleeping there. Jim confesses that he has run away because Miss Watson was about to sell him down the river. Huck and Jim join forces, fish, paddle round the island, and wander over it. One morning, after a violent storm, they see a farm house floating on the river. They paddle out to examine it and find a dead man in the house. Jim looks closely, covers the face with rags, but won't let Huck look at it.

Huck feels things are getting dull, so he slips on one of the dresses salvaged from the floating house and goes to the Illinois shore. He makes an unconvincing girl. The answers he invents when a shrewd farm woman questions him, though admirably quick, are contradictory. She exposes him easily by dropping a lump of lead into his lap and watching him clap

---

* See *The Adventures of Tom Sawyer.*

his legs together. A girl would have reacted by spreading them, she points out. However, Huck quickly shifts his line and tells the woman that he's a runaway apprentice. He learns that people are out looking for Jim—and for the $300 reward offered for his capture. Many think that Jim killed Huck. Pap is also suspected. There is a $200 reward offered for him— since he has gone off with a couple of hard-faced characters and hasn't been seen since.

Returning to the island, Huck rouses Jim, telling him that they must shove off if they are to elude capture. Piling their possessions on a raft they have salvaged, and trailing the canoe, they set out along the Mississippi for Cairo, Illinois where they can enter the mouth of the Ohio River. They run at night and rest during the day, sometimes "borrowing" a watermelon or a chicken from the farms they pass.

Now follow a series of turbulent adventures on the river. The earliest is almost the last. Below St. Louis, Huck and Jim encounter a steamboat, apparently foundered on a rock. They board her and find two bandits who have bound a third and are about to leave him, knowing that he will drown when the boat cracks. Huck and Jim are almost caught when their raft breaks loose, but they grab the bandits' skiff, leaving the would-be abandoners themselves abandoned.

Jim proves to be a devoted comrade. He shields, protects, and even instructs Huck. Once, after Huck's canoe is separated from the raft, Jim agonizes about Huck's safety, worries himself sick because he thinks Huck is lost. Huck suddenly appears, however, and pretends that Jim has been sleeping and has dreamed the whole episode. Jim, at first almost convinced, realizes when he sees the evidence of leaves and rubbish on the raft, that Huck has been fooling him. He rebukes Huck for his callous behavior. Huck apologizes.

On another occasion, just after Huck has suffered pangs of conscience at helping a slave escape, some men approach the raft, searching for escaped slaves. Huck tricks them into believing that his father is on the raft, sick with smallpox. The men gingerly leave some money for him and hastily push off.

Matters become worse. Huck and Jim bypass Cairo—Jim's great hope—in the night, and their raft is cut in two by a steamboat. Huck dives and escapes the wheel, but he can't find Jim. He goes to shore and is at once taken in by the

Grangerfords, a "mighty nice family": the aristocratic and benevolent Colonel Grangerford and his wife, two daughters, and three sons, one of them, Buck, a boy of Huck's age. The Grangerfords are engaged in a senseless blood feud with the Shepherdsons, another family whom they rather admire but persist in killing (and being killed by). The origins of the feud have become somewhat vague to both sides. A Grangerford girl and a Shepherdson boy fall in love and elope, precipitating a murderous ambush in which Buck, his father, two brothers, and a cousin are killed—along with some Shepherdsons. Huck feels the worse about this episode since unwittingly he has helped trigger this phase of the feud by delivering a message in which the two lovers arranged their elopement. Huck learns more about the cruelty that obsesses even "good" people.

Jim has escaped, too, and makes contact with Huck through the assistance of some of the Grangerford slaves. Together they return to the river, board their raft, and slide along the river. But their peace does not endure for long. Huck takes aboard two fugitives who are being chased by a mob, and they shortly reveal themselves to be two complete rogues—confidence men, each of whom has escaped a crowd eager to tar and feather him. One of them, about thirty, sells patent medicines, acts, teaches singing, "slings" lectures—does "most anything that comes handy, so it ain't work." The other—"about seventy," Huck says, perhaps inaccurately—doctors, cures by laying on of hands, tells fortunes, but thinks preaching is his special vocation. Soon each begins to demonstrate his talents. The younger asserts that he's the Duke of Bridgewater, falsely deprived of his high estate; the elder identifies himself as "the pore disappeared Dauphin, Looy the Seventeen." Huck and Jim, of course, feel it necessary to wait upon them hand and foot, a service they accept as their aristocratic due.

In one town a camp meeting is in process and the king passes himself off tearfully as a pirate converted by the preacher at the meeting and eager to leave for the Indian Ocean to convert other pirates—a statement of intention that proves very profitable, since the audience contributes generously to the project. In another town the pair of mountebanks put on a bizarre version of the balcony scene from *Romeo and*

Juliet, and almost get themselves run out of town for following it with *The King's Cameleopard* ("Ladies and children not admitted"). The latter performance consists solely of the king capering about the stage naked except for being painted in rainbow fashion. The pair might have been run out of town on a rail if one of the audience hadn't suggested that the same trick be played the next night on the rest of the townfolk. The audience accepts the suggestion and waits for revenge the next night. But the duke and king make their getaway after collecting the receipts for the second performance.

Huck sees another frightening instance of pride and cruelty. In one river town a harmless drunk named Boggs hurls dire but meaningless threats at a Southern aristocrat, Colonel Sherburn. The Colonel, after warning him to stop, shoots him. An aroused mob goes to the Colonel's house to lynch him—but he turns them away, scornfully telling them it needs a man to lynch someone, not a mob—unless the lynching is done Southern fashion, in the dark and with masks.

The two rapscallions (Jim's characterization of the royal pair) next try their most odious gambit. Waiting for a steamboat near a small town, they learn from a departing resident that his fellow townsman, Peter Wilks, has died, leaving behind three nieces and considerable property. The king learns further that Peter's two brothers, Harvey and William, are expected from England but haven't arrived. Immediately the king's plan is formed: he will be Harvey, the duke will be William (deaf and dumb), and Huck their servant. They easily deceive the innocent girls and gullible townspeople. Mary Jane, the eldest, whom Huck is attracted to, in order to show her faith in her "uncle," turns over the inheritance to the king. But Huck tells her the truth, and the king, despite his eloquence, doesn't get away with the scheme. The real brothers appear and identify themselves. Again only an expeditious retreat saves the two from a lynching party.

The most monstrous act of the charlatans is to turn Jim in as an escaped slave for forty dollars. Huck discovers Jim's whereabouts. His conscience has been troubling him. He believes it wrong to help a slave escape—almost an abolitionist act. Now he writes Miss Watson, informing her that a Silas Phelps has Jim and will give him up for the posted reward. Then, after writing the letter, he thinks of how good Jim has been to him, how steadfast through all their adventures. He says to himself, "All right, then, I'll *go* to hell," and he tears the letter up.

Arriving at the Phelps farm, Huck—much to his amazement —is enthusiastically greeted as Tom Sawyer, the nephew of Aunt Sally Phelps and Uncle Silas Phelps. He accepts the identification, hoping it will help him to engineer Jim's escape, and is able to answer all questions about the Sawyer family. The reason for Huck's being mistaken for Tom Sawyer is cleared up by Tom's sudden arrival. The Phelpses were expecting Tom, their nephew, whom they had never seen. Tom sizes up the situation with his customary acuteness and declares himself to be Sid Sawyer, Tom's brother. To Huck's astonishment, Tom eagerly enters into the "immoral" scheme of freeing Jim—but insists that the freeing has to be done in style, the style he has learned from his avid reading of the literature of escape. Tom's plan involves saws, chains, journals, magic, and some anonymous letters of warning. When finally the boys help Jim escape, the letters of warning that Tom has lavishly distributed, alert the neighbors who gather at the Phelps farm. Tom receives a bullet in the leg from one of them. Jim again displays his heroism by refusing to escape while Huck goes for a doctor. Instead he stays to nurse Tom tenderly and is captured. But Tom now springs his surprise: Old Miss Watson is dead, and she has set Jim free in her will. All of Tom's rigmarole and stratagems have been put on for sheer fun and adventure.

At this juncture, Aunt Polly appears. She has been puzzled about the letters she has received referring to Sid who has remained at home with her. She soon clears up the identities of Tom and Huck. Jim, now a free man, tells Huck that "Pap" Finn is dead: he was the man in the floating house, the man whose face Jim would not let Huck see. As for Huck, he thinks he must light out for the "territory" because Aunt Sally wants to adopt him and civilize him, and he's "been there before."

Critical Opinion

"All modern American literature," Ernest Hemingway wrote,

"comes from one book by Mark Twain called *Huckleberry Finn* . . . it's the best book we've had." Hemingway's comment stretches things a little, but *The Adventures of Huckleberry Finn* is, in fact, a marvelous book—"a joy forever," to quote Dixon Wecter, and "unquestionably one of the masterpieces of American and of world literature."

A sequel to *Tom Sawyer*, it is a much better book because Huck is far more interesting and complex than Tom; because Huck, who tells the story in his own wonderful vernacular, almost never strikes a false note; because Huck's experiences are deeper-going and his moral travails more meaningful. "A great-spirited boy among mean-spirited men," one critic observes, "Huck stands alone and ponders a decision usually left to those much older and more experienced—the reconciliation of piety with human decency." And his decision—to follow his own moral impulse rather than village morality—amounts almost to a vindication of what Mark Twain called "the damned human race," damned for its comfortable hypocrisies, its thoroughgoing dishonesties, and its pervasive cruelties, all of which Huck plentifully observes on his river odyssey with Jim.

Jim is as great a creation as Huck. Bernard De Voto calls Jim the only heroic character Mark Twain ever drew in his novels. Jim's heroism lies in his kindness, endurance, courage, and essential humanity. He contrasts dramatically with the scoundrels of the Mississippi frontier, with Pap Finn, the "Duke," and the "Dauphin," as well as with its aristocracy, Colonel Sherburn, the Grangerfords, and the Shepherdsons.

The Mississippi itself functions as a character in the novel, its greatest character some readers feel. The river gives form to the wanderings of Huck and Jim and from it arise the fun and the horror, the beauty and the color, of the book. To it Huck and Jim return gratefully after each unhappy adventure on shore, to move with it peacefully and freely once more.

The entrance of Tom Sawyer toward the end of the novel is perhaps a blight on an otherwise perfect book. The uproar and intrigue that Tom introduces shatter the tone of the story, shift it from high comedy to low farce.

Huckleberry Finn, however, is so great that it rises above even Tom and his shenanigans.

The Author

Samuel Langhorne Clemens was born in Florida, Missouri, in 1835. Four years later his family settled in Hannibal, Missouri, a sleepy river town where he led the romantic boy's life described in *Tom Sawyer* and *Huckleberry Finn*. His father, an unsuccessful lawyer turned unlucky merchant, died in 1846. Before Sam was twelve, his schooling was over, and he became a printer's apprentice and, not long after, the author of occasional newspaper pieces.

At eighteen he set out on his travels. He worked as a journeyman printer in a number of large cities from St. Louis eastward to New York. In 1857 he took passage at New Orleans, intending to proceed to South America. But luckily he met Horace Bixby, a river pilot, who agreed to teach him piloting, fulfilling Sam's boyhood ambition. As Bixby's apprentice, he learned to navigate every inch of the 1,200-mile Mississippi River. This was the happiest period of his life, he recalled in *Life on the Mississippi*. In his four years on the river, he acquired "his richest store of literary material." Here, he derived, too, the name "Mark Twain," from a river cry signifying two fathoms (or twelve feet).

With the advent of the railroad, the demand for river pilots declined. So Clemens went westward in 1861 to Nevada. There he tried his hand at mining, worked as a journalist on the Virginia City *Enterprise*, and engaged in some unsuccessful speculation. Here he also met the first of several literary advisers, "Artemus Ward" (Charles Farrar Browne), a famous humorist. When Clemens pushed on to San Francisco to work on the *Morning Call*, he submitted a story to Ward for a collection the latter was editing. It arrived too late, and the "villainous backwoods sketch"—"Jim Smiley and His Jumping Frog" (1865)—appeared in the *Saturday Press*. Widely circulated, it gave Samuel Clemens his first recognition.

Clemens' reputation grew substantially during the next decade. In 1865 he went to the Hawaiian Islands as a newspaper correspondent. The humorous lectures he delivered upon his return were enormously popular. In 1867 he traveled in Europe and the Holy Land. His hilarious if philistine record of the trip in *The Innocents Abroad* (1869) swelled his reputation and bank account. Following his romantic courtship of and marriage to Olivia Langdon, daughter of a wealthy coal dealer in Elmira, New York, Clemens moved to Hartford. There he produced his three most memorable books: *The Adventures of Tom Sawyer* (1876), *Life on the Mississippi* (1883), and *The Adventures of Huckleberry Finn* (1885).

Royalties from his books and proceeds from his lectures made Clemens an extremely rich man. His unfortunate investments, however, left him bankrupt. In 1895, at the age of sixty, he set out to pay his creditors and recoup his fortune. Through a triumphal lecture tour and the continued success of his books, he managed to do this.

Clemens built a magnificent home at Redding, Connecticut, and lived there in princely style. But, despite the adulation of his multitude of readers, the honors showered upon him at home and abroad, and the warm friendship of some notable men, his last years were melancholy, sometimes desperately unhappy. The death of his wife and all but one of his children left him lonely and deepened the pessimism that underlay his humor. He died in 1910. A number of his books have appeared posthumously; the most important of them, *The Mysterious Stranger* (1916), is also his bleakest and most despairing view of man.

Samuel Clemens was a matchless humorist. But he was also a gifted creator of memorable characters like Huckleberry Finn and Tom Sawyer. "Increasingly," writes Walter Blair, "Clemens' countrymen appreciate the charm of his personality, the breadth and depth of his richly native experiences, the unostentatious artistry revealed by his best writings." He is, William Dean Howells adds, "sole and incomparable, the Lincoln of our literature."

The Rise of Silas Lapham

by

WILLIAM DEAN HOWELLS (1837–1920)

Main Characters

Silas Lapham—A self-made man, an American go-getter, fundamentally sound, honest, and brave.

Persis Lapham—His wife, loyal, loving, and a moral prod to Lapham.

Irene Lapham—Their beautiful, efficient, but not especially intelligent younger daughter.

Penelope Lapham—Their droll, perceptive, humorous, though not particularly pretty elder daughter.

Tom Corey—Member of a wealthy upper-class Boston family who seeks employment in Lapham's paint business.

Mr. Corey—Tom's father, a charming dilettante.

Mrs. Corey—Tom's mother, conventional, aristocratic, good-natured.

Jim Rogers—The unscrupulous businessman whom Silas has once taken advantage of.

Mr. Sewell—The intelligent minister, foe of cant and sentimental humbug, who advises Silas and his wife at a critical period.

The Story

Silas Lapham, as he appears to a journalist who interviews him, is a solid, self-made man, perhaps a bit smug but none-

theless shrewd and enterprising. Though the journalist is right,
there is more to Silas Lapham. He has every reason to be satisfied with himself. He is wealthy because he aggressively and
proudly sells a superior paint, manufactured from minerals he
has discovered on the Vermont farm inherited from his father.
He has married a schoolteacher, Persis, who has proved a loyal
and loving wife as well as a moral guide—almost a conscience. Lapham has two affectionate daughters: Irene, the
younger, is not only a beauty but also a capable "manager"
about the house; Penelope, the elder, is a droll and perceptive young lady. Finally, Lapham has served his country, becoming a colonel during the Civil War.

Lapham suffers from a secret shame, though he never admits it, despite his wife's prodding. He once took on a partner, Jim Rogers, whose money helped him exploit the paint.
Then, partly because Rogers was a drag on the business and
partly because Lapham could not stand sharing the ownership
of his beloved paint with anyone, he crowded Rogers out. The
maneuver, while perfectly legal, was morally suspect, as his
wife and occasionally his conscience remind him.

Since Lapham and his family have moved to Boston, he has
developed social ambitions. Three Boston Brahmins—Mrs.
Corey and her two daughters—come to call in belated ac-
knowledgment of the kindness that Mrs. Lapham had shown
them at a resort where they had met. While perfectly polite,
Mrs. Corey had intimated that none of their friends lived in
Lapham's part of town. The hint is enough. Silas determines
to build on a lot he owns in the fashionable Back Bay area.
He is mildly supported by his wife, Persis, but not by Irene
or Penelope whose education for fashionable society has been
neglected.

Silas intends to build a big house. His excellent architect
helps him. One day, as they visit the site of the construction,
they see Rogers. Persis is deflated and declares that she will
not live in the house, but Silas grimly denies having wronged
Rogers and persists in his project.

On another occasion, Irene accompanies her parents to the
site. They are surprised by the appearance of Tom Corey, a
young Brahmin whom Irene finds extremely pleasant. After
some casual talk, during which Silas brags a good deal, as is
his habit, Corey leaves and the Laphams return home. Irene

confides to her sister, though indirectly, that she is smitten with Tom Corey.

As for Tom, he tells his father—a charming and cultivated dilettante who has refrained from work all his life—that he would like to get a job, preferably with Lapham. Having received his father's quizzical blessing, Tom applies to Silas directly, much to the latter's gratification since his wife regards young Corey as belonging to another social sphere. Tom's plan is to serve as foreign representative after he has learned the business.

Silas takes Tom to his summer home at Nantasket to discuss the matter. It is the first of many visits, for even after Tom's proposition has been accepted, he returns frequently. All the Laphams, including Irene, suppose that he admires Irene—although it is Penelope whom he always talks about and to whom he listens delightedly.

After a while the Coreys feel obliged to invite the Laphams to dinner. Penelope, who has disliked Mrs. Corey from the start, refuses to go, but the others accept eagerly, though they are uneasy about their social ineptitude. The dinner is a fiasco. Silas, unused to wine, drinks to excess and begins to brag obnoxiously. The next day, of course, Silas is desperately unhappy. He is not comforted by Tom's assurances that everyone at the party understood the reasons for his unseemly behavior. Silas offers Tom an opportunity to resign, but he refuses it and will not listen to Silas's self-abasement.

Some hours later Tom comes to the conclusion that he has not shown Silas enough sympathy, and sets off to visit him. Silas is not home—but Penelope is. She greets him amiably and, as always, chatters amusingly. Before very long, Tom finds himself telling Penelope that he loves her. She is amazed, bewildered, but not altogether unhappy. Like all the Laphams (and the Coreys, too), she supposed that Tom was paying court to her far more beautiful sister. She sends him away. Next morning Penelope conveys the news of Tom's preference to her mother who tells Silas. Puzzled about the course they ought to take and deeply unhappy about the necessity of inflicting pain on one of their daughters, they recall a minister, Mr. Sewell, whom they met at the Coreys' dinner party. His commonsense denunciation of sentimental novels and their false solutions to human problems especially impressed Silas.

They call on him, and his advice immediately appeals to them. One must suffer rather than three, he says, if none is to blame. The principle of the economy of pain would be obvious if false tradition did not prevail.

To Persis falls the duty of telling her daughter Irene that Tom loves Penelope. She performs it bluntly. Irene takes it without tears, presents to Penelope the mementos of Tom that she has cherished, and returns to her room. She cannot respond to Penelope's compassionate attempts at reconciliation or her parents' either. As soon as she can, she leaves for their Vermont farm.

Silas runs into serious financial troubles. To please Persis and perhaps to ease his own conscience, he has lent Rogers $20,000 on securities worth only a fraction of that amount. Moreover, Rogers has involved him in disastrous financial speculations. Especially disheartening to Silas has been his discovery that some mills given to him by Rogers as collateral for the loan are on the line of a railroad that has been purchased by a powerful combine that can force sale of the mills whenever it chooses, at whatever price it sets. Tom offers to lend Silas $30,000, but Silas gallantly refuses.

Silas hopes to get some money to buy out a new company that can produce paint as good as his but at a lower cost. He decides to sell the elegant house he has been building. But luck has turned against him. Because of his own carelessness, the house—on which he has allowed the insurance to lapse— burns down. Rogers meanwhile has located some Englishmen who are willing to buy the mills even when they are informed (as Silas insists they must be informed) that the railroad controls the value of the property. Silas discovers that the Englishmen are acting as agents for wealthy men who would be cheated if he sold them the mills. He rises to the moral challenge, rejects the deal, and goes bankrupt.

The affair between Tom and Penelope is happily resolved. Tom persists in his proposal even after Silas's bankruptcy, and Penelope ultimately consents to marry him. Irene, who has returned from Vermont upon hearing of her father's misfortunes, gives the lovers her blessing. After their marriage, Tom and Penelope leave for Mexico, a move that will minimize family friction (for the Coreys cannot wholly approve of Penelope nor she of them) and further Tom's business career. And Silas, much poorer but not poverty-stricken, retires to his Vermont farm. He finally sells his mines and works to the firm he had once hoped to purchase—but he still produces a special high-grade paint, the Persis brand. Both he and his wife are content with the moral choice that he so courageously made.

Critical Opinion

The Rise of Silas Lapham has not been exempt from the attacks commonly launched against Howells' fiction. Critics have deplored its lack of passion, its unvarying restraint, its refusal to explore the depths. Some have assailed it for its "unfavorable picture of the modern industrial and financial order" and others for its superficial analysis of the predatory nature of big business. Nevertheless, it has been said that "it has every appearance of being an American classic."

The reasons are plain. Howells' double plot—the temptations of Silas Lapham and the winning of Penelope—is expertly constructed. The characters, especially Silas Lapham —the self-made American businessman, honest, awkward, innocent in social relations despite his shrewdness in business affairs, fundamentally moral despite his single lapse from probity—are thoroughly realized. The style is graceful, flexible, tinged with humor.

It is Howells' ethical theme, however, that is most important. More than one critic has thought the title ironic, supposing that *rise* implied "social ascent." And at least one critic thought it misleading, supposing that *rise* alluded to Silas's business success. Howells himself, though, specifically declared that he conceived the rise to be a moral one. Silas, having learned from sad experience, rejects expedient solutions, refusing to wear moral blinders, to cheat even through a substitute. There are, Howells seems to insist, no substitutes for honesty—nor anything so valuable.

The commonsense formula of Mr. Sewell, the minister, underlines the same principle in a different context: If none is to blame, one must suffer rather than three. This lucid doctrine—"the economy of pain"—illustrates Howells' stand against romantic illusion and for truth, in life as in literature.

The Author

William Dean Howells, who was born in Ohio and died in New York, wrote about eighty books. He was, one commentator says, "in himself almost an entire literary movement." He early developed a love of books, and working in the office of his printer-father, educated himself intensively by a long course of reading. Beginning his career as a journalist in Ohio, he soon developed a reputation for competence. As a reward for writing a campaign biography of Lincoln, he was given a consulship in Venice. Returning to the United States in 1865, he joined the staff of the *Nation* and later the *Atlantic.* In 1871 he attained the highest editorial post in the country as editor of the *Atlantic,* where he remained until 1881. In 1885 he left Boston for New York, the new literary capital, and wrote "at large" for *Harper's.*

Meanwhile Howells had been pouring forth a stream of books—essays, criticisms, autobiographies, short plays, poetry, and novels. He became the acknowledged "dean of American letters," a position that nobody has quite filled since. He deserved his eminence for introducing Americans to foreign writers—about everyone of real importance, from Goldoni to Tolstoi—and for advancing the careers of such writers as Frank Norris, Stephen Crane, and Hamlin Garland. Moreover, he fought the good fight for realism in American literature, and opposed the cult of sentimentality that was restricting the growth of American letters.

Howells' own novels are not thrilling productions. In all forty of them, O. W. Firkins writes, "adultery is never pictured; seduction never; divorce once and sparingly . . . ; marriage discordant to the point of cleavage, only once and in the same novel with the divorce; crime only once with any fullness . . . ; politics never; religion passingly and superficially; science only in crepuscular psychology; mechanics, athletics, bodily exploits or collisions very rarely." Because so many of the basic themes that intrigue us are missing from Howells, his influence and popularity have declined. Yet in *A Hazard of New Fortunes* (1890), *A Modern Instance* (1882), and above all in *The Rise of Silas Lapham,* he has explored lucidly and attractively aspects of American life seldom touched on earlier and never in quite the same way.

These novels have been read for three-quarters of a century, and they still are engrossing documents. They go far to justify Carl Van Doren's observation that Howells "produced in his fourscore books the most considerable transcript of American life yet made by one man."

The Portrait of a Lady

by

HENRY JAMES (1843–1916)

Main Characters

Isabel Archer—A twenty-three-year-old American girl, pretty, confident, and determined to discover for herself the limits of freedom and responsibility.

Gilbert Osmond—Isabel's husband, dilettante expatriate, cruel and vain, who tests Isabel's psychic endurance.

Mme. Serena Merle—Osmond's former mistress and mother of their illegitimate child, Pansy. A deeply emotional woman, Serena is sympathetic, yet wholly unscrupulous where her daughter's interests are involved.

Ralph Touchett—Isabel's gentle English cousin, an invalid who tries to live vicariously through her. Mature and knowledgeable, he prepares Isabel for the world she must face.

Henrietta Stackpole—A brash American journalist, sure she can outwit and outmaneuver any "foreigner."

Lord Warburton—An affable but ineffectual young nobleman who would like to marry Isabel.

Caspar Goodwood—A forthright, vigorous American who pursues Isabel before her marriage and again after it founders, an ideal hero who never wins the heroine.

The Story

In the summer of 1872, Isabel Archer, a young, beautiful American from Albany, New York, is a guest at the country home of her wealthy English cousins, the Touchetts. In accepting her aunt's invitation to make her first trip abroad, Isabel explains that being abroad will deepen, not alter, her fundamental purpose in life—to live fully and independently. "I always wanted to know the things one shouldn't do. . . . So as to choose," Isabel remarks. During the first stage of her European experience, Isabel acquires the knowledge she needs to make her ultimate choice. Before the novel ends four years later, she understands what her invalid cousin Ralph Touchett said in the beginning about her fund of worldly knowledge, "Yes, of happy knowledge—of pleasant knowledge. But you haven't suffered, and you're not made to suffer."

Isabel's experiences at Gardencourt, the Touchett estate, cause her little suffering. Old Mr. Touchett enjoys her freshness and forthrightness. A liberal young aristocrat, Lord Warburton, falls in love with her and unsuccessfully proposes marriage. Her cousin Ralph, who also loves her deeply but vainly, instructs her in the nuances of European custom. Isabel also has on hand two old American friends, Henrietta Stackpole, a journalist who is wholly insensitive to subtleties in human relationships and disapproves of Americans living abroad, and Caspar Goodwood, Isabel's indomitable suitor. Rejected by Isabel before her trip, Caspar pursues her to Gardencourt. She dismisses him again, insisting he leave her for at least two years, until she probes the limits of her freedom.

Ralph persuades his dying father to leave Isabel a fortune of £60,000 to enable her to test her theories of independence. Just at this point Isabel meets Mme. Merle, an American-born cosmopolite who attracts and disarms Isabel by candidly confessing that she is a parasite. The worst of her type—as well as the most fascinating and delightful—Mme. Merle assures Isabel, is Gilbert Osmond: "No career, no name, no position, no fortune, no past, no future, no anything." Yet he is, Mme. Merle adds, "a man made to be distinguished" and a man Isabel must meet.

In Italy, six months after she has become an heiress, Isabel meets Osmond, as Mme. Merle has intended. Mme. Merle's purpose in bringing the two together is simple. As the mother of Osmond's illegitimate fifteen-year-old daughter, Pansy (who lives with Osmond), Merle hopes to assure the child of economic security. Isabel, however, knows only that Osmond appears to be mature, intellectual, and suave. She sharply denies the criticism of Osmond's superficiality and selfishness offered by Ralph, Caspar, and Mrs. Touchett. A few months later she marries Osmond.

Three years later the results of Isabel's marriage begin to emerge indirectly. Osmond and Mme. Merle have been trying to prevent young Ned Rosier from wooing Pansy. Rosier is not poor, but Merle and Osmond hope for a better match. When Lord Warburton comes to visit, they see the perfect suitor, titled and wealthy. Because Isabel is unaware that Pansy prefers Rosier, she agrees to Osmond's demand that she encourage Warburton's suit, even if she has to use as leverage Warburton's still warm affection for her.

At this point Isabel engages in a long internal monologue, sitting before the fire and reviewing the events of her past three years. Only vaguely conscious of some link between Osmond and Mme. Merle, she is profoundly aware of disappointment and anguish in her own life with Osmond: "Suffering, with Isabel, was an active condition . . . it was a passion of thought, of speculation, of response to every pressure." She knows that Osmond desired her once as an addition to his art collection. Because she has displayed a mind of her own, Isabel realizes, this complete egoist's hatred "has become the occupation and comfort of his life."

When Isabel realizes that Pansy does not love Warburton, she tries to break up the relationship. Though Osmond's fury is cool and controlled, Isabel has wrecked his plan completely. He retaliates by forbidding Pansy's marriage to Ned Rosier and shipping her off to a convent. Although Mme. Merle is disappointed, she cannot be so cruel. She, too, manages to wound Isabel by making it clear that she has engineered Isabel's fate from the outset. To Osmond, Mme. Merle makes yet more explicit her estimate of his viciousness ("Have I been so vile all for nothing?").

From England comes word that Ralph Touchett is dying

and wishes to see Isabel. Osmond refuses to let her go, but
when Isabel learns from Osmond's sister, Countess Gemini,
that Mme. Merle and Osmond were once lovers, she feels no
guilt about disobeying Osmond. In her final talk with Ralph,
Isabel admits that she has been used, and apologizes for
having disappointed him. Ever generous, Ralph reassures her:
". . . if you've been hated you've also been loved." Soon
Caspar Goodwood proves that such love can still be hers. Like
the others, Caspar has suspected her unhappiness but has
been powerless to interfere. Now he demands that she admit
her affection for him. Guardedly she does so, and Caspar
embraces her passionately. Isabel nevertheless leaves him and
returns to Osmond. As the novel closes, Henrietta Stackpole
says to Caspar, ". . . just you wait!" But Caspar recoils from
such optimism "shining at him with that cheap comfort."
Henrietta's "key to patience" opens no door to a happy ending.

Critical Opinion

Henry James regarded *The Portrait of a Lady* as his first
"big" novel. His critics have generally agreed, and some
believe James never surpassed his achievement in this work
of his "middle period." Certainly, in plot, characterization, and
technique, *The Portrait* deserves high praise. This masterly
sketch of a young woman determined to choose her fate
rather than have it thrust upon her stirs compassion without
sentimentality. The focus remains sharply and objectively on
Isabel's inward imagination and her preparation for the ordeal
she must endure.

The stages that precede Isabel's becoming an heiress and
choosing Osmond have been carefully plotted to reveal the
possibilities before her: the gentle but colorless charm of Lord
Warburton, and the attractive but frightening virility of
Caspar Goodwood. Because she is, as James notes, still "too
young, too impatient to live, too unacquainted with pain,"
there is also Ralph Touchett to serve as guide and commentator. Thus James mounts a subtle setting of American
and European taste, culture, and morality against which his
young heroine stands in sharp relief. Together scene and

character operate to shed brilliant light and ominous shadow on Isabel as she in turn casts her own luminous glow.

Though few critics disagree about the psychological implications of the first half of the novel, they are often in conflict about the latter half, especially about such questions as these: Why does Isabel choose Osmond? Why, after her disillusionment, does she reject Caspar and return to Osmond? About her original choice, some critics say it represents her proud rejection of those who would too rigidly direct her destiny. Leon Edel argues that Osmond represents a "safe" choice between the social commitments posed by Warburton's aristocratic world and the personal commitment demanded by Caspar Goodwood.

Isabel's determination to stay with her loathesome husband poses a more difficult problem. The range of theories here is great: Isabel has too much respect for the marital vow to abandon it; her sense of duty, especially to Pansy, is overpowering; her dread of an intense emotional involvement with Caspar makes even Osmond endurable; her moral values demand that she pay full retribution for her error. Whatever conclusion the reader reaches, he will find it difficult not to respect this young heiress whose integrity never falters even when her intelligence and imagination seem to waver. Surely no reader can forget her remarkable internal monologue (one of the first in modern fiction) as she sits alone before the fire and inwardly confronts the knowledge her freedom has purchased. It is a passage of surpassing beauty and tragic awareness.

The Turn of the Screw

by

HENRY JAMES

Main Characters

Governess—The spinster whose diary recounts the strange experiences of the children, the adults, and the ghosts.

Miles and Flora—The charming, precocious children in the governess' charge.

Mrs. Grose—The earthly, simple housekeeper who tries unsuccessfully to maintain a balance between the real and the spectral.

Peter Quint (a ghost)—Redheaded, sensual, evil, the deceased ex-steward of the estate.

Miss Jessel (a ghost)—Former governess of Miles and Flora and mistress of Quint.

Douglas—Reader of the tale and owner of the governess' diary. He knew her when she was his sister's governess and he was a college student.

Narrator—A liberal-minded fellow now in possession of the original manuscript.

The Story

On a Christmas Eve, long after the event, Douglas reads to an assembled group of friends the governess' diary, a meticulously written narrative of macabre events.

The governess, twenty-year-old daughter of a country parson, is hired by a handsome gentleman (her diary suggests that she is infatuated with him) to attend to the education of his late brother's two children. At Bly, a country estate, the youngsters live with a plain, motherly housekeeper, Mrs. Grose, and a large staff of servants. The governess is wholly enchanted with eight-year-old Flora—"the most beautiful child I had ever seen"—and looks forward to meeting

66

ten-year-old Miles who is away at school. Two days later she meets him unexpectedly, for he has been expelled from his boarding school as a bad influence. Can one so young corrupt others? she wonders. Mrs. Grose defends the boy vigorously and positively. The governess swiftly surrenders to his charm and beauty: "Everything but a sort of passion of tenderness was swept away by his presence."

She has already shown some curiosity about her predecessor, Miss Jessel, learning from Mrs. Grose only that she was pretty and that she is dead. Now the governess immerses herself in the joys of teaching her bright and lovable charges. They fill her present as nothing has filled her "small, smothered" past.

Strolling on the lawn one afternoon, enjoying a reverie about meeting a handsome man on the grounds of Bly, she looks up and sees—beyond the lawn, atop a tower—a strange man, his gaze fixed upon her, his appearance neither familiar nor agreeable. Troubled but determined not to worry Mrs. Grose or the children, she keeps silent. A few days later, when the same face appears at the dining-room window, she is horrified because the face seems to be searching for someone. She rushes outside but discovers no one. Suddenly she encounters the startled Mrs. Grose, who asks what has happened. The governess describes her two visions of the man who is "a horror"—red-haired, pale-faced, tall, well-dressed, but ghastly. Shaken, Mrs. Grose groans that the figure is that of Peter Quint, the master's valet, and adds, "Mr. Quint is dead."

Mrs. Grose now tells the governess that Quint is probably seeking the children, particularly little Miles, with whom he was friendly, too friendly and too free, as Quint was with everybody before he was found dead in a ditch one wintry morning. The governess determines to protect Miles at any cost, keeping him indoors yet telling him nothing to arouse his fears. With Flora, however, she continues to walk about the estate. A few day later, standing beside Flora at the edge of the lake, the governess senses another presence. Across the lake she sees staring at them "a woman in black, pale and dreadful." More terrible than the vision is the governess' sense that Flora has also seen the figure but pretends not to. The governess tells poor Mrs. Grose of her latest experience. By persistent questioning she elicits from Mrs. Grose the admission that the woman in black may be Miss Jessel, the former governess—and the mistress of Quint—who died while giving birth to his illegitimate child. What horrifies the governess most is her inner conviction that Miles and Flora are in league with the ghosts.

Meanwhile the children behave as winningly as ever. Their gaiety and sweetness are in utter contrast to the corruption the governess senses everywhere. A night later, hearing a rustling on the stair, the governess rushes out and confronts Quint on the stairwell. She rushes to Flora's room and discovers her bed empty. The child, unharmed, is at the window. She explains that she thought someone, possibly the governess, was walking about the grounds and had merely come to look. The governess does not challenge the explanation. A fortnight later, however, the governess, awakening shortly after midnight, steals to a window and sees an incredibly eerie sight: Flora gazing down from her terrace upon the moonlit lawn where Miles stands, transfixed, staring at the tall tower where Quint stares back at him.

Despite Miles's insistence that he and Flora have made up this "game" to show her how, for a change, they can be "bad," the governess remains certain that her charges are thoroughly infected with evil. Though Mrs. Grose urges her to tell her employer about the situation, she insists it is her duty not to bother him. She must save them herself. During the succeeding weeks she tries to keep the children as close to her as possible. Each conversation convinces her that their damnation is near. When Miles protests that she has become too possessive, she takes his complaint as further evidence of his attachment to Miss Jessel and Quint.

Completely distraught, the governess resolves to leave her post, but when she sees Miss Jessel seated in the children's schoolroom one afternoon, her determination is renewed. She writes to her employer, inquiring why Miles was expelled from school. As she sits writing the letter, Miles joins her. They talk for a while, pleasantly (almost like "honeymooners," James suggests), and suddenly she embraces the boy passionately, pleading with him to let her save him. At that moment, though the windows are shut, a shrill gust sweeps the room and the single candle is snuffed out. Miles shrieks, but insists he has blown it out himself.

Influenced by the governess' suggestions, Mrs. Grose also believes that the children are possessed by the infernal presences. The governess' letter to her employer, for example, has disappeared, apparently stolen by Miles. At the lake, Mrs. Grose's terror deepens when the governess suddenly asks Flora where Miss Jessel is, grasps the child's arm, and points to where Miss Jessel is standing across the lake. Mrs. Grose does not admit she sees Miss Jessel, and neither does Flora. Instead, the child demands to be taken away from the governess. The next day Mrs. Grose reports to the governess that Flora, sick in bed and feverish, has spoken "horrors," using bad language about the governess. The governess persuades Mrs. Grose to take Flora away to her uncle for the time being.

Alone now with Miles, the governess resolves to make him confess so that she can save him. She asks him why he stole her letter. Would that also explain his expulsion from school? He admits taking the letter ("To see what you said about me"), but denies that he stole at school. Rather, he admits, though evasively, to saying "things" to a few friends who then repeated them. As the governess presses Miles to reveal the nature of those "things," the face of Quint appears to her at the window. Hysterically, she clasps the boy to her. Miles whispers, "Is she *here*?" and then, "Miss Jessel, Miss Jessel." The governess cries that it is not Miss Jessel. "It's *he*?" the boy asks, and the governess flashes back at him, "Whom do you mean by 'he'?"

"Peter Quint—you devil!" Miles exclaims, demanding to know where the vision is. Hearing the boy speak the name convinces the governess that she has wrung the confession she needs to save him. Triumphantly she points to the window. Miles cries out and seems to fall, but she catches him and holds him close to her. Only her final sentence remains: "We were alone with the quiet day, and his little heart, dispossessed, had stopped."

Critical Opinion

One may read *The Turn of the Screw* on a number of levels. James, for example, said it was "a piece of ingenuity pure and simple, of cold, artistic calculation . . . to catch those not easily caught." Thus a reader may appreciate the story as sheer entertainment, enjoying it as a tour de force of suspense and horror, without ever knowing what the horror really is. The details are always wholly realistic and yet the effect is thoroughly romantic, because James writes about those things that, as he said, "we cannot possibly ever directly know."

Many critics insist, however, that the story's artistry is felt only when the reader recognizes the psychological aberration implicit in the governess' behavior. As Edmund Wilson and others argue, she is a sexually frustrated woman suffering from delusions and able, with fatal effect, to persuade others to share her delusion. Leon Edel adds that James's own disappointment as a dramatist is reflected in the haunted anguish of the governess.

Beyond the Freudian analysis lie other plausible interpretations. For example, the story has overtones of religious import: innocent children in a country Eden corrupted by evil (Quint in red and Miss Jessel in black—devil and death). The governess becomes, in this theory, a savior who fails because the force of evil is too great.

Readers must decide for themselves whether Quint and Miss Jessel really appear or are hallucinations. Are the children as innocent as they seem? Whatever the answer, most readers, like most critics, will find *The Turn of the Screw,* whether simple ghost story or complex psychological or theological narrative, a superbly wrought, absorbing tale.

The Author

Henry James was less than a year old when his wealthy parents first took him abroad. Of the seventy-three years that remained to him, James would spend fifty in Europe, and shortly before his death, he would become a British subject. It was not that James despised America, but rather that as an artist he decided that Europe, and especially London, held "the biggest aggregation of human life—the most complete compendium in the world." Out of that decision came some of the finest fiction of an age: *The Portrait of a Lady* (1881), *The Wings of the Dove* (1902), *The Ambassadors* (1903), and *The Golden Bowl* (1904).

James's boyhood and youth were years of rich intellectual ferment. His father, a friend of Emerson's, delighted in stirring debate between Henry and his brother William (later the famous psychologist). Throughout their lives a kind of lively competition animated their relationship.

Since James's back injury disqualified him for service in the Civil War, he was free to turn his attention exclusively to writing. After several early efforts, he won his first real fame with *Daisy Miller* (1878), a short novel about an American girl abroad. Working with great ardor at his craft, he found no time for marriage. His biographer, Leon Edel, recently published evidence of a close liaison between James and an American woman writer, Constance Fenimore Woolson, who later committed suicide.

As James's art matured, it became subtler, more complex, and more intricate. Although readers grew less receptive, James worked determinedly (despite profound depression) to penetrate the surface of reality and to disclose the core of the human heart.

James's productivity staggers the imagination: more than one hundred novels and stories, as well as plays, biography, travel books, and criticism. For the twenty-four volumes that comprise the New York edition of his novels, he prepared prefaces that rank with the finest critical essays about his work. An artist of great sensitivity, James paved the way for some of the major psychological novelists of the twentieth century.

The Red Badge of Courage

by

STEPHEN CRANE (1871–1900)

Main Characters

Henry Fleming—A young Union volunteer ("the youth") who loses his illusions about the glory of war and matures into manhood after his first experience in combat.

Jim Conklin—An older soldier ("the tall soldier"), knowing and patient, from whose death Henry learns much.

Wilson—"The loud soldier," a terrified braggart who helps Fleming understand the nature of courage.

The Tattered Man—A wounded soldier whose concern for Fleming increases the youth's sense of guilt.

The Story

On the day before initiation into battle, a company of Union soldiers conceal their fear underneath their cocky bragging. The boasts of Wilson, "the loud soldier," and the more reasonable observations of Jim Conklin, "the tall soldier," lead young Henry Fleming to wonder how he himself will respond to combat. Will he prove himself a hero, or will he run in terror? "He was an unknown quantity," Crane observes.

As a yellow sun blots out the red eyes of the night fires, the first day's battle begins. Fleming's imagination never has a chance to function during the skirmish. Curiosity, rage, and above all, the momentum of the mob carry him along. During those early hours, Fleming sees his first corpse and watches the boastful Wilson break down in fear. But because Fleming was "not a man but a member," part of a "subtle battle brotherhood . . . a mysterious fraternity born of the smoke and danger of death," he passes safely through his initial encounter.

His joy in his triumph over terror is, however, short-lived. Minutes after it has been repulsed, the Rebel army regroups for a counterattack. Now, for the first time, Fleming's imagination stirs and he begins "to exaggerate the endurance, the skill, and the valor of the onrushing enemy." He envisages them as dragons, machines of steel—unconquerable. Suddenly the soldier beside him howls and flees. Frenzied, abandoning cap and rifle, Fleming runs away, too. Ironically, the enemy attack is unsuccessful.

Ashamed and resentful, Fleming plunges into a forest, "going from obscurity into promises of a greater obscurity." Deep in the forest, "where the high arching boughs made a chapel," Fleming discovers that nature offers no real solace. For there, propped against a tree, mouth agape, eyes sightlessly staring upward, is a corpse.

Awed and horrified, Fleming flees the appalling spectacle. The stillness about him is shattered by the violent sounds of men in flight. A host of wounded soldiers join him in retreat, but he takes little comfort from the contrast between their wounds and his wholeness. "He wished that he, too, had a wound," Crane writes, "a red badge of courage." But before he can succumb to self-pity, he is catapulted into his first personal experience with death. He has seen men die, but never any who have been intimate friends. Now he watches the mortally wounded Jim Conklin stagger toward some isolated place where he may die without being run over by passing artillery wagons. Jim's grotesque dance of death awes him and adds to his growing sense of guilt. Unwittingly a tattered soldier who expresses concern for Fleming's welfare adds to his anguish.

At the deepest level of his inward torment, Fleming wins some respite. The regiment, now in full flight, overtakes him. Fleming seizes one soldier to ask what has happened. Hysterical, the man smashes his rifle butt into Fleming's skull. When Fleming recovers consciousness, he has a "red badge." Led back to his own company by a soldier with a cheery voice, Fleming is greeted by all as a wounded veteran. Inwardly, however, he remains disconsolate, aware that more struggle, more suffering lie ahead.

In the final battle, Fleming wins his real red badge. This time he fights neither as a member of a mob nor as an enemy of the universe. Rather he is an angry man, devoured by a vengeful fury directed against the living men who are trying to destroy him. He fights, as his officer notes, like a wildcat, a war devil. He leads a futile charge, wholly unconscious of any purpose except the need to destroy. When a color sergeant is shot, he plunges into murderous fire to retrieve the flag from the enemy. At the end of the battle—which the Northerners have neither won nor lost—Fleming discovers that the true significance of his badge has nothing to do with courage. It is not a blow on the head or a sacrifice to patriotic frenzy, but a freedom from illusion about great deeds or chances for survival. It is an acceptance of the simple fact that death, after all, is only death. Knowing this, Fleming, as the novel ends, has attained his maturity and become a man.

Critical Opinion

When it was first published in 1895, *The Red Badge of Courage* won praise from many reviewers, especially in England where H. G. Wells and Joseph Conrad admired its profound sensibility and fertile imagination. More recently, critics have disagreed about its theme and its art, though most acknowledge that it is a masterpiece.

Many early critics argued that Crane's war novel is dominantly naturalistic, i.e., as Crane had written of his earlier *Maggie*, "it tries to show that environment is a tremendous thing in the world and frequently shapes lives regardless." Today critics believe that Fleming is not merely a wisp in a turbulent universe. At least he does not sink in ignoble defeat. He learns much about himself and the universe during the novel, and most important, he manages to achieve maturity and a kind of dignity by asserting his will. The novel seems, then, to be closer to realism—an objective study of the conflict between man's will and his fate.

Crane's wealth of colorful imagery (suggested by the paintings of the French impressionists) has also aroused wide discussion. Are Crane's images merely the extravagant excesses of a gifted amateur? Or are they related organically to Crane's theme? Thus, the color red, which dominates the novel ("red cheers," "red sun," "red eyes," "crimson roar"), is linked to themes of terror and guilt, rage and heroism. Similarly, innumerable *animal* and *machine* images suggest the bestiality and impersonality of war. Some critics have analyzed the imagery even further, hinting that Christian themes of sacrifice and redemption or ritual patterns of initiation lie embedded in such symbols as the death of Jim Conklin or Fleming's journey to the forest.

The Red Badge of Courage is, as Ernest Hemingway observed, "all as much one piece as a great poem is." In a great poem, the synthesis of the parts adds up to an inescapable truth. Although Crane's novel challenges one with its broad range of possibilities, the perceptive reader never loses sight of its core: the emerging character of Henry Fleming. Structure, imagery, character contrasts—all contribute to the vivid portrait of a young man discovering himself under the most trying of all human conditions—war.

The Author

"I decided that the nearer a writer gets to life, the greater he becomes as an artist," *Stephen Crane* once wrote. Ironically Crane, born six years after the close of the Civil War, drew upon imagination rather than experience to write his great novel of that war, *The Red Badge of Courage.* His brief life was not, however, without excitement. Crane grew up in a literary environment. Both of his parents were writers. But the boy rebelled against the restrictions imposed by his stern Methodist parents. He read novels and plays and, worse, he played baseball. Indeed, Crane's ambition was to be a professional ballplayer.

Crane's dedication to sports rather than to studies cut short his college career. In his early twenties he turned to journalism, which was to be his life work. From his newspaper assignments emerged some of his most notable fiction. While covering the Bowery, he lived briefly as a derelict and gathered material for his moving story, *Maggie: A Girl of the Streets* (1893). In the Far West he studied lonely frontier men and produced two memorable short stories, "Blue Hotel" and "The Bride Comes to Yellow Sky." During the Spanish-American War, as a correspondent on a gun-running boat, Crane was shipwrecked. Soon afterward, he wrote his great short story about men against nature, "The Open Boat."

Crane's life was filled with action. It was also, unhappily, filled with much sadness and frustration. His war experiences undermined his health and left him with incurable tuberculosis. His love for Cora Taylor, who had once run a sporting house, earned him much ridicule and social censure. For a short time, he and Cora found refuge and happiness in England, but it was too late for the ailing Crane. At twenty-eight he died. His work, however—vigorous, realistic, poetically imaginative—helped open the way to modern American fiction.

Looking Backward

by

EDWARD BELLAMY (1850–1898)

Main Characters

Julian West—A conventional young Bostonian of 1887 who is precipitated 113 years into the future.
Edith Bartlett—His fiancée.
Dr. Leete—The patient physician who explains carefully to Julian the social organization of America in the year 2000.
Edith Leete—Dr. Leete's kind and sympathetic daughter, a source of comfort and stability to Julian West.
Mrs. Leete—The doctor's amiable wife.

The Story

Julian West, in 1887, when the story opens, is an upper-class Bostonian, engaged to the charming Edith Bartlett. Save for his occasional concern about industrial unrest, he is a quite ordinary American who shares the ideals and prejudices of his time and class. Plagued by insomnia, he builds beneath his house a soundproof sleeping chamber hermetically sealed with stone slabs. Occasionally he summons a hypnotist who effectively puts him into a deep sleep. He has instructed his Negro servant in the technique of waking him.

After visiting his fiancée one night, Julian returns home and, unable to sleep, has resort to his hypnotist. When he awakens, he is surprised to see a man and two women near his bed. He makes inquiries—and to his utter disbelief, at least initially, discovers that he has been asleep for 113 years. Presumably his house burned down and his servants died in the flames. Julian, in his secret subterranean room, was untouched by the fire and continued to sleep right through the century. Then, in the year 2000, Dr. Leete, the gentleman at his bedside, a retired physician, while excavating in order to build an underground laboratory, discovered the chamber and revived the sleeper.

Julian slowly accepts his situation, the more easily because of the presence of Edith Leete, the doctor's lovely and sympathetic daughter. In the society to which he has awakened, the state owns all the means of production and distribution. The change was effected without violence. The absorption of business into ever-larger monopolies, a tendency already apparent in the nineteenth century, resulted in one huge syndicate that consolidated the entire capital of the nation. The nation took over the syndicate, thus becoming one great business corporation. All citizens, whatever their work, now share equally in the profits and economies of the new society. Though money as such has been abolished, each citizen receives an amount of credit in the government storehouse. The title to such equality is simply the worker's humanity. Moreover, each worker can live in luxury because the elimination of competition has brought shoddy or useless production to an end.

It is no longer necessary to maintain a vast army. Other nations have followed America's lead, and cooperation among nations is now the universal rule. The police force is greatly diminished. Since the economic motives for crime have largely disappeared, so has crime. Of course, there are instances of "atavism" or regression. These people are treated in hospitals, not jails.

Julian's bewilderment and disorientation, especially when he sets out alone to explore the new Boston, almost shatter him. But the kindness and sympathetic understanding of Edith and her mother and father save him.

The explanation of the new society continues, Dr. Leete serving as the chief expositor. Education, broadly based and liberal, is the same for everyone. All men go to school till they are twenty-one. Then for three years they engage in menial service, to which no onus is attached. Dr. Leete, for example, served as waiter in one of the enormous, superbly constructed and expertly managed restaurants where the citizens generally take at least one of their meals daily. When a man is twenty-four, ability and inclination determine his career. Some citizens receive further education to prepare them for a profession. Others enter the industrial army, rising as high as their skills and talents permit. If anyone chooses to change his vocation, he is given every opportunity to do so. If a man, for example, thinks that he would like to become a physician, his way is smoothed, provided he can meet the severe academic qualifications. As a rule, such shifts in vocation are discouraged after a man becomes thirty-five. The reason is obvious. Except for judges and some administrative officers, all men retire at forty-five.

How are the disagreeable jobs filled? By lowering hours and improving conditions to the point at which enough men will volunteer for them—even if this entails an hour a day (or less, conceivably) of tedious labor. And what makes men strive to attain superiority when it brings them no monetary rewards? Their commitment to their society: service to the nation, patriotism, passion for humanity—all fostered and encouraged by their education and training.

The President of the United States is chosen by a method that ensures his qualifications. He is elected by the chiefs of the ten grand divisions of the industrial army. These, in turn, are chosen by the chiefs of each trade or guild. And to prevent intrigue, the chiefs of each guild are elevated not by its active members but by its retired or honorary members. The President is usually about fifty when he assumes office, an honorable exception to the rule of retirement at forty-five. He serves for five years and is responsible to a national Congress which may approve him for another five years or, as seldom happens, refuse to approve. The latter circumstance is rare because the President has risen through the ranks, amply demonstrating his fitness and devotion all along the way.

Women participate fully in the new society's benefits and contribute fully to its wealth. Only while they bear and rear children do they leave active service. Most serve from five to fifteen years; those without children fill out the full term.

Relieved from a servile or degrading dependence, women are
more cultivated, more vigorous, freer than ever before. They
even have a representative in the Cabinet, chosen on the same
principle as the chiefs of the industrial army. The representative may veto measures respecting women's work, pending appeals to Congress. There are no lawyers in this society. Instead, three judges—sober, intelligent, acute people who are
also an exception to the practice of retirement at forty-five—
investigate thoroughly and dispassionately the merits of the
cases before them and render their decisions. If the cases involve women, the judges are women. If they involve a man
and a woman, a man and a woman judge must consent to
the verdict.

Edith Leete seems to Julian West to prove the virtues of
the new society. Intelligent, sensitive, deeply understanding,
she arouses his love. He wants to confess it, but the thought
of his deficiencies as a man from an inferior, antiquated world
prevent him. After he listens to a sermon over the telephone-
radio, on the principles of the new Christianity, in which love
is the touchstone and guiding principle, his feelings of in-
adequacy deepen. But Edith's gentleness and compassion
break through his reservations. He tells her of his love and
she responds gladly. She has always loved him, she says. She
is the great-granddaughter of his nineteenth-century fiancée,
Edith Bartlett. The letters he had written to Edith have been
passed down to her; and even before meeting him, she had
determined to marry only another Julian West. Dr. and Mrs.
Leete cheerfully give their formal consent. Julian, however,
will be no drone in the twenty-first century. He will assume a
position for which he has the most valid credentials of any
man in the new century: professor of nineteenth-century
history.

Critical Opinion

During the first year of its publication, *Looking Backward*
sold slowly; then it began to catch on sensationally. In 1890
the *Literary Bulletin* of Houghton Mifflin, its publishers, declared: "*Looking Backward* holds in American literature an
almost unique place in character and popularity. Of only one

The Twentieth
Century

The Octopus

by

FRANK NORRIS (1870–1902)

Main Characters

Presley—A thirty-year-old poet settled in California to write a romantic epic of the West, graduate of an Eastern college, sensitive, hopefully committed to beauty as an alternative to evil.

Vanamee—Presley's friend, a shepherd, a wanderer, and a mystic with "an almost abnormal capacity for great happiness and great sorrow." He tries desperately to evoke the spirit of his brutally ravished dead sweetheart, Angele.

Annixter—A young rancher, college-educated but rough-hewn, a stanch and courageous fighter for his cause.

Hilma Tree—A pretty nineteen-year-old working girl at Annixter's Quien Sabe Ranch. Fresh, unassuming, and generous, she is a perfect foil and mate for Annixter.

Magnus Derrick—Called "Governor" since he long ago ran unsuccessfully for that office. Owner of the Los Muertos Ranch, an honest, earnest man lacking the decisiveness needed to guide the community that looks to him for leadership.

Mrs. Derrick—His wife, a handsome woman, hopelessly out of place in the harsh world of the West and willfully isolated in her private realm of decadent poetry and fiction.

Harran Derrick—The youngest son, Magnus' favorite, and manager of Los Muertos, eager to fight for the farmers' rights.

Lyman Derrick—The eldest son, a corporation lawyer, ambitious, unscrupulous, ready to cooperate with any power that will lead him toward his goal—the governorship his father failed to attain.

S. Behrman—President of the Loan and Savings Bank of Tulare County, leading real estate and mortgage broker in town, fat, oily, and ruthlessly effective as the chief local agent of the railroad.

Shelgrim—President of the Pacific and Southwestern Railroad, the "octopus" company whose tentacles crush the wheat ranchers. An elderly but articulate and powerful man who believes himself wholly innocent of malice and sees the struggle between railroad and farmer as one of natural forces.

Dyke—A former railroad engineer, now a hops grower caught in the vise of freight costs.

Hooven—A German wheat farmer, vigorously and openly antagonistic to the railroad powers, and willing to fight to the death to protect his interests.

Osterman, Broderson, Dabney—Wheat farmers.

Ruggbag, Delaney, Christian—Agents of the railroad.

Genslinger—Editor of the local newspaper, a hireling of the railroad.

The Story

In late September, toward the close of the nineteenth century, Presley walks along the sun-baked farm land of Bonneville in California's San Joaquin Valley. The grimy farmers seem brutish to him, hardly the sort of people he hopes to include in his proposed poem about the romance of the West. And their problems, too—surviving increases in freight rates, mortgage commitments, and land grabs—seem alien to his vision of the beautiful countryside. He listens with barely controlled impatience to the complaints of farmer Hooven, fired after seven years from Magnus Derrick's ranch because Derrick can no longer afford outside help, and to those of Dyke, released after ten years as a railroad engineer because he has refused to accept a sharp paycut. Presley finds more comfort with his old friend Vanamee, working as a shepherd on Buck

Annixter's ranch, who urges him to put his hexameters to work on an epic of the West in which problems of the present will recede into a panorama of the land and of all nature. But even as Presley dreams, a train hurtles by and massacres a group of Vanamee's sheep that have stumbled onto the tracks. This grim, bloody episode adds to Presley's imagination a less tender but more compelling image: ". . . the iron-hearted Power, the monster, the Colossus, the Octopus."

Of the railroad's many tentacles, the one most threatening to the farmers is a proposed regrading of their land. Years earlier, farmers had taken advantage of the Government's invitation to settle and develop the rich valley land. They were aware even then that not all of the land was legally theirs, but the possibility of making a quick fortune in wheat overcame their fears. What now keeps them from absolute ownership of their ranches is the bonus the Government had given the railroad for constructing the road: vast tracts of land overlapping the farmers' holdings. Originally the Government had intended that the farmers ultimately repurchase the railroad's holdings at about two dollars and a half per acre. The railroad, however, conscious of the improvements wrought by the farmers, shrewdly plans no such modest price. Doggedly and unrealistically, the farmers cling to their slender hope that the announced price will not exceed five dollars an acre.

To assure themselves a fair chance of winning their battle, the farmers determine to place one of their own men on the powerful railroad commission that sets freight rates and approves land-regrading plans. However, as one of them, Osterman, points out, the only way to obtain that post is to bribe the appropriate officials in San Francisco. Magnus Derrick vehemently opposes such underhanded actions; his wife, less from scruple than from fear, encourages Magnus to submit rather than fight the railroad. Caught between the arguments of his fellow ranchers, his own integrity, and his wife's importuning, Magnus vacillates.

Meanwhile the seeding goes on; the farmers hope for rain and try to order their private lives. The brusque Annixter has the most difficult time. Apart from his difficulties as a farmer (the bank has already refused his offer to repurchase all of its holdings on his ranch at the original price), Annixter finds himself emotionally disturbed by the presence of Hilma Tree.

Her pleasant exchanges with Delaney, one of Annixter's hands, goad him to jealous fury, and he angrily fires Delaney. Clumsily and boorishly, he makes a befuddled and unsuccessful attempt to embrace Hilma, managing only to frighten her. But during the great barn dance he holds for everyone in the neighborhood, Annixter learns that Hilma returns his affection. At the height of the party, Delaney, drunk and belligerent, rides into the barn, gun in hand, and threatens Annixter who until that moment has been dancing with Hilma. As Annixter starts to thrust Hilma toward safety, they exchange a brief but significant glance that assures Annixter of her affection. Then he shoves her away and, while the guests cringe, shoots Delaney in the hand and emerges as the local hero.

At the very climax of the gaiety, however, the tentacles of the railroad reach in to destroy the farmers' good cheer. Word arrives that the railroad has set the price for repurchase of the land at between $22 and $30 per acre, and has expressed willingness to sell it to anyone who will pay the price. Momentarily struck dumb by the horror of their situation, the farmers decide to establish a "League," with Magnus Derrick as president, to battle the railroad and keep it from taking over the land. All of the members except Magnus sign, but this time, as his wife once more tries to dissuade him, the men crowd about him, sweep his wife away, and Magnus affixes his signature. As the first book ends, Vanamee says to Presley, "I think that there was a dance in Brussels the night before Waterloo."

By this time, too, Presley's romantic notions about the West have begun to disappear. Increasingly he has come to sympathize with the farmers and to hate the inequities that cripple them. At the same time he knows that the farmers have also been opportunists and have loved profits more than they have loved the land. In conversation with Cedarquist, a wealthy manufacturer, he learns that the great struggle in American life is against exploitation, and that the struggle must continue so long as no way is found to rouse the public from apathy or to quell the aggressiveness of the monopolistic trusts. Above all, Presley now realizes that his poem must be about the people he has hitherto ignored, not just a vague tribute to the land.

To press their interests, the farmers manage to place

Lyman Derrick on the commission. This feat is accomplished by a sizable bribe arranged and paid for by Magnus. The railroad, using dummy buyers (like Delaney, who bids on Annixter's ranch), has already instituted eviction proceedings against the farmers and has won its initial test cases in both the local and circuit courts. Dyke, the ex-engineer, believes himself fortunate in having begun as a hops farmer, thus avoiding the predicament of his friends. Thinking that he will avail himself of the cheap freight rate quoted by the railroad, Dyke has mortgaged his home to S. Behrman to raise money for seeds and supplies, and contracted with several dealers for delivery of his crop at a low but profitable price. But when Dyke comes to Behrman to arrange final details for shipping his crop, he discovers that the freight rate has more than doubled, wiping out not only his profits but also any remote chance of financial survival. What, he demands of Behrman, does the railroad base its rates on? Emphasizing each word with a tap of his finger, Behrman replies, "All the traffic will bear."

In the midst of all the turmoil, Annixter carries on his amorous pursuit of Hilma. Although, in a tender scene she admits her love for him, he tells her that what he has in mind is an affair, not marriage. Astonished and hurt, she leaves his ranch with her parents to go to San Francisco. Alone in the fields that night, Annixter suddenly realizes that he, too, is in love. At the moment of his awareness, he notes that the wheat has just broken through the ground. In another part of the dark wheatfield, Vanamee, seeking mystically to recall his dead beloved, calls forth her daughter who sleepwalks across the field toward him.

Annixter follows Hilma to San Francisco and persuades her to marry him. After a brief and happy honeymoon, they entrain for Bonneville and the ranch. En route, the train is stopped and the mail train held up, a brakeman fatally wounded, and $5,000 stolen. The dying brakeman identifies the holdup man as a former employee of the railroad, and Annixter knows at once that Dyke is the culprit. After his experience with Behrman, Dyke talks with everyone in town about his misery, but it is while listening to Caraher, the local bartender and anarchist, that Dyke settles upon his foolhardy plan to take his revenge on the railroad. While Dyke hides in the mountains, where Behrman's deputies search for him, Annixter and Hilma take his mother and child to Quien Sabe Ranch.

Presley completes his poem, now entitled "The Toilers," and at Vanamee's urging, publishes it in the daily press rather than in a literary magazine so that the masses may read it. The poem wins national acclaim as a cry of the downtrodden, but Presley still finds himself personally apart from the people he has come to admire, unable to join them in any specific action in their cause.

Some weeks pass, during which the farmers learn to use the rifles Annixter has had shipped to his ranch, and then Lyman Derrick arrives to announce the new freight rates. He assures the farmers that the commission has managed to obtain an average 10-per-cent decrease in rates, but a quick examination of the freight charts reveals that all of the major decreases are assigned to those points from which almost no shipments are made. No changes of any kind have been made in Bonneville's rates or in those of any other community where trade is active. Even Magnus recognizes that his son has sold out the farmers and when Annixter punches Lyman, the disillusioned father cannot bring himself to intervene.

Later that same evening, the newspaper editor, Genslinger, confronts Magnus with evidence of the bribery that gained Lyman his post and demands $10,000 not to print the story. To make the barb even more painful, he tells Magnus that Lyman had been pledged to the railroad long before the bribery. Alone in his desperation, Magnus decides to send the money to Genslinger. Ironically he gives it to Presley to deliver at the same time the poet is sending off the manuscript of "The Toilers" to his publishers.

The next day, Hilma's birthday, as Annixter tells Presley how his love for her has enriched his life, Dyke rides wildly onto the ranch begging for a fresh horse. Annixter provides one and Dyke dashes off, pursued by Delaney, Behrman, and others. At the rail depot, Dyke leaps aboard an engine and tries to escape with it, but the railroad men signal ahead for a derailment. Seeing what they have done, he backs up, exchanges shots with his antagonists, is wounded, and leaps from the train, running to hide in the tall wheat of Annixter's farm. Trapped when he falls from a stolen horse, Dyke finds himself only a few feet from Behrman and feels elated that at least he can kill this monster. But his gun misfires, and though he struggles valiantly and savagely, he is subdued. Some months later Dyke is sentenced to life imprisonment.

With the wheat at its summer-ripe fullness (Hilma, incidentally, is now pregnant), the farmers take time out from their worries to have a jack-rabbit hunt and barbecue. After they have flushed out tens of thousands of rabbits and corralled them, they allow the Portuguese laborers to slaughter them brutally. Again, however, as earlier at Annixter's barn dance, the railroad interrupts the festivities. A messenger tells Annixter that Delaney has moved into his house and thrown out all of Annixter's possessions, and that another group of railroad men is heading toward Magnus Derrick's Los Muertos Ranch for the same purpose. The railroad has simply decided not to bother waiting for the Supreme Court decision, convinced that it will win and has the right to proceed as it wishes.

Aroused and determined to prevent the intrusion, Annixter and Derrick try to call the men together to fight the interlopers. But instead of the 600 Leaguers they had counted on, they can rally only nine men to go with them. The men intercept the marshal, accompanied by Behrman, Delaney, and several other railroad hirelings. A heated argument takes place between Magnus and the railroaders, and a shot fired by Hooven sets off an exchange of volleys. When the smoke clears, Delaney and another railroad agent lie dead. Among the five dead farmers are Annixter, Harran Derrick, Hooven, and Osterman.

That night Hilma suffers a miscarriage. That same night Presley enters in his journal his sense of horror at what the people of America have allowed to take place. ". . . it is Lexington," he writes. "God rouse us from our lethargy. . . ." To himself he vows revenge on Behrman and Shelgrim, the president of the railroad.

At a protest meeting the next evening, the Leaguers ironically blame Magnus for not having avoided violence by gathering all 600 men to face the railroaders. Presley harangues the crowd about the need to overwhelm their oppressors, but as he finishes amid their wild applause, he realizes that their response has been but an emotional outburst of momentary conviction, that an hour later they will once more subside into apathy. Taking full advantage of the farmers' indecisiveness, some railroad agents in the audience distribute hundreds of copies of the Genslinger newspaper telling the full story of Magnus' bribery in behalf of Lyman. Again Magnus has been sold out. The beaten old man is left abandoned by those who had hitherto looked to him as their leader. Later that night Presley acts for the first time as he has always hoped he would. He hurls a bomb through the window of Behrman's dining room. The room is totally wrecked, but Behrman miraculously escapes unharmed.

What remains of the novel is for the most part a tying together of the shreds and tatters of human aspiration. The Supreme Court finds in favor of the railroad, and the farmers are either dispossessed or reduced to leasing their own land from the railroad. Magnus Derrick, almost senile, accepts from Behrman a job as assistant freight manager at fifty dollars a week. Hooven's wife and daughters try to survive in San Francisco, but the elder daughter is swiftly reduced to prostitution, and the mother, accidentally separated from her, dies in the streets of starvation, her younger daughter beside her. Lyman Derrick, enjoying a happier fate, has become the railroad's candidate for governor of California.

Presley, too, is in San Francisco, waiting for a ship to take him to India. Before sailing, he calls on Shelgrim and discovers that the tycoon is not at all the monster he has anticipated. Intelligent and even charitable, Shelgrim points out to Presley that the wheat and the railroad are forces governed not by men but by the laws of supply and demand. "Blame conditions," he argues, "not men." S. Behrman is also in San Francisco, paradoxically to supervise the loading of wheat aboard the ship that will carry Presley to India. As he watches the wheat pour into the hold, Behrman loses his footing and falls into the hold. What ensues is a hysterical dance of death as Behrman claws and crawls trying to avoid sinking beneath the dusty cargo. The dance ends as the wheat runs into his gaping mouth, suffocates and buries him.

As the boat sails, Presley asks whether anything is left and finds his answer in a recollection of Vanamee's mystical faith in the ultimate triumph of good and truth. The individual may die, but the race lives on.

Critical Opinion

Despite its extravagant melodrama, *The Octopus* has its base in solid fact—the historical event known as the Mussell Slough affair of 1878, during which almost all of the catastrophic events cited in Norris' story did in fact occur. Had Norris rigorously followed the disciplines of naturalistic fiction laid down by Emile Zola, *The Octopus* would have emerged as a purely scientific sociological document. But though critics continue to disagree about the novel, they are in accord on one point—that Norris is not detached about the people or the events that fill his broad canvas.

Presley's slow but inevitable development into conscious sympathy with the downtrodden farmers is evidence of Norris' own compassion. It is not, however, an uncritical sympathy, for Presley (whose real-life counterpart, incidentally, is Edwin Markham, "The Toilers" being the counterpart of Markham's "Man with the Hoe") recognizes the economic opportunism of the farmers, too. What confuses the issue and diminishes the impact of the novel is the intrusion of the quasi-mystical thesis about pervasive forces in nature that move man despite his will. On the surface, such an approach seems conventionally naturalistic, but Norris refuses to see the forces as indifferent, insisting through both Vanamee and Presley that nature ultimately works for good and for truth. If nature is all good, then it is man—both railroader and farmer—who has interrupted the perfection of the world. Thus, Norris fuses his philosophic idealism with his sociological sympathy for the underdog and achieves a fundamentally distorted and unconvincing outlook.

However illogical Norris' thinking, his narrative force compels the reader to continue without loss of enthusiasm to the very last page of the long novel. *The Octopus* is rich in memorable episodes—the dance at Annixter's barn, the jack-rabbit hunt, the pitched battle between the farmers and the railroad men, and the death of S. Behrman—and in a host of unforgettable, if often overdrawn, characters. Its greatest weakness is the overly long, rhapsodic passages about Vanamee and his dead love, Angele. Yet even these have at times a lyric tenderness.

Norris spent four months in the library researching the facts for *The Octopus*. Whatever the weaknesses of the book, it easily transcends mere reportage. William Dean Howells admired it when it was published, H. L. Mencken and Theodore Dreiser in the years that followed. Today it continues to merit the attention of anyone interested in man's greed and compassion, inhumanity and idealism, struggles, defeats, and aspirations.

The Author

Frank Norris' mother was a well-known actress, his father a successful jewelry man. In 1884, when Norris was fourteen, the family moved from his birthplace, Chicago, to San Francisco where he attended preparatory school before going to Paris to study art. In Paris he became a dilettante, more fascinated with atmosphere than with his studies. He nevertheless began to write romantic stories and sketches that were published in California newspapers. Norris' father, alarmed that his son might become a writer rather than a businessman, brought him home to enroll at the University of California. Norris managed to pass nothing during his four years there and earned no degree. But he did discover the writings of Emile Zola (as well as those of Kipling and Richard Harding Davis) and begin work on one of his finest naturalistic studies, *McTeague*, published in 1899. During a year at Harvard, he came under the influence of Lewis Gates, a teacher of creative writing, and wrote *Vandover and the Brute* (published posthumously in 1914) while continuing his work on *McTeague*.

For a year Norris covered the Boer War for the San Francisco *Chronicle*, writing several articles and a few stories and, unhappily, falling victim to a fever that undermined his health. For the next few years he worked again as a journalist in California but also completed another novel, *Moran of the Lady Letty* (1898). In 1898, while covering the Spanish-American War, he met Stephen Crane whose writing he admired but whose callous attitude toward war he despised.

Back in America, Norris found himself becoming increasingly conscious of social and economic problems. While working as an editor for Doubleday, Page, he conceived the idea of an "epic of the wheat," a trilogy of which he completed both *The Octopus* (1901) and *The Pit* (1903) before his death, which followed an attack of appendicitis. The last novel of the trilogy, to be called *The Wolf*, was never written.

Norris wrote enough during his short life to fill a ten-volume edition of collected writings, including critical essays and short fiction as well as novels. As an editor, too, he left a memorable heritage, for it was through his efforts that Theodore Dreiser's novel *Sister Carrie* was published.

The Call of the Wild

by

JACK LONDON (1876–1916)

Main Characters

Buck—The 140-pound dog, powerful, loyal, endowed with
almost human intelligence, who reverts to savagery.
François—A French-Canadian dog-sled driver.
Perrault—His companion on the trail.
Spitz—A huge, crafty Spitzberger dog, Buck's deadly rival.
John Thornton—The kind master, wise in the ways of dogs,
whom Buck loves.

The Story

Buck, a powerful 140-pound dog, a cross between a St.
Bernard and a Scotch shepherd, is the trusted and valued
companion of Judge Miller and his family. He roams the Miller
acres in the Santa Clara Valley of California, an aristocrat rejecting all attempts to make him a pampered kennel dog. It is
the year when the Klondike strike makes dogs like Buck valuable as never before. One of Judge Miller's gardeners, a gambler sorely in need of money to pay his debts, sells Buck to a
man who specializes in procuring dogs able to survive in
Alaska. Trusting at first, Buck soon protests against the in-
dignity of a rope around his neck. But he is choked into in-

sensibility, caged, hurled into a train, and arriving at Seattle, taken by wagon to a trainer.

Hungry and parched, Buck by this time is a demon. Released from the cage, he furiously hurls himself at the trainer. He never reaches him. The man hits him hard with a club. As often as Buck charges, he is struck. Finally he loses consciousness. He has learned his first great lesson: a man with a club is master.

Before long he is sold to two French-Canadians, Perrault and François, and suffers through a terrifying voyage to Alaska. The ferocity of the huskies is beyond his comprehension. One attacks and kills a large, friendly Newfoundland dog who had been on the boat with Buck and who is torn to pieces by the fierce pack that gathers. Another dog, a snow-white Spitzberger who has had some arctic experience, incurs Buck's enduring hatred by enjoying the savage spectacle.

One morning Buck is harnessed and set to work hauling a sled. Shocked, he knows enough not to rebel. François, the driver, and the other dogs soon teach Buck how to pull the sled and stay clear of the traces, how to dig in the snow for shelter when sleeping, how to steal without being caught.

Perrault and François carry mail to the prospectors in distant areas. The team must traverse difficult and dangerous trails, often running forty miles a day on a pound or a pound and a half of sun-dried salmon. From the beginning Buck resents Spitz's leadership, though he tolerates it. But Spitz's sly malignance infuriates him. Attacked by a group of starving huskies from some Indian village, Spitz seizes the opportunity to spring on Buck. Only by bracing himself to withstand the charge and then fleeing does Buck save himself. His hatred grows. He does all he can to undermine Spitz's leadership. The two must fight, and fight to the death. When Spitz kills a rabbit Buck has been chasing, the time arrives. Spitz is a clever and practiced fighter, but Buck crunches his forelegs with his teeth and topples his enemy. After the battle the other dogs tear Spitz apart.

Buck silently demands the leadership of the team, refusing to enter harness until he receives it. The drivers capitulate, and Buck becomes a severe taskmaster, literally whipping the dogs to a new solidarity.

At Skaguay, after three days of rest—hardly enough, considering that the dogs had made a record run of 560 miles in fourteen days—the team is turned over to a Scotch halfbreed. The new run is to Dawson, and the sled carries a heavy load of mail. Buck has developed pride in his leadership, and his task, arduous as it is, gives him satisfaction. But often a strange atavistic dream comes to him: visions of a primitive world and of primitive men with whom his ancestors had hunted.

After only two days' rest at Dawson, the dogs are back on the trail to Skaguay. Arriving there thirty days after they had left it, they are sold so that fresh batches may take the place of the overtired dogs. Buck and his mates are purchased by two men and a woman who know nothing of the frozen country or of dogs. They overload the sled, mistreat the dogs, overfeed them at first—and then, when provisions run short, nearly starve them. Many of the dogs die, others become so weak that they can hardly draw the sled. By sheer luck the party arrives at the camp of John Thornton who advises them not to continue because the ice over the river is too thin. But the men do not listen to Thornton. One of them whips Buck, whose mistreatment has reduced him to a virtual skeleton. Buck refuses to respond, and his tormentor trades his whip for a club. Thornton can no longer bear to witness this cruelty and springs on the man, pushing him away from Buck. Then he cuts Buck's traces. The group continues on its way. Before they are quite out of sight, a section of ice gives way; both dogs and human beings disappear under water.

John Thornton nurses Buck back to strength. Buck conceives for the man a deep and abiding love, greater than he has ever felt before. Only Buck's adoration prevents him from answering "the call of the wild," to return to the primitive life that now beckons him insistently. After Thornton's partners arrive, the men break camp and Buck goes with them. While poling a stretch of rapids, Thornton falls overboard. Following Thornton's orders, Buck swims to shore where a rope is fastened to his shoulders and neck. Despite the current, which threatens to submerge him, he swims back to Thornton who grabs him. Together they make their way to shore, nearly smashed by the rocks and half-drowned.

Thornton's pride in Buck grows. In town he boasts that Buck can "break" a sledge loaded with a thousand pounds from ice, start it, and walk with it for a hundred yards. Chal-

lenged, he accepts a wager of $1,200 on Buck's ability to per-
form a task suitable for a team, not a single dog. Nevertheless,
by a tremendous effort, Buck accomplishes the incredible feat.

With the money, Thornton and his two partners go in
search of a fabled mine. They never find it, but their wanderings lead them to a broad valley where, in a shallow place,
gold lies like butter. The men take thousands of dollars in gold
each day. While they work, Buck answers the call of the wild.
He absents himself from the camp for days, runs with a wolf,
hunts as his remote ancestors once did—and with all their
cunning. Returning after a long absence, he finds Thornton
and his friends murdered. The Indians who killed them are
still in the camp, dancing their victory. Filled with frenzy,
Buck hurls himself on one of the Indians, ripping his throat
open. Without a pause, he plunges at the rest until panic seizes
them, and, convinced that an evil spirit is attacking them, they
flee in terror.

Buck now joins the wolf pack. Proving his right by combat,
he becomes their leader, crafty and strong beyond any of his
fellows. The pack prospers. The Indians are certain that Buck
is a Ghost Dog, a demon come to torment them. But on one
day each summer, Buck comes across the valley to the stream
where John Thornton lies. Here he sits musing for a time. Before he departs, he howls once, long and mournfully.

Critical Opinion

His compassion and his intelligence may have prompted Jack
London to enlist on the side of the underdog. But emotionally,
he seems to have been drawn to the raw, primitive power and
the figure of the superman. This idealized creation of the
German philosopher, Friedrich Nietzsche, became for London
the peak of the evolutionary process and the hero of his novel
The Call of the Wild.

This saga of Buck, the "civilized" dog who reverts to the
savagery of his wolf ancestors, has been abundantly criticized.
It has been described as a callow and brutal romance, as an
icebound pulp story, and as an extreme expression of the
"cult of raw meat and red blood."

Not many defenders of *The Call of the Wild* would be

likely to deny that the novel is generally sensational, often incredible, and sometimes even a bit ludicrous. Why, then, is it the most widely read, most fondly remembered of Jack London's fifty books? The answer is: Buck, the heroic dog who embodies all the virtues we most admire—courage, loyalty, endurance, determination, and intelligence. Against a strange and intriguing background, he moves through a series of rousing, blood-tingling adventures, and emerges from them in a way that gratifies and delights us. Like the heroes of the great novels of the Western world, Buck develops an acute and sure knowledge of his powers and his defects.

After we have read the novel, we may balk at the lack of realism and logic in Buck's brooding introspectiveness, his long memory (not only of his own life but of the "life of his race" as well), and his extraordinary strength. But while we are reading—while we strain with Buck as he attempts to pull the sled held fast by ice and loaded with a thousand pounds of flour, or circle with him as he seeks an opening in the defenses of the sly and malignant Spitz—neither realism nor logic seems relevant to us. It is here in the directness and immediacy of our irresistible response to *The Call of the Wild* that we see the triumph of Jack London's storytelling art.

The Author

Jack London's life was as turbulent as any described in his fifty books. Born in San Francisco in 1876, he was the illegitimate son of Flora Wellman and Professor W. H. Chaney. His father, an itinerant astrologer, deserted Flora Wellman while she was pregnant. Eight months after the birth of her son, she married John London, a kind man whose commercial activities were doomed to failure. Jack London's early life was passed in dire poverty along the waterfronts of San Francisco and Oakland. He sold newspapers in saloons, worked in canneries, set up pins in a bowling alley.

By the time he was eighteen, London had been a hobo, an oyster pirate, a longshoreman and (as he said of himself) "a drunken bum." At the urging of his family, he set out to sea on a whaling vessel. He returned from the cruise determined to "live by his brain," and at nineteen began high school. At some point in his brief career, he had been converted to socialism. During his studies he made speeches for the cause, one of which landed him in jail. He entered the University of California but left before completing his first year, partly because he wanted to help support his mother, partly because he detested college. In 1896 he set out for the Klondike to prospect for gold, but scurvy forced him to return before he had washed a trace of metal.

By this time Jack London had developed into a kind of intellectual. He had read Marx, Darwin, Spencer, Nietzsche, and out of their works had forged his own private philosophy. He began writing and was successful nearly from the beginning, his Alaskan stories appearing in the *Overland Monthly*, the *Black Cat*, and in 1899, *The Atlantic Monthly*. His first book, a collection of stories entitled *The Son of the Wolf*, was published in 1900. Soon others followed: *A Daughter of the Snows* (1902), *The Call of the Wild* (1903), *The Sea Wolf* (1904), *White Fang* (1906)—all extremely popular works.

London wrote too much, however, to maintain a high level of craftsmanship. He drove himself to produce in order to earn the money to support his extravagant style of living. Moreover, personal crises interfered with his art. In 1900 he married Bessie Maddern, and divorced her three years later to marry Charmian Kittredge. He continued to drink too much, despite his novelistic tract (drawn from experience), *John Barleycorn* (1913). In 1916, following the lead of his fictional hero in *Martin Eden*, another autobiographical novel, he committed suicide.

Of his many books, only a handful continue to be widely read in the United States. Abroad, especially in the Soviet Union, though he abjured socialism in his later years, London ranks much higher than in his own country. However, his remarkable anticipation of fascism, *The Iron Heel* (1907), his socially conscious *The People of the Abyss* (1903), and the Klondike takes—particularly *The Call of the Wild*—are still very much alive.

Ethan Frome

by

EDITH WHARTON (1862–1937)

Main Characters

Ethan Frome—At fifty-two, a man with the look of one who has long lived in a special hell of his own.

Zenobia (Zeena)—His querulous, demanding, shrewish wife (seven years older than he) whose hypochondria enables her to control her husband.

Mattie—Zeena's graceful, pretty cousin whose coming to the farm provides the only bit of brightness in Ethan's existence.

The Narrator—An engineer working for a time near Starkfield, Massachusetts, who pieces together the story of Ethan Frome.

Denis Eady—The well-to-do Irish owner of the Starkfield livery stable, once Mattie's admirer.

Ruth Hale—Mattie's friend from whom the narrator gleans the hints that help him reconstruct the story.

The Story

The setting of *Ethan Frome* is Starkfield, Massachusetts. The narrator, an engineer, is for a time working in Corbury Junction and living in Starkfield (the nearest habitable place). In that town one day he sees a striking figure, the magnificent ruin of a man, tall and powerful, but stiff-jointed and maimed.

Curious, the narrator inquires about him, but gets only bits of information. The man's name is Ethan Frome. He lives on his farm with his wife Zeena (Zenobia), "the greatest hand at doctoring in the country," and his cousin Mattie. He had a smash-up twenty-four years ago.

Chance helps the narrator learn more. The horses that he has been hiring to take him to the train for Corbury Junction fall ill. The Irish stable owner, Denis Eady, suggests that Ethan Frome's bay still has legs and that its owner will be glad to earn a dollar. The narrator approaches Frome who agrees to drive him to the train daily. One stormy day the train is stalled, and Frome takes his passenger to Corbury Junction, a considerable distance away. Returning in a blizzard, Frome invites him to spend the night at the farm which is nearer than Starkfield. He gladly accepts the invitation. That night he finds the clue to, and gradually reconstructs, Ethan Frome's story.

It begins on Ethan's starved farm and sawmill, from which he barely ekes out a living. He is trapped by circumstances he cannot control. First his father, then his mother, fall ill. He cares for them. Ethan, a native says, "always done the caring." During his mother's illness, his cousin Zenobia Pierce comes over from the next valley to help nurse her. Seven years older than Ethan, gaunt and angular, she nevertheless brings a touch of femininity into the house, and she manages it efficiently. Ethan, who began a technical course before his father's illness, still wants to be an engineer. He feels sure that with Zeena's help he can leave the farm to live in a town where there are lectures and libraries and where people do things. Moved partly by this hope and partly by gratitude, he marries Zeena.

The dream vanishes soon. Zeena has an affinity for sickness. Whining, utterly self-centered, she renders Ethan's existence bleaker than ever. Into this cheerless household some brightness penetrates when Ethan's wife's cousin Mattie comes to live with them and to aid Zeena. Mattie's father has died after appropriating (perhaps misappropriating) his relatives' money, and she has been left nearly destitute. Her grace and sweetness, so different from his wife's chill rigidity, captivate him. He calls for Mattie on the rare occasions of a Starkfield dance or other festivity. He assists her with the chores that sometimes

overwhelm her. He suffers agonies of jealousy when smart
Denis Eady, the Irish grocer's son, flirts with her.

When Ethan walks her home from a dance one night, his
arm encircles her. He promises her that on the next moonlit
night he will take her coasting down the steep Starkfield hill.
Zeena is waiting up for them and receives them more sullenly
than ever. She informs Ethan that she is going to town to
consult a new doctor. Though he dreads the thought of the
expense—for Zeena is unrestrained in her hypochondria—
he consents because it will give him his first opportunity to
be alone with Mattie. He arranges for the hired man to drive
Zeena to the train, pretending that he must collect a debt from
the local builder.

With Mattie, his innocent companion in the house, Ethan
experiences a strange new joy. But bad luck mars it. The cat
breaks Zeena's treasured pickle dish which Mattie has taken
down from its high place in the cupboard. Ethan puts the
pieces together carefully and replaces the dish. The rest of the
evening passes delightfully, though Ethan approaches Mattie
no closer than to kiss the edge of something she is sewing.

Back from town, Zeena tells Ethan that the doctor says she
must have someone in to "do" for her; she may not work at
all about the house. Ethan is dismayed. He can't afford a
hired girl. Zeena tells him that Mattie, of course, must go. That
ought to save something at least; and besides, she intimates
significantly, Mattie has been with them too long. Ethan tries
to plead for Mattie, but Zeena is adamant, especially after she
discovers the broken pickle dish. Ethan desperately tries to
run away with Mattie, but is brought up sharply by the hard
realities. How will they live? He hasn't even enough money
to pay their fare out West. And how will Zeena manage? The
farm and the mill are so heavily mortgaged as to be worth
next to nothing.

Over Zeena's querulous objections, Ethan drives Mattie to
the train. Both are in despair: he, because with Mattie goes all
that makes life endurable for him, and she, because she loves
Ethan and because she is utterly without resources. Their
embraces are interrupted by tears. When the horse reaches
School House Hill, Ethan determines that he and Mattie will
have their long-delayed coast. In a nearby sled, they make
their descent, Ethan easily avoiding the great elm that looms

at the foot of the hill and that has worried Mattie. Ascending with Ethan, she is mastered by a fresh hope. She has before tearfully exclaimed that she wished she were dead. Now she suggests that they coast down the hill again—and never come up any more. Ethan hesitates, then agrees. But their fate is grimmer than death. They crash into the elm; Mattie and Ethan survive despite their terrible injuries but remain invalids for the rest of their lives. Zeena emerges from her self-imposed illness to care for them—complainingly but resolutely.

The narrator sees the three tragic victims of life together: Mattie as fretful and shrill as Zeena ever was, Ethan's face showing the pain that racks his body and spirit, Zeena cranky but enduring. "I don't see there's much difference," says Mrs. Hale, an old friend of Mattie's, "between the Fromes up at the farm and the Fromes in the graveyard; 'cept that down there they're all quiet, and the women have got to hold their tongues."

Critical Opinion

Ethan Frome is widely regarded as "securely on the level with the few great tragic novels in English," as a New England tragedy of greater "power and elevation" than any novel since Hawthorne's *The Scarlet Letter*. But there are those who differ sharply with this view. While acknowledging the technical expertness of the novel, Bernard De Voto insists that it is not "a transcript of human experience" or "an exploration of or comment on genuine emotion." Alfred Kazin, too, feels that *Ethan Frome* fails ultimately because its world is abstract. Edith Wharton "never knew how the poor lived in Paris or London; she knew even less of how they lived in the New England villages where she spent an occasional summer." Others have criticized the "literary" quality of the villagers, the "contrived" plot, the "synthetic" New England dialect.

It is true, of course, that *Ethan Frome* departs from the norm of Edith Wharton's fiction, which usually involves meticulous analysis of the crumbling of fashionable society as a result of its own inner corruption and of the onslaught of vulgar "new riches." Whether she is accurate in her

description of life in a small New England town may be
questioned. Literary sociologists have presented evidence to
show that she is not. But such evidence hardly touches the
heart of the novel. The doom that hangs over men, the dark
force that threatens them always and that may at any time
descend—this is the true center of the novel. The New England scene is the backdrop, not the meaning of the novel. As
an ironic tragedy of love, *Ethan Frome* transcends particular
places and people.

The Author

Edith Wharton was born in New York in 1862, the daughter
of wealthy and socially prominent parents. She was brought
up in New York, receiving her early education from private
tutors and governesses. It was a life, she recalled much later,
"safe, guarded, and monotonous," its pattern broken by
frequent journeys abroad and summer holidays in Newport.

Her life after her marriage to Edward Wharton in 1885
seemed likely to follow the same pattern. A Bostonian, descendant of an aristocratic Virginia family, he was independently wealthy. Together they spent a good deal of time
traveling in Europe. But from 1900 on, Edward Wharton
suffered from mental illness, and in 1906 his condition was
judged hopeless.

Edith Wharton had attempted some writing earlier—some
criticism of current modes of interior decorating and several
stories. Now, perhaps on the advice of physicians, she started
writing seriously. In 1902 she published her first novel, *The
Valley of Decision*, a re-creation of the Italian courts on the
eve of the French Revolution. Her first really important novel
was *The House of Mirth* (1905), an affecting portrait of a
woman in fashionable society that created something of a furor
in its day. The years of her greatest achievement were 1911,
when she published her grim New England study, *Ethan
Frome*, and 1920, when she completed her Pulitzer Prize-
winning *The Age of Innocence*, another of her "inside" portraits of New York society.

After her great period, her creative powers declined, though
there were occasional evidences of her earlier talents in *The*

Writing of Fiction (1925), a fascinating discussion of her literary credo, and *A Backward Glance* (1934), an interesting but too reticent biography.

Edith Wharton's efforts for the Allies during World War I brought her the Legion of Honor and other awards. For the most part, she lived her last years quietly in France, years rendered tolerable by her intimate friendship with Walter Berry, an American international lawyer, and her friendship with other writers. She died in France and was buried in the Protestant Cemetery at Versailles.

My Ántonia

by

WILLA CATHER (1876–1947)

Main Characters

Jim Burden—The narrator, a successful railroad lawyer who
   looks back nostalgically to the golden years of his youth on
   the Nebraska prairies.
Ántonia Shimerda—A Bohemian girl, vital, strong, warm,
   who accepts adversity as a condition of life and triumphs
   over it.
Mr. Shimerda—Ántonia's father, a frail, sensitive man, incapable of surviving the harsh realities of pioneer life.
Mrs. Shimerda—Ántonia's mother, a greedy, ungrateful,
   shrewd woman.
Ambrosch Shimerda—Ántonia's brother, surly, suspicious,
   sullen.
Marek Shimerda—Ántonia's imbecilic brother.
Krajiek—A Bohemian, greedy and unscrupulous, who cheats
   the Shimerdas.
Mrs. Herling—The amiable and musical next-door neighbor
   of Jim's grandparents in Black Hawk.
Lena Lingard—A pretty Norwegian farm girl who opens a
   successful dressmaker's shop in Lincoln and with whom
   Jim has a love affair.
Mr. Cutter—A lecherous, avaricious, unscrupulous money-
   lender.

108

Mrs. Cutter—His aggressive, masculine wife with whom he is
continually at war.

Larry Donovan—A ne'er-do-well who seduces Ántonia and
deserts her.

Mr. Cuzak—Ántonia's husband, a strong, lively, good-natured
farmer.

Jim's Grandparents—Good, kind, religious folk.

Jake Marpole—One of Jim's grandfather's hands, a friend and
ally to Jim.

Otto Fuchs—Another hired man, who instructs Jim in the
ways of prairie life.

The Story

Jim Burden, a successful railway lawyer married to an
unsympathetic wife, tells the story of his youth on the
Nebraska prairies and of the vital Bohemian girl whom he
has never ceased to love. At ten, after the death of his parents
in Virginia, he travels to Nebraska to live with his grandparents. Accompanying him on the long train journey is Jake
Marpole, one of his father's hired hands, who is going to
work for Jim's grandfather. They hear of a Bohemian family,
their train companions, who are going to settle on a Nebraska
farm, but not until they arrive at Black Hawk do they actually
catch a glimpse of them.

Jim's grandparents are active people, kind and religious,
and Jim speedily comes to love the brilliantly colored, ever-
moving, limitless prairie lands. Before long his grandmother
suggests that they visit their new Bohemian neighbors, the
Shimerdas. They are driven there by their hired man, Otto
Fuchs, an Austrian who teaches Jim much about prairie life.
The Shimerda family consists of the father, frail, melancholy,
elderly, and dignified, obviously unused to farm work; the
mother, shrewd, grasping, sharp; two sons—Ambrosch, a suspicious and surly youth of nineteen, and Marek, an imbecilic
boy; a small girl, Yalka, mild and obedient; and the fourteen-
year-old Ántonia, vibrant, warm, joyous. The Shimerdas have
been duped by a countryman, Krajiek, who has overcharged
them for their farm, equipment, and animals. They are living
in a sod dugout in the utmost poverty and eagerly welcome

the Americans and the food they bring. None of the Shimerdas knows more than a few words of English. The father asks Jim to teach Ántonia his language.

Through glorious afternoons of their first autumn, they explore the prairie, seeing the prairie-dog villages, once killing a snake, but mostly reveling in the magnificence of the country. Winter does not wholly cut them off, except when the snowfall is too heavy. Mr. Shimerda cannot adjust to the rough life of the new land. He makes two friends, Russian bachelors who speak something of his language. But one of them leaves Nebraska after the other dies seeing terrifying visions of wolves: once, driving the lead sled in a wedding party, he had thrown the bride and groom to the pursuing wolves in order to lighten the load and ensure his escape. His only friends gone, Mr. Shimerda's desolation deepens until, able to bear it no longer, he shoots himself. He is buried on the farthest southwest corner of the Shimerda acres, where eventually two roads would cross, in accordance with Bohemian custom.

Following her father's death, Ántonia works in the fields with her brother Ambrosch, doing a man's work, reveling in her strength. Jim's lessons stop, especially after the ingratitude and boorishness of Ambrosch lead to a fight with Jake. Jake knocks him off his feet and pays a fine in town for breaking the peace.

Soon after, Jim moves to the town of Black Hawk with his grandparents who are getting too old to work the farm. He makes friends with the Herlings, their next-door neighbors, a gay and intimate family. Though Jim likes town, he misses the prairie and Ántonia. When the Herlings' cook leaves, his grandmother suggests they try Ántonia. She soon becomes one of the Herling family, enjoying their talk and music and doting on their children. Other farm girls migrate to town, too. With Lena Lingard, a pretty Norwegian girl who works for the town's dressmaker, Ántonia becomes especially chummy. When a dance pavilion is set up in town, the girls become wildly excited, eager to finish their chores and go dancing—Ántonia most eager of all.

One night Mr. Herling catches Ántonia slapping a young man who has escorted her home and has attempted to kiss her. The fresh, vivid country girls always seemed a threat to their languid town sisters, and Mr. Herling insists that Ántonia stop attending the dances or seek another job. Ántonia does not hesitate. She leaves, to accept a place with the Cutters, a couple in a continual state of matrimonial discord. Mr. Cutter is a lecherous, greedy moneylender. On one occasion Jim saves Ántonia from being attacked by him.

Jim graduates from school as class valedictorian, studies hard during the summer, and in the fall goes to Lincoln to attend the state university. Here he comes under the influence of Gaston Cleric, a brilliant, dedicated scholar who opens up vistas of classical learning for Jim, though he knows that he himself can never become a scholar. Jim's devotion to his studies is interrupted when Lena Lingard moves to Nebraska to open her own dressmaking establishment. Jim forms a deep attachment for her, taking her to the theater, breakfasting with her Sundays, relaxing in her company. Parting is a wrench for both of them, but Jim—nineteen now—has decided to follow Cleric to Harvard and complete his education there.

For the next two years, Jim remains at Cambridge. Before entering law school, he returns to Black Hawk for a visit. There he hears what has happened to Ántonia. She fell in love with the ne'er-do-well Larry Donovan, who promised to marry her, but delayed, living on her money till it was gone, and then deserted her while she was pregnant. Ántonia returned to the Shimerda farm and worked hard in the fields until her baby was born. Now her life is centered on her daughter, though she still labors as hard as a man on the farm. Jim visits her briefly and their deep friendship for each other reasserts itself. He promises to see her again.

It is twenty years before Jim keeps the promise. During those years he has become a successful, if perhaps spiritually unfulfilled, railway lawyer. On his way East from California, he interrupts his journey to visit Ántonia. She has married and raised a swarm of children. She greets him joyfully, proud of her family, happy in her life. She has worked with her husband, a Bohemian, encouraged him, persevered with him. They are not rich, but they have enough to make them happy. Jim enters fully into the family life during his three-day stay, enjoying Ántonia's radiant delight in her lot. He leaves, promising to return next summer to take the boys hunting. He stops for a while at Black Hawk and gazes at the prairie (now highway and plowed land), musing—with some sadness but with acceptance—about his destiny and Ántonia's and the past they had possessed together.

Critical Opinion

My Ántonia is representative of Willa Cather's interest, early and late, in the theme of the immigrant pioneers—the Swedes, Norwegians, Poles, Slavs, Bohemians, and French who bravely make "a new settlement of the frontier." *My Ántonia* glosses over none of the unpleasantness of pioneer life, nor does it fail to recognize that there were many unpleasant pioneer folk— the greedy, repellent Krajiek, for example; or the sullen, ungrateful Ambrosch; or the wheedling, crafty, and foolish Mrs. Shimerda. But Willa Cather writes from a depth of affection and understanding that converts the bleak and often deadly pioneer experience into something rich and warm. Surely every reader comes increasingly to admire Ántonia, the strong, brave, enduring woman who suffers and triumphs, who loses her teeth but keeps "the fire of life."

The flaw in the novel, critics point out, is that its center of gravity shifts from Ántonia to Jim. Thus in the third section of the book, Ántonia nearly disappears and Jim emerges as the focal figure. However, we should be aware of the significance of the *My* of the title: Ántonia is central to the novel only when she is central to Jim. When Jim leaves Black Hawk for the university, Ántonia recedes—in the story as in Jim's life. She returns at the end because she evokes Jim's past, because her battered yet vital person makes him recall how much he has lost through his "success."

With some exceptions, critics concede that Willa Cather's *My Ántonia* is "the most masterly of her novels and one of the classics of our literature." It is, says Henry Seidel Canby, "the story of a great woman ennobling common things and a common struggle by elemental passion." T. K. Whipple more succinctly calls it an instance of "the victory of mind over Nebraska."

The Author

Willa Sibert Cather was born in Winchester, Virginia, in 1876, but her formative years were spent in Nebraska where her father owned a ranch. She at once fell in love with the country, still a pioneer territory, and its people. "I have never found any intellectual excitement more intense than I used to feel when I spent a morning with one of these pioneer women at her baking or buttermaking. I used to ride home in the most unreasonable state of excitement; I always felt as if they told me so much more than they said—as if I had actually got inside another person's skin."

Her elementary schooling was presided over by her mother. Not till the family moved to Red Cloud, Nebraska, did she have any formal education. But her mother's teaching, based on the English classics and on Latin, was sound enough to enable her to perform excellently at high school and at the University of Nebraska.

Because of her passion for music, which she retained all her life, Willa Cather determined to move to a city where she could hear it. She chose Pittsburgh and there found employment as editor and theater critic for the *Leader*. Newspaper work proving insufficiently attractive, she taught English at Allegheny High School from 1901 to 1906. Then the publication of a book of poems, *April Twilights* (1903), and a collection of stories, *The Troll Garden* (1905), both well reviewed, led to her obtaining an editorial position on *McClure's* magazine in New York. From 1906 to 1912, she was its managing editor.

The success of her novels made it possible for her to quit her magazine work and devote herself exclusively to writing. She continued to live in New York but took frequent trips abroad, to the prairies, and finally to the Southwest desert country (which almost replaced the prairies in her affections). She remained Miss Cather till her death in 1947.

Except for *One of Ours* (a Pulitzer Prize winner in 1922) and *The Professor's House* (1925), Willa Cather's novels characteristically are devoted to the themes of the immigrant who

pioneers in a new and hard land—*O Pioneers!* (1913) and
My Ántonia (1918); and of the quest for stability as represented by the Catholic Church—*Death Comes for the Arch-
bishop* (1927) and *Shadows on the Rock* (1931).

Winesburg, Ohio

by

SHERWOOD ANDERSON (1876–1941)

Main Characters

George Willard—A young reporter, eager to set forth from Winesburg to encounter the world. His sensitivity and receptivity make him the confidant of most of the characters in the book.

Elizabeth Willard—His mother, once ebullient and vibrant, now, at forty-five, physically and psychically shriveled.

Tom Willard—His father, an ambitious hotelkeeper, passionate about politics but almost wholly indifferent to his wife.

Dr. Reefy—A doctor, sympathetic and compassionate, the only adult love in Mrs. Willard's life.

Wing Biddlebaum—A berry picker, once a gifted schoolteacher, gentle, timid, lovable, and the possessor of extraordinarily expressive hands. His real name is Adolph Myers.

Dr. Parcival—A doctor no longer in practice, who has retreated in terror and guilt from all experience.

Jesse Bentley—A farmer, obsessed by God and money, determined to use his grandson, David, to open a path between himself and God.

Kate Swift—A schoolteacher, stern, but deeply aware of promise in the young and dedicated to encouraging any sign of genius.

Alice Hindman—A spinster oft disappointed in love and bursting with unsatisfied passion.

Wash Williams—The telegraph operator, a violent anti-feminist and a hater of life.

The Rev. Curtis Hartman—Pastor of the Presbyterian Church, quiet and devout but also filled with soul-shattering carnal urges.

Enoch Robinson—A would-be artist and *bon vivant* who has failed in both roles and finds himself frighteningly alone and embittered.

Louise Trunnion—The serving girl at the Willards' who initiates George into sex.

Belle Carpenter—The flirtatious daughter of a bookkeeper and George's second conquest.

Helen White—Daughter of the town banker, educated and sophisticated, who gives George his last and most significant sexual experience.

The Story

(Note: Because *Winesburg, Ohio* comprises several connected short stories, the relevant story titles have been supplied in parentheses at appropriate points.)

Although Elizabeth Willard's girlhood dreams of becoming an actress and living an excitingly romantic life have been pulverized by the drab routine of her marriage to an insensitive husband, she refuses to abandon her hopes for her only son, George. Above all, she dreads the possibility that her husband will force George into a career that will keep him in Winesburg and suffocate his will and his imagination ("Mother"). Only once in her married life does Mrs. Willard know release from the stultifying world of Tom. With Dr. Reefy (whose own marriage, though happy, ended after a year with the death of his wife—"Paper Pills"), she finds herself able to speak of her early dreams and aspirations, and of the marriage she foolishly allowed herself to make. For a brief moment, in Dr. Reefy's arms, she finds respite. But the moment—interrupted by the noise of a clerk dumping rubbish outside the door—is short-lived and the two are never to meet again, for Mrs. Willard dies a few years later.

Ironically the $800 she has hidden in the wall behind her bed, money intended to help George get away from Winesburg, remains there unknown to all ("Death").

Mrs. Willard's fears that George will remain in Winesburg were not well founded. Even as she fretted about what her husband might insist upon, George was telling his father that he did not want an ordinary "successful" career. Above all, he knows that when he comes of age, he wants to go away, to "look at people and think." Only sixteen when he tells his father of his intention, George has already begun work on the local newspaper. His assignments bring him in touch with everyone in town, and from them he learns the poignant lessons of loneliness and frustration that lead him toward maturity and the day when he must leave Winesburg.

Wing Biddlebaum ("Hands"), the best berry picker in Winesburg, urges George to forget the routine world and learn how to dream. He reaches out and touches the young man's shoulders, almost caresses him, then, with a look of horror on his face, leaves. George cannot wholly understand the old man's terror and anxiety but suspects Wing's problems have something to do with his hands, "the piston rods of his machinery of expression." What George does not know is that years earlier Wing, as Adolph Myers, had been an inspired and inspiring teacher. Boys loved his gentleness, accepted his warm and friendly touch, and under his tutelage learned to dream. Unhappily, one half-witted boy who also loved Wing dreamed that his relationship with his teacher was sexual and told his parents about his dream as if it were true. As a result, Wing was accused of immorality and driven out of town, barely escaping hanging.

Other men in Winesburg have turned their backs on life, too, each for a different reason. Dr. Parcival ("The Philosopher") fills George with stories of his unhappy boyhood: a lunatic father, a drunken brother, an impoverished mother. "I want to fill you with hatred and contempt so that you will be a superior being," he tells George. So complete is Parcival's withdrawal from life that when a child is killed by a runaway horse, he refuses the pleas of the townsfolk to examine her. Yet he expects retribution, perhaps (he suggests) by lynching. Frightened as he is at the prospect, Parcival is convinced that the outcome will support his vision of life—"that everyone in the world is Christ and they are all crucified."

Enoch Robinson ("Loneliness") confides to George his life-long determination to be admired by all for his talents as an artist and a conversationalist. He went to New York and joined bohemian art circles, but neither his painting nor his talk held anyone's interest. He tried marriage but found it stifling, and at last sank into a self-pitying isolation in his Greenwich Village room. Into that room came a woman, a violinist, who often sat in silence with Enoch. At first Enoch believed that he might be able to lose his identity in her presence, but suddenly one night he felt compelled to make her understand who he was and how important his existence was. As he raved on about himself to the woman, he sensed that she understood him, but ironically, her understanding became a threat to his independence and impelled him to a frenzied verbal assault upon her. When he drove her from the room, however, Enoch realized that he was forever alone. And thus he returned again to Winesburg, the town he had many years before tried to escape.

Wash Williams, the old telegraph operator ("Respectability"), had loved his wife with a jealous passion which turned to bitter loathing when he discovered that she had several lovers. Yet even after he dispatched her home to her mother, he continued to send almost every cent he earned or saved. A few years later the girl's mother sent for Wash to visit. Lonely, he was determined to accept his faithless wife once more. As he waited in the living room, Wash heard mother and daughter conversing, and knew that if the girl were simply to enter and touch his hand, he would forgive and forget. What he had not expected, however, was that the girl would enter the room stark naked, pushed across the threshold by her mother. As the chilled George listens, Wash says he wanted to kill the mother, but succeeded only in hitting her with a chair before the neighbors intervened. Now, he moans, he can never get to kill her because she died of a fever only a month later.

Bitterness and frustration afflict many of the women of Winesburg, too. Alice Hindman ("Adventure") was a lonely woman in her late twenties, in love with the young man who had seduced her many years before, left town, and never returned. When her mother remarried, Alice became even more deeply aware of her isolation, clasped a pillow to her breast and even arranged the bedclothes to resemble a human form. One rainy night, desperate with longing, Alice rushed into the street naked, calling to a passer-by to wait for her. The passer-by proved to be an old man, deaf, who shouted back asking her what she wanted. Alice collapsed on the ground, then crawled on hands and knees back to her house. In bed, she turned her face to the wall and "began trying to force herself to face bravely the fact that many people must live and die alone, even in Winesburg."

Kate Swift ("The Teacher") had been George's teacher and he had often as a boy dreamed of making love to her. Neither pretty nor very young, Kate, despite a forbidding exterior, was "the most eagerly passionate soul among them." She had recognized in George's writing the possibilities of genius and had tried to make him conscious of the challenge and responsibilities of the artist. One evening when George, now a young reporter, came to her room to borrow a book, she began anew her impassioned appeal about art. Suddenly she kissed the embarrassed youth, then dismissed him by telling him it would be ten years before he understood what she was saying to him. The next evening, however, she came to George's office at the *Winesburg Eagle* and allowed him to embrace her. Almost ready to yield to him, Kate could not and struck George repeatedly in the face until he released her and she ran home.

Later that same evening, as George paced his office angrily after his rejection by Kate, the Reverend Curtis Hartman burst in, his hand dripping blood, and shouted at George that God had manifested Himself to him in the shape of a naked woman. Unhappily married to a frigid wife, unable to win his battle with his sensual yearnings, Hartman had some time earlier broken off a bit of stained glass in his church-office window and was thus able to peep across the walk into Kate Swift's bedroom. He struggled with his temptation, but on several occasions yielded and watched the teacher reading in her bed, yearning to see her body naked. On the night that Kate fled from George's arms, however, Hartman's desires were fulfilled. In her room, Kate flung herself naked upon the bed and, in tears, beat her fists upon the pillows. As Hartman watched, she suddenly rose and began to pray. Convinced that her gesture was a symbolic signal from God, Hartman smashed his fist through his window, knowing that now he would have to replace it and thus no longer be able to peep ("The Strength of God").

George's initiation into sex is achieved callously and unemotionally with Louise Trunnion, the Willards' maid ("Nobody Knows"). He makes merely a casual gesture of interest, and the girl easily though dispassionately gives herself to him. When she leaves, George laughs self-assuredly to himself that nobody knows what has happened and thus Louise cannot really cause him any trouble. In his succeeding affairs, however, George learns that love is more than a minor carnal episode. With Belle Carpenter ("An Awakening"), he senses a deeper, almost mystical, sense of being in "touch with something orderly and big that swings through the night like a star." But he experiences humiliation in his affair with Belle, too, for even as he holds Belle in his arms, her other lover, Ed Handby, the local bartender, comes by, pushes George into the bushes, and marches Belle off.

At eighteen, shortly after his mother's death and just before he leaves Winesburg, George knows that he is ready to share his brief but already rich past with another person. He has now come into sharp contact with love and death and has acquired knowledge about the joy and pain of human experience. He is, in brief, nearly mature, and ready for an experience that is tender and gentle. With Helen White ("Sophistication") he has that consummate experience. Helen is bored by her college-teacher suitor's pompous verbosity. She runs from him to find George and together, thoroughly conscious of their oneness though unable to express or explain it, they wrest from "their silent evening together the thing needed."

Early one morning in April, George takes the train that will carry him to the world beyond Winesburg ("Departure"). His mind filled with memories of the past and dreams of the future, George strays from the present momentarily, just long enough so that when he looks at the real world outside the train window, he has left Winesburg.

Critical Opinion

"I am a child, a confused child in a confused world . . . ," Sherwood Anderson wrote in his *Notebook* in 1916. In *Winesburg, Ohio* he translated that sense of isolation and alienation, the confusion between self and society that has long been the hallmark of American literature, into a high artistic achievement. The stories of *Winesburg* tell of the failure of both emotional and intellectual communication, not merely in a small town but among all men. All of the characters strive toward that maturity that is the high-water mark of psychological development, but only George Willard can possibly achieve it in the future. And Anderson provides no sentimental assurance that George will fulfill his promise.

All of the other characters are, as Anderson called them, "grotesques." In the prologue to the book, Anderson explains that a "grotesque" is a person who has falsely shaped his life about an assumed and all-embracing truth. Actually what cripples these people is not so much their addiction to a particular truth as their failure to communicate to others their most deeply felt emotions. As a result they drift in a terrible void of aloneness, helpless by themselves, unable to be helped by others. They inhabit a kind of twilight world where they can neither see nor be seen.

Readers of *Winesburg, Ohio* will, of course, recognize that Anderson knew Edgar Lee Masters' *Spoon River Anthology*, the poetic rendering of the sterility and blighted hopes of small towners. But Anderson gave to his tales a kind of narrative unity lacking in Masters' poem. Certainly the form of *Winesburg, Ohio* is loose, hardly what one normally expects in a novel. Yet, as Anderson has written: "Life is a loose, flowing thing . . . but the whole . . . leaves a definite impression. . . ." Thus, for Anderson and for most readers, the diverse stories of *Winesburg, Ohio* form a cohesive unit, and the separate lives fall together into an unmistakable pattern of human sadness.

The Author

With almost no formal education, *Sherwood Anderson* became one of America's finest storytellers. Born in Camden, Ohio, he wandered restlessly from job to job, starting at the age of fourteen. After serving for a short time in the Spanish-American War, he returned to Elyria, Ohio, married, and briefly settled down as manager of a paint factory. But he was already planning a literary career, and, when he had enough money, he left the factory to try his luck in Chicago. There, working as an advertising writer and meeting major literary figures like Carl Sandburg and Floyd Dell who encouraged him, Anderson finished his first novel, *Windy McPherson's Son* (1916). But neither this initial venture nor its two successors won him the fame that came with the publication of *Winesburg, Ohio* in 1919.

In *Poor White* (1920), another successful novel, he studied the effects of industrialism on small-town life, and in a superb volume of short stories, *The Triumph of the Egg* (1921), he exploited still further the Freudian implications of personal frustration. Although he wrote and published many more books before his death (he choked on a toothpick), none matched the power and insight of these earlier works. Nevertheless, several of his writings merit attention, especially his autobiographical works: *Tar: A Midwest Childhood* (1926) and *A Story-Teller's Story* (1924). Also of interest for their comments about contemporary writers (he was a good friend of Gertrude Stein's and gave much help to young writers like Ernest Hemingway and William Faulkner) are his critical volumes: *Sherwood Anderson's Notebook* (1926) and *The Modern Writer* (1925).

After four marriages (his novel *Many Marriages*, 1923, depicts some of the difficulties he encountered) he settled near Marion, Virginia, to edit two newspapers, one Republican, the other Democratic.

Jurgen

by

JAMES BRANCH CABELL (1879–1958)

Main Characters

Jurgen—A pawnbroker and "the remnant of a poet"; witty, learned (especially in the lore he invents), skeptical. His three favorite sayings: "I am willing to try any drink once"; "Of course you may be right; and certainly I cannot go so far as to say you are wrong; but still, at the same time—"; and "I shall deal fairly with you."

Dame Lisa—Jurgen's shrewish yet fond wife.

Koshchei the Deathless—The Supreme Being (as far as we know) "who made things as they are."

Mother Sereda—Earth Goddess—also known as Aesred and Aderes (all anagrams for *Dea Res*, "the thing Goddess")—who has all Wednesdays in her keeping, the middle of working days and of all middles. Her function is to bleach all the colors of life; she is Gray Conformity.

The Centaur Nessus—A creature from Greek mythology, who takes Jurgen to the Garden between Dawn and Sunrise and gives him a magic shirt to wear.

Dorothy la Désirée—The first love of Jurgen, who deserted him to marry a nobleman whom she now regularly deceives with younger lovers.

Guenevere—The wife of Arthur, later the mistress of Lancelot, once the innocent if slightly obtuse beloved of Jurgen.

123

Anaitis—The Lady of the Lake, embodying the principle of desire and fulfillment.

Chloris—A Hamadryad whom Jurgen marries and lives with placidly.

Helen of Troy—The avatar of beauty, dream of the poet realized.

Florimel—A vampire on vacation in Hell, whom Jurgen meets while sojourning there.

The Story

The scene is Poictesme (a land of Cabell's creation) during the middle ages. Jurgen, a middle-aged pawnbroker who still retains something of his gift for poetry, passes a monk who has tripped over a stone and is roundly cursing the devil who placed it there. Jurgen defends the devil's industry and energy and walks on. Shortly he meets a black gentleman who thanks him for his good word and promises to reward him.

Returning home, Jurgen is unable to find his wife, Lisa, a lady "with no especial gift for silence." Though he bears her disappearance manfully, he is finally persuaded by his sister-in-law to seek Lisa who has been seen walking on a local heath. He follows her into a cave, and there sees not Lisa but the centaur Nessus, who gives him a bright shirt (perhaps the emblem of imagination or fantasy) and offers to carry him to the Garden between Dawn and Sunrise. It is a place of romantic illusions bred in youth. There Jurgen encounters Dorothy la Désirée—not as she is now, the faithless wife of the rich Heitman Michael, but as she was at eighteen, tender, vivid, and loving. Unhappily, though, Jurgen is no longer twenty and she does not respond to the poetry of a middle-aged pawnbroker.

The radiance of the garden vanishes, and Nessus changes into an ordinary riding horse. Jurgen mounts and rides until he comes to a great stone house where he sees an old woman bleaching. She is Sereda whose function is to turn all color or beauty gray. Jurgen makes a song for her and in exchange she gives him a Wednesday of his twenty-first year to relive, for she is the mistress of all Wednesdays, "Time's middles."

She also gives him a shadow—her shadow—which accompanies him everywhere.

The bygone Wednesday to which Jurgen returns is again presided over by Dorothy, his beloved, who is being courted by Heitman Michael. This time, however, Jurgen is not defeated; three times he drives his dagger into the undefended back of his rival and then disposes of the body. He embraces his sweetheart just as Wednesday passes. The middle-aged Countess Dorothea is in his arms. Jurgen draws away with a shiver, reads her a brief lecture on morality, and resumes his journey.

Fortunately, Jurgen keeps his youth, and fortune stays with him. He comes upon a lovely young woman in a trance and awakens her with a long kiss. She proves to be Guenevere, not yet the bride of King Arthur or the mistress of Lancelot. With exceptional bravery he conducts her to Camelard, where her father, Gogyrvan Gawr, reigns. The king is a remarkably tolerant father. Though Guenevere is engaged to Arthur, Gogyrvan is willing to allow her to have an affair with Jurgen, who now calls himself Duke of Logreus, since he has certain rights as a champion. Gogyrvan insists on a promise, nevertheless: in all matters concerning his daughter's honor, he expects Jurgen to lie like a gentleman. Jurgen agrees, and nightly in the deserted Hall of Judgment Guenevere and he converse lovingly. Still, when Arthur arrives to claim his bride, Jurgen does not mourn. Guenevere, while charming, is a bit obtuse. (And even when most committed to her, Jurgen does not reject the love of Dame Yolande, another lady whom he has befriended.)

In the wedding party is the Lady of the Lake, Anaitis, enchanting and perverse. She is Queen of Cocaigne and directs erotic rituals throughout the world. She and Jurgen marry (despite the fact that he is theoretically still married to Dame Lisa) and they experiment continually. At first Jurgen is intrigued, but he becomes progressively less enthusiastic. Consequently, when he has to leave Cocaigne at the Equinox, Jurgen is quite prepared "to taste a new drink." He chooses the country of Leukê, where Helen of Troy, the poet's ideal of beauty, reigns with Achilles in their palace at Pseudopolis. Before he sees the Queen, however, he quickly establishes a relationship with a tree nymph, the comfortable, plump and pretty Hamadryad Chloris to whom he identifies himself as King Jurgen. Since she desires it and no local legislation prohibits it, he marries her, living in her tree house. When conjugal happiness palls a little, he searches out Helen, but she is perfectly mated to Achilles. Jurgen sadly realizes that she must always remain an ideal for him, a perfection not to be attained, for once attained, she would make all other beauty seem flat and insipid.

But the forces of Philistia, the enemies of Romance, have no high illusions of beauty. They invade and burn Pseudopolis as a sacrifice to their god Vel-Tyno. Though Helen, Achilles and their retinue rise gleaming from the ground to escape their Philistine foes, the latter burn the tree of Chloris and kill her. Jurgen may still manage to survive in Philistia, for he has caught the fancy of its queen and has delighted her in his fashion, but he will strike no compromise with dull conformity. And two days before Christmas he is dispatched to the Hell of his fathers.

Jurgen adjusts quickly—this time as Emperor of Noumaria. He learns that Hell has been created by Koshchei the Deathless to satisfy the demands of ancestral conscience. His own particular father, Coth, is present, too, tormenting the devils with his insatiable demands for punishment. Coth conjures into existence—through his heated imaginings—a vampire, Florimel, whom Jurgen takes as his mistress. In short, he suffers not at all, except from the religion of Hell, which is patriotism, and from the government, which is an enlightened democracy.

Yet Jurgen wants to visit Heaven, giving as his unconvincing reason his desire to seek out Dame Lisa. With the aid of Jacob's ladder, he ascends to Heaven as Pope John XX. The boy angel who procures the ladder from one of Heaven's storerooms is—Jurgen himself, as he was. The affection of his grandmother, Steinvor, who visualized him as an angelic boy, is responsible for his being in Heaven. For Heaven, as the God of Jurgen's grandmother informs him, has been created by Koshchei according to the specifications of Steinvor. But none of the illusions that formed Heaven are Jurgen's, and so he departs to the heath from which he began his journeyings.

On the heath Mother Sereda is waiting. She takes back her shadow and takes away Jurgen's youth, leaving him as he

was—which is what he wanted; familiar reality appeals more
than glamorous illusion, for a youthful body and a middle-aged
mind go poorly together. Nor does Koshchei, whom Jurgen
stumbles upon immediately after, change his mind. And
Koshchei does try, producing in turn Guenevere, the distilla-
tion of romantic faith; Anaitis, the emblem of desire; and
Helen, the supreme embodiment of beauty. Jurgen longs for
his termagant wife, Lisa. She appears, scolding furiously—
overwhelming Jurgen and astonishing even Koshchei. Yet Jurgen is firm and Koshchei releases him to Lisa. As he enters his
snug home, where she has preceded him, he is nearly content
with domesticity, though he sighs a little.

Critical Opinion

When *Jurgen* was published in 1919, it met with three di-
vergent responses. Critics like Carl Van Vechten, V. L. Par-
rington, Burton Roscoe, H. L. Mencken, and Sinclair Lewis
hailed the book rapturously. Benjamin de Casseres called the
author "the Watteau of ironists, the Debussy of prose, the
Spinoza of word-magic, the Prometheus of an American
Renaissance." And even so temperate a scholar as Carl Van
Doren found the book to be "a progression full of beauty and
pity and mirth, as if a huge organ should burst into laughter."

Another group of readers was less enthusiastic for varying
reasons. Clifton Fadiman observed that the world of Poictesme
has "the beauty and formal perfection of a well-known soap
bubble." Others denounced it as veiled obscenity, as obses-
sively preoccupied with sex, as archaic in style and trivial in
philosophy. William Summer brought suit against *Jurgen* for
the New York Society for the Suppression of Vice, an action
that failed after two years and triggered the enormous success
of the book.

A very few perceived Cabell's *Comedy of Justice,* as the
subtitle had it, for what it was: a witty, suggestive, and
fundamentally moral tale. For though the hero is sufficiently
libertine in his progress, he does finally prefer his wife and the
dullness mingled with the delight of domesticity. "*Jurgen,*"
says Joe Lee Davis, the most recent and scholarly of Cabell's

critics, was ". . . as convincing a defense of monogamy as
Homer's *Odyssey*."

The reputation of Jurgen has suffered through the years,
partly because it was originally so overinflated, partly because
the years themselves, years of depression and devastation, have
been ruinous to witty fantasy. Contemporary historians of literature tend to dismiss the novel casually. Yet in the past
decade Edmund Wilson has lauded it for its grace and imagination; there has been a spate of critical studies and re-
evaluations of Cabell. Though it hardly seems likely that
Jurgen will again be so generally and so generously praised
as in the twenties, it surely will long be admired as a commentary, at once mordant and gay, on our impossible dreams
and inevitable compromises.

The Author

James Branch Cabell once noted that his last name rhymed
with "rabble." The observation was perhaps to be expected
from the scion of one of the First Families of Virginia, an
aristocrat reared in the ante-bellum tradition and always conscious of his distinguished lineage. This consciousness may
indeed account for his long professional labors (from 1901
to 1911, and periodically throughout his career) as a genealo-
gist—labors that produced three volumes on the Branch family and its connections. It accounts, too, for Cabell's lifelong
interest in Virginia history and his appointment as editor for
the Virginia War History Commission (1919–26).

After graduating from the College of William and Mary
with high honors (as an upperclassman he was hired to teach
other undergraduates French and Greek), Cabell worked for
newspapers in Virginia and New York, engaged in genealogical
researches, and began his career as a writer with some graceful but sentimental romances. In 1913 he married a widow four
years his senior. Though his wife was less than fascinated by
his writing, she proved a superb helpmate. Cabell partly
repaid her by establishing her notable ancestry in *The Majors
and Their Marriages* (1915). When she died in 1949, he was
shattered. But the next year he married another, much younger

Virginia lady with literary aspirations, Margaret Waller Free-
man.

Since Cabell wrote more than fifty books, clearly his dedication to literature is the most important fact in his long life.
Though some of these books—his memoirs and his trilogy
(*Smirt, Smith,* and *Smire,* 1934–37)—are remarkable achievements of wit and style, his huge epic of Poictesme in eighteen
volumes is his enduring monument. Conceived as the "Biography of the Life of Manuel," the volumes trace the history
of that mythical dignitary and of his descendants from 1234
to 1750. Cabell called on his vast knowledge of myth, story,
folklore, legend, and history to fill in the imaginary terrain of
Poictesme. Where knowledge failed, invention came to his
rescue. Cabell never hesitated to invent myths, any more
than personages or places. His expertness in genealogy and
his predilection for anagram are also evident in his epic.

Of all of Cabell's work, *Jurgen* (1919) has achieved the
greatest fame, not only because of its delightful satire but also
because of the attempt by the New York Society for the
Suppression of Vice to ban the book. It was triumphantly
cleared in court, and its erudition and subtle eroticism have
since delighted all but the most prudish readers.

Sister Carrie

by

THEODORE DREISER (1871–1945)

Main Characters

Caroline Meeber—"Sister" Carrie, a young country girl whose
single, compelling drive is to possess whatever lies beyond
her reach. She longs for love, fame, and wealth. She gets
all of these, but at the end she is still yearning for the un-
attained and the unattainable.

George Hurstwood—Carrie's lover and "husband," a man of
average sensibilities and passions trapped by hostile forces
that undermine his will and turn him toward self-
destruction.

Charles Drouet—Carrie's first lover, a stereotype of the traveling salesman: elegant, suave, sensual, shallow.

Mr. and *Mrs. Vance*—High-living neighbors of Carrie and
Hurstwood in New York, who first expose Carrie to the
temptations of New York's night life.

Robert Ames—A genial young man-about-town, with excellent
taste in food, entertainment, and women—qualities that
make him increasingly attractive to Carrie.

Julia, George, and *Jessica Hurstwood*—Hurstwood's wife, son,
and daughter. Each is spoiled, selfish, and vindictive.

The Story

Aboard a train en route to Chicago, Caroline Meeber, aged eighteen, excitedly conjures up a romantic vision of the dynamic metropolis where she hopes to discover romance and wealth. She takes her first hesitant step toward fulfillment when she promises a train acquaintance, Charles Drouet, a young traveling salesman, to let him show her the city.

But Carrie's excursion with Drouet is temporarily postponed, as are her hopes for swift success. Living with her married sister in a tiny, drab apartment, Carrie feels too ashamed to have Drouet call and writes to put him off. Shocked by the grim drudgery of her sister's lot, Carrie is determined to shape a happier life for herself. Her initial efforts bring her little reward. In 1889 Chicago boasts an expanding economy for its half million inhabitants but has few jobs for inexperienced or unskilled girls. After days of jarring refusals, Carrie gets a job as an assembly-line worker in a shoe plant. Ill-paid, harshly overworked, she despairs of achieving the glamorous life she had envisioned. But she struggles on until she falls ill for a few days. Fired, she loses even the tenuous hold on economic security her job afforded.

A chance meeting with Drouet shortly thereafter measurably brightens Carrie's prospects. With his flair for ostentation (to Carrie, he seems at first a shining knight), Drouet takes her to dinner, to the theater, buys her clothes—and offers pointedly to take care of her. Thus, as Drouet's mistress, Carrie takes her first significant step toward reaching her goal. As a lover, Drouet is kind and thoughtful, but Carrie soon ignores his virtues and fixes upon his obvious shortcomings—lack of wit, showy taste, and a basic mediocrity.

Ironically, Drouet paves the way for his own defeat and for the progress of his successor, George Hurstwood. Hurstwood, manager of Fitzgerald and Moy's fashionable bar, is a reserved but personable man just short of forty. Married to a hostile, unlovable wife, and father of two grasping and disagreeable children, Hurstwood finds refuge among his friends and clients at the saloon. There Drouet lightheartedly and proudly introduces Carrie to Hurstwood. Occasionally, thereafter, Hurstwood visits Carrie and Drouet, joins them at the theater, and soon impresses Carrie as far superior to Drouet. One afternoon when Drouet has been called away on business, Hurstwood makes his first gentlemanly advance; Carrie's rebuff is ladylike but not sufficient to discourage Hurstwood.

In the months that follow, Hurstwood's passion increases. His aim is to have an affair, Carrie's to win marital status. (She is ignorant of Hurstwood's family life.) Meanwhile both Drouet and Mrs. Hurstwood grow suspicious of their respective partners. Mrs. Hurstwood boldly locks her husband out and institutes a lawsuit. Drouet tries to win back his mistress by informing her of Hurstwood's marital problem. Even after Drouet and Carrie have argued violently, he offers to allow her to use the apartment for which he pays rent. Carrie remains curiously unmoved by either Drouet's anger or gallantry: "It was not for her," Dreiser observes, "to see the wellspring of human passion."

A quick series of accidents thrusts the plot toward its turning point. First, Drouet returns to patch up his quarrel with Carrie, but finding her gone (she is out seeking a job), he leaves in anger. Then Hurstwood, seeing Drouet register at a hotel, concludes that Carrie and Drouet have broken, leaving the way open for him. Finally, Hurstwood, alone in his employer's office, discovers that the safe has been left open, and $10,000 in receipts is readily at hand. As he vacillates, now holding the money in his hand, now replacing it, a chance gust of wind swings the safe door shut, leaving him with the money.

Stirred into almost hysterical action now, Hurstwood seeks Carrie and deceives her into believing that Drouet has been hurt. Supposedly in search of Drouet, he takes her aboard a train headed for Montreal. At first irritated at the deception, Carrie yields to the lure of a new life in New York. Then she relents and consents to marry Hurstwood, each of them conveniently ignoring the obvious bigamy. Hurstwood's love for Carrie is sincere, but she knows only "a semblance of affection" created by "the drift of things and this man's proximity."

The two embark on a new life in a new metropolis. Carrie does not know, however, that detectives have already trapped Hurstwood in Montreal and compelled him to return all but a thousand dollars of his loot. Hurstwood must, therefore, begin life in New York without the essential ingredients of his success in Chicago: money and reputation. Like Carrie when she first walked the alien streets of Chicago, Hurstwood feels trapped by an environment in which "the great create an atmosphere which reacts badly upon the small." He tries earnestly but unsuccessfully to find a place in this new society. An investment in a new bar turns out disastrously, the income from various jobs disappears in extensive gambling bouts, the periods of unemployment grow longer and longer. As Hurstwood's fortunes dwindle, his manhood also declines. Once proud of his appearance, he now neglects to shave regularly, and he makes no protest when Carrie has him sleep in a separate room. Gradually he abandons even his quest for work, and rocks silently in a chair near a window. Once, humiliated, he serves as a scab during a trolley strike.

Carrie, meanwhile, flourishes. Fascinated by the city and by her lively neighbors, the Vances, she demands more and more of the material pleasures she dreamed of during her girlhood. When Hurstwood fails to provide more than a marginal living, her mild affection turns to contempt. Determined to make her own way, she becomes a chorus girl, advances rapidly to speaking parts and, at last, achieves stardom as a comedienne. By this time, she has decided to leave Hurstwood who sits pitiably in his rocker muttering, "I tried, didn't I?"

As Carrie's fortunes soar, Hurstwood's sink. Reduced to beggary in Stuyvesant Park, he thinks of suicide but lacks the fifteen cents for the gas jet in a Bowery flophouse. One snowy evening as Carrie leaves the theater surrounded by a throng of admirers, Hurstwood tries to push through to see her. He is summarily cast aside and tumbled headlong in the snow. Later that night he obtains the money he needs to carry out his suicide plans. Ironically, as the novel ends Carrie sits alone in a rocking chair, surveying her success, thinking of her lover, Bob Ames. Apparently successful, she remains discontented, yearning still for something elusive, something that, as Dreiser suggests, will forever remain just beyond her grasp.

Critical Opinion

Literary naturalism—as derived from the theory and practice of Emile Zola—commonly assigns to the novelist the role of dispassionate observer, of scientific recorder of the impact upon men of heredity and environment. To many critics, Theodore Dreiser remains the first and greatest of America's naturalists. His novels do record the effect of "chemisms," inner forces that enslave the will (for example, Carrie's "rudimentary mind" and Hurstwood's bodily "poisons" generated by remorse). Similarly, he describes the powerful impact of natural surroundings that produce "desperate results in the soul of man."

Had Dreiser been absolutely loyal to such a theory, however, he would probably not occupy his present place in American letters. For one thing, despite the massive—usually too massive—documentation with which he burdens his reader, Dreiser cannot suffocate his own passion or compassion. More than a scientist, he is a man of feeling. As he details Hurstwood's decline, Dreiser himself feels and communicates the pathos of human degradation. His own youthful ambitions for success and power are mirrored in Carrie's surge upward. But though he cannot resist admiring her rise, he understands the spiritual emptiness accompanying her triumph. Thus Dreiser humanizes the mechanistic thesis and makes memorable in his fiction the deeper, more lasting tones of humanity.

H. L. Mencken called *Sister Carrie* a "broken-backed" novel because the second half—for many readers the more interesting—concentrates upon Hurstwood, as the first does upon Carrie. This criticism has never been satisfactorily answered in literary terms. But then Dreiser cannot effectively be judged on purely esthetic grounds. The novel's structure is certainly faulty, and even more painful are its lumbering sentences, bad grammar, and ornately rhetorical images. For a few critics, these defects diminish Dreiser's stature as a great novelist. To many others, Dreiser's blunders contribute to his titanic force. Tragic reality beckons the creative writer to approach however he may. Dreiser plods and plunges, striking here at social and economic inequity, blasting there at false gentility and timidity. Relentlessly, however, he presses inward toward the inevitable center of experience, the human heart, driven by illusion, maimed by reality. Few American writers before or since have dramatized that tragic dichotomy more movingly.

An American Tragedy

by

THEODORE DREISER

Main Characters

Clyde Griffiths—The protagonist, a weak-willed materialist who awakens tragically from dreams of lavish economic and social success.

Roberta Alden—Clyde's gentle mistress, an innocent caught and destroyed in Clyde's tragedy.

Sondra Finchley—Clyde's ideal woman. Fascinated by her beauty and wealth, Clyde is utterly blind to her vanity, silliness, and irresponsibility.

Elvira and *Asa Griffiths*—Clyde's parents, poverty-ridden evangelists whose naïveté and unworldliness spur his desires for material things.

Esta Griffiths—Clyde's sister, whose seduction and abandonment foreshadow his own tragic future.

Samuel Griffiths—Clyde's wealthy uncle in Lycurgus. Shrewd and conservative, he is also more compassionate than his counterparts in high society.

Gilbert Griffiths—Samuel's son, young, aggressive, vain, a successful businessman and a snob.

Hortense Briggs—Clyde's first girl, a rapacious tease.

Orville Mason—The prosecuting attorney at Clyde's trial. Frustrated in his own life, he resents Clyde's amorous conquest.

Alvin Belknap—Clyde's defense attorney. With no special sympathy for Clyde, he recognizes Clyde's situation as one

he himself experienced in youth, and thus brings a mildly
ironic compassion to the case.

The Rev. Duncan McMillan—A dedicated zealot who tries to
bring solace to Clyde in his last hours.

The Story

At dusk on a summer evening in Kansas City, homeward-
bound office workers pause in the street to observe a strange
family group. The father announces a hymn, the mother sings,
a fifteen-year-old daughter plays the organ, and three younger
children stand about. Only one of them, Clyde Griffiths, seems
restless and ill at ease. At twelve, Clyde already feels out of
place, his vanity and pride offended by his parents' poverty.
Everywhere the boy senses the excitement of the city and
yearns to share its wealth and beauty.

At sixteen, an attractive, well-mannered but ill-educated
youth, Clyde is a bellhop at the Green-Davidson Hotel, gog-
gling at men and women of the world and aspiring to their
grace and mobility. With several of his fellow bellhops, he
imitates them in the rites of liquor and sex. At a party he meets
a rapacious young woman, Hortense Briggs, who brazenly
teases him. Though Clyde thinks of Hortense romantically,
she sees him as a source of cash. To give Hortense the price
of a fur coat, Clyde must deny his sister Esta the money she
needs for medical care. (She has been abandoned, pregnant,
by her lover.) The climax of Clyde's adolescence occurs during a wild ride with Hortense and some other irresponsible
youths. Their stolen car kills a child and crashes into a lumber
pile. Clyde, concerned chiefly for his own safety, crawls away
and escapes to Chicago.

Three years later, Clyde's mild sense of guilt disturbs him
far less than his failure to make progress toward his social
and economic goals. A chance meeting, however, with his
uncle Samuel Griffiths sets him on his path. At his uncle's
suggestion, Clyde leaves Chicago and journeys to Lycurgus,
New York, where Samuel Griffiths' Collar and Shirt Company
has won the family a solid place in the community. Given a
virtually menial job in the factory, Clyde determines to forge
his way upward. His prospects are less happy than he sus-

pects, for the caste-conscious Griffiths clan looks upon him as a poor relative and dispenses condescension along with charity. Clyde's promotion to an assistant foremanship, for example, results less from recognition of his ability than from familial concern about outward appearances.

Few of the local people appeal to Clyde's yearning for high life, and he avoids the easy advances of the factory girls. His longing for society grows after the Griffithses (to fulfill a family obligation) invite him to dinner. There he meets Sondra Finchley, the "most adorable feminine thing he had seen in all his days," and he leaves determined to invade at any cost this world of luxury and beauty. For a time his determination is sidetracked by a chance encounter with one of the less aggressive factory girls, Roberta Alden, an attractive and gentle young woman. Drawn together by their mutual loneliness, Clyde and Roberta drift into a love affair. Roberta yields to Clyde hesitantly, her strong moral training urging her to caution. When at last she does accept him as her lover, however, her passion is sincere, her love profound. Clyde, though fond of Roberta, is chiefly proud of the amorous conquest he has made.

Lacking any real depth of feeling for Roberta, Clyde is easily drawn from her by Sondra who decides to "take him up . . . just for fun." Sondra's attentions reawaken Clyde's dream "to be lifted from the lowly state in which he now dwelt." Clyde continues to see Roberta, though Sondra, now charmed by her suitor, shows him warm affection. The double amour comes to its inevitable crisis when Roberta tells Clyde she is pregnant.

Failing to persuade Roberta to have an abortion and loath to marry her (especially since marriage with Sondra now seems a strong likelihood), Clyde grudgingly agrees to a "secret" marriage, suggesting that for the time being they live apart. Clyde promises to give Roberta the details of his proposal during a day's outing they are to share. By this time Clyde has determined never to marry Roberta. He tries—unsuccessfully—to thrust aside recurrent dreams and thoughts of murder. A newspaper account of a tragic lake drowning is too suggestive for Clyde's comfort as he contemplates his proposed rendezvous with Roberta at Big Bittern Lake. During their journey to Big Bittern, the water, the cries of the birds

overhead, all echo dark thoughts of death. As he and Roberta
row on the lake, his agony contorts his face. Frightened, Roberta beseeches him to speak, then crawls toward him to take
his hand. Half in shock, he twists from her, swinging his
camera-laden hand so that it strikes her across the face. Then,
standing, half-prompted to help, half to apologize, he cap-
sizes the boat. As they flounder in the water, the wale of the
boat strikes Roberta in the head. She cries to Clyde for help.
An inner voice also cries out to him to leave her; her death will
seem accidental; he will be free. As he struggles to decide
what to do, Roberta drowns. Once ashore, Clyde hastily and
ineffectually hides the evidence of their visit, then heads back
toward Lycurgus.

The third book (nearly half the length of the novel) concerns itself with Clyde's arrest, trial, and doom. At first confident that he has covered his tracks with masterly skill, Clyde
feels safe. But once Roberta's body is discovered, mounting
evidence points to Clyde's guilt. Arrested at a beach party
with Sondra, Clyde insists that what occurred at Big Bittern
was an accident, not murder. But since both the coroner and
the district attorney, Orville Mason, scent political gain in a
strong indictment, they decide to ignore truth and justice to
pursue a conviction. Ironically, Clyde's defense attorney,
Alvin Belknap, similarly hopes to benefit from a powerful ex-
hibition of his skill. The trial degenerates into a travesty. The
jury reaches its conclusion before the case begins. The press
sensationalizes everyone, especially the mysterious "other"
woman, Sondra, whose name both sides agree not to reveal.
The lawyers match bravura performances.

Mason argues that Clyde at best willfully let his pregnant
sweetheart drown. Belknap argues that Clyde is not a criminal
but "a mental as well as a moral coward." In his carefully re-
hearsed testimony, Clyde gets little chance to search inwardly
for the truth. His sole preoccupation is survival, and he lies
witlessly, pitiably, and futilely. He is found guilty and condemned to death.

While Clyde is in jail, his mother preaches and writes to
raise money for an appeal, even though she, too, has begun to
doubt his innocence. She enlists the aid of the Rev. Duncan
McMillan who volunteers to try to bring solace to Clyde
during his last days. It is during his long conversation with

McMillan that Clyde gains some insight into his deepest motivations and learns that beneath his shabby protest of innocence lies a hard core of guilt. True, he did not murder Roberta, but he did wish her dead. And worse, his sorrow since has been less for her death than for the loss of his dream. Clyde never achieves a clear understanding of himself. He is never able to get the whole thing straightened out in his own mind.

Clyde goes to his death urging all young men to lead good Christian lives, but a hesitant, skeptical note jars the sentimental harmony of his appeal. A like note of bitterness pervades the closing scene as the Griffiths family gathers once more to sing hymns in the street. The youngest among them —Esta's illegitimate son—begs to be allowed a dime for ice cream—and the terrible cycle seems about to begin anew.

Critical Opinion

Dreiser's *An American Tragedy* is not a tragedy in the conventional sense. Although Clyde is ambitious, his ambition lacks the comprehensive force and energy to make it a "tragic flaw" in the same sense as, for example, Macbeth's ambition. Furthermore, Clyde lacks the tragic hero's nobility of mind and strength of will. Though he enlists sympathy, Clyde fails to win respect, for he is both weak and shallow. Nevertheless, most readers will share F. O. Matthiessen's judgment that in *An American Tragedy*, Dreiser has "written out of a profoundly tragic sense of man's fate."

That fate, as Dreiser expresses it, involves not only Clyde Griffiths but also the nation whose youth he represents. The sources of Clyde's failure are many, but chief among them is the fatal illusion of success through wealth. Blinded to more substantial values, Clyde sacrifices his single real possession— personal identity—to the god of money. Nothing in his society encourages or recognizes anything more worthwhile than the pursuit of material gain. The family unit collapses; religion fails because of its narrow extremism; and even the law, during the trial, perverts truth. Nor are there among Clyde's peers any who offer him a better way of life. They seem incapable of love. They sink into a nameless ooze of impersonality, "absorbed," as Robert Penn Warren has observed, "by the great machine of modern industrial secularized society." The tragedy thus extends beyond the failure of the hero. It is the social and moral tragedy of an age, a people, and a nation—an American tragedy.

Dreiser's novel is bulky and at times tedious. Especially in the account of the crime and the trial (which he took from newspaper stories of an actual murder), Dreiser piles up indigestible chunks of data and dialogue. Despite this, the reader finds himself propelled by the novelist's intensity and dramatic urgency. Dreiser possesses "a Balzacian grip on the machinery of money and power," and as he moves in on a scene or withdraws to survey it, he sweeps the reader along with him. Action and imagery catapult the reader along with Clyde toward the abyss lying beneath a world of shattered illusions and false dreams.

The Author

As a child in Terre Haute, Indiana, *Theodore Dreiser* knew almost daily hunger and poverty. Once he was even sent home from school because he had no shoes. The roots of Dreiser's passion for material success grew out of this arid soil. At sixteen, after the family had broken up several times, Dreiser set out for Chicago alone, hoping to discover a career for himself. It was a false start, for although he was, like Sister Carrie, fascinated by the metropolis, he could find only a succession of menial jobs.

After a year back in Indiana at the university, Dreiser ventured once more toward the city, this time to try his luck at journalism. For the next twenty years he worked at various journalistic tasks—from reporting to editorial work—in the Midwest and in New York. In 1898, shortly after he had begun work as a reporter, he married a woman he did not love, and for the next forty years she refused him the divorce he pleaded for. Not until her death in 1942 could Dreiser marry the woman he had really loved during this period.

The publication of *Sister Carrie*, his first novel, in 1900, did little to buoy Dreiser's hopes or fortunes. Because the publisher's wife was shocked by Dreiser's portrait of an American girl, she persuaded her husband not to distribute the novel. For nearly a dozen years, the novel went without an American reading public. Not until he had achieved a national reputation as the editor of the famous Butterick fashion magazines did Dreiser gain an audience for his novel. By that time, however, he had survived his misfortunes and had achieved the wealth and fame he had yearned for since boyhood.

Beginning in 1911, Dreiser wrote four novels in as many years: *Jennie Gerhardt, The Financier, The Titan,* and *The Genius.* These, too, encountered resistance from publishers and self-appointed censors, but Dreiser, aided by distinguished critics like H. L. Mencken, fought the oppressive forces. Disgusted with the narrowness of the society of his time, he published only one more novel during the remaining thirty years of his life. That one, however, was his masterpiece, *An American Tragedy* (1925). Two of his novels were published posthumously.

At the height of his fame in the twenties, Dreiser dressed like a dandy, affecting a cane and leading a Russian wolfhound on a leash. He praised American rugged individualism and attacked the Soviet system after he returned from a trip to Russia. But during the 1930s, Dreiser grew increasingly disenchanted with American capitalism and began to support left-wing causes. In his social and political essays ("Tragic America"), he attacked the inequities created by the same individualism he had supported all his life. Just before his death, Dreiser joined the Communist Party, apparently convinced that the hope for economic and spiritual salvation no longer could be left to the will of the individual. His dream of material success turned at last into a nightmare.

Babbitt

by

SINCLAIR LEWIS (1885–1951)

Main Characters

George F. Babbitt—Prototype of the American bourgeois in
his comfortable mid-forties, solidly anchored to the standardized virtues of work, duty, and morality—yet somehow
restless, with a romantic urge to rebel.

Myra Babbitt—Babbitt's wife, "as sexless as an anemic nun,"
bursting with maternal instincts toward her husband as
well as toward her three children.

Verona, Ted, and *Tinka Babbitt*—Babbitt's brood. Verona,
twenty-two, a recent Bryn Mawr graduate dedicated to advanced notions about literature, sex, and social reform;
Ted (christened Theodore Roosevelt), a teen-age fraternity
man dedicated to the advance of school spirit and the re-
tardation of intellectual growth; Tinka, at ten, dedicated to
ice-cream sodas and candy.

Paul Riesling—Babbitt's best friend and alter ego. A would-
be artist (violinist), crushed by the twin molds of business
and marriage, Paul rebels, briefly but violently.

Tanis Judique—A widow, lonely, attractive, and liberated,
who helps Babbitt strip away a few layers of his hidebound
conventionality.

Vergil Gunch, Chum Frink, Orville Jones—Luminaries of the
Zenith Athletic Club and the Boosters' Club, outstanding

examples of what Lewis calls the "Standardized American Citizen."

Charles and *Lucille McKelvey*—Members of the aristocratic Union Club, a niche above and forever beyond the reach of the Boosters. McKelvey owns a construction company. His wife has elevated notions about art. Neither suffers from moral scruples.

Sir Gerald Doak—A visiting businessman, the British equivalent of Babbitt.

Seneca Doane—The radical idealist, a lawyer who challenges Zenith reactionaries but wins few adherents.

The Story

Just beyond the urban limits of Zenith (a thriving Midwestern metropolis of nearly a half-million people) lies Floral Heights, the home of George Follansbee Babbitt. Like the streets and skyscrapers of Zenith, the houses of Floral Heights are smugly the same, utterly devoid of individuality. To Babbitt, however, his house (in no sense a home) symbolizes the world of progress. His possessions—porcelain bathtub, fancy alarm clock, electric fan, percolator, toaster, and most sublime, his automobile—attest to his elevated status in Zenith.

To achieve his place as a solid citizen of Zenith (including membership in the Athletic Club and the Boosters' Club), Babbitt has worked diligently and aggressively as a real estate salesman, raised a reputable if undistinguished brood, and espoused the right causes. Whether in politics, art, or education, Babbitt detests socialists, foreigners, and reformers. (To be one of these, he feels, is probably to be the others as well.) Babbitt supports efficiency and laissez-faire, a "business Administration" like Warren G. Harding's. He favors but does not observe Prohibition, believes in the sanctity of marriage but yearns after his secretary. In brief, when forty-six-year-old George F. Babbitt wakes early one morning in April, 1920, his pink and pudgy countenance expresses the zesty energy, uncritical optimism, and innocent hypocrisy of the typical American bourgeois.

But a rebellious scowl lurks behind Babbitt's serene mask, a rejection of domesticity and a doubt about the worth of ma-

terial success. Outwardly, Babbitt observes the forms. He
urges his reluctant son toward college, nags his daughter toward social conformity, invites the snobbish McKelveys to dinner in a vain attempt to climb the social ladder, and ingratiates
himself sufficiently with his peers to win a vice-presidency in
the Boosters' Club. The seed of discontent, nevertheless, bur-
geons; rebellion threatens to sprout. The catalyst, strangely, is
Paul Riesling, Babbitt's college classmate and closest friend.

Once an aspiring concert violinist, Paul has descended to
selling tar roofing during the day and battling nightly with his
wife, Zilla, who despises but will not divorce or desert him. A
kind of mirror-image of Babbitt, Paul reflects an extreme form
of Babbitt's own marital dissatisfaction. Moreover, Paul's
refuge from the horror of his marriage—the clandestine love
affair—rouses Babbitt's latent passions. From the outset of the
novel, Babbitt has cherished a recurrent dream of a lovely
girl, a "fairy child" who will love him gently and deeply.

Babbitt's revolt begins simply. He turns on Zilla sharply
and denounces her for nagging Paul. To his own wife, Myra,
he says he is "sick of everybody and everything" and wants to
be left alone for a while. Shocked by his own audacity and
by the readiness with which Zilla and Myra yield to him,
Babbitt feels reduced to "primitive terror . . . wondering what
he could do with anything so unknown and so embarrassing
as freedom." What he does with his new freedom is merely to
go off with Paul for a joyous week of fishing and talk before
their wives join them.

His rebelliousness momentarily quenched, Babbitt bows
once more to middle-class convention. But when, during a trip
to Chicago, he encounters Paul with one of his mistresses,
Babbitt again grows restive. Two unexpected events convince
him he must make "a terrifying, thrilling break with everything that was decent and normal." Paul shoots Zilla and is
sentenced to three years in jail. Myra goes East for a visit,
leaving Babbitt entirely alone. Isolated, deprived of his alter
ego, Babbitt must face himself. The confrontation convinces
him that "perhaps all life as he knew it and vigorously practiced it was futile." When he wakes the next morning, Babbitt
is a conscious rebel.

At a party a few nights later, he makes his first ineffectual
pass at a neighbor's wife. Some days later he takes a young

manicurist to dinner and makes a fumbling, unsuccessful attempt to seduce her. With Tanis Judique, a widow approaching middle age, Babbitt at last discovers his "fairy child" in the flesh. Lonely and compassionate, Tanis brings to Babbitt an interlude of fulfillment. Even after Myra returns, he finds reasons to stay away from home to be with Tanis alone or with her bohemian friends. Boldly, Babbitt dares to dine with Tanis publicly within the sight of shocked Boosters.

Babbitt's revolt assumes a socio-political guise as well when he supports the town radical, Seneca Doane, during a workers' strike. To his fellow Boosters, Babbitt seems increasingly a "crank," and they apply intense pressure upon him to return to the fold. In fact, Babbitt has already found freedom most uncomfortable, but is too proud to yield to social pressure. Gallantly, Tanis releases him from his sexual adventure and returns him to his marital bondage. His friends, however, lack her delicacy and press him to acknowledge the social and political rightness of conventional thinking. Ironically, Myra's sudden illness provides the avenue for Babbitt's escape back to the "paralyzed contentment of middle age." As his old friends rally to his side during his siege of worry about Myra, Babbitt swears renewed allegiance "to his wife . . . to Zenith . . . to business efficiency . . . to the Boosters' Club . . . to every faith of the Clan of Good Fellows." To prove himself a worthy prodigal, Babbitt now campaigns vigorously against Doane.

Outwardly, the ending is happy. Myra recovers. The children marry. Business is booming. Inwardly, Babbitt keenly feels a sense of loss. To his son Ted, who has left college to marry the girl next door, Babbitt confides: "I've never done a single thing I've wanted to do in my whole life. . . . But I do get a kind of sneaking pleasure out of the fact that you knew what you wanted to do and did it." Perhaps, Babbitt tacitly suggests, another generation may discover a way to crash the barrier of "sound citizenship."

Critical Opinion

E. M. Forster, the distinguished British novelist and critic, once wrote about Sinclair Lewis that he was neither poet nor preacher, "but a fellow with a camera a few yards away." The candid photography in *Babbitt* captures unforgettably the banal and the absurd in Midwestern American life: the Babbitts' living room and the main street in Zenith; the boys at the club and the Babbitts at breakfast—all enlargements of false heartiness and empty-souled optimism. At the center of the group stands the man whose name has become an American byword for the essentially decent fellow who believes so deeply and uncritically in the values of his society that he forgets his own individuality.

The weakness of Lewis' novel lies in Babbitt's achieving a dimension beyond our expectation by undertaking to rebel. No one would have expected Vergil Gunch or Chum Frink to rebel, or George Babbitt either. Because he does, the reader may become confused. Is Lewis satirizing Babbitt as a conformist or as a rebel? Is he satirizing him as both? Or is he sympathizing with him as both? Most critics believe that Lewis never truly resolved his attitude toward Babbitt—that he simultaneously admired and despised Babbitt's bourgeois soul, approved and censured his brief revolt. That such indecision affected Lewis is not difficult to understand, for in many ways Babbitt and his creator are one and the same—a combination of philistine and rebel.

Babbitt does not, as H. L. Mencken claims, represent all there is to tell about the real America. Rather it shows us what Lewis' biographer, Mark Schorer, significantly describes as a half-truth. Lewis' vision is narrow, his emotion shallow. He shows us that we are spiritually sterile and to some extent even suggests why. What *Babbitt* achieves is a shrewd criticism of the surface of American experience, but the depths remain unplumbed.

Arrowsmith

by

SINCLAIR LEWIS

Main Characters

Martin Arrowsmith—The protagonist, a young medical researcher, torn between commitment to his ideal—the lonely path of pure science—and the worldly goal of science for profit.

Leora Tozer—Martin's wife, unsophisticated, utterly feminine, forthright and unaffected, warm and unswervingly loyal.

Dr. Max Gottlieb—Martin's scientific mentor and idol. A refugee German-Jew, he is shy, austere, dedicated, an "authentic scientist" and a decent human being.

Dr. Gustaf Sondelius—Another of Arrowsmith's heroes, a crusty but kindly Swede, a pioneer in battling disease epidemics and an indefatigable fund raiser.

Terry Wickett—Arrowsmith's closest friend, an uncomplicated man and a doggedly honest research worker.

Almus Pickerbaugh—The Babbitt of the medical world. Director of Public Health in Nautilus, Iowa, later U.S. Congressman, a preposterous but exuberant booster of good health and good business for wholesome, respectable Americans.

Ross McGurk—Millionaire founder of the McGurk Institute for Medical Research, unscrupulous in business but absolutely pure in his support of science and of Dr. Gottlieb.

Capitola McGurk—His wife, "a complete controller of virtuous affairs," including insufferable dinner parties, a dispenser of "cooing staleness."

Dr. A. DeWitt Tubbs—Director of the McGurk Institute when Arrowsmith arrives there, a man of little scientific knowledge but of considerable talent for high-level medical politics.

Dr. Rippleton Holabird—Head of the department of physi-

ology at McGurk, a youthful, charming, tweedy protégé of
Dr. Tubbs, destined for mediocrity and success.

Madeline Fox, Orchid Pickerbaugh, Joyce Lanyon—The
other women in Arrowsmith's life. Their roles, respectively:
Martin's college girlfriend; his first post-marital flirtation
("She's no orchid," Leora observes, "she's a bachelor's but-
ton"); Martin's second wife. All are more attractive physically than Leora, but also more superficial, less understanding.

The Story

From early adolescence, Martin Arrowsmith worships science and those who pursue its truths. As a fourteen-year-old,
he idolizes and is inspired by Doc Vickerson, a brilliant, alcoholic village physician. Seven years later, as a medical student
at the University of Winnemac, Zenith's proud education factory (its students are "beautifully standardized, with perfectly
interchangeable parts"), Martin discovers a new idol, Dr. Max
Gottlieb, a crotchety genius and professor of bacteriology and
immunology. Gottlieb's implacable insistence upon patience
and skepticism as the only paths to scientific truth challenges
Arrowsmith's youthful arrogance and agonized sense of in-
feriority. Doggedly he struggles to rise to Gottlieb's demands,
sloughing off the many temptations of the "men of measured
merriment"—the facile, graceful, empty-headed and hollow-
souled seekers after easy success. To win from Gottlieb an encouraging smile spurs Martin to renewed and enthusiastic
effort.

During his junior year, when he is Gottlieb's assistant, Martin becomes entangled with two fiancées: Madeline Fox, a glib
graduate student in English, and Leora Tozer, an unsophisticated student nurse. Absurdly he brings them together, hoping they will understand his plight. Madeline does not and
stalks off, leaving Martin to Leora, who accepts her triumph
with unaffected delight. Their marriage plans are temporarily
postponed when family illness compels Leora to return to her
home in Wheatsylvania. Lonely and irritable, Martin grows
careless at his work, defies Gottlieb and the dean, and is fired.
In anger and despair he turns for a time to the road, drifting

and drinking, but before he hits bottom, he flees to Leora. Despite the opposition of her limited and provincial family, they marry.

Determined now to earn a living, Martin returns to the university, apologizes to the dean (but not to Gottlieb), and works to complete his medical degree. Though he yearns above all to work with Gottlieb, he is too proud to apologize, and rationalizes about the superiority of his country medical practice in Leora's hometown in North Dakota. His year there proves frustrating and infuriating. Neither his patients nor his fellow-practitioners respect truth, preferring epidemics to preventive injections. The only significant event all year is his meeting with a visiting lecturer, Gustaf Sondelius, a famous epidemiologist, who reawakens Martin's dormant love for research. At the end of the year, encouraged by Leora, Martin writes to Sondelius, and, with his help, wins a post as an assistant director of public health in Nautilus, Iowa, a small-scale Zenith.

Martin's superior, Dr. Almus Pickerbaugh, is a "man of measured merriment." He never talks. ("He either bubbled or made orations.") Though he thwarts Martin's attempts to establish citywide pasteurization or the elimination of tenements where tuberculosis is breeding, Pickerbaugh does initiate several projects of his own, such as "Swat the Fly Week" and an "Open Your Window Parade." His "Eugenics Week" narrowly escapes disaster when members of the "model" family turn out to be epileptic, illegitimate, and wanted by the police. For a time Martin tries to fight Pickerbaugh, but at last he succumbs and learns how he too may smile with measured merriment. Part of the reason for his surrender may be his infatuation with Pickerbaugh's night-blooming nineteen-year-old daughter, Orchid. Pickerbaugh's election to Congress (his platform: "Just elect him for a term and all through the nation he'll swat the germ") solves the problem of Orchid but catapults Martin into a new challenge by making him the director of public health.

Martin meets the challenge honestly and energetically. He undertakes research once more and writes and delivers a learned paper. But whenever his plans endanger business, the politicians and churchmen of Nautilus block his efforts to improve public health. At last they force his resignation. Beaten and dismayed, Martin accepts a routine testing assignment at a clinic in Chicago. His idealism seems atrophied, his hopes diminished. Only his relationship with Leora thrives. Out of the gloom and chaos, however, comes an invitation from Gottlieb (who has read Martin's recently published paper) to join him at the distinguished McGurk Institute of Research in New York.

Gottlieb himself has experienced reverses. An impassioned but tactless appeal to the administration at Winnemac in behalf of a research institute lost Gottlieb his post. A drug company hired him, but he left when they tried to commercialize a vaccine he had discovered but not yet fully tested. Family problems have also beset the old man: his wife died and his son turned wastrel. But the offer from McGurk brought Gottlieb economic and scientific security, both of which he now eagerly offers to share with the protégé he has always most admired and loved.

From the moment of his arrival at McGurk (nearly two-thirds of the way through the novel), Martin is the kind of man he always wanted to be. "I've found my work, I've found my work," he exults, forgetting even to ask about his salary. For months—serenely oblivious of the cliques and factions seething about him—he works feverishly on an experiment that promises to prove revolutionary: the discovery of a virus that destroys other viruses. When word of his progress leaks to Dr. Tubbs, the director, Martin is pressured to publish his findings before he has administered all the tests Gottlieb has urged him to employ. Choosing integrity rather than fame, he plods on with his work, only to have a scientist in France publish a paper anticipating his findings.

Deflated but undismayed, Martin turns next to testing his "phage" (as he calls the anti-bacterial serum) as a possible weapon against specific disease. Now, because Gottlieb assumes the directorship of the Institute (Tubbs, a man of measured merriment, goes on to a more glamorous post), Sondelius, Martin's idol of earlier years, arrives to become his noisy but dedicated co-worker. Together they study the startlingly destructive effect of phage upon the bacilli of bubonic plague.

The outbreak of plague on the island of St. Hubert in the British West Indies provides the occasion for a large-scale test of Martin's vaccine. Martin agrees to test the serum provided that rigid experimental conditions are observed: only half of the natives will be inoculated; the others, as controls, will receive no protective inoculation. Sondelius objects to these terms on humane grounds, but agrees to go along on the expedition to exterminate rats, one of his specialties. What he categorically refuses is to allow himself to be inoculated against plague until Martin promises to drop his system of controls. One last problem remains before the expedition leaves: What to do about Leora? She solves the difficulty swiftly and efficiently; she will go wherever Martin goes.

On the island of St. Hubert, bureaucracy rages as devastatingly as the plague. Once the reluctant governor admits the reality of the situation, he must fight all those who want tourist and export "business as usual." By cajolery and sheer lung power, Sondelius wins the right to exterminate rats. Martin, however, encounters stiffer opposition when he demands the right to inoculate only half the population. "I'm not a sentimentalist; I'm a scientist," he argues, and gets his way. Aided by a local native physician, he administers the serum and keeps meticulous account of the results, turning aside all pleas of those who must die because of his determination to be scientifically accurate. He withstands even the shock of Sondelius's death. But when Leora dies as a result of a careless infection through a cigarette, Martin's courage fails, and he inoculates everyone. Acclaimed as the hero of the island, he regards himself as a failure.

Back in New York, Martin is shocked and saddened to find Gottlieb lost in the shadowy mists of senile dementia. The man whose censure Martin most dreaded cannot even recognize him. Alone now, except for Terry Wickett, Martin plunges into research with an ardor that would have cheered Gottlieb. Almost whole again, Martin encounters another temptation: Joyce Lanyon, a wealthy, beautiful, socially important widow he meets at St. Hubert. Martin cannot resist Joyce, and for a year their marriage seems a possible way for him to survive the loss of Leora. Joyce gives Martin a son, but in return she takes from him his independence and individuality. His work suffers. He rebels, leaves her, and goes off to the Vermont hills to continue his research. With Terry Wickett as his only companion, Martin rededicates himself to the ardors and rewards of pure research, freed at last from men and the women of measured merriment.

Critical Opinion

Arrowsmith, some critics agree, is Sinclair Lewis' best novel. A long novel, it lacks the concentration *Babbitt* achieves by focusing upon a single region of the Midwest. In *Arrowsmith*, Lewis hunts quarry that lurk in no single lair, for Zenith does not contain all of the evils that beset the dedicated scientist. The entire nation, as Lewis shows, abounds in commercialism, quackery, political chicanery, social snobbism. Universities, medical schools, hospitals, all tempt young idealists to abandon honesty in exchange for money or fame. Lewis lances his prey with septic wit and irony. The Pickerbaughs and the Tubbs, Holabirds and Capitola McGurks have all been inoculated against sincerity and idealism, but they are no match for Lewis' satire.

The novel is not, however, merely a broadside attack. Nor does it suffer from the ambivalence in attitude that undermines *Babbitt*. Martin Arrowsmith, like Babbitt, is drawn to material success, but Martin "succumbs to his own integrity" and forces himself to continue his struggle. In his delineation of Martin, Lewis etches not only the true scientist's passionate devotion to research, but also the growth of a gifted man with very human weaknesses. Many people contribute to Martin's development, none, of course, more selflessly than Leora, one of the most luminous creations in American fiction. Through Leora's death, Martin learns to face reality on his own. Until her death, she had always been beside him at critical moments to share his burdens. Similarly, Max Gottlieb, high priest among Arrowsmith's demigods, must leave his protégé to find his own way. The scientist, like all men, must learn that his path is lonely.

Only occasionally does the novel falter. Sometimes, for example, Lewis digresses too long in his denunciation of social villains; the plot calls him back long before he is ready to return. Sometimes, too, the butts of his ridicule lack dimension and credibility.

Another weakness of Lewis' grows, ironically, from a source

of his strength. For his almost Zolaesque accuracy in scientific detail, Lewis turned to Dr. Paul de Kruif, the famous author of *Microbe Hunters.* What de Kruif provides is, of course, valid information, and for the most part it creates the suspense of research. But insistence upon rigid controls during the epidemic results almost in a caricature of the "inhumane" scientist. Such incidental failures do not really diminish the stature of the novel. It has, as Lewis Mumford has rightly observed, "that additional quality which belongs only to the higher levels of literature, the sense of facing the issues of life and death, and creating, in the very face of defeat, an inner assurance."

The Author

Sinclair Lewis was born in Sauk Center, Minnesota, the son of a country doctor and a consumptive mother who died when he was six. Tall and spindling, ugly, his face ravaged by acne, Lewis led a lonely, introverted youth. At Yale he refused to fit into conventional molds, tramping off one summer to Panama, another to Upton Sinclair's socialist community, Helicon Hall. He seemed alternately to burst with coarse, inexhaustible energy, and to withdraw into agonized moodiness. The cycle was to persist throughout his life.

After his graduation from Yale (1908), Lewis worked for several years variously as reporter, editor, advertising manager, and even as an idea man, selling plots for novels to Jack London and Albert Payson Terhune. His first novel, *Our Mr. Wrenn* (1914), won him enough praise to convince him that his future lay in fiction. Just married, he pressed on to write more fiction, but success and fame did not come until 1920. With *Main Street,* Lewis exploded upon the literary scene. His satirical account of Carol Kennicott's revolt against Gopher Prairie, the universal small town, brought him almost unanimous acclaim, abroad as well as at home. Within the next five years, Lewis added two more figures to his chronicle of the American middle class caught in the stultifying net of conformity: the protagonist of *Babbitt* (1922) and *Arrowsmith* (1925).

These three works rank as Lewis' finest. His later work—nearly a dozen novels, all financially successful—deteriorated in quality, though it never lost its vigor. Descending sometimes to caricature, sometimes to sentimentality, occasionally to both, Lewis nevertheless created memorable characters like Elmer Gantry, the rapacious preacher, and Sam Dodsworth, the henpecked automobile manufacturer. But Lewis himself became trapped by the success myth he had satirized and found it difficult at last to detach himself from the values of Gopher Prairie.

Outward success—the Nobel Prize, travel, marriage to famous journalist Dorothy Thompson, wealth—all these seemed increasingly empty as the years passed. Lewis' second marriage failed, his drinking got out of control, his friendships disintegrated. What remained was the early conflict between his enormous zest for life and his inward despair. Unfortunately, his fiction reflects little of the torment he felt when, shortly before he died, he said, "Oh God, no man has ever been so miserable." Ironically, Lewis' life, even more than his fiction, testified to the cruel gap between happiness and material success.

The Great Gatsby

by

F. SCOTT FITZGERALD (1896–1940)

Main Characters

Nick Carraway—The critical but compassionate narrator.

Jay Gatsby—Born James Gatz, he is the tragic hero who, paradoxically, is also a bootlegger and peddler of phony stocks. Reckless and romantic, he suggests the emptiness of the American success myth.

Daisy Buchanan—Nick's cousin. Once about to marry Gatsby, now wed to Tom Buchanan, she is lovely, exciting, and shallow. But for Gatsby she represents the fulfillment of his false dreams.

Tom Buchanan—Handsome, wealthy, and athletic, but also insensitive to the point of stupidity and cruelty.

Jordan Baker—Friend of Daisy and occasional girl friend of Nick; petulant, spoiled, and an incorrigible liar.

Myrtle Wilson—Tom's mistress. Wife of a garage owner, she is attractive, tasteless, and dismally vulgar.

George Wilson—Myrtle's browbeaten husband. Devoid of will and purpose, he becomes, ironically, the agent of the tragic climax.

The Story

The year is 1922, the setting Long Island, New York. At West Egg live Jay Gatsby and his neighbor, the narrator Nick

155

Carraway; Gatsby in a staggeringly elegant mansion, Nick in a small cramped cottage. Across the Sound in more fashionable East Egg live Daisy and Tom Buchanan. Midway between West Egg and New York City lies a vast ash dump near which are the garage and home of George and Myrtle Wilson. Significantly, all of the characters pass through this "valley of ashes," symbol of the barren spiritual wasteland they inhabit. It is here, too, that the terrible climax of the novel occurs. Upon this bleak setting stare the sightless blue eyes of Dr. T. J. Eckleburg—a grotesque billboard advertisement placed in the ash dump by an oculist. These blank eyes mirror unfeelingly the tragic events that pass before them.

After serving in World War I and getting an education at Yale, Nick begins work as a bond salesman. Settled in West Egg, he renews his acquaintance with his cousin Daisy and her husband Tom. From Daisy's friend, Jordan Baker, Nick learns that Tom is unfaithful and that Daisy is agonizingly aware of his infidelity. Tom boldly insists that Nick meet his mistress, Myrtle Wilson. Reluctantly, Nick joins Tom and Myrtle for a noisy party at their private New York apartment. The climax of the party occurs when Tom breaks Myrtle's nose for daring to mention Daisy's name.

Caught up in the bitterness of the Buchanans' turmoil, Nick finds himself almost immediately trapped as well in Gatsby's turbulent life. Gatsby's is a lavish world of weekend parties attended by guests who rarely meet their host, yet speculate freely upon the shady sources of his wealth. Gatsby's showy parties fail to satisfy his central, all-consuming passion—to reclaim Daisy whom he won and then lost while he was abroad during the war. To this purpose he enlists the aid of both Jordan and Nick who both know Daisy. A meeting is arranged at Nick's and soon Daisy is again Gatsby's mistress. For a short time Gatsby and Daisy share a happiness neither has known since their first encounter.

Gatsby's innocent assumption that he can sustain this idyl is short-lived. Reality intrudes as both Tom Buchanan and George Wilson discover almost simultaneously that their wives are unfaithful. Though Wilson has learned of Myrtle's trespasses, he does not know that Tom has deceived him. To Wilson, Tom is merely a customer at the garage and a potential source of used cars. Tom, however, suffers the "hot whips of panic" as he confronts the possible loss of a wife and a mistress. In a suffocatingly hot hotel room in New York, Gatsby demands—in the presence of Tom, Daisy, Nick, and Jordan—that Daisy leave her husband and admit that she has never loved him. Willing to acknowledge that she loves Gatsby and that she no longer loves Tom, Daisy cannot say that she has never loved her husband. Tom uses this wedge to expose and denounce Gatsby as an underworld creature. Daisy's silence before Tom's attack and her refusal to deny having loved Tom shatter Gatsby and wreck his illusions.

Earlier, when the five set out for New York, Tom's jealousy rages, inflamed by Daisy's insisting upon riding with Gatsby in the Buchanans' car while Tom and the others follow in Gatsby's. Now, triumphant and scornful, Tom encourages Gatsby to use his own car to drive Daisy back to West Egg. They leave together. Catastrophe awaits them on the road.

Beaten by her husband and locked in her room, Myrtle Wilson forces her way out and dashes into the road. Seeking refuge, she encounters violent death under the wheels of Gatsby's car which careens on without stopping. Soon after, Tom, Nick, and Jordan arrive at the now crowded garage where Tom discovers his mistress dead, her husband distraught. Tom's whispered words to Wilson (unreported until the closing pages of the novel) provoke a swift and terrible climax. First, however, Nick learns from Gatsby that Daisy, not he, drove the car that killed Myrtle. Gatsby announces his intention to assume all responsibility for Daisy's action. He never gets the chance. As he leaves Gatsby, Nick shouts to him across the lawn: "They're a rotten crowd. You're worth the whole damn bunch put together." The compliment wins from Gatsby a radiant smile—his last. A few hours later he is dead of a gun wound inflicted by George Wilson who then takes his own life.

Only Gatsby's aged father and a few servants join Nick at Gatsby's funeral. No other friends or former guests attend, despite Nick's earnest pleas. And Daisy and Tom have already left on a trip. Several months later Nick meets Tom and forces him to admit the truth: that he told Wilson that Gatsby was driving the death car. Obviously Daisy has never contradicted the lie. Furious, then compassionate, Nick realizes that it was "all very careless and confused. They were careless people,

Tom and Daisy—they smashed up things and creatures and then retreated back into their money or their vast carelessness, or whatever it was that kept them together, and let other people clean up the mess they had made...."

Soon after, Nick breaks off his relationship with Jordan, conscious that she resembles Daisy too closely to share a vital human relationship. His last gesture, however, reaches beyond denial to awareness. Returning for a last look at Gatsby's mansion, Nick stands at the shore and recalls that centuries earlier Dutch sailors had looked upon this island, their eyes and hearts filled with illusions that prepared the way for Gatsby's hopeless dream, a dream whose doom had already been foretold long ago.

Critical Opinion

The Great Gatsby was published in April, 1925, enjoyed enthusiastic reviews, and won Fitzgerald warm praise from writers he deeply admired. T. S. Eliot, for example, wrote Fitzgerald that *Gatsby* "has interested and excited me more than any new novel I have seen, either English or American, for a number of years . . . it seems to me to be the first step that American fiction has taken since Henry James. . . ." But sales failed to match critical acclaim. From a disappointingly modest beginning, *The Great Gatsby* reached fewer and fewer readers until, by 1937, Fitzgerald reported that he could not find a bookstore that stocked even a single copy. Today, nearly forty years after its initial publication, *Gatsby* sells about 50,000 copies a year, more than twice its original sale.

What has assured *Gatsby* its command of a larger audience is a clearer understanding of Fitzgerald's achievement. *Gatsby* is not—as many earlier critics wrongly assumed—an uncritical study of manners during the Jazz Age. It is a penetrating analysis of the failure of the Jazz Age to produce significant or lasting values. Despite his personal ambivalence toward wealth, Fitzgerald achieved in *Gatsby* enough detachment to expose the disease corrupting the social and moral fiber of the American spirit. That disease lay deep in the distorted imagination of Jay Gatsby. Duped by the dream of material success, Gatsby succumbed to warped fantasies, equating present with past and love with wealth. Gatsby symbolizes America enslaved, as Fitzgerald writes, in "the service of a vast, vulgar, and meretricious beauty." In Gatsby's pitiable disillusion and defeat, Fitzgerald illustrates the fever that burns away the spiritual strength of so many Americans.

Although it attacks conventional values, *Gatsby* opens rather than shuts the door to change. Nick's growing awareness of the Buchanans' destructiveness and Gatsby's blindness offers hope. As the novel ends, Nick achieves maturity: he stands free of illusion yet capable of compassion. He can never become a Jay Gatsby or, far worse, a Tom or Daisy Buchanan. If then, as one critic has observed, *The Great Gatsby* dramatizes "the withering of the American dream," it offers also a more substantial alternative to it.

A brief note on the craft of Fitzgerald's finest novel: neither plot nor characterization is outstanding; elements of melodrama mar the narrative, and the characters are too foreshortened to possess depth. Nevertheless, Fitzgerald uses his selective technique creatively. From Joseph Conrad and Henry James he learned to employ an outside observer (Nick) to vivify portraiture and to create suspense. But above all, *Gatsby* is a triumph of mood and tone. Character, symbol, and image blend uniformly to produce a quality of lyric sadness that pervades the whole work. For its moral criticism and technical artistry, then, *The Great Gatsby* emerges, as Malcolm Cowley has observed, as "a fable of the 1920s that will survive as a legend for other times."

The Author

Great-grandnephew of Francis Scott Key, *F. Scott Fitzgerald* was born in St. Paul, Minnesota, to Catholic parents of Irish and Maryland-English stock. After completing a parochial education with indifferent success, Fitzgerald entered Princeton (1913), where his grades continued to suffer as he pursued extracurricular rather than academic interests, writing plays for the Triangle Club and poems and stories for the college literary magazines. A timely illness followed by enlistment in the Army saved him from failing out of college, but Fitzgerald's love for Princeton lasted throughout his life.

As a second lieutenant, Fitzgerald never served abroad, spending most of his time at training camps. With ample leisure but small funds at his disposal, he wrote his first novel and courted Zelda Sayre, the woman who proved one of the most powerful influences in his life. Not until his novel, *This Side of Paradise,* was published in 1920 did Zelda consent to marry her no longer impoverished suitor. *This Side of Paradise* established Fitzgerald as the voice of the Jazz Age and brought him, at the age of twenty-four, the wealth and fame he hungered after. For several years he and Zelda lived abroad, chiefly in Paris and on the French Riviera, luxuriously, extravagantly, and always hopelessly beyond their means. Many of his short stories were potboilers written to meet expenses. Some of them, however ("The Diamond as Big as the Ritz" and "Babylon Revisited"), rank with the finest short fiction of the century and compare favorably with his best novels.

From 1927 on, Zelda's mental health deteriorated and Fitzgerald's drinking habits worsened. By the mid-thirties he had become an alcoholic. His productivity had diminished, his debts had risen, and his reputation had faded. The final years, dramatically recorded in *The Crack Up* (1945), testify to Fitzgerald's courage as well as to his despair. With Zelda institutionalized (she died in a fire a few years after Fitzgerald's death), he struggled to support their daughter, Scottie, by writing scripts for Hollywood. But the machine had worn down. At the age of forty-four Fitzgerald died in Los Angeles of a heart attack. In his last incomplete novel, *The Last Tycoon,* Fitzgerald reveals that despite many failures, he retained both the integrity and the penetrating vision of a true artist.

The Sun Also Rises

by

ERNEST HEMINGWAY (1899–1961)

Main Characters

Jake Barnes—The hero, a journalist, made impotent by a war wound, in love with the beautiful, promiscuous Brett Ashley. A defensive cynicism, drinking, the outdoor life, and friendship help him live with his inner torment.

Brett Ashley—A cultivated Englishwoman, in love with Jake, but compulsively involved in a series of sterile love affairs.

Robert Cohn—A novelist and a doggedly persistent, briefly successful suitor of Brett, once a boxer and intellectual at Princeton, now a brooding moralist (despite his mistresses), and as a Jew, a defensive outsider in Brett's coterie.

Bill Gorton—Jake's friend, fellow journalist, and confidant, good-natured, tolerant, and humorous.

Mike Campbell—Brett's fiancé after her divorce from Lord Ashley, a heavy drinker and an economic and spiritual bankrupt infected with a vengeful anti-Semitism.

Pedro Romero—A young bullfighter in love with Brett. A brave and honorable matador, he narrowly escapes corruption of the traditions he most values.

Montoya—Proprietor of the Pamplona hotel where Jake and the others stay during the fiesta, a true *aficionado* of the traditions and tragic grandeur of the bullfight.

Count Mippipopolous—Worldly, wealthy friend and would-be lover of Brett. A veteran of seven wars and four revolutions, he believes in nothing but love.

The Story

Paris after World War I is the scene of the first of three sections of the novel, each narrated from the point of view of Jake Barnes. Despite a minimum of action, the opening section communicates the disillusion and discontinuity pervading the lives of a group of American and British expatriates who drift from bar to bedroom.

Jake and Robert Cohn represent irreconcilably opposed philosophies. The thirty-four-year-old Cohn, divorced, afflicted with a petulant, hysterical mistress, Frances Clyne, yearns for a happier existence. Inspired by W. H. Hudson's romance, *The Purple Land,* he dreams vaguely of starting afresh in South America. Cohn has money, talent, and intelligence (a moderate amount of each), but he cannot bring them simultaneously to bear upon reality. Foolishly he demands that life conform to his dream, making Brett Ashley his epitome of the dream woman who will share with him a better, more ennobling life.

Jake, on the other hand, elects to live with what is. When Cohn urges him to share the trip to South America, Jake replies: "You can't get away from yourself by moving from one place to another." Despite his seeming detachment, it is Jake who feels the agony of life more deeply and perceives it more sharply. Alone at night, the worst time for him, he lies awake and weeps despite his efforts "not to think about it." His inability to make love to Brett shatters him. When he is not alone, he endures his fate sardonically, as when he puts off a prostitute with the admonition that he is "sick"; stoically, as when he embraces Brett but insists that she simply not think about the absurdity of their love. Unlike Count Mippipopolous, Brett's epicurean admirer, Jake cannot compensate for the denial of his love by enjoying other women. Yet Jake and the Count are alike in their love for food, wine, adventure, and above all, in their determination not to complain about inescapable reality.

As the second section of the novel opens, others join Jake, Brett, and Cohn in Paris to plan a journey to Pamplona, Spain, for the annual July fiesta and bullfight. Before they leave, however, Jake learns with dismay that Brett has had a brief affair with Robert Cohn because "it would be good for him." Since Brett's drunken and abusive fiancé, Mike Campbell, will accompany them on the excursion, Jake tries unsuccessfully to dissuade Cohn from coming along. Cohn not only refuses to be put off, but even cancels a scheduled fishing trip with Jake to remain near Brett. That nobody wants him around fails to deter him. Silent, sober, and dour, he hangs on—watching and hoping.

Planning a reunion with the group in Pamplona, Jake goes off with his friend Bill Gorton (a fancier, when drunk, of stuffed animals) for five days of trout fishing in the Spanish hill country. Free of the tensions induced by Paris, Jake exults in the masculine out-of-door pleasures he shares with Bill. With almost total abandon, they fish, drink, and banter. Only when Bill tentatively probes his feelings about Brett or about his dormant Catholicism does Jake become evasive and withdrawn. Sensitive to Jake's pain, Bill quickly stops. Their affection for one another is deep, their brief holiday a success.

Soon thereafter Jake must forsake the ease of a world of men without women. At Pamplona, at the Hotel Montoya, the group once more gathers a few days before the opening of the fiesta. As they watch the unloading of the bulls, Jake, knowledgeable about such matters, explains how the docile steers quiet the angry bulls and guide them to the corral. The episode stirs Mike Campbell to bait Cohn by comparing him with a steer: "They never say anything and they're always hanging about so." Relentlessly and viciously, Mike taunts Cohn about his sobriety, his Jewishness, his affair with Brett. Only Brett can silence Mike. Bill Gorton leads Cohn off to calm him. Bill's good nature helps to restore some kind of harmony to the tense group.

That night, alone in his room with the light on, Jake lies in bed thinking about Brett, the others, and his own place among them. He concludes that despite the bitterness of his draught, it is worth drinking. Life is worth living if only for its occasional good moments. What one must do is learn to recognize and appreciate them. Universal truths are neither possible nor even necessary. "All I wanted to know," he tells himself, "was how to live in it."

A few days later the fiesta bursts into life and rockets noisily and violently for the next week. As the crowds throng into the street, one group dances about Brett, presses her into a bar and enshrines her atop a wine cask. Cohn, like Homer's Elpenor, falls asleep and is laid among the wine casks in the rear of the shop. Later, the friends watch the bulls chase the mob through the streets and even see one reveler gored to death. The great moments, however, occur in the arena. There, tutored by Jake in the nuances of bullfighting, they marvel at the skill and courage of Pedro Romero, a handsome young *torero*. Even Cohn, who had expected to be bored, admits his interest in the spectacle. Brett exceeds them all in her ardor. She confesses her desire for Romero to Jake and begs him to help her win him. Jake arranges a meeting and leaves the youth with Brett.

Hours later, seated with Mike and Bill, Jake faces an enraged Cohn. Horrified by his guess about Brett and Romero, which is confirmed by the complaisant Mike Campbell, Cohn calls Jake a pimp and knocks him out. Cohn discovers Brett in Romero's room, Jake learns later, and proceeds to beat the bullfighter mercilessly. When Brett denounces Cohn, he turns pitiably to Romero and offers to shake hands. Romero smashes Cohn's face. Cohn apologizes to Jake, and says goodbye, giving up all hope of winning Brett.

On the final day of the fiesta, Romero, his face battered, nevertheless performs magnificently in the arena, his grace and assurance inspiring the crowd to prolonged applause. The judges award him the coveted ear of the dead bull. That evening he and Brett leave Pamplona together. Jake, Mike, and Bill remain, drinking absinthe, Jake drunker and more depressed than ever.

The final, and briefest, section of the novel opens the day after the fiesta. In the anticlimactic stillness of Pamplona, the friends separate. Jakes goes off to San Sebastian to swim, catch up with the newspapers, and drink. Again, however, his respite is brief, for he receives a telegram from Brett urging him to join her in Madrid at once. When they meet, Brett tells him that she has left Romero. She has decided not to destroy his decency and innocence and, more important, weaken his power as a *torero*. Lacking Jake's formal religion, Brett believes that her gesture of renunciation brings her as near to religion as she can come. Jake merely urges her not to spoil the power of her emotion by discussing it.

The two ill-starred lovers ride together in a cab and sit tormentingly near one another. Brett exclaims in despair that she and Jake might have been wonderful for each other. Jake's rejoinder closes the novel: "Yes. Isn't it pretty to think so?"

Critical Opinion

The title of Hemingway's novel comes from a passage in the Old Testament, *Ecclesiastes*: ". . . vanity of vanities; all is vanity. . . . The sun also ariseth, and the sun goeth down, and hasteneth to his place where he arose . . . and that which is done is that which shall be done: and there is no new thing under the sun."

Like the Preacher of *Ecclesiastes*, Hemingway addressed a generation socially and morally disillusioned, and also like the Preacher, he seems at first glance to urge men to eat, drink, and be merry. Some critics of *The Sun Also Rises* consider it a defense of hedonism. Others, however, have found a truer, deeper meaning, a meaning clued by Hemingway's own statement that he did not regard his generation as lost or his novel as a hollow satire of his fellow man.

Stunned but not downed by adversity, Hemingway's heroes must learn the "code": to live and, if necessary, to die with courage and with dignity. Those who master the mystique of the code become Hemingway's elect, the initiated. Some, like Romero for example, are born initiates; they have inherited a tradition that enables them to confront the world bravely. Others, like Robert Cohn and Mike Campbell, fail because they cling, like Cohn, to false ideals, or like Mike, to sheer self-indulgence. Brett, some critics argue, belongs in the same category as Mike; others insist that her final renunciation of Romero lends her a kind of grandeur. Jake Barnes is the "code" hero in the making. His castration—a symbol of the sterility of the age—prevents his achieving fulfillment. But he can and does attain the self-knowledge that enables him to endure the frustration of his life with dignity.

The structure and style of *The Sun Also Rises* serve its theme very effectively. "Prose," Hemingway once wrote, is "architecture, not interior decoration." And Hemingway builds simply but soundly. Thus the apparent rambling of the early parts of the novel reflects the lack of direction in the characters' lives. As they discover purpose, the structure tightens and the plot surges ahead vigorously. At the end an aimless pattern follows the chaos of shattered dreams. Sentence style and language are part of Hemingway's purpose. The simple sentence and the monosyllabic word help him re-create the "feel" of the experience in all its immediacy. Hemingway's world is a violent world; to reproduce it poignantly and memorably, he uses staccato rhythms and unadorned language. At its best, his style is superb; at its worst, it parodies itself. In *The Sun Also Rises*, Hemingway is very much at his best.

A Farewell to Arms

by

ERNEST HEMINGWAY

Main Characters

Frederic Henry—An American lieutenant serving in the Italian ambulance corps during World War I. Uprooted, haunted by life's emptiness, disheartened by his own cynical escapism, he searches—at first indifferently, then desperately—for a truth to sustain his spirit.

Catherine Barkley—Frederic's love, a beautiful English volunteer nurse on duty in Italy. Serenely selfless, incapable of cynicism, she focuses every facet of her profoundly feminine sensibility upon her lover.

Rinaldi—An Italian Army surgeon and Frederic's best friend. Disillusioned, like Frederic, he has settled for the supreme beauty of successful surgery and the lesser joys of liquor and sex.

Priest—An Italian Army chaplain, devout, patient and gentle, unmoved by the gibes of his irreverent fellow officers.

Count Greffi—An aged aristocrat, wise in the ways of a brutal world, but firm in his conviction that love, not cynicism, sustains the human spirit.

Ettore Moretti—A young Californian enlisted in the Italian Army. Brash, boastful, and a bore, his highest goal is military promotion.

Helen Ferguson—Catherine's friend, a dour Scottish nurse, much concerned about the morality of Frederic's liaison with Catherine.

Bonello, Piani, Aymo—Enlisted Italians under Frederic's command, all socialists, all without illusions about the war they are trapped in, and all ready to spring themselves from the trap at the first opportunity.

The Story

Awaiting an Alpine thaw that will permit an offensive against the Austrians, a company of Italian troops in the Udine Valley of northeastern Italy passes its time drinking and wenching. Among the officers, an additional pastime is baiting the chaplain, an earnest young Abruzzi priest. Frederic Henry, the American officer and narrator, respects the priest for his untroubled faith and his quiet love for the clean, cold country of his birth. Yet when Frederic goes on leave, he fails to visit the priest's home. Instead, he wanders about Italy, drifting into bars and brothels. The priest, he realizes, "had always known what I did not know . . . although I learned it later."

A few days after his return to his post, Frederic meets Catherine Barkley whom he at first regards merely as a beautiful and available woman. When, at their second meeting, she sharply rejects his advances, then a moment later accepts his embrace and speaks prophetically of their future love, he decides that she is "probably a little crazy"—perhaps out of remorse for the war death of her fiancé. Frederic's interest remains detached, yet he feels "lonely and hollow" when he is away from Catherine.

Less than a week after their first meeting, Frederic is ordered to the front. During a mortar attack, he and his ambulance drivers crouch in a shallow dugout munching cheese and macaroni. A shell explodes nearby, killing one of the men and seriously wounding Henry in the head and legs. En route to the field hospital in an ambulance, the soldier in the stretcher above Frederic begins to hemorrhage, the blood dripping steadily down on him. When the ambulance arrives at the hospital, the soldier is dead.

Before he is shipped to the general hospital in Milan, Frederic receives visits from his surgeon friend, Rinaldi, and from the priest. Rinaldi teases him about sex. The priest urges him to seek a nobler kind of love, preferably of God but at least beyond lust. At the hospital in Milan, where Catherine is a nurse, she comes to him and he realizes that he is really in love with her. They consummate their love in Frederic's hospital bed.

The next morning a trio of windy, ineffectual doctors consult about Frederic's leg and agree that he must wait six months before his mutilated knee can be operated on. When Frederic protests, another doctor, Valentini, decides to operate the next morning. Like Rinaldi, Valentini is brisk, witty, and efficient. He needs no consultation. As Rinaldi says, "I don't think; I operate."

During the long summer of his successful convalescence, Frederic and Catherine are lovers. He wants to marry her, but she sees no need: "We are married privately," she says, and adds, "It would mean everything to me if I had any religion. But I haven't any religion." In contrast to the purity of their relationship is the tainted materialism of the world symbolized in Ettore who wants glory and recognition as a hero, and the crooked horse races, rigged for profit but devoid of any excitement.

Before Frederic returns to the front, Catherine tells him she is pregnant. Momentarily disturbed, he soon agrees that he, too, wants the child. Knowing the depth of her love as well as her fears about death, he is awed by her courage when she assures him during their last meeting that all will go well with her while he is away.

Frederic returns to the front and to the terrible retreat from Caporetto. He finds Rinaldi despondent because he has too few patients for surgery. Only when he is at work does Rinaldi's life take on meaning. Otherwise there is only sex and with it the dread of venereal disease. The priest, too, is depressed by the interminable war, his hope for peace growing dim. Soon, however, there is no time for talk, for the Germans break through the Italian lines and force a general retreat.

Columns of peasants join the troops along the jammed, muddy highways. When Frederic's truck gets stuck, he orders two sergeants to cut brush to support the wheels. When they ignore him and walk off as deserters, he shoots and wounds one of them, and Bonello, his sergeant, finishes off the other man. Afoot, Frederic and his three loyal noncoms try to avoid encounters with the Germans. Ironically, they are fired upon by Italians, and Aymo is killed. Bonello leaves, determined to save his life by surrendering.

Alone on the road with Piani, Frederic encounters throngs of Italians joyously deserting to return home. At a bridge across the river Tagliamento, he is arrested by Italian battle police assigned to capture and shoot deserting officers. As he awaits questioning, Frederic suddenly ducks away and plunges into the river. In the line of fire, he swims to safety, throws away his uniform, and rides to freedom beneath the canvas-covered guns on a gun train. "You were out of it now," Frederic thinks. "You had no more obligation." He has made his farewell to arms and a "separate peace."

In Milan, Frederic learns that Catherine and Helen Ferguson have gone to Stresa in the Italian lake country. He follows them and when he is reunited with Catherine, knows that only with her does the world seem real. He realizes, too, that the world will not abide such happiness. "If people bring so much courage to this world the world has to kill them to break them, so of course it kills them."

Their few days at Stresa are happy. One evening Frederic plays billiards with Count Greffi and listens to the aged philosopher distinguish between wisdom and cynicism. Like Catherine, Greffi lacks orthodox faith, but he believes firmly in life and in living it as well and as honestly as possible. The same evening Frederic is warned by the hotelkeeper of his imminent arrest as a deserter. A boat is provided for Frederic and Catherine and in the rain and wind they row across Lake Maggiore to Switzerland. Briefly detained by the Swiss customs, they persuade the officers that they are cousins traveling to enjoy the winter sports. Released, they find refuge in a lovely chalet overlooking Montreux.

Their winter is idyllic. But with the spring rain, the time arrives for Catherine's delivery and they leave for Lausanne. At the hospital Catherine's labor is slow and intense. As her strength wanes, the doctor suggests a Caesarean delivery. The child is stillborn and Catherine lies at the threshold of death. Terrified that she will die, Frederic tries to pray. In despair he recalls once having watched some ants atop a burning log. As the log burned, the ants fled—some to the fire, some to the end where they fell off into the fire below. For a moment Frederic knew the sensation of playing God. He thought briefly of lifting the log from the fire and saving the ants. Instead, he threw a cup of water on the log and merely steamed the ants. "You never had time to learn," he thinks. "They threw you in and told you the rules and the first time they caught you off base they killed you."

When he returns to Catherine, she knows she is dying. Denying that she is afraid, she admits only that she hates death. Then she dies. Frederic pushes the nurses out of the room. He wants his farewell to be private. But the parting seems senseless, like saying goodbye to a statue. Frederic leaves and walks back to his hotel in the rain.

Critical Opinion

For many readers, *A Farewell to Arms* is Hemingway's most appealing and affecting novel. The courage of Frederic and Catherine and the tragic consequences of their love, the atmosphere of the Italian war front and the powerful scenes of the debacle at Caporetto—these remain etched in memory long after other details have slipped away. Some critics have objected that Catherine is too idealized, too romantically compliant, too sentimentally a "code" heroine. As a result, they believe, Frederic's development proceeds with a slick, movie-script glibness different from the rough-edged force of *The Sun Also Rises*. For other critics, the emotional force of the novel as a whole transcends its several weaknesses.

Like most of Hemingway's novels, *A Farewell to Arms* is about love and death and the kind of courage one needs to experience them. In the beginning, Frederic lacks commitment of any kind. He cannot find in love of man, woman, or God any compelling reason for existence. Until he meets Catherine, he drifts with the moment. Afterward he moves inevitably toward an understanding of the fullness as well as the emptiness of life. He learns about the hollowness of abstractions: medals do not prove valor; a wedding need not signify a true marriage. He learns from Catherine—and from Rinaldi and Greffi as well—the potential force of the individual spirit. And he learns, above all, that those who undertake a "separate peace" win no lasting victory. By deserting the army to be with Catherine, Frederic symbolically bids farewell to military arms. Ironically, when she dies, he must bid yet another farewell—to the arms of his love.

The novel is rich in symbols. For example, the rain that opens and closes the book symbolizes death as well as life. What Frederic learns, then, is that a "code" hero must accept the truth that all stories end in death. That truth understood, life has moments of beauty and significance well worth the living.

The Old Man and the Sea

by

ERNEST HEMINGWAY

Main Characters

Santiago—A Cuban fisherman, old yet still rugged in body, young and indomitable in spirit.

Manolin—A Cuban boy, Santiago's companion. Too young to comprehend fully either the joy or the anguish of experience, he is sensitive enough to recognize the old man's wisdom.

The Story

Luckless but undaunted, old Santiago has fished the Gulf Stream off Havana for eighty-four days without catching a fish. For the first forty days, the boy Manolin went with him, but now his parents have sent Manolin to another boat. Still the boy serves the old man, bringing him food, beer, bait, and helping him carry his tackle to the skiff. In the old man's shack, they discuss baseball, the great Di Maggio, the splendid hauls they have made in the past. Alone, the old man sleeps and dreams of his youth in Africa and of the lions who played on the beaches.

At dawn on the eighty-fifth day, Santiago sets sail again, confident that somewhere in the sea he loves like a woman is the big fish he must catch. He sails far out into the Stream, baits and sets his lines, and drops them into deep water. Waiting, he watches a school of dolphin pursue flying fish and he curses a malevolent Portuguese man-of-war that drifts near by. He catches a small tuna and waits hopefully for the big strike. When it comes, it is deceptively gentle, the merest tug, but Santiago knows that it is a marlin nibbling his bait 600 feet below. Speaking aloud, the old man urges the marlin to sample more of the bait. When he senses the right moment, Santiago pulls hard and settles the hook. The long battle has begun.

With the noon sun high and hot, Santiago feeds his marlin the line it needs as it swims off towing the skiff northwest, away from land. Santiago can do nothing except wait for the fish to tire. Meanwhile, he grips the heavy line in his callused hands and braces it across his naked shoulders. All afternoon the fish tows the boat, then after sunset and into the chill night. Although he wishes he had Manolin with him to help, the old man is determined to conquer the fish alone. At the same time he begins to think about the fish at the end of his line and about other great fish he has caught. During the night the fish lurches, pulling Santiago down on his face and cutting his cheek. But the old man never relaxes his vigil.

By morning the old man is stiff as well as hungry. Still he cannot exert tension on the line lest the fish break it. As Santiago talks to the birds overhead, the fish suddenly surges and the line cuts through the old man's hand. Despite his pain, the old man is pleased, for he senses that his prey has begun to tire. He wonders what the fish intends and what he will do. He wishes that he might feed the fish, his brother, but knows that his own strength must be the greater if he is to prevail, and worries about the paralyzing cramp that stiffens his left hand.

Suddenly the line grows slack; the fish surfaces, leaping out of the water. It is the largest marlin Santiago has ever seen, longer even than his skiff. Santiago prays for victory, sure that he can "show him what a man can do and what a man endures." All afternoon and again into the night the fish tows the skiff, now to the east. To bolster himself, Santiago recalls a titanic hand wrestle he won years ago at a tavern. Hungry, he catches and eats a dolphin. During the night the marlin jumps again, cutting Santiago's hands once more. He dreams of Africa and the lions.

At sunrise on the third morning, the line almost tears through Santiago's hand as the fish begins a series of leaps. Now the old man begins to shorten the line even though each tug lacerates his hands anew. He washes his bleeding hands in the sea, then continues to draw in his line as the fast-tiring marlin circles the skiff in ever-narrowing arcs. Just before the fish is close enough to harpoon, the old man pleads with it not to kill them both. For a fleeting moment, in admiration— almost in love—he exclaims that he would not care if the noble creature, at once his brother and his enemy in nature, killed him. But the old man knows that he must overwhelm the marlin. He harpoons the mighty fish and lashes it to the side of his boat.

The return to Havana is a nightmare that begins an hour after the marlin has been tied to the skiff. A Mako shark attacks the corpse and mutilates it before the old man can kill it. As other sharks come, the old man fights them off tenaciously, defending not only his own victory but the dignity of the dead marlin. He wonders whether it was a sin to kill his fish, but he realizes that man must struggle against defeat by nature. Sorry that the fish is dead, its corpse ravished, he knows also that he had to do what he did. Although he continues to battle the sharks, his struggle is in vain. His knives break, and his torn hands will not even hold the club he tries to wield. All he can do is steer his boat toward harbor as the ravenous sharks strip the marlin to a skeleton. To himself, Santiago says that he went out too far. That was why he suffered defeat.

His boat beached, only the head and tail of his catch remaining, the old man shoulders his mast and climbs slowly up the hill to his shack. Once he stumbles and falls, but he rises and struggles on. He sleeps sprawled face down on his bed, his arms outstretched, his palms turned up. Manolin comes to the old man in the morning and tends to him. Despite Santiago's insistence that his luck has turned bad, Manolin says that it will turn good again and that he wants to sail again with the old man. As the novel ends, the old man sleeps, dreaming about his lions. Manolin sits beside him.

Critical Opinion

Read literally as an adventure yarn, *The Old Man and the Sea* grips young and old. The prose is simple, the approximations of Spanish dialogue poetically affecting and appropriate, the narrative pattern lucid and economical. Santiago's stubborn courage, rugged strength, and marvelous skill sustain suspense till the tragic end. As almost every critic has noted, however, the reader who casts for subtler meanings may net a more rewarding haul. Hemingway said of the story that the old man, the boy, the sea, the fish, and the sharks were all real. "But if I made them good and true enough," he went on, "they would mean many things."

For some readers the novel has deep, religious implications. Santiago's scarred palms, the crosslike mast he carries up the hill—these symbols suggest the Christian overtones that sound throughout the tale. Although Santiago loves the fish, his pride compels him to destroy it—a human failure for which both man and nature suffer.

Others see the struggle between man and nature as the ancient bond between hunter and hunted. Respecting his prey, the hunter must nevertheless assert at any price the power of man. Ironically, the price is often death or defeat for the hunter as well. Santiago becomes an embodiment of all of Hemingway's "code" heroes—the first of them, however, as Philip Young observes, to have grown old.

The Old Man and the Sea is also significant as a study of initiation, for in it the boy Manolin learns what it means to be a man. He has been consummately tutored in the craft of big-game fishing. More important, however, he has, like all of Hemingway's initiates, absorbed knowledge about love, death, courage, and endurance.

The Author

In *Death in the Afternoon* (1932), a study of the art of bull-fighting, *Ernest Hemingway* wrote: "All stories, if continued far enough, end in death, and he is no true storyteller who would keep that from you." Violent death, often the subject matter of his fiction, shaped Hemingway's life. It also triggered his exit—with a blast from a shotgun he held in his mouth.

Hemingway's boyhood in Oak Park, Illinois, was quiet, his chief enthusiasms fishing and hunting trips in northern Michigan or making medical rounds with his father, a physician (who years later committed suicide). Shortly after his high-school graduation, Hemingway joined the Italian Army, first as an ambulance driver, then as an infantry officer. In 1918, at nineteen, he was almost killed by a shrapnel burst. For the rest of his life, Hemingway flirted with destructive forces, both human and natural. As a journalist after the war, he reported battles in the Near East. During the twenties and thirties, he divided his time between bullfights and wild-game safaris in Africa. He was in Spain during the Civil War and in Europe (often farther ahead of the lines than the Allied troops) during World War II. In 1954 he survived two plane crashes in the African jungle. Throughout, Hemingway's code was courage in a world of crisis. Almost compulsively he sought danger in order to prove himself man enough to face —perhaps to overwhelm—the threat of extinction.

In Paris after World War I, Hemingway joined the expatriate group of artists and writers described by Gertrude Stein as "the lost generation." From her as well as from Ezra Pound and others, he learned the discipline of his craft—the taut sentences, monosyllabic vocabulary, stark dialogue, and understated emotion that are the hallmarks of the Hemingway style. His earliest stories foreshadow his mature technique and his concern for values in a corrupt and indifferent world.

With the publication of *The Sun Also Rises* (1926) and *A Farewell to Arms* (1929), Hemingway's fame was secure for the rest of his life. But until *For Whom the Bell Tolls* (1940), his succeeding novels added little to his stature, though some of his short stories, notably "The Snows of Kilimanjaro" (1936) and "The Short Happy Life of Francis

Macomber" (1936), are distinguished and memorable. After *For Whom the Bell Tolls*, only *The Old Man and the Sea* (1952) approached the force of Hemingway's early genius. In 1953 *The Old Man* won him the Pulitzer Prize. A year later he was awarded the Nobel Prize

Some observers have commented that Hemingway's suicide resulted partly from his awareness that he was no longer, in his favorite term, "the champion." Although it is true that some of his late works seemed parodies of himself, in the pages of the posthumously published memoir of his early years in Paris, *A Moveable Feast* (1964), a reader may discover once more strong traces of Hemingway's deep sensibility, sinewy style, and resounding courage.

The Bridge of San Luis Rey

by

THORNTON WILDER (1897–)

Main Characters

Doña Mariá, Marquesa de Montemayor—An unprepossessing, eccentric woman who is also a superb letter writer, an intensely devoted mother who has compassion for no one but her daughter.

Doña Clara—Doña Mariá's daughter, beautiful, cold, intellectual.

Camila Perichole—An extraordinarily talented actress (called "the Perichole") whose social ambitions help to destroy her individuality and to mar the lives of other people.

Abbess Madre Mariá del Pilar—Directress of the Convent of Santa Rosa de las Rosas, an extraordinarily perceptive woman supremely dedicated to the church, to the poor and the outcasts.

Pepita—An orphan girl, the particular object of the Abbess's solicitude, who is being trained to carry on the Abbess's work.

Esteban—One of twin brothers, racked by excessive guilt for his brother's death.

Manuel—His twin, silently and unavailingly in love with the Perichole.

Uncle Pio—An adventurer endowed with the gift of love—
especially for beautiful women and beautiful language.
Jaime—The sickly young son of the Perichole.
The Viceroy—An aristocrat, now old and suffering from the
gout, but still charming and capable of ruling.

The Story

The bridge of San Luis Rey, a slat bridge with vine hand-
rails, was the most famous bridge in Peru. On Friday, July 20,
1714, at noon, it broke, and five travelers were hurtled into
the gorge it spanned. It was a deeply impressive event, and
Brother Juniper, who had long wanted theology to be an exact
science, felt that this was his opportunity to demonstrate
God's wisdom with laboratory precision. By gathering all
possible data about the five people who had fallen to their
deaths, he would be able to show the outline of His purpose,
the pattern of His providence.

Doña Maríá, Marquesa de Montemayor, is the most important personage of the five. She is remembered for the wit
and brilliance of her letters to her daughter. The Marquesa's
life is marked by almost unvarying suffering. An ugly child
without grace or charm, she grows into an equally unprepossessing young woman. Only her father's great wealth
procures her a husband. She gives birth to an exquisite
daughter, Doña Clara, who regards her adoring mother
with a cold indifference that develops into repulsion. Deliberately she accepts the offer of marriage that will require her
removal to Spain. The agonized mother—after one disastrous
visit—returns to Lima to write the letters that establish her
enduring fame.

Though ill and unhappy, she forces herself to go everywhere and to see everything that might be converted into
amusing material for her letters. She pours her love, her very
life, into these masterpieces. Her daughter answers seldom,
briefly, distantly. Increasingly the Marquesa finds relief and
oblivion in drinking wine.

Desiring a companion, she applies to the devout and saintly
Abbess Madre Mariá del Pilar, directress of the Convent of
Santa Maria Rosa de las Rosas. The latter chooses Pepita, a

twelve-year-old orphan whose devotion and intelligence have moved the Abbess to train her as a potential successor. Pepita's service in a great house, the Abbess believes, will further her education. But the Marquesa is willful, eccentric, and often unintentionally cruel to the young girl who suffers additionally from the contempt and practical jokes of the servants.

A curt letter arrives from Spain in which Doña Clara briefly announces her pregnancy. The Marquesa becomes frantic with worry over her daughter's well being. She deluges her with unwanted counsel, prays hysterically, even succumbs to pagan superstitions in the attempt to ensure a safe delivery. On a pilgrimage to a great shrine, the Marquesa and Pepita stop at an inn. Pepita, during a pause in her duties, begins a letter to the Abbess, a letter that cries out with her unhappiness at being with the Marquesa and away from the Abbess. The Marquesa reads it by accident. In it she finds revealed not only her wanton neglect of Pepita but also her oppressive love for her daughter—never brave and generous, always greedy. She prays to be allowed to begin again. Two days later the bridge falls as she and Pepita are crossing it.

Esteban is the third victim. He is one of twin boys, foundlings reared by the Abbess. He and his brother Manuel have been fused into a spiritual unity, a oneness for which the word love is too shallow. After leaving the Abbess, they earn their living as scribes, though sometimes they work at other jobs. Always they are together; all other men are strangers.

One day Manuel is asked to write a letter for Camila Perichole, the first actress of Peru. Idolized by her public, she is the mistress of the Viceroy but is having an affair with a matador. At her dictation, Manuel writes a very different letter to each lover. When he has finished his task, he is wholly infatuated with her. He broods over her continually, haunting the places where he is likely to see her. Esteban soon realizes his brother's condition and is saddened by the breach that follows. Sometime later, the actress visits them in their room. She wants Manuel to write an angry letter to the matador, who has failed to keep a rendezvous. He complies and she steals away. But Manuel has sensed the misery of his brother and by a powerful exercise of will he renounces her, telling Esteban that he will write no more letters for her.

Esteban realizes the nature of Manuel's sacrifice and refuses to accept it. Manuel, however, insists.

Sometime later, Manuel cuts his leg which swells painfully. Esteban nurses him faithfully through his delirium during which he curses Esteban violently for coming between him and the Perichole. In his lucid intervals Manuel grieves over his outbursts. When Manuel dies in agony, Esteban is inconsolable. He wanders desolately over Peru, seeking lonely and difficult jobs, and once tries to commit suicide. At the instance of his old guardian, the Abbess, a sea captain persuades Esteban to join him in a voyage. It is on the way to the ship that Esteban crosses the bridge of San Luis Rey at the fatal moment.

Uncle Pio and Camila Perichole's young son, Jaime, are the last victims. Uncle Pio ("Uncle" because of his willingness to listen and advise—if also to profit) is a witty, acute, somewhat disreputable adventurer. Almost successful in a variety of undertakings, he seems at the last juncture to will his own downfall. The great passion of his life—a life devoted to beautiful women and the theater—is for the actress Camila Perichole. He finds her singing in cafés at the age of twelve and undertakes her training. He teaches her to speak distinctively, to convey the essential quality of a song, and to act with fervor and understanding. She becomes the best actress in Peru, perhaps in the Spanish-speaking world. As she develops into a woman, she has intermittent love affairs (never with Uncle Pio, though, for their attachment is deep but passionless). Ultimately she attracts the Viceroy himself. For a long time she admires him, even adores him, and learns from him the habits and carriage of a great lady. She bears him a son who is legitimized. Unhappily, however, she turns from the stage to seek a place in society. Uncle Pio is heartbroken and attempts to convince her of her supreme talent, but she spurns him. Shortly afterward she contracts smallpox and her face becomes hideously marked. She goes into seclusion, hiding herself from the world. By a stratagem Uncle Pio manages to see her. He has only one request. For one year he wants to take her young son, Jaime, who remains secluded with her into the world to teach him fencing, Latin, music—all that a gentleman should know. Reluctantly she agrees, and together Uncle Pio and Jaime return to Lima.

They start across the bridge of San Luis Rey in the company
of the Marquesa, Pepita, and Esteban.

The Perichole comes to the funeral service for her son
and Uncle Pio. She visits the Abbess, tells of her profound
despair, and is comforted. She enters the service of the Church
as aide to the Abbess. Doña Clara, too, comes to see the
Abbess. The daughter at last realizes the greatness of her
mother, not merely as a writer but as a person. And the Abbess
muses over the meaning of all that has befallen, concluding
that love is the only meaning, the only answer to the tragedies
of life.

The large book that Brother Juniper wrote was seized by
the Inquisition—all but one copy, upon which the narrator
draws. The others were burned, together with their author.
His deductions were perhaps too scientific—or too incon-
clusive.

Critical Opinion

The Bridge of San Luis Rey is generally considered Thornton
Wilder's best novel. It is certainly his best known. It seems a
slight-enough work: three "case histories" and a somewhat
ironic commentary. But the case histories are not only acute
psychological studies. They also illuminate, though they
hardly solve, an age-old philosophical problem: Is there a
reason for man's suffering in this world, for his blighted hopes
and shattered purposes?

The findings of Brother Juniper, Wilder's theological investi-
gator, are deliberately withheld. Yet while Wilder "spares"
us the generalizations, he tells us that Brother Juniper "thought
he saw in the same accident, the wicked visited by destruction
and the good called early to Heaven." Brother Juniper, however, has decided in advance; he is scarcely to be trusted.

Through the Abbess, who seems to speak for Wilder, we
may infer the answer that the book projects to the problem
of man's pain-fraught existence. It is that there is no answer
—or else that the answer is shrouded in darkness. In the last
sentence of the novel, the Abbess insists that "love is the only
survival, the only meaning."

The Bridge of San Luis Rey is a remarkable achievement.

The incisive portraits, especially of the Marquesa (modeled after Mme. de Sevigné), the sensitive, slightly ironic style, which reaches a real eloquence, the deft evocation of the atmosphere of a different era and an exotic place—these continue to make the book a rich and absorbing experience.

The Author

Thornton Wilder has won the Pulitzer Prize three times: twice for plays—*Our Town* (1938), a glowing, sentimental, but not cloying piece of nostalgia, and *The Skin of Our Teeth* (1942), "a sort of Hellzapoppin with brains"—once for *The Bridge of San Luis Rey* (1927). In almost any year in which he has written either novel or play, he has been a contender for the prize.

The Cabala (1926), his first published novel, describes the fragmented lives of aristocrats in Rome as viewed by a young American. *The Woman of Andros* (1930), though based on a play by the Roman dramatist Terence, is a contemporary novel on the values of love. *The Ides of March* (1948) is a witty and serious fictional study of the life of Julius Caesar. Wilder's first novel of the contemporary American scene, *Heaven's My Destination* (1934), a comic story about a traveling salesman, deals with the problem of belief in an unbelieving age.

Wilder's plays, perhaps more derivative than his novels, are still admirable creations. *The Matchmaker* (1955) reworks an earlier Wilder play, *The Merchant of Yonkers* (1938), which was adapted from Johann Nestroy's farce. Currently Wilder is working on a cycle of fourteen plays, the first three of which have had a successful off-Broadway production under the title *Plays for Bleecker Street*.

Thornton Wilder, born in Wisconsin, grew to young manhood in China where his father was American Consul General. In America he attended Oberlin College (1915–17), interrupted his academic studies to serve as a corporal in the Coast Artillery during World War I, and completed the work for his bachelor's degree at Yale in 1920. He did post-graduate work at the American Academy in Rome, taught French at the Lawrenceville School, took his master's degree at Princeton (1925), and then became a member of the University of

Chicago faculty (1930-36). In World War II he served as an Air Force intelligence officer in Africa and Italy, and was discharged with the rank of lieutenant colonel. He has lived most of his life in a suburb of New Haven, reading at the university library and frequently lecturing abroad.

Wilder, it has been remarked, "is a curious anomaly in the American literary scene, a widely cultured man who writes as he pleases and yet has managed to captivate the masses in his best work." He has written broadly and in a half-dozen fields. Moreover, he has several absorbing literary hobbies, ranging from the analysis of Joyce's *Finnegans Wake* to the tracing of Lope de Vega's dramatic productions. His scholarly avocations and his vocation as writer, however, dovetail, for, he has commented, "My writing life is a series of infatuations for admired writers."

Giants in the Earth

by

OLE EDVART RÖLVAAG (1876–1931)

Main Characters

Per Hansa—A Norwegian pioneer farmer in the Dakota Territory, proud, independent, resourceful.

Beret—His wife, deeply in love with him but assailed by a profound melancholy.

Ole ("Olamand") and *Hans*—Their stalwart young sons, happy in the new life on the prairie.

Anna Marie ("And-Ongen")—Their small blonde daughter.

Hans Olsa—A loyal friend to the Hansas, a kindly, hard-working giant.

Sorine—Olsa's sweet-tempered, dutiful wife.

Syvert Tönseten—Another Norwegian settler, short, stout, excitable, self-important.

Kjersti—Tönseten's sharp-tongued but good-hearted wife.

The Solum brothers—Two Norwegian settlers, bachelors, who unlike the other pioneers can speak some English.

The Minister—An itinerant minister, ungainly, ill-dressed, spiritually gifted.

The Story

In 1873 Per Hansa, a Norwegian immigrant, moves west by ox wagon from Minnesota to the Dakota territory, with his family: his wife, Beret, a loving, deeply religious woman, who at times becomes deeply melancholy; his two sons, Ole (or "*Olamand*") and Hans, the former about nine, the latter seven—both stalwart, eager boys; and his small blonde daughter, Anna Marie (pet-named *And-Ongen*, "The Duckling"). The family arrive at a fertile spot where they have been preceded by friends who now joyfully welcome them: the kindly giant, Hans Olsa; his devoted wife, Sorïne, and their ten-year-old daughter, Sofie; Syvert Tönseten, a short, stout man, perpetually excited and garrulous, and his good-natured but sharp-tongued wife, Kjersti; and two bachelors, the Solum brothers, the only settlers who can speak English at all.

Per Hansa falls in love with the stretch of land that has been set aside for him. With one of the Solum boys he travels to Sioux Falls, a fifty-two-mile journey, to file an application for his quarter section, his new "kingdom." On his return he sets to work in an indomitable mood, brooking no opposition from man or nature. He dreams of his land at night and awakens at daybreak to labor on it—fourteen, then sixteen hours a day. He begins building an enormous sod house and completes it in an astonishingly short time, making an arduous trip to another settlement to get timber for the house and young trees to plant around it. He enlists all his family, but especially Ole and Hans, for his eager labors.

Once Indians come when Per's comrades have made a trip to town. The settlers are terrified, but Per visits the Indians, cures a sick chief, and receives a pony as a gift.

Life in the settlement is a continual struggle. Even little events seem very important, for on them depend the life of the community. Per prospers and everyone regards him as a fortunate man. He plants potatoes, raises a good crop, sells it profitably. He catches a large quantity of fish and ducks. He is the first man to whitewash the interior of his sod house. Because of his extraordinary energy and resourcefulness, he is admired by his sons, looked up to by his neighbors.

But there is a deep sorrow in Per's life. His wife, Beret, has never been happy on the prairie. The great expanse of flat, lonely land, the frontier mores, the lack of religious dedication among the settlers all distress her. Per, who has found markers

left by earlier pioneers, destroys them, then repulses the settlers when they return. He is legally justified, since they have
not filed official claims, but Beret fears the vengeance that
must follow such a sinful act. She recalls, too, her passionate
love for Per, her child born out of wedlock, her desertion of
her parents to follow him. Pregnant now, she is sure that a
terrible punishment awaits her guilt, sure that she will "fall
into the hands of the living God." And in fact she almost dies,
as tended by Sorïne and Kjersti, she gives birth to the child
while Per waits in agony of spirit outside the house.

But Beret lives and the child is chistened Peder Victorious
—a heathen name, Beret thinks, and the ceremony, performed by Hans Olsa, is unhallowed. After the birth of the
child, Beret sinks into a more profound melancholia. Just after
the wheat that her husband had so proudly and joyfully
planted is destroyed by great swarms of locusts, Beret, quite
mad, prepares for death. She lies down in the huge chest that
they had brought from Norway, her baby in her arms and her
daughter And-Ongen at her knees. His heart bursting with
grief, Per rescues them.

An itinerant minister comes to the settlement. Ungainly and
ill-dressed, he nevertheless has a real spiritual gift. His understanding counsel, his intense sincerity, his powerful preaching,
and, not least, his approval of the name Peder Victorious
and his christening of the child, help to remove the pall that
has fallen over Beret's spirit. Though she recovers her sanity,
she remains always touched with sadness, and her religious
fervor increases.

The settlement suffers from a plague of locusts, from rain,
snow, and freezing cold. But it endures. Tragedy, never far
distant, falls upon Hans Olsa. Attempting to repair his cattle
shed, he is prevented from making his way home by a fierce
blizzard. He spends the night in the shed. When he returns
home it is clear that the exposure to the blizzard has made
him deathly ill. Beret decides that he must be saved and
earnestly begs him to repent. Hans asks for the doctor, but
Beret insists on a minister. And she prevails upon Per to go
after one, despite the weather. Tenderly bidding his children
goodbye but saying nothing to Beret, Per sets forth on skis

for the long journey to fetch the minister. But with evening, the snow begins to fall and the drifts become deeper.

One day, during the spring after Hans Olsa died, two boys find the body of a man with his back against a moldering haystack. Though it is May, there are two pairs of skis with him, one on the ground, the other on his back. His eyes are set toward the West.

Critical Opinion

Giants in the Earth, a "Saga of the Prairie," is dedicated "to those of my people who took part in the great settling, to them and their generations. . . ." Like all of Rölvaag's works, it was written in Norwegian and translated with astonishing skill by the author in collaboration with Lincoln Colcord—a collaboration, it has been said, as remarkable "in its way as that of Joseph Conrad with Ford Madox Ford."

Giants in the Earth is not so widely read now as it used to be, perhaps because the American pioneer experience has faded, perhaps because it has so frequently been recounted— by Hamlin Garland, Willa Cather, Ruth Suckow, and others. But the novel has not sunk into oblivion, nor does it deserve to. It has been called "the fullest, finest, and most powerful novel that has been written about pioneer life in America. . . . a great and beautiful book that suggests the wealth of human potentialities brought to America year after year by the peasant immigrants who pass through Ellis Island and scatter the length and breadth of the land."

Giants in the Earth is an American book, too, despite its high position in Norwegian literature. To know that, Lincoln Colcord suggests, one has merely to look at Johan Bojer's *The Emigrants*, which explores a similar theme and which Rölvaag's novel anticipated by only a month. As both Bojer and Rölvaag agreed, they had wholly different perspectives: "Bojer saw it from the viewpoint of Norway, not of America." To him, it was a story of emigration; to Rölvaag, one of settlement. It fulfilled Rölvaag's ambition from student days: to become the spokesman of one people to another, to tell them "the immigrant's part in the making of the great new nation."

The Author

Ole Edvart Rölvaag was born in Norway, on the island of Dönna, "just south of where the Arctic Circle cuts the coast of Norway." His parents, like all the people on the island, were fishermen. He went to school for seven years, nine weeks a year, walking seven miles each way to and from the schoolhouse. Ole, however, seemed to have no aptitude for learning, though he read widely and indiscriminately.

After five years as a fisherman, Rölvaag decided to go to America. An uncle in South Dakota sent him a ticket, and in 1896, aged twenty, he came to America. He farmed for three years, an occupation he thoroughly disliked. Then, without much confidence or inclination, he entered Augustana College, a preparatory school in South Dakota. There he performed brilliantly, and upon graduation entered St. Olaf College in Northfield, Minnesota (1901–05). Despite poverty and ill health, he was graduated with honors, and set off for graduate study in Norway with five hundred borrowed dollars. Upon his return to the United States, he was offered a post at St. Olaf teaching Norwegian literature. He remained at the college for the rest of his life, dying from a heart attack in 1931.

All Rölvaag's books were written in Norwegian and gained their first recognition in Norway, yet he belongs to American literature. As his translator comments, he deals with American life and characteristically American episodes; his "material is altogether American." His most important works bear this out: *Giants in the Earth* (1927), *Peder Victorious* (1929), and *Their Father's God* (1931), an epic trilogy depicting in harsh, realistic detail the struggle of the Norwegian pioneer to survive on the American prairie—and the terrible human cost of that struggle.

Look Homeward, Angel

by

THOMAS WOLFE (1900–1938)

Main Characters

Oliver Gant—A huge, exuberant, eloquent man, harried by his wife and children, often drunk.

Eliza Gant—Oliver's wife, a sharp-tongued, shrewd, avaricious woman.

Steve Gant—Their eldest son, a foul-mouthed, dishonest braggart.

Daisy Gant—Their eldest daughter, timid, conventional, dutiful.

Helen Gant—Their third child, temperamental, unstable, loving, the father's favorite.

Grover Gant—One of the twins, a sad, gentle boy who dies young.

Ben Gant—His twin, a tormented, proud, independent man, Eugene Gant's beloved brother.

Eugene Gant—The youngest of the family, a brooding dreamer, hungry for life, love, beauty.

John Leonard—Principal of the private school that Eugene attends, a good but not very intelligent man.

Margaret Leonard—Eugene's teacher, who recognizes his talent and encourages him to develop it.

Laura James—A guest at the Dixieland, with whom Eugene falls madly in love.

The Story

Oliver Gant is a huge, haunted man driven by undefined longings. After the death of his wife, he wanders into Altamont, a small mountain town in North Carolina. There he marries Eliza Pentland, a shrewd, calculating woman, amassing property with almost insane greed. Oliver works as a stonemason, often interrupting his labors to go on drinking sprees, returning to denounce his wife in madly inflated rhetoric. The Gants steadily produce children of whom the seventh is Eugene, born when Eliza is forty-two and Oliver fifty.

Through Eugene's childhood run three memories: his father's violent, drunken rages and his mother's terrified responses; his love of words and his joy on learning to write; and the affection, alternating with cuffs, showered on him by his elder brothers and sisters. They are an eccentric and unstable crew. Steve, the eldest, is the one unregenerate member, foul-mouthed, foul-minded, whining, crooked. Daisy, next born, is timid, dutiful, industrious. Helen, the third child, is passionate, dissatisfied, loving, fiercely devoted to her father who in his debauches will be quieted only by her. Grover and Ben are twins, the former sad and gentle, the latter tormented, proud, afflicted. Luke, the youngest except for Eugene, is clever and sharp. He shares, beyond the others, his mother's lust for possessions.

When Eugene is four, Eliza takes all her children, except Daisy, to St. Louis, the world's fair city, to open a boardinghouse. Daisy stays behind to finish school and keep house for Oliver who opposes Eliza's venture. But Eliza soon returns to Altamont, for Grover contracts typhoid fever and dies.

There, at the age of six, Eugene begins school. He is tormented by his schoolmaster, who senses that he is different. Eugene is dark, brooding, given to fantasy. Nevertheless the books he now begins to devour make school tolerable. And after a while, too, he becomes part of a boy's gang and so is able to inflict pain on people even more helpless than he.

Eugene is soon forced to endure more serious suffering. From childhood Ben had delivered newspapers and Luke had been an energetic agent for the *Saturday Evening Post*. As a result of Eliza's insistence, Eugene also becomes a wage earner. First he assists Luke; later he gets a newspaper route of his own. Eugene hates his jobs which expose him to danger when he delivers his papers to the worst parts of town. Only Ben seems to sympathize with him, upbraiding their mother for her neglect.

Before Eugene is eight, Eliza buys Dixieland, a large boardinghouse in town. The purchase means her separation from Oliver. Helen, who is hostile toward her mother and adores her father, stays to keep house for him. Eliza takes Eugene with her, while Ben and Luke float from one house to the other. Steve has already begun his vagabondage, existing by odd jobs and small forgeries. Daisy marries a grocery clerk and moves to another town. Eliza regularly complains of her hard lot despite the fact that it is self-imposed. Working from early to late at the Dixieland, engrossed in land speculation, she can devote little attention to her family.

In his eleventh year, Eugene wins a school essay contest. The principal, John Leonard, about to start a school of his own—the Altamont Fitting School—prevails upon Eliza to enroll Eugene. There, for the next four years, he comes under the spell of a highly gifted teacher, Margaret Leonard, the principal's wife. She recognizes and directs his passion for knowledge and beauty, his confused gropings toward understanding and self-realization. Eugene reads hungrily, memorizes great quantities of poetry, learns Latin and some German. At the same time he continues to work his paper route. It is small wonder that at fifteen he has only 130 pounds of flesh on his six-foot-three frame.

Eugene is tortured by erotic desire, but is at the same time plagued by sexual fears. Once, when he stops to make a collection on his paper route, a Negro prostitute arouses him. But he runs away. On a trip to Charleston, he has an affair with a waitress, but again he does not consummate it.

Eugene is not quite sixteen when he enters the state university. He is happy to go. Eliza has become richer and more grasping and miserly than ever. His brother Ben, whom he loves more than any other member of his family, suffers from weak lungs. Oliver, the powerful, raging man, is debilitated by cancer. Steve, though he has married a sluttish older woman with a small fortune, keeps returning to the Dixieland—and with him he always carries the stench of rottenness. Helen has become a professional singer and, as one of the Dixie Melody Twins, is touring the South with indifferent success.

At college, Eugene at first seems out of things. He is the victim of practical jokes. His gullibility and ignorance of college traditions are exploited unfeelingly. But gradually he adjusts to college life. He joins the staff of the student literary magazine, does well in his studies, especially in English literature and in Greek, subjects in which he has imaginative teachers. He makes some disreputable friends and visits a brothel where his fear and revulsion make him impotent.

During his first summer holiday, Eugene falls in love with Laura James, a guest at the Dixieland. But he is fifteen, she twenty-one. They have a brief but intense love affair. Then she returns to her home in Richmond—for a week, she promises. But from Richmond she writes to tell him that she has been engaged for a year and is to be married the next day. He is sunk in despair which is intensified by the malicious teasing that he gets from his family.

Eugene's sophomore year is uneventful. He is accepted by his fellow students, joins clubs and societies, promises to become a "big man" on campus. He spends a desolate summer working at several jobs in Richmond where he has gone in the forlorn hope of somehow seeing Laura. Returning home, he is further depressed by his father's decline and his mother's callous pursuit of money.

In October of his third year at college, Eugene is summoned home. His brother Ben is dying of pneumonia; Eliza had neglected to call a doctor till too late. On his deathbed, Ben rejects Eliza's faltering attempts to approach him. After his death, he is given an expensive funeral. The Gant family spends more money on Ben dead than they ever did when he was alive.

At the university, Eugene becomes editor-in-chief of the newspaper, does brilliantly in his courses, and is graduated with honors. He returns home to his family which has grown more divided than ever, each suspecting the others of wanting more than a just share from the estate of their dying father. Eugene remains aloof. After Eliza promises to send him to Harvard for a year's graduate study, Luke asks Eugene to sign a paper acknowledging that the college fees and expenses he had received eliminate him from sharing in the estate. He signs the release willingly.

On his last night in Altamont, under a blazing moon, Eugene has a vision of his beloved brother, the dead Ben. Ben tells him that there is only one voyage, that there is no happy land, that the world is always within—that there is no more to be found in life than Eugene has found so far. But Eugene, filled with hope, looks forward to the great voyage of discovery he is about to take, the voyage that is life.

Critical Opinion

Thomas Wolfe's *Look Homeward, Angel,* a biographer points out, "fell on critically evil days and they have taken their toll of his reputation, if not of his steadily increasing number of readers." Published in 1929 in the month of the stock-market crash, it was regularly attacked by the critics of the thirties for its lack of social commitment. The attacks have never ceased. Only recently an influential English critic has said that Wolfe is not a novelist at all: "He is an obsessional neurotic with a gift for words who could write only about himself and who could not create other people."

The charges against Wolfe vary, but those most frequently leveled are that he is guilty of "sprawling profusion," that he is "monstrously rhetorical and oratorical," that he constructs formless, bulging pseudo-narratives that he then calls "novels." Not all the charges are baseless. Wolfe himself divided writers into two classifications—those who "take out" and those who "put in," and named as the great practitioner of the selective novel, Flaubert and of the inclusive novel, Tolstoi.

Wolfe further wrote, to Margaret Roberts (the model for Margaret Leonard), that *Look Homeward, Angel* was the story of a powerful creativity "trying to work its way toward an essential isolation; a creative solitude; a secret life—its fierce struggles to wall their part of life away from birth, first against the public and savage glare of an unbalanced, nervous, brawling family group, later against school, society, and all the barbarous invasions of the world." And this analysis may indicate the reason for the novel's continuing appeal. *Look Homeward, Angel* is intense autobiography, the record of the author's struggle for self, for individuality. People, especially but not exclusively young people, identify with that struggle, feel the novel with a force and directness that make negative criticism largely irrelevant. The novel still proves for them a vitalizing, even a liberating experience, and they still find their way to it in undiminished numbers.

Besides, the novel has three qualities that make it rise above its faults: its lyrical, soaring prose which forms an effective counterpart to its harsh and bitter realism; its moving, pungent dramatic dialogue; its vivid portraiture, which has etched for us a gallery of real, memorable people. Few American novelists can boast a greater accomplishment.

The Author

Thomas Wolfe was born in Asheville, North Carolina, and died in Baltimore, Maryland, of a brain infection. The thirty-nine years of his tumultuous life are chronicled in his four novels: *Look Homeward, Angel* (1929), *Of Time and the River* (1935), *The Web and the Rock* (1939), and *You Can't Go Home Again* (1940). Though the last two novels have a different hero (George Webber displaces the Eugene Gant of the earlier novels), all are essentially autobiographical.

Thomas Wolfe's father was a stonecutter, fond of reciting Shakespearean verses and impelled from time to time to go on roaring drunks. His mother ran a boardinghouse. In Asheville, Wolfe attended first a public school, then a private school where he came under the influence of a superb teacher, Margaret Roberts. He escaped a tempestuous family life by going to the University of North Carolina where he "joined everything" and wrote prodigiously. Two of his plays were produced at the university. Later he studied playwriting at Harvard under George Baker who conducted the famous "Workshop 47" course. The plays were not important in themselves, but they developed in Wolfe the dramatic sense that informs his novels.

The rest of his life Wolfe dedicated to writing, though he taught intermittently at New York University (1924–30) and went abroad several times. The stage designer Aline Bernstein, with whom he had a long love affair, showed the manuscript of his first novel, *Look Homeward, Angel,* to Maxwell Perkins, editor of Scribner's. It was a huge, sprawling, shapeless, unpublishable work, but Perkins saw in it the marks of genius. Together with Wolfe, he edited the novel, eliminating, condensing, sharpening. Their "creative partnership" was generously acknowledged by Wolfe in *The Story of a Novel* (1936). The manuscript, one wit commented, was brought to Perkins by truck and he returned it by taxi.

Despite the unfortunate timing of publication—the month of the 1929 stock-market crash—*Look Homeward, Angel* was successful. Wolfe worked for the next six years on the monumental *Of Time and the River,* the second installment of his vast fictional autobiography, publishing in the interval some stories and one excellent short novel, *A Portrait of Bascom Hawke.*

After his second novel, Wolfe changed publishers, perhaps because it had not been as favorably received as his first, perhaps because he resented the frequent remark (originating in jealousy) that Perkins ought to be listed as co-author at least. In any event, Edward C. Aswell of Harper and Brothers proved a splendid editor, too. Wolfe's untimely death prevented the kind of intimate collaboration that he had had with Perkins, but Aswell expertly sifted through the huge stack of manuscript that Wolfe had left and from it shaped three novels: *The Web and the Rock, You Can't Go Home Again,* and *The Hills Beyond* (1941), the last a book of stories. Together with the Eugene Gant novels, they form a vivid, astonishingly full account of one man's artistic growth and fulfillment.

The Sound and the Fury

by

WILLIAM FAULKNER (1897–1962)

Main Characters

Jason Compson, Sr.—The alcoholic head of the Compson family. Weak and cynical, he loves his brood but lacks the initiative to do more than advise them of the futility of struggling against life.

Caroline Bascomb Compson—His wife, a selfish hypochondriac, more concerned about her status than the psychic welfare of her children. Her favorite child is Jason.

Quentin Compson III—The eldest son, born 1891, a Harvard undergraduate, obsessed with tradition, purity, and death, a suicide at nineteen.

Candace Compson—Nicknamed Caddy, beautiful, indiscriminately amorous, but capable of profound self-sacrifice.

Jason Compson—Brutal, devoid of human feeling, responsive only to money.

Benjy Compson—Youngest of the children, born 1895; a gelded idiot who loves three things: the Compson pasture, Caddy, and firelight.

Miss Quentin—Caddy's seventeen-year-old daughter, separated by family will from her mother, living with Mrs. Compson, Jason, and Benjy. She is headstrong and rebellious, beautiful and promiscuous.

Uncle Maury—Mrs. Compson's only brother, handsome, lecherous, and always unemployed.

Dalton Ames—Caddy's lover, probably young Quentin's father, as stereotypically Southern as his name—romantic, bold, and egotistic.

Herbert Head—Caddy's husband, an Indianan, a former Harvard undergraduate, remembered at college for cheating at cards and during examinations.

Gerald Bland, Spoade, and *Shreve*—Quentin's classmates. Bland and Spoade are Southerners, the former a shallow parvenu, the latter a lazy man but a sexual athlete. Shreve, a Canadian and Quentin's roommate, remains an outsider.

Dilsey—The Compsons' Negro housekeeper. Strong of will and faith, she scolds and submits as circumstance demands and struggles to keep the declining Compsons together.

Roskus—Dilsey's husband.

Luster—Dilsey's grandson. Aged fourteen, he is assigned the man's task of caring for Benjy.

Frony—Dilsey's daughter and Luster's mother.

T.P., Versh—Dilsey's sons.

Deacon—A Negro factotum at Harvard who earns his living by providing for Southern students the Uncle Tom image they seem to need.

The Story

The Sound and the Fury is divided into four books, each narrated from a different point of view, each told on a different day. Thus the opening section takes place in the mind of the idiot Benjy on Holy Saturday, April 7, 1928. The second section is a record of Quentin's stream of consciousness on June 2, 1910, the day Quentin commits suicide. Jason narrates the third section on Good Friday, April 6, 1928. The final section, dealing with the events of Easter, April 8, 1928, is told from an external point of view.

The first two sections present difficulties for the reader. The latter two are readily comprehensible. Benjy's tale—since he is an idiot—shifts time and events rapidly and apparently incoherently. Moreover, Benjy's responses to stimuli are sensory, never rational. Quentin, despite his highly sophisticated intelligence, is obsessed by memory, compelled by suicidal drives. As a result he, too, fuses time and freely associates words, things, and episodes so complexly that his narrative may confuse the reader even more than Benjy's. To enable the reader to follow the sequence of events in these first two sections, the following summary chronologically orders the events. Such an arrangement, of course, is a convenience, not a substitute for Faulkner's brilliantly realized evocation of dislocation and decay.

Benjy, April 7, 1928

a. The Present.

On his thirty-third birthday, Benjy, attended by Luster, watches the golfers across the fence from the Compson yard and moans as they call for their caddies. (The word reminds him of his sister.) Luster has lost a quarter he needs for the visiting carnival that evening and, while searching for it, keeps Benjy quiet by giving him a jimson weed to chew on. They reach the creek and Luster takes off Benjy's shoes so he can wade. Thinking that he may have lost his quarter elsewhere, Luster leaves Benjy alone and goes off to search further. Benjy wanders off to a grove where Miss Quentin and a carnival pitchman are embracing. When Luster—still without his quarter—arrives, Quentin berates him for letting Benjy intrude on her.

Luster tries without success to sell the pitchman a golf ball for twenty-five cents. A few minutes later, a golfer takes the ball from him without paying anything. Frustrated and angry, Luster relieves his boyish irritation by tormenting Benjy. He overturns the bottle in which Benjy keeps his weeds and whispers "Caddy" in his ear.

Benjy's howls reach the house and Dilsey calls the two back, then placates Benjy by sitting him before the oven fire and lighting the candles on his birthday cake. When Dilsey leaves the kitchen, Luster mischievously closes the oven door and blows out the candles. Benjy howls and Dilsey returns to open the door and warn Luster. Again, however, with Dilsey's back turned, Luster shuts the door, and this time Benjy reaches out for the fire and burns his hand on the oven. Dilsey slaps Luster, salves Benjy's burn, and gives him Caddy's old slipper to appease him. Moaning softly, clenching the slipper, Benjy sits before the library fire.

At dinnertime Jason refuses Luster's request for a quarter

and warns Quentin to stay away from her carnival boyfriend. Quentin defies Jason and when he ridicules her, throws a glass of water at him and runs from the room.

At bedtime Benjy looks at his gelded body and cries. Luster, putting Benjy's nightclothes on him, hears a noise and, together with Benjy, watches Quentin climb down a tree from her window and walk out across the lawn.

b. The Past.

In 1898, while all the children are playing in the creek, Caddy, squatting, wets her dress and takes it off despite Quentin's protest. Quentin slaps her and she falls, muddying her drawers. Angrily, she splashes water on Quentin. Jason says he will tell his parents what they have done and as soon as the children return home, he tells his father. Sent to bed after supper, the children, led by Caddy, sneak out to the Negroes' cabin to play. Later, Caddy climbs a tree to see what the adults are about. The children below look up at Caddy's muddy drawers—all except Quentin, who remains aloof and sullen. What Caddy thinks is a party is in fact a funeral gathering for her dead grandmother, "Damuddy."

The years of Benjy's adolescence are dominated by memories of Caddy's smelling like rain, her gentle embraces, and her sleeping beside him. Other memories also intrude: delivering Uncle Maury's love notes to a neighboring lady and seeing Maury's eye blackened by her husband; watching his beloved paper dolls being cut up by Jason; crying when Caddy, at fourteen, first uses perfume, and again, after discovering her in a swing with a boy who tries to kiss her, and still again, when at the age of thirteen, he is forbidden to stay in Caddy's bed.

At fourteen Benjy howls when Caddy returns home after losing her virginity. He tries to pull her into the bathroom to wash, as before when he cried at her using perfume and her being kissed. The next year, at Caddy's wedding party, T.P. gets Benjy drunk on champagne in the cellar. Standing atop a box to look inside, Benjy sees Caddy in her wedding dress and cries. Then he slips, hits his head, and begins to bellow. Quentin discovers Benjy and T.P., beats the Negro boy sober, and watches as Benjy vomits and passes out.

With Caddy gone, Benjy stands sobbing at the Compson

fence. When Quentin's body is sent home from Harvard a month later, Benjy is kept from the house. Just a few weeks thereafter, Benjy chases some girls passing along the fence and touches one of them. Yielding to town pressure, the family sends Benjy away to be castrated. Two years later Benjy smells death once more, this time the death of his father. Holding a flower in his hand, Benjy rides to the cemetery in a horse carriage with his mother and T.P. On the way they drive through the town square of Jefferson to pick up Jason at his store, but he refuses to attend the funeral. The carriage drives on.

Quentin, June 2, 1910

a. The Present.

It is the last day of Quentin's life. He awakens early, hears his watch ticking, and turns it face down. His roommate, Shreve, urges him to hurry lest he be late for Harvard chapel. But Quentin lingers, watching Spoade dawdle across the campus. Then he breaks his watch crystal and twists off the hands, cutting his fingers in the process. He packs his trunk, addresses some letters indicating to whom his clothes are to be given, and lays out a fresh change of clothing. After bathing and shaving, he rides the tram to Boston, breakfasts, and brings his watch to a jeweler, noting with interest that none of the clocks in the jeweler's window has the correct time.

At a hardware store he purchases two six-pound flatirons (to weight his body) and reboards a trolley for Cambridge. At the Charles River, the drawbridge opens and Quentin gets off the trolley to watch Gerald Bland row by. Within the next hour, he mounts and leaves several trolleys, each headed in a different direction. At last, just after noon, he rides to a stop in the country near a stone bridge that seems right for his purpose. Under one edge of the bridge he hides his flatirons.

He stands at the bridge with three boys watching a trout swim by and then begins to walk toward the adjacent town, guided by the church steeple whose clock face he tries not to see. At a bakery where he stops to buy a bun for lunch, he meets a little girl, buys her a bun, too, and then some ice cream as well. The child follows him silently despite his efforts to get her to leave. Two men suggest that he take her to the section of town across the tracks. He does, but the child refuses to tell him where she lives or to leave him. Quentin climbs a wall to elude her but finds her waiting for him on the other side. Together they approach the river, and there the sheriff and the child's brother accuse Quentin of having assaulted the girl.

Quentin laughs wildly at the charge, but he is nevertheless arraigned before a justice of the peace. Spoade and Shreve arrive to pay the six-dollar fine. As the three leave, they find Gerald Bland, his mother, and two girls waiting to take them all to a picnic. Angered by Gerald's cynical remarks about women's purity, Quentin punches him, but is himself battered, his nose bloodied, his eye blackened. Quentin returns to Cambridge alone at dusk, hiding his bruised eye from the passengers on the trolley but watching his own reflection merge with a woman's hat feather in the car window.

Back in his dormitory, Quentin changes into the clothes he had laid out early in the morning, and pauses to clean his vest with gasoline. As the campus clock tolls, he puts a letter to Shreve on the table and his watch in Shreve's drawer. He brushes his teeth, rubs up the nap on his hat, dons it, and leaves—to commit suicide.

b. The Past.

Like Benjy, Quentin recalls first the episode of Caddy's dirtying her drawers on the day of Damuddy's death. All his subsequent recollections spiral outward from that primal stain upon his sister's purity. When Caddy at fifteen kisses a boy and twits Quentin, saying she made the boy kiss her, Quentin rubs her face in the grass. She taunts him further by reminding him that he kissed a girl named Natalie not long before. In that episode Quentin and Natalie kissed and childishly imitated the gestures of intercourse, unaware that Caddy was watching. After the incident Quentin, humiliated and ashamed, threw himself into the hogwallow. Then, seeing Caddy, he tried to make her understand what happened. When she turned away from him, he grabbed her, knocked her down, and smeared her with the mud from his body. Caddy scratched his face, apologized, and together they washed themselves in the creek.

Quentin's central memory is of Caddy's loss of virginity to Dalton Ames. When Benjy howls at Caddy's new smell, Quentin, who understands Benjy's strangely perceptive sensory insight, determines to ask Caddy whether she yielded or was forced. Finding Caddy squatting in the creek, he asks her, swears to kill Ames if he has harmed her, and offers to run away with her. When she asks him whether he has ever experienced sex, he weeps, and recalls for her the day she muddied her drawers. He presses a knife to her throat, offering a death compact, but she rightly doubts his willingness to go ahead with his offer.

Failing to dissuade Caddy from meeting Ames, he goes along with her and watches as they embrace. He runs off distraught, and Caddy follows him to the creek and offers herself to him. Torn between desire and horror, he shakes her and bids her be still. A few days later Quentin confronts Ames alone and threatens him. Ames gently dismisses Quentin's warnings, reminding him that all women are bitches. Enraged, Quentin tries to hit Ames but is easily held off. Ames takes a pistol and shoots a bit of wood in the river, then offers the pistol to Quentin. Quentin takes it, but trying again to hit Ames, he faints. Caddy, hearing the shot, runs to the scene, thinking Ames has hurt Quentin. She sends Ames away forever, she says, but when Quentin asks her later whether she still loves Ames, she admits that she does.

Mrs. Compson (who wore black the day she first knew Caddy had kissed a boy) now takes Caddy away hoping to find her a husband other than the unacceptable Ames. While they are gone, Quentin tries to convince his father that he, not Ames, has made love to Caddy. Aware that his son is a virgin, Mr. Compson tries to help Quentin gain perspective on Caddy's loss of virginity as a normal process, one hardly conducive to thoughts of suicide. All of this is temporary, Mr. Compson argues, persuasively but unavailingly.

Just before the wedding, back from Harvard where he enshrined the wedding invitation on his desk as an altar for the dead, Quentin meets Herbert Head, Caddy's fiancé, and despises him for his flattery and ostentation (he has bought Caddy a car for a wedding present and promised Mrs. Compson to give Jason a job in his bank) and for his attempt to bribe Quentin not to tell about his reputation at Harvard. When he is alone with Caddy, he begs her not to marry Head, but Caddy insists he let her have her chance for marriage. The night before the wedding, she asks him to care for their father and for Benjy. Again he pleads with her not to marry Head but rather to go away with him. As he tries to embrace her, Caddy pushes him away, telling him that she is pregnant and must marry, and that she has had other lovers, too. Quentin's responsibility, she insists, is to finish college and help the family.

Jason, April 6, 1928

With Quentin and his father dead and Caddy exiled, Jason is the head of what is left of the Compson family. "You are the only one of them that isn't a reproach to me," his whining mother tells him. Jason's thoughts ("Once a bitch always a bitch, what I say . . . ." is the opening phrase in this section) and actions do little to support his mother's misplaced faith. Deprived of his promised banking post when Herbert Head abandons Caddy, Jason has compensated by stealing for fifteen years the monthly $200 checks Caddy has sent Mrs. Compson to care for her daughter Quentin. Though Mrs. Compson knows about the money, Jason has kept the authentic checks aside, giving his mother worthless forged copies which she innocently burns, proud of her refusal to accept money from her sinful child.

Once partner in a general store, Jason has sold the interest his mother had purchased for him to buy a car. He remains as a clerk just to keep his mother ignorant of what he has done with her investment. Ironically, the car yields Jason more grief than pleasure, for he is allergic to gasoline fumes and cannot venture any distance without carrying along as antidote a camphor-soaked handkerchief. His attempts to make money on the cotton market meet with little more success, for he is so busy spying on Quentin that he misses opportunities to buy and sell at a profit. Thus, on Friday, April 8, while the market fluctuates wildly and demands his constant attention, Jason pursues Quentin up and down back alleys, trying to trap her with her boy friend from the carnival. Not only does he fail to catch her, but he misses an important message about a stock transaction. When he does at last try to telegraph his instructions, the stock market has closed. His revenge is to taunt

Quentin at dinner with thinly veiled obscene allusions to her activities.

Jason's bitterness extends beyond his family: he hates Jews and Negroes, because he fancies that the former control the stock market and the latter his life. He resents Dilsey's place in the family pattern and regards all Negroes as stupid or stubborn or both. When Luster, still hoping to attend the carnival even though he has lost his quarter, asks Jason for one of the two passes he has, Jason retorts that he needs cash and will sell one pass for a nickel. Despite Dilsey's anger, Jason baits the boy, rejects his fervent promises of repayment, and at last drops both passes into the fire.

Easter Sunday, April 8, 1928

Three episodes are interwoven in this brief final section. Ironically contrasted with the chaos of the Compson family is Dilsey's orderly preparation of breakfast and her trip with her family to Easter services conducted by a wizened, inspired Negro preacher from St. Louis, Rev. Shegog. After the service, her face tear-streaked, her head held high, Dilsey walks toward home and says, prophetically, "I seed de beginnin', en now I sees de endin'."

Meanwhile, Jason discovers that Quentin has run off with the nearly $7,000 Jason had hidden beneath a plank in his room. When the sheriff refuses to join in a chase on evidence he regards as too circumstantial, Jason drives off alone—without his camphor-soaked handkerchief. His headache rages even when he tries to think about his weekends with his blowzy mistress Lorraine. At the carnival, where he hopes to find Quentin and her pitchman lover, Jason irrationally demands of an elderly cook that he produce the couple. The cook has no notion of what Jason is talking about, but when Jason strikes him, the cook goes berserk and chases him with a rusty hatchet. Others prevent the cook from killing Jason after Jason falls and strikes his head. Exhausted, unable to carry on his search or to drive his car back to Jefferson, Jason offers various Negroes a dollar to drive him home. All refuse until one stops by and demands four dollars. Jason counters with an offer of two, but the Negro insists upon and gets what he asked for.

In the final scene, Dilsey allows Luster to drive Benjy to town. Holding a narcissus in his hand, Benjy sits quietly as the carriage moves toward the town square in Jefferson. Suddenly determined to show off, Luster decides to turn the carriage to the left, counter to traffic. Unaccustomed to seeing objects in reverse order, Benjy bellows. Just back from his unhappy trip, Jason hears the noise, leaps across the square, turns the horse about, pounds Luster on the head, and directs him to return to the house. As the pattern returns to normal, Benjy sinks into a serenely quiet blankness, the broken narcissus stem clenched in his fist.

Critical Opinion

Life, says Macbeth, is "a tale told by an idiot, full of sound and fury, signifying nothing." In Faulkner's complex paraphrase of Shakespeare's grim utterance, man's prospects grow no brighter. True, Dilsey endures and seems a symbol of man's endurance. But Dilsey is a Negro housekeeper, courageous yet subjugated and oppressed by the white society she lives in. Her strength is internal. Its impact on the world outside is small.

One cannot turn away, however, from a work of literature because its author's vision of life is neither idyllically happy nor glowingly hopeful. Critics have argued lengthily about theme and technique in *The Sound and the Fury*, but only a few have denied its overpowering force. Unquestionably a difficult book, it rewards the painstaking reader with deep insight into the private and public life of a degenerating Southern family. A haunting sense of the glories of their ante-bellum past torments the Compsons, and their failure to adjust to a modern world hastens their decay. False views of caste, chivalry, morality, and love distort Quentin's approach to experience as thoroughly as Jason's total absence of any but material values distorts his. Caddy, like her daughter Quentin, is essentially a decent human being trapped by the inflexibility of outworn or inhumane conventions. Poor Benjy, though he understands nothing, feels and smells the effects of the disorder that surrounds him. His tale, a tale told by an idiot, nevertheless signifies much.

To tell his powerful story, Faulkner uses his novelistic techniques with consummate skill. Structurally, he moves from the disordered, irrational world of Benjy's uncomprehending consciousness to the lucid, objective, external narrative of the final section. Some critics have argued that the novel would read better were the order reversed. Others have justly shown that the small gain in clarity would be offset by great loss of perspective, mood, and insight.

Other devices also add density to Faulkner's searching revelation of the fate of modern man. The novel is rich in symbols that render concrete many of the abstract problems Faulkner treats. Thus, Quentin's obsessive interest in time is imaged in his broken watch—a sharp contrast, incidentally, to Dilsey's faulty alarm clock which never disturbs her assurance about time. The theme of incest is presented against the sensually aromatic background of honeysuckle. Jason's materialism evokes the noxious odor of gasoline. And there is, of course, the central myth of Easter to underscore the agony of man and to hold forth in Dilsey's experience at the service the possibility of resurrection.

The Sound and the Fury, then, affords the reader a rich and complex philosophical and psychological perception of life. Its art orders a chaotic universe, and though it provides no final answers to man's problems, it dramatizes them with power, insight, and understanding.

Light in August

by

WILLIAM FAULKNER

Main Characters

Joe Christmas—The protagonist, an agonized spirit, violent, rebellious, destructive, unable to discover his identity, and doomed to wreak vengeance on himself as well as on others.

Joanna Burden—Joe's mistress, a forty-one-year-old New Englander whose moral inheritance commits her to helping the Negro even though she believes him inferior.

Gail Hightower—Once a Presbyterian minister, now a recluse willfully isolated from the world of reality and from all possibility of either pleasure or pain.

Lena Grove—Pregnant with an illegitimate child, yet the symbol of natural innocence, never questioning the essential goodness of life and man.

Lucas Burch—Alias Joe Brown, the father of Lena's child. Shiftless and irresponsible, he wants from life only the pleasures of sex and drink.

Byron Bunch—Until he meets Lena Grove, he is lonely, austere, dutiful, bound by moral strictures and social taboos.

Doc Hines—Joe Christmas' grandfather, a sin- and race-obsessed fanatic who hovers over Joe like an avenging angel.

McEachern—Joe's foster father, a bloodlessly religious and ruthless tyrant.

Mrs. McEachern—Gentle, maternal, but wholly submissive to her husband's will.

Bobbie Allen—Joe's first woman, a waitress and prostitute, capable of both affection and cruelty.

Percy Grimm—A young National Guardsman, a chauvinist and a racist.

The Story

Although the stories of Joe Christmas, Gail Hightower, and Lena Grove are entirely separate, during the eleven eventful August days in Jefferson, Mississippi, their lives intersect dramatically and bring to the novel a powerful unity. At the beginning Lena Grove has been walking from Alabama toward Jefferson for nearly a month to find Lucas Burch, the father of her unborn child, rumored to be working at a lumber planing mill in Jefferson. Ignoring her swollen, uncomfortable body, Lena plods along the road, gratefully accepting a wagon ride or a night's hospitality. Lacking these, she trudges on serenely, confidently, resting and sleeping in the open fields. One Friday morning she arrives in Jefferson where she sees columns of smoke rising from a burning house in the distance.

Three years earlier—also on a Friday morning—a silent young stranger named Joe Christmas was hired at the mill. Just six months before Lena's arrival, another young man, brash and talkative, calling himself Joe Brown (he is, in fact, Lucas Burch), also began work there. For some months before the novel begins, neither Burch nor Christmas has worked at the mill, being partners in a lucrative bootlegging operation. A third millworker is Byron Bunch who has labored there for nine years. The men at the mill respect Christmas for his diligence but dislike him for his rude aloofness. They ridicule Lucas' laziness and despise his loudness, and they wonder about Byron who is friendly and hard-working but reticent about his personal life.

Only one townsman, the Rev. Gail Hightower, knows about Byron's private life: on weekends Byron drives to the country to sing with a church choir, and several nights a week he spends hours in conversation with Hightower. Thus on the evening of Lena Grove's arrival in town, Bunch tells Hightower about certain significant events of the day: Lena's visit to the mill, the murder of Joanna Burden, and the burning of her house. At the mill, Lena has spoken with Bunch about Lucas. Byron, knowing of Lucas' involvement in the Burden case, regrets now that he did not deny to her that Lucas and Joe Brown are the same man. Byron tells Hightower only that he wants to shield Lena from knowing the grim sequence of events coincident with her arrival. But Hightower senses what Byron himself does not yet realize—that he has already fallen in love with the tranquil but determined girl. About Joanna Burden's death, Byron tells what he has learned from the townspeople. Having heard of a reward for the capture of Joanna's murderer, Lucas has told the police that Joe Christmas is the culprit and lived with Joanna for three years even though he apparently merely shared with Lucas a cabin on her property. Finally, he has told the police that Joe has admitted he is a Negro, despite his coloration.

During Byron's recital, Hightower sits silent, rigidly erect, his expression one of "denial and flight." Years have passed since he came with his young wife to preach in Jefferson, since he abandoned his ministry, and since he has accepted reality. From the outset, parishioners found his sermons too frenzied, as if he sought to find religion rather than to dispense it. And Hightower's wife, too, seemed objectionably strange, rarely attending service, disappearing on weekends, and once interrupting services by screaming hysterically. Briefly confined as a mental patient, she was soon thereafter discovered in a Memphis hotel room with a strange man and leaped from a window to her death. Despite pressure from his flock, Hightower refused to resign his post. But at last, accused of relations with his Negro cook, beaten by Klansmen, he yielded. In time the townfolk came to ignore him and to accept his self-imposed isolation.

Now, listening to Byron's narrative of love and violence, Hightower is afraid these events may disrupt his determination to turn away from experience. Ironically, he also fears that Byron's involvement—especially with Lena—will deprive him of his single remaining human companion.

The novel now shifts to Joe Christmas, tracing in multiple flashbacks his recollection of the past and the events leading to his murder of Joanna Burden. He recalls first a key episode during his fifth year when he lived in a white orphanage. Hidden behind a curtain in the room of Miss Atkins, the dietitian, Joe sits eating toothpaste and, when Miss Atkins and a young doctor unexpectedly enter, uncomprehendingly hears the sounds of their lovemaking. When the toothpaste sickens him, Joe vomits and thus is discovered by the woman. Angered, distraught, she calls him a spy and, in an outburst of rage, "nigger." Joe understands only that he is being punished for eating toothpaste, but the trauma of sex and racial identity stirred by this episode haunts him forever.

Afraid that Joe will tell and cause her to lose her post, Miss Atkins seeks help from Doc Hines, the janitor, who began work at the orphanage just after Joe's arrival. Since then, as Miss Atkins says, Hines has stayed on just "to watch and hate" the child. Though he regards Miss Atkins as a harlot and her discovery by Joe as a triumph for God, he nevertheless tries to steal the child and place him in a Negro orphanage. Meanwhile Miss Atkins, hoping to have Joe sent away, tells the matron of the orphanage that he is a Negro. Hines's kidnaping venture is unearthed, the child brought back, and the matron, believing that a shift in Joe's racial identity will hurt him, places him with a white family, the McEacherns.

Joe's years in the McEachern home harden the mold of his sexual and racial bitterness. As a child of eight he is mercilessly beaten by his rabidly moralistic foster father for failing to learn his catechism. At fourteen, confronted with the possi-

bility of his first sexual experience, he kicks and beats the
Negro girl his white friends have been making love to. At
seventeen, after arduous daytime work on McEachern's farm,
Joe begins to slip away at night to meet Bobbie Allen, a woman in her thirties, with whom he has his first sexual experience. During one of their amorous moments, he tells her of his
belief that he is part Negro. Shocked but not entirely convinced, she continues with their affair. When Joe learns that
Bobbie is really a prostitute, he beats her brutally, yet remains
her lover, but he pays her each time, using money he has
stolen from his kindly foster mother.

One night McEachern follows Joe and finds him at a dance
with Bobbie. McEachern denounces the girl as a whore and
attacks Joe who fells him with a chair. With Bobbie's impre-
cations roaring in his ears, Joe returns home, steals his foster
mother's money as she looks on (he has loathed her kindness
even more than her husband's brutality), then steals and beats
the horse he rides to Bobbie's house. He spills the stolen money
on her bed, then punches her viciously. She calls out for help,
denounces Joe to her friends as a Negro, and watches as he
is beaten up.

For the next ten years Joe drifts through the country, working at several jobs, sleeping with innumerable women, afterward telling them he is a Negro and suffering the curses or
beatings that follow. One woman shows indifference to his
race and he nearly beats her to death, sickened at the possibility of her lack of prejudice. For two years after this experience, he lives as a Negro in the North, his mistress an ebony-
hued girl. But he fails here again to prove his racial identity
to himself.

At last—at the age of thirty-three—he arrives in Jefferson.
Attracted by the large house just beyond the town, he walks
there. Once inside the gate, Joe smells food and steals into the
kitchen. He is eating when the lady of the house, Joanna Burden, discovers him. She allows him to stay on and live in a
cabin across the field from her house. Although they rarely
meet, Joe is always infuriated by her aloofness. His rage increases and one night he rapes her, startled by her "hard, un-
tearful and unself-pitying and almost manlike yielding." Joe
expects that Joanna will seek revenge for what he has done to
her. He is shocked when nothing happens. He continues to

work at the mill and to live at the cabin, wondering what his strange benefactor and victim will do next. Some time later, Joanna comes to his cabin and in great detail recounts her history: her abolitionist forebears, the murder of some of them who moved to Jefferson to help Negroes, and her ancestrally imposed task—to expiate the guilt of her race at whatever cost to herself.

Her confession over, Joanna initiates the "second phase" of her relationship with Joe. The days remain as before, but at night—in her bed and sometimes even in the fields—she forces him beyond sin, demanding of him total corruption in word and deed. Always during their lovemaking, she whispers, "Negro, Negro, Negro." Her passion and fury terrify Joe. Yet knowing he should escape, he stays on, not understanding why.

Two years later, the third and final phase begins—Joanna's quest for salvation. Pregnant, desperate to be forgiven her carnal sins yet unwilling to forego them, she turns to prayer. Trying to force Joe to share her expiation, she urges him to attend a Negro college or, since he refuses, at least to pray for his soul. Again Joe refuses. The struggle grows in intensity until one night Joanna points a Confederate revolver at him, and Joe cuts her throat. The next morning, after Joe has fled, the drunken Lucas Burch discovers the body and accidentally sets fire to the house.

Catastrophe follows Joe swiftly in his flight. Bloodhounds and posse pursue him while Lucas clamors for the reward money. Along his way, Joe bursts into a Negro revival meeting, knocks the preacher from the pulpit, and looses a tirade against God. When the preacher's son tries to slash Joe with a razor, Joe fractures his skull with a bench leg. The flight and pursuit continue, the dogs thrown off the scent when Joe dons a Negro's shoes. Running, no longer aware of time or place, Joe enters Mottstown, twenty miles from Jefferson, on Friday morning, just seven days after his flight began. In Mottstown, Joe has his hair cut by a white barber, buys new clothes, and then walks the main street until he is recognized and arrested.

Among the would-be lynchers in the mob that quickly gathers, none is more eager for Joe's blood or more difficult to restrain than Doc Hines. The erstwhile janitor of Joe's orphanage has for the past thirty years been a preacher in Mottstown, his gospel—white supremacy as the price of salvation; his audience—Negroes. A lynching is averted and Joe is returned to the jail in Jefferson. Doc Hines and his wife follow the prisoner, Doc to try once more to stir the crowd to action, his wife to learn the truth she has never heard about the boy whose existence Hines has kept hidden from her since the child's birth. She reveals the tale to Hightower after Byron Bunch brings her to him.

The truth about Joe's origins emerge. The Hineses are Joe's grandparents. Their daughter Millie bore a son from her affair with a man she described as a Mexican. Doc Hines killed the man and, denying his daughter the post-natal care she needed, allowed her to die. Then he stole the newborn child and deposited it on Christmas Eve on the doorstep of a brothel, later telling the madam its name was Joseph. Once Joe went off with the McEachern family, Doc thought his God-assigned task of revenge was complete. Soon, however, his haunted sense that Joe was "a pollution and an abomination" returned to torture him until the climax of Joe's final arrest.

As Joe is led from his cell across the square to the courthouse for arraignment, he breaks and runs. Handcuffed but with a gun gripped between his hands, he clears a path through the stunned crowd. Alone among the pursuers, Percy Grimm keeps Joe in sight, chasing him from behind a Negro's cabin and finally into Hightower's house. Inside the house, Joe cracks his gun against Hightower's face and runs into the kitchen, overturning the table and taking refuge behind it. When Grimm enters the house, Hightower, who has sworn to Byron Bunch that he would not help Joe in any way, now cries to Grimm that Joe is innocent, that he was with Joe the night of the murder. Grimm, disgusted with the pretense, brushes Hightower aside and enters the kitchen firing. When the other deputies arrive, they discover Grimm bending over the dying but still conscious Joe and castrating him.

As Joe dies in Hightower's house, Lena Grove gives birth to her child in the cabin Byron Bunch had sheltered her in, the same cabin Joe and Lucas had shared on Joanna Burden's property. Mrs. Hines, sent by Bunch to attend Lena, helps deliver the child. Then, crazed by her recent knowledge, she mistakes the child for Joe, Lena for Millie. Despite Byron's love for Lena, he has the sheriff bring Lucas (who thinks he is being taken to receive his reward) to Lena's cabin. Within a very few minutes, Lucas leaves, promising to return. Instead, he escapes, chased by Byron, who catches him near the railroad. But Byron is no match for the aroused Lucas. Beaten, Byron watches as Lucas leaps aboard a departing freight.

Thus Joe Christmas dies, Lena Grove bears her child, and the Rev. Hightower is thrust reluctantly, and at best temporarily, back into the agony of life. As the novel ends, a furniture dealer from the eastern part of Mississippi, lying in bed with his wife, tells of picking up in Jefferson and carrying along to Tennessee in his truck a young woman with a baby in her arms and, with her, a nervous young man. He recalls how, when the truck paused for the night, the young man (whose name, the dealer recalls, was Bunch) crawled in to lie beside the young woman and was promptly ousted. The next morning only the girl and the baby were aboard the truck as it drove off. But around the bend, the dealer found the young man waiting. When he jumped aboard, the young man said to the girl, "I done come too far now. I be dog if I'm going to quit now." The girl's reply was, "Ain't nobody never said for you to quit."

Critical Opinion

Acknowledged as one of Faulkner's finest and most readable novels, *Light in August* is nevertheless a difficult work. The sources of its difficulty are many: complex structure, diversity of points of view, intricate imagery and symbolism, and involved themes. A summary merely suggests the novel's dazzling technical complexity and its profound insight into human behavior.

Critics have taken pains to demonstrate how Faulkner's technique serves his theme in the novel. The separate plots about Joe, Lena, and Hightower, for example, testify powerfully to man's isolation. And even when people do meet, or, as with Joe and Joanna, collide, they never do really communicate with one another. Each is sealed off in his own traumatic world of self. The same fate befalls even the minor characters: Doc Hines, McEachern, and Percy Grimm. By keeping characters like Joe and Lena from ever meeting, Faulkner not only underscores the theme of alienation and frustration, but counterpoints Joe's agony against Lena's serenity.

Similarly, the varied points of view used to narrate the story suggest how impossible it is for any single mind to comprehend the range of experience. Shifting from Lena's intuitive mind to Joe's inwardness and then to Hightower's agonized detachment, the reader begins to appreciate the kind of omniscience required to understand the power and weakness of man.

Many critics have seen in the story of Joe Christmas an ironic parallel to the New Testament account of Jesus Christ. Among the more obvious analogies are these: Joe's initials, Lucas' Judas-like betrayal of Joe for money, Joe's wanderings in his early manhood, and his inevitable progress toward crucifixion during the last seven days of his life. But Joe is no savior. His death saves no soul, frees no spirit. Indeed, as Edmond Volpe points out, Joe alone finds release, not the society whose racist concept crucifies him: "The fear and guilt of his society . . . are reinforced . . . and the concept will be imposed, during childhood, for the heirs of the executioners and make these victims, in their turn, executioners." Joe cannot save the South from its puritanical mentality. He can serve only as a scapegoat, suffering torment for a tormented people, white and black alike.

Joe dies trying to discover some justification for living. Hightower, on the other hand, surrenders his quest. "I am not in life any more," he says, rejecting at last the forces of life and death symbolized by Lena and Joe. Only Byron Bunch and Lena Grove survive to face the future. Yet Faulkner holds forth no shining promise for them: Lena is too primitive, Byron more dogged than delighted about his commitment to experience. Lena's delivery of her child is only an affirmation of a natural process—she is "light in August," as a cow might be; she has delivered her bodily burden. But no other "light" shines through to beckon her or the others. The "shadow" of Joe Christmas still falls darkly across the land when the novel ends.

The Author

Since the Civil War, the Faulkner family has been distinguished in Mississippi history. None, however, has attained the eminence of *William Faulkner,* winner of both the Pulitzer and the Nobel prizes for his fiction. Although he never graduated from high school and failed the only English course he took at the University of Mississippi, Faulkner tirelessly labored at the craft of writing and won recognition as one of the finest American novelists of the first half of the twentieth century.

After World War I, during which he trained as a pilot for the Canadian Air Force, Faulkner determined to be a writer. He started out as a poet, but soon after he met Sherwood Anderson in New Orleans, he began work upon his first novel, *Soldier's Pay* (1926), later published with Anderson's help. Though it brought him no fame, it encouraged him to go on writing. Three years later, with the publication of *The Sound and the Fury,* his finest work, Faulkner had arrived as a major writer.

That same year Faulkner married and found himself compelled to undertake odd jobs to earn a living. In 1931 he published *Sanctuary,* a novel avowedly written to make money. The brutal portrait of the degenerate Popeye and of the charming young decadent Temple Drake produced a sensation and earned Faulkner the fortune he sought. Shortly afterward he began the first of several jaunts to Hollywood, where, as he later noted, "I made me some money and had me some fun."

Such instances of potboiling, however, are fleeting and minor in Faulkner's creative life. Most of the years after 1930 found him living quietly and working diligently in his old colonial house in Oxford, Mississippi, the town where he grew up and where he spent most of his adult life. Out of that town and its environs he fashioned the mythical world of *Yoknapatawpha,* its inhabitants a cross section of the rigidly stratified Southern society. The Sartoris and Compson families, for example, represent the genteel aristocracy, a shade above Faulkner's own upper-middle-class origins. The Snopes stand at the other extreme, a clan of grasping, virulent usurpers.

And always there are the Negroes, embodying the qualities of human endurance and, by their very existence, nagging the dormant guilt and fear of the white man.

A small but handsome, quiet man, Faulkner—until his very last years—avoided publicity. Only intense family pressure persuaded him to go to Sweden, don formal attire, and accept the Nobel Prize. When he did go, however, he delivered a memorable acceptance speech. In it he declined to accept the doom of man: "I believe that man will not merely endure, he will prevail."

The 42nd Parallel

by

JOHN DOS PASSOS (1896–)

Main Characters

Mac—Restless, socially conscious, and theoretically committed
to the cause of the proletariat, but unable to act creatively.
Janey Williams—The epitome of the career girl who ineffectually apes her betters.
J. Ward Moorehouse—An opportunist, the symbol of the
corruption destructive to both capital and labor.
Eleanor Stoddard—Dedicated to the pursuit of a sterile
estheticism that can never turn her into a warm human
being.
Charley Anderson—A talented young mechanic with a zest
for ideas and experience who is still emotionally uncom-
mitted.

The Story

The 42nd parallel is a latitudinal line along which American climate travels from west to east. In Dos Passos' novel, it
is also the imaginary track along which most of his characters
travel. To tell his story, Dos Passos uses four different simul-
taneous narrative techniques. Each of these appears within the
first thirty pages of the novel.

The novel opens with a *Newsreel,* a composite of headlines, songs, speeches suggesting the national mood at the opening of the twentieth century. Carefully selected, the items of the *Newsreel* record the political, social, and cultural chaos of American life until 1917, when the novel ends. *The Camera Eye* follows immediately, an autobiographical stream-of-consciousness treatment of the themes of idealism and frustration in Dos Passos' childhood, adolescence, and young manhood. With *Mac*, the third and most conventional of the narrative devices begins. Mac is one of five characters whose lives are presented in the course of the novel. Each characterization is complete in itself, yet all the lives are interrelated. Finally, there are the *Living Biographies*, free-verse sketches of businessmen, scientists, and politicians drawn from contemporary history: case studies of notable Americans who represent the possibilities and the dangers along the 42nd parallel. Included are Andrew Carnegie, Minor Keith, Edison, Steinmetz, Debs, Bill Haywood, LaFollette, and William Jennings Bryan.

No summary can effectively represent either the *Newsreel* or the *Living Biographies*. Because the interspersed sections of *The Camera Eye* would interrupt the fictional narrative, a brief, general summary of that material has been appended to the summary below which concerns itself with the fictional narrative.

Mac

Fainy McCreary, known as Mac, is the son of poor Connecticut parents. Daily, as a child, he fights the sons of his Polish and Bohemian neighbors, finding moments of peace only in his own back yard. When his mother dies and his father loses his job during a strike, Mac's uncle Tim O'Hara, a printer and a socialist, takes him and his sister to live in Chicago. There Mac grows up, learns the printing trade and the principles of socialism.

When his uncle is driven out of business by anti-labor forces, Mac ventures forth alone, guided by Tim's words: ". . . read Marx, study all you can, remember that you're a rebel by birth and by blood." Hired by an unctuous lecher, the Rev. E. R. Bingham, with whom he travels, Mac soon learns that most of the books he is supposed to peddle are pornographic. When an irate farmer discovers Bingham with his wife and chases him with a shotgun, Mac's career as a book salesman ends.

For several months thereafter, Mac rides the rails westward, working at lumber camps and on railroad jobs. By late fall, 1905, Mac reaches San Francisco and finds work again as a printer. He attends socialist meetings, hears Upton Sinclair lecture about Chicago's stockyards, and meets Fred Hoff, a member of Bill Haywood's newly organized I.W.W.— the Industrial Workers of the World. Hoff invites Mac to join him and others in Nevada in publishing a newspaper supporting a miner's strike. Though he wants go, Mac has become amorously involved with Maisie Spencer, a pretty salesgirl.

Having seduced Maisie, Mac promises to marry her, but first he leaves for Nevada. Several months after he learns that Maisie is pregnant, he returns and marries her. Settled now in a printing job in San Diego, Mac assumes a domestic role for at least another year, long enough for Maisie to have a second child. Increasingly, however, he frets about having sold out to the bourgeois world. When Maisie's brother makes it possible for them to move into a suburban cottage, Mac's rancor mounts. Everywhere about him he hears about the Mexican revolution, the fall of Diaz, the murder of Matero, the revolutionary leader. When Maisie berates him for drawing from their savings to pay for Uncle Tim's funeral, Mac uses the quarrel as an excuse to leave for Mexico.

Americans in Mexico assure Mac that Zapata is vicious, the revolution an affair for bandits. But Mac is resolutely determined to join the fighting forces of revolution. Somehow Mac never gets beyond talk. Instead he settles for a printing job with a newspaper in Mexico City, a mistress, and a comfortable apartment. A few months later he buys a bookstore: "It felt good to be his own boss for the first time in his life." Ironically, Mac's shop specializes in radical literature. Grudgingly Mac admits a kind of admiration for J. Ward Moorehouse who is trying to work out major investment deals in Mexico for American firms. Still committed to the revolution, however, Mac fails to help Moorehouse. When Zapata comes into Mexico City, Mac sells his bookstore and flees with Concha and her mother. Once in Vera Cruz, he buys a single steerage passage for the United States, planning to abandon

Concha. But he has a change of heart and remains in Vera Cruz. From that point on, settled with his Mexican girl, Concha, in Vera Cruz, Mac and his friends serenely and safely toast the coming of reform in the new Mexico.

Janey Williams

Janey Williams, a plain, sandy-haired girl from Georgetown, Washington, D.C., adores her older brother Joe and despises their father for beating him. In her adolescence Janey falls in love with Joe's best friend, Alec, though Alec knows nothing of her infatuation. When Alec is killed in a motorcycle accident, Janey feels emotionally dead. She never really recovers.

When Joe joins the Navy, Janey, now a stenographer, lives vicariously the excitement in his postcards. For a brief period she comes close to a life of her own when Jerry Burnham, a genial, left-wing cynic, tries to win her. Almost in love with him, she resists his lovemaking and frightens him away. Janey decides to become a career woman instead of a woman. She bleaches her hair, smokes, and flirts mildly and safely.

When the war in Europe starts, Janey leaves her job because her employer is pro-German. After a brief period of unemployment and a single day's work for G. H. Barrow (an unscrupulous publicist and labor organizer, more gifted as a lecher than as a leader), Janey comes to work for J. Ward Moorehouse. When Moorehouse's secretary is injured, Janey becomes his private secretary and goes off with him on his trip to Mexico.

When she returns to New York, infatuated with Moorehouse, who barely acknowledges her existence, Janey aspires to a better set of friends. When Joe comes home (he has deserted from the Navy, joined the merchant marine, and been torpedoed twice), Janey is too embarrassed to invite him to her apartment lest her friends see her sailor brother. But the next evening she goes with Joe to a restaurant and listens disapprovingly to his vitriolic attack upon the war as fraudulent and crooked. Janey shares Moorehouse's patriotism.

G. H. Barrow, who has been dating Janey during this time, proposes marriage to her. Janey considers him briefly—especially after finding him listed in *Who's Who*—but decides she cannot love him and refuses. The wisdom of her decision is confirmed when Moorehouse (strictly for business reasons) makes her a member of his new corporation. Her affection for him doubles because of this action and because she knows that his wife has started divorce proceedings over an alleged affair with Eleanor Stoddard.

J. Ward Moorehouse

Ward Moorehouse was the eldest and brightest of six children. As school marble champion he rented marbles to his peers. Winner of a college scholarship, Ward leaves college after a year when his father, drunk, suffers an injury that prevents his working. Determined to rise in the world, Ward gets a job with a real estate firm and impresses his employers with his energy and insight. In Maryland, where he has been sent to report on some company holdings, he meets and falls in love with wealthy Annabelle Strang. Not long after their honeymoon abroad, Ward discovers Annabelle with another man and leaves her.

In Pittsburgh, Ward works briefly as a reporter, then gets a job as a publicist for a steel company. He rises swiftly in the esteem of his employers, and again a lucky match—at least financially—helps him on his way up. This time he marries Gertrude Staple, a millionaire's daughter. Now thirty-two and wealthy, he returns from Europe and his second honeymoon, ready to move to New York to set up his own firm. With G. H. Barrow, he devises a plan for labor-capital rapport during the war, a plan that has nothing to do with principle but much with profits.

Eleanor Stoddard

From childhood on, Eleanor Stoddard has hated the smell and sight of blood. Nightly her father brought home with him the stench of the Chicago stockyards. What Eleanor loved was the exquisite purity of pre-Raphaelite art and the idealism of the poets her high-school English teacher introduced her to. Mobs and sex also frightened and sickened Eleanor. After her mother died, Eleanor found peace working in a lace shop, and beauty in her courses at the Art Institute.

A friendship with cultured Eveline Hutchins leads to their establishing an interior-decorating shop in New York where they barely cover expenses. When a Shubert play for which they designed the costumes fails, Eveline returns to Chicago, but Eleanor rents an apartment in Greenwich Village. Her opportunity comes when Ward Moorehouse commissions her to decorate his summer home on Long Island.

Eleanor and Ward become close friends, though she is shocked to learn that his wife suspects an affair. One afternoon Eleanor decides to confront Mrs. Moorehouse and tell her how purely platonic the friendship is. But before she can, she learns that the United States has entered the war. Ward tells her that he has offered his services free to the Government. Eleanor, after confronting Mrs. Moorehouse, says that she will join the Red Cross to serve in France.

Charley Anderson

When Charley Anderson is growing up in Fargo, North Dakota, his mother, owner of a railroad boarding house, takes note of him only on Sundays when she marches him diligently to church. But Charley's interests are mechanical, not theological. From his earliest years he tinkers with machinery. At fourteen he works in a garage, and at seventeen he is busy in an amusement park repairing the roller coaster.

For a passing moment a girl almost snarls Charley's career. Having teased Charley, she sleeps with his friend, becomes pregnant, and traps Charley into a promise of marriage. At the last possible moment, Charley escapes.

On the road toward New York, Charley absorbs much socialist indoctrination and almost as much sexual experience. Just before he leaves the Mardi Gras in New Orleans, he meets Doc Rogers, a Floridian on his way to enlist in a volunteer ambulance corps. Doc has no patriotic motives but wouldn't dream of missing a big war. Charley has no feeling about the war, but after a few days in New York, where he listens dispassionately to violent pro- and anti-war arguments in bars and on street corners, he decides to join Doc. As the novel closes, Charley stands at the bow of a liner bound for France.

The Camera Eye

In Holland during the Boer War, the "narrator," aged four, walks carefully to avoid hurting the tender grass blades. All about him an angry Dutch mob stones a mother and child suspected of being English. Thus the conflict between poetic sensibility and harsh reality enters Dos Passos' consciousness in childhood, never to end, never to be resolved. He hears among his countrymen clichés about racial equality but sees actions that rob the clichés of meaning. Negroes, Mexicans, Poles, Bohemians—all are treated as inferior; only the English and the Americans are thought to be truly civilized.

School, church, and home fashion him according to the dictates of the upper class. But his private dreams deny his caste, and his personal experiences disprove the stereotypes. The brutality of a streetcar strike, the poverty of a Southern farm during a drought, contrast sharply with the portrait of America others have drawn for him. At Harvard he spends "four years under the ether cone," encouraged to be a good student but not too good, and to avoid being seen with Jews and socialists.

Just before the war, he attends a pro-Russian rally at Madison Square Garden and also hears Emma Goldman. At the end, like Charley Anderson, he stands aboard a troopship heading for France.

Critical Opinion

To comprehend the full impact of Dos Passos' study of despair, defeat, and disillusion, one must read all three volumes of the trilogy *USA*, of which *The 42nd Parallel* is the first volume. *1919* and *The Big Money* (published in 1932 and 1936) round out the portraits begun in the earliest novel and add several others. But even in the initial work, the sustaining purpose is clear, the pervasive technique manifest. All four narrative techniques merge to shape a nightmare vision of human exploitation.

Dos Passos' method, as critics have noted, enables him—except in *The Camera Eye*—to stand apart and record events dispassionately. The testimony of history thus indicts the capitalistic system without reducing the novelist to the role of propagandist. Unhappily, the results do not entirely fulfill the promise of Dos Passos' purpose. Too often his carefully selected characters lack flesh to body forth their symbolic intent; they seem clinical specimens rather than full-blooded human beings. Similarly, in choosing subjects for his *Living Biographies,* Dos Passos has ignored many who have survived or prevailed in our society without selling out or being sold out.

Before the trilogy ends, the reader becomes aware that Dos Passos has not intended to indict only capitalism. Acts of betrayal and distortion indict Communism as well. What Dos Passos seems to argue for most passionately is the dignity of man and his right to freedom from the encroachments of any ideology that diminishes him. Precisely how to achieve his goal Dos Passos fails to make clear, but his nobility of motive and dramatic force move the reader.

The Author

Of Portuguese ancestry and fairly wealthy parentage, *John Roderigo Dos Passos* studied abroad and at Harvard. In 1916 he went to Spain to continue his studies in architecture, but a year later, like many other American writers—Hemingway and e. e. cummings, for example—he volunteered in World War I as an ambulance corpsman. Out of his war experiences grew his first novels, *One Man's Initiation—1917* (1920) and *Three Soldiers* (1921).

In New York after the war, Dos Passos published several volumes of poetry, produced some plays, and was one of the founders of the Marxist periodical *New Masses.* His novel *Manhattan Transfer* (1925), written during this period, was his first attempt to master the technical form he perfected in *The 42nd Parallel.* Later in the twenties, Dos Passos worked actively in behalf of Sacco and Vanzetti—writing, picketing, and even going to jail.

Throughout the 1930s, his most creative years, Dos Passos dedicated himself to such causes as miners' strikes, the defense of political prisoners, and support of the Spanish Loyalists. In the 1940s, Dos Passos increasingly wrote historical tracts as well as novels, again arguing the case for the rebel, the outsider. Today the onetime radical of the left has swung so far to the other side (a supporter of Taft and later of Goldwater) that many of his former admirers find his position intolerable. Whatever Dos Passos' political views, they continue in one way or another to reflect his original dedication to protest against whatever threatens to silence the affirmation of the individual voice.

The Good Earth

by

PEARL BUCK (1892–)

Main Characters

Wang Lung—A poor Chinese farmer, devoted to his land above all else.

O-lan—His wife, a faithful, self-sacrificing, and seldom-appreciated helpmate.

The Sons—Nameless in the novel, they are nevertheless sharply distinguished. The *eldest* is an unfulfilled scholar whose overriding ambition is to establish a great house. The *second* is a shrewd merchant whose main concern is profit. The *third* is a passionate young man whom his father intends to be his successor to the land but who wants to be a soldier.

Lotus Blossom—Wang Lung's concubine, pretty and ineffectual, with whom he is for a time infatuated.

Wang Lung's Father—An old man who once toiled unremittingly on the land and now sleeps peacefully in the sun.

Wang Lung's Uncle—A lazy good-for-nothing member of a robber band, whom Wang Lung supports partly out of respect but mostly out of fear.

Wang Lung's Cousin—The son of his uncle, an insolent and immoral young man who plagues Wang Lung and his eldest son.

Pear Blossom—The lovely, timid young slave who is Wang
  Lung's last love.
Cuckoo—Once the concubine of the master of the House of
  Hwang, finally the paid companion of Lotus Blossom.

The Story

Wang Lung, a poor Chinese farmer living in a house made
of earthen bricks, has for the past six years since his mother
died cared for his old father, rising early in the morning to
light the fire and boil hot water for him to drink and, after
laboring in the fields all day, preparing his simple evening
meal. Now Wang Lung's domestic labors, at least, will be
eased, for he has persuaded his father to choose a wife for him.
She is to be a slave from the House of Hwang, not too young
and not too pretty (for a pretty one would be no virgin, since
the Hwang men had their will with female slaves).

After washing his whole body, Wang Lung sets out to fetch
his bride. He is overwhelmed by the great family—even by
the gatekeeper. The old mistress of the house, smoking her
opium pipe, receives the awed farmer and allows him to take
her slave, but orders him to return when their first child is
born. Wang Lung and his bride stop at the temple to light
sticks to the god of the fields and his lady. It is their only
marriage ceremony.

The woman, O-lan, is not beautiful. She has square cheeks,
a strong, graceless body, and large feet (they have not been
bound)—but she is hard-working and good-tempered. Not
only does she perform all her domestic tasks expertly and serve
Wang Lung and his father devotedly, but she helps him in the
fields each day. Before long a son is born to O-lan. She will
accept no aid during the birth. The next day she waits upon
the men, and soon after she works in the fields again. On the
second day of the New Year, the three, dressed in new clothes,
go to the House of Hwang to pay their respects.

Wang Lung, who has had a good harvest, learns during their
visit that the great house feels pinched and is willing to sell
land. Eagerly he buys. The buying is a symbol of his lust for
land. The next year O-lan bears a second child. Again the
harvests are good, but this time Wang Lung does not buy

more land because his rascally uncle borrows money from him, ostensibly for a dowry for his daughter, actually as a gambling stake.

Wang Lung's fortunes decline. A third child arrives, a girl this time and a simple-minded one, as the years prove. The earth is parched, the crops scanty. Wang Lung nevertheless buys another, larger field from the House of Hwang. Famine comes to the province. The family eats its ox and then nearly starves. Another baby girl is born, but O-lan chokes the meager life from it. Desperate as he is, Wang Lung will not sell any of his land to the shrewd, grasping men who offer only a fraction of its value. But he does sell them his few furnishings for two pieces of silver.

Finally Wang Lung and his family decide to go south where they hope somehow to find food. They join a multitude of others on the same quest. In a large city in the south they build themselves a fragile house of reed mats and go to the public kitchen for rice. O-lan and the children beg each day, and Wang Lung pulls a rickshaw. Still, they have scarcely enough for rice, and Wang Lung is in danger of being seized for the Army, for there is a war going on. Finally, as the enemy approaches, people flee from the city. There is no work to be found nor anyone to beg from. Wang Lung wants to return to his good land, but O-lan asks him to wait a little longer.

When the enemy enters the city, the poor of the slums break the gates of rich men's houses. Carried along by O-lan's directions and by the surging mob, Wang Lung enters one such house and encounters a terror-stricken fat man who has lingered and who offers him money to spare his life. Thinking of his land, Wang Lung grabs the money, gathers his family, and hurriedly goes back to his land.

Wang Lung finds his old house looted, but with the silver he has acquired, he purchases everything he needs. He discovers, too, that O-lan has been even more successful than he at the rich man's house. She has found a collection of precious jewels. Wang Lung allows O-lan to keep two pearls, and with the rest of the treasure he makes his way to the House of Hwang, deserted now save for the old master and his shrewd concubine, Cuckoo. Without difficulty Wang Lung buys the land belonging to the great house. After that he prospers. He hires men to work in his fields, employs the honest farmer

Ching to be his overseer, and builds additions to his earthen dwelling. His two sons he sends to school so that they will not be unlettered like himself.

Seven years later the river bursts its bounds and floods Wang Lung's lands. Though he does not worry, he grows restless, finds fault with his sons, and sees all at once that O-lan is no longer beautiful. He begins to frequent the new tea house and looks longingly at the pictures of beautiful women hanging on the walls. Cuckoo, who works for the tea house now that her old lord is gone, tells him they are portraits of women in the rooms who may be had for silver. He buys the favors of the beautiful Lotus Blossom. Soon he finds that he cannot live without her.

Meanwhile, his uncle, aunt, and their son have moved into his house, much to his disgust. But now he finds a use for his aunt. She bargains with Cuckoo. For a large sum Lotus Blossom, attended by Cuckoo, comes to live with Wang Lung. He sets her up in a special court, for O-lan, from whom he has heartlessly taken the two pearls to give to Lotus Blossom, will not recognize her presence or her companion's.

Now that Lotus Blossom is easily accessible, Wang Lung's infatuation cools. Peace, however, does not settle on his house. His eldest son demands a woman, and Wang Lung arranges a marriage for him with a grain dealer's daughter. The marriage is to take place in three years. The young man is restless and sullen. One day Wang Lung catches him in Lotus Blossom's court, talking and laughing. Furious, Wang Lung whips both, then sends his son off to the South. To prevent difficulties with the second son, he apprentices him to the grain merchant.

For a long time O-lan has been ailing. Her health worsens. Wang Lung goes for the doctor who pronounces her condition hopeless. Though he has no love for her any more, Wang Lung is deeply unhappy at O-lan's illness and feels guilty about the way he has treated her. He buys two coffins, one for her and one for his now ancient father. But O-lan refuses to die until her eldest son is married. The latter is recalled, an elegant marriage takes place, and that night O-lan dies. Wang Lung's father dies soon after.

Wang Lung's uncle and his uncle's son behave grossly, but Wang Lung dares not oust them, for he has learned that his uncle is second in command of a robber band that has been terrorizing the village but so far has never harmed Wang Lung's house. At the suggestion of his eldest son who is angry with his cousin because the latter has been ogling his wife, Wang Lung buys opium for them. Before long they are addicts, too engrossed in dreams to threaten his peace again. Next, at his eldest son's urging, he once more rents the inner courts of the House of Hwang and furnishes them expensively. His second son marries a good and careful village maid, as he had desired. A sumptuous wedding is held in the new residence. His eldest son's wife and then his second son's wife bear him grandchildren. Wang Lung seems ready to pass into a contented old age, especially when his uncle's son joins the Army.

But the sons and the sons' wives bicker continuously. His youngest son, who, Wang Lung has hoped, will take his place and care for the family's lands, resents his fate bitterly. When Wang Lung, his desires returning for a season, takes Pear Blossom, a lovely young slave, as his concubine, the youngest son, who had longed for her, runs off to join the Army. Finally the vicious cousin returns with a troop of soldiers and arrogantly quarters himself in Wang Lung's courts for a month and a half. Only the old man's simpleton daughter and Pear Blossom offer him comfort. His sons have deeply disappointed him.

One day Wang Lung walks over his land accompanied by his sons. He overhears them speaking softly of the fields they will sell after he is gone. Trembling, he protests that the land is their source of unity and stability. They comfort their father, assuring him they will not sell the land—but over his head they smile at each other.

Critical Opinion

The Good Earth is the first of a trilogy, *House of Earth*. The second novel, *Sons* (1932), traces the destinies of Wang Lung's three sons, an idle man of wealth, a merchant, and a war lord. The third, *A House Divided* (1935), carries the story forward to the decline of the family in revolutionary China. The trilogy, a historian of the American novel observes, "is more epic than dramatic in its development." Nevertheless, there are dramatic episodes—war, famine, pestilence—all intensely projected through the experience of the characters. They live, they suffer, they love, they sometimes are briefly visited by happiness, they die; and then the cycle is continued through their descendants.

Clearly *The Good Earth* is the best novel of the three—so good, in fact, that it has been suggested that the others seem unfulfilled beside it. Some scholars have challenged the accuracy of Pearl Buck's description of Chinese life and customs. She has vigorously rebutted these objections. For the American reader the argument does not seem especially significant. As Oscar Cargill points out: "The great merit of *The Good Earth* . . . is the conviction it carries of verisimilitude to all the vicissitudes of Chinese life—nothing changes or passes which does not seem probable."

The Biblical simplicity of Pearl Buck's language, her gift for making the strange and distant appear familiar, her feeling for the fundamental truths of life—these have established *The Good Earth* as a contemporary classic. Though she has sunk in critical esteem—the two largest histories of American literature give her no more than a few sentences of consideration— Pearl Buck is still an enormously popular author, both in America and abroad. "*The Good Earth* was almost the first book to unlock for the West the interior of China. . . ." It remains one of the very best.

The Author

Pearl Buck, born in Hillsboro, West Virginia, was brought up in China. (She would have been born there if her missionary parents had not come home on furlough.) Both father and mother—about whom she has written two "passionate but critical biographies," *The Exile* (1936) and *Fighting Angel* (1936)—belonged to liberal, distinguished families. "From my ancestors," she writes, "I have the tradition of racial equality."

Living in the far interior of China, Pearl Buck learned Chinese before she learned English. She delighted in the marvelous Buddhist and Taoist stories she heard as a child from her Chinese nurse. Indeed, she came to think of herself as Chinese.

When she was seventeen, she was taken to England and then America where she entered Randolph-Macon College. Earlier, save during her stay at a boarding school in Shanghai, her mother was her chief teacher. Apparently she was an excellent one, too, for Pearl Buck gives her mother high praise, particularly for teaching her "the beauty that lies in words and in what words will say." Pearl Buck did extraordinarily well at college, becoming president of her class and in her senior year winning two literary prizes.

Returning to China after graduation, she married Dr. John Lossing Buck, whom she describes as a "soil missionary." For five years they lived in a town in North China, then came to Nanking. There, from 1921–31, she taught English at the University of Nanking, at Southeastern University, and at Chung Yang University; and there she gave birth to two daughters. In 1934 she came back to New York alone and joined the editorial staff of John Day, the publishing company. The next year, after obtaining a divorce, she married Richard J. Walsh, president of the publishing company.

Pearl Buck began to write as a girl in China. She published articles and stories, and her first book, *East Wind, West Wind* (1930), achieved critical recognition. Not till 1932, however, when *The Good Earth* appeared and won for her the Pulitzer Prize, did she become a significant figure in American letters. Since then she has written many novels (the best of them with Chinese settings), plays, essays, and biographies, and translated the Chinese classic *All Men Are Brothers* (1933). She was awarded the William Dean Howells medal by the American Academy of Arts and Letters in 1935, and in 1938 she became the first American woman and the third American to win the Nobel Prize for literature. Over 70 now, she still writes with distinction on such varied subjects as racial unity, retarded children, and of course, China.

Mutiny on the Bounty

by

JAMES NORMAN HALL (1887–1951)

and

CHARLES NORDHOFF (1887–1947)

Main Characters

Roger Byam—A young man of seventeen when he first sails from England, he already shows the integrity, courage, and firmness that mark his whole career. As an old man, retired from the British Navy, he narrates the *Bounty* story.

Mrs. Byam—Roger's mother.

William Bligh—A superb mariner, resolute and forceful, but as captain of the *Bounty*, petty, harsh, and tyrannical.

Fletcher Christian—Master's mate, brave and generous, whose fatal flaw is excessive pride coupled with a capacity for fierce resentment.

John Fryer—Master, an honest, fair, capable officer.

Robert Tinkler—Midshipman, carefree, good-humored, and good-hearted.

Thomas Hayward—Midshipman, vengeful and untrustworthy, a bully and a coward.

John Hallet—Midshipman, like Hayward, less than brave and less than truthful.

Thomas Huggan—Surgeon. Whiskey is his sovereign cure for all troubles, his own as well as other people's.

David Nelson—Botanist, a quiet, dedicated scientist.

James Morrison—Boatswain's mate, a sound-hearted, wholly honest, steadfast man, Byam's good friend.

Sir Joseph Banks—President of the Royal Society, a good man, a devoted worker for science and a staunch friend to Byam.

Tehani—Byam's wife (through a Polynesian ceremony), a lovely, sweet-tempered, charming, faithful young woman.

Hitihiti—The noble Tahitian chief who becomes Byam's loyal friend.

The Story

In 1787 Lieutenant Bligh visits Mrs. Byam and her seventeen-year-old son, Roger. Bligh has come at the suggestion of Sir Joseph Banks, President of the Royal Society, friend of the late Mr. Byam, an astronomer who has done important navigational research. Bligh has just been given command of the *Bounty* and is scheduled to sail to Tahiti to procure breadfruit trees which West Indian planters hope will prove a cheap and wholesome food for their Negro slaves. Bligh invites young Byam to join his crew. Since the boy has a gift for languages—a gift that Sir Joseph thinks will enable Byam to compile a dictionary and grammar of the Tahitian language—he gladly accepts.

The *Bounty* sails. It will be four and one-half turbulent years before she returns to England. The voyage out is fairly uneventful, marked chiefly by Bligh's at-times insane ferocity. For the slightest infractions or insubordinations, he orders men flogged. He is insufferably rude to his officers, insulting and upbraiding them before the crew. Petty, avaricious, unaffected by the needs of others, he doles out short rations to the crew and pockets his small gains.

Gradually Byam learns his duties and gets to know the crew. The master's mate, Fletcher Christian, a stalwart young man of twenty-four, is bold, fair, resolute but excessively proud, fiercely resenting the wrongs inflicted by the captain. The master, John Fryer, is a bluff, steady, capable officer. The surgeon, Thomas Huggan (nicknamed "Old Bacchus"), prescribes brandy for everyone and especially for himself. Of Byam's fellow midshipmen, two prove ultimately to be enemies —Thomas Hayward and John Hallet, a cowardly pair. The

others turn out to be his firm friends, particularly the carefree
and brash Robert Tinkler and the solid and generous George
Stewart. Three others are on his side: James Morrison,
boatswain's mate, a steady and cool but deep-feeling Scotsman;
William Muspratt, a loyal and conscientious able seaman; and
Thomas Ellison, a foolish, brash, light-hearted boy.

When Tahiti is sighted, Byam is struck by the loveliness of
the island and its inhabitants. He goes ashore to begin learning
and recording their language, a task for which he will have
several months, since it will take that long for the botanist to
collect young breadfruit plants. Almost immediately he finds
his island *taio*, or intimate friend, an important chief, Hitihiti,
a middle-aged man of superb bearing. With him and his large
family, Byam spends an idyllic season and learns to love the
land and its people, while working steadily and productively
at his language lessons. Unlike Christian and some others,
he does not choose a sweetheart.

The voyage homeward begins unhappily and grows tragic.
Bligh has regularly annexed the gifts that the Tahitians have
offered to the crew—pearls as well as pigs, cloth, fruit. Christian has bitterly resented this highhanded action. A day out
from the island, Bligh falsely accuses Christian of stealing
some coconuts, cursing him in front of crew members.

That night at watch, Christian asks Byam to notify his people in Cumberland if anything happens to him. As Byam says,
"You can count on me" and shakes hands, Bligh appears on
deck. He exchanges some words with the two officers, then
retreats. Midshipman Tinkler, lying in the shadow of the guns,
has witnessed the brief, apparently innocuous episode.

Before daybreak Byam is awakened by two of the crew—
one bearing a pistol, the other a musket with fixed bayonet.
The explanation soon becomes terribly clear: a mutiny has
broken out, led by Christian. Four officers and twelve seamen
have seized all weapons, tied Bligh up, and disarmed the
twenty-eight loyal members of the crew (of a ship's company
numbering forty-four). Bligh cajoles, snarls, promises. To no
avail. Christian is adamant. "I have been in hell for weeks
past," he declares.

At first a rotten cutter is allotted to Bligh, but at Byam's
intercession, a small launch is substituted. Bligh and eighteen
of his loyal men board it. There is less than eight inches of

freeboard amidships. Byam, Stewart, Morrison, and seven others who have been delayed want to enter the launch, but it will hold no more. Cursing bitterly, Bligh and his men sail away.*

The mutineers with the nine loyal men who remain aboard turn back. Christian regrets his action, but is determined to do what he can for his co-conspirators. After voyaging among the islands, he attempts a settlement on one, but the Indians are hostile. He sails to Tahiti again, and several weeks later allows Byam, Stewart, Morrison, and more than a dozen others to stay on Tahiti—though he realizes that he endangers himself and his followers by the act, since the Navy search for the *Bounty* will surely begin at Tahiti. Eight Englishmen remain aboard ship with him, plus eighteen Polynesians, twelve men, and six women (among the latter his sweetheart). Together they will seek an uninhabited island in the South Seas.† Before he leaves, he again asks Byam to tell his people the story as Byam knows it. Christian assures him that the mutiny was not planned, that ten minutes before Bligh was seized, Christian's only intention was to cast himself on a raft he was having built, hoping it would take him to a nearby island.

On Tahiti, Byam and his companions soon adapt themselves to the tranquil ways of the islanders. Byam falls in love with Tehani, niece of an important chief, and fathers a girl. He continues working devotedly on his Tahitian dictionary, but the days slip by imperceptibly in a land where it is always summer. In March, 1791 a British frigate, the *Pandora*, anchors off Tahiti. As duty commands, Byam paddles out to her, identifies himself, and is promptly clapped into chains by the captain, Edward Edwards. So, too, are thirteen others of the crew—some of them, ironically, seized while attempting to return to England on a craft they had painstakingly constructed.

During the return trip they suffer a variety of hardships, not least among them the severities of the captain and the sadism of one of the officers. Only the ship's surgeon is Byam's friend, informing him of the charges against him. Bligh, on the night of the mutiny, heard his innocent words to Christian—"You

---

* After fantastic hardships, they manage to reach England. The details of the amazing journey are recorded in the authors' *Men Against the Sea,* the second narrative of *The Bounty Trilogy.*

† *Pitcairn's Island,* the concluding narrative of the trilogy, tells the fascinating history of their quest and settlement.

can count on me"—and afterward wrongly deduced Byam's complicity. Since everyone who can give decisive testimony to his innocence is with Christian, Byam is in an exceedingly dangerous position.

Fifteen months after they are placed in irons—four and one-half years after their initial departure—Byam and his crewmates return to England. Though Byam has devoted and influential friends—Sir Joseph Banks, especially—the court, composed of eleven sea captains and presided over by a vice-admiral, is clearly unsympathetic. The malicious testimony of Hallet and Hayward, midshipmen on the *Bounty*, seems final, since none of the crew who sailed from the *Bounty* with Bligh can prove Byam's innocence, though most are morally certain of it. Midshipman Tinkler, who overheard Byam's conversation with Christian, is the desperately needed witness, but he has been reported lost at sea.

The court finds not only the mutineers guilty but also Muspratt, Morrison, and Byam. All are sentenced to be hanged. The first two, after enduring agonies of suspense, are granted unconditional pardons at the recommendation of the court, apparently activated by more than a suspicion of doubt concerning their guilt. Byam's case, though, appears hopeless, and he resigns himself to his fate. But his fortunes take a spectacular turn. Tinkler has been rescued at sea, has landed in England, and has been seized by Sir Joseph who immediately carries him to the admiral. Examined by the Admiralty Commission, he easily persuades them of Byam's innocence. They reverse the decision of the court-martial. Byam is free.

Byam intends to return to Tahiti, but is induced to continue his naval career so that he may remove any trace of dishonor clinging to his name. He serves gallantly during England's wars with the allied nations of Europe, attaining captain's rank. Not till sixteen years later, in 1809, does he have the opportunity to sail to Tahiti. En route he touches Port Jackson in New South Wales, there briefly glimpsing Bligh again. Bligh's notable tactlessness has again bred insurrection. Appointed governor of New South Wales, he has alienated the settlers who have revolted and imprisoned him. He has been relieved of his post and is sailing for home, once more to figure in a dramatic trial.

In Tahiti, Byam discovers that his wife and nearly all his friends are long since dead, his daughter married. He sees her and her child without identifying himself. Sadly he returns to England, and as an old man writes his recollections of the mutiny.

Critical Opinion

Mutiny on the Bounty is a splendid novel of adventure on the high seas and on the islands of Polynesia. The narrative is compounded of shadow and light, of gallantry and romance, steadfast courage and cowering fear, nobility and villainy. It has impressed an image of the lovely islands of the South Seas on the American imagination, an image that seems likely to last for a long time to come. In the snarling Captain Bligh, the resolute mate Christian, the enchanting Tehani, the noble Hitihiti, the harsh Captain Edwards, the cheerful "Bacchus," Nordhoff and Hall have projected a gallery of memorable, vividly realized characters.

Mutiny on the Bounty is not only an exciting sea story. It is also a completely documented account of a real voyage. To discover the facts of the mutiny, the authors ransacked libraries, photostatted every page of the court-martial report, even prevailed upon the British Admiralty first to make copies of the deck and rigging plans of the *Bounty* and later to make a detailed model of the ship. Books, charts, maps, photographs were collected and painstakingly studied. Though *Mutiny on the Bounty* is fiction, it is fiction with the authority of comprehensive and precise scholarship behind it. While the authors invented episodes, conversations, and characters, they nevertheless produced a history that is truer than a flat, unadorned recital of facts could possibly be.

The Authors

James Norman Hall and *Charles Nordhoff* have become in the public mind a fused novelist whose specialty was romantic adventure. Hall, born in Colfax, Iowa, in 1887, attended public school in his home town and later Grinnell College.

thority on baseball. Curious about the activities of the gang, he remains aloof from their excesses and is often the butt of their games.

Davey Cohen—A Jewish member of the gang, tolerated in most activities, but ostracized from others.

Paulie Haggerty, Kenny Killarney, Red Kelly, Tommy Doyle —Members of the Prairie Avenue gang.

T.B. McCarthy, Three-Star-Hennessey, Johnny O'Brien, Jim Clayburn—Members of the Indiana Avenue gang, the latter two more or less outsiders because they go on to high school.

Lucy Scanlan—Studs' girl friend, a sweet, proud girl.

Helen Shires—The local tomboy and confidante of Studs.

Iris—A fourteen-year-old nymphomaniac.

The Story

The events of the novel take place within a six-month period beginning June, 1916, the day that Studs Lonigan graduates from St. Patrick's Grammar School in Chicago and Woodrow Wilson is nominated for a second-term as President. As the novel opens, Studs is in the bathroom secretly smoking, assuming various expressions of leering toughness as he studies himself in the mirror, and delighting in the prospect of being free of the intellectual, moral, and physical discipline imposed by the nuns and priests of St. Patrick's. Outside the bathroom door, his sister Frances loudly complains about Studs' keeping the bathroom to himself. While the argument goes on, Studs tries to clear the room of smoke.

Meanwhile Patrick Lonigan sits contentedly on the back porch smoking his cigar, glancing at the pages of the Chicago *Evening Journal* and sentimentally recalling his own childhood and his achievements since then. He alone of his family has had any real success. One of his brothers ran off to sea, another was killed in the Spanish-American War, a third married unhappily, and a fourth struggled along as a motorman. His sister became a prostitute. Mr. Lonigan and his wife feel proud of their accomplishments, confident that they have done right by their children.

During Father Gilhooley's delivery of the St. Patrick's

Grammar School commencement address, the bored graduates tickle one another, whisper obscenities, and indulge in
all sorts of horseplay. Studs feels a certain sentimental appeal in the proceedings, but sternly represses the emotion
as unworthy. After the ceremonies several of the children
come to the Lonigans' for a party. While the older Lonigans
and Reilleys sit in the living room discussing the marvels of
parochial education, the youngsters experiment with a variety
of kissing games, Studs and Lucy delicately and timidly,
Weary Reilley and Helen Borax passionately, almost brutally.
After the party Studs' parents discuss his prospects with him,
Mr. Lonigan wanting him to go on to high school and then
enter the painting trade, Mrs. Lonigan beseeching him to
think seriously about the priesthood. Studs listens to both
with feigned interest. His real aim is to become as tough
as Weary Reilley. In his bedroom later Studs and Frances,
roused by the light sexual play at the party, find occasion
to study one another surreptitiously, even to knock against
each other accidentally. Horrified and self-reproaching, Studs
leaves and kneels beside his bed praying that his soul may
be washed of sin.

A month later, having abandoned his lackadaisical efforts
to secure a job, Studs lies in bed late each morning shadow-
boxing and scowling for a while before the mirror, then wanders along the streets kicking cans and batting stones. He
wonders about the "goofy" middle-aged music teacher, Leon,
who strokes his arm and urges him to visit and begin to learn
about the more beautiful things in life. Disgusted by Leon,
Studs feels comfortable with tomboy Helen Shires. Helen
tells him about Weary's attempts to make sexual advances
to her and how she has put him off. While Helen and Studs
dribble a basketball (at which she is far better than he),
Weary comes along to join them. Even less skilled with the
basketball than Studs, Weary irritatedly smashes his shoulder
into Helen's breast. Hurt and angry, she hits Weary in the
mouth with the ball and he rushes toward her furiously.
When Studs interferes, Weary curses them both and a fight
ensues between Studs and Weary. Helen—as well as Danny
O'Neill and Lucy Scanlan, who happen by—cheers Studs
on during the long and brutal fracas. A host of spectators,
young and old, gathers to watch the smaller Studs give

Weary a thorough beating. When the fight is at last stopped by Diamond-Tooth, a detective, Studs emerges as the "champ fighter of the block." His reward at Helen Shires' party is a shower of kisses from Lucy Scanlan.

As the pride of Indiana Avenue, Studs occupies a niche he has aspired to, and he enjoys its minor rewards of respect and admiration. He still finds little that holds his interest for any length of time. He presses the less combative into wrestling and boxing matches with each other and, when he cannot match their skills in another sport, makes them box with him so that he can prove his superiority. Thus when Danny O'Neill repeatedly beats him at stoop ball, he decides to teach Danny how to box. Although he batters and humiliates the younger boy, he cannot reduce him to tears and concludes merely that Danny, like so many others, is "goofy." At home Studs resents his father's increasing insistence that he find a job, come home earlier, and occupy himself more usefully. When his father gives him a baseball novel to "improve his mind," Studs dutifully reads for ten minutes, then leaves to rejoin his friends at the playground.

A day in early July brings complete happiness to Studs. On that day he and Lucy Scanlan walk hand in hand through the park, climb a tree together, and sit there sharing an idyllic dream of love. Though they kiss, Studs represses the passion that surges through him. He thinks of how he would like most to win her as his pure love, yet he cannot bring himself to speak about his feelings. When at last they return home, Studs is in a joyous daze, but tells himself that he is a "Goddamn goof." The lyric episode is short-lived, for the next day Studs finds chalk signs everywhere announcing that Studs and Lucy love each other. When Danny O'Neill laughs at Studs' discomfiture, Studs beats him. At home he lashes back at the family's teasing, and when Helen Borax, Lucy's girl friend, twits him, he insults her obscenely. When Lucy learns how he has treated Helen, she snubs him in the street.

By the end of July, the promise of a happy summer has faded. Studs is conscious only that he wants something, but he cannot articulate what it is. Though he now knows that he loves Lucy, he has not seen her; and as a hard-boiled youth, he refuses to seek her out. Drifting from his haunts on

Indiana Avenue, he seeks adventure on Prairie Avenue. By fighting and beating Red Kelly, the champion of that block, he gains acceptance. But with his new friends, Davey Cohen and Paulie Haggerty, the games are essentially the same, though they promise a deeper plunge into degradation. After Studs twists the arm of a youngster who will not obey him, Studs feels a certain renewal of assurance. As he gains mastery of the skill of spitting tobacco juice from either side of his mouth, he senses that passers-by will recognize that he is a young man to be reckoned with. Unfortunately, Lucy Scanlan happens by and rebukes him for being a show-off.

In addition to their usual escapades of hitching rides and stealing candy and fruit, Studs' new friends prove even more effective than his former cronies in baiting Jews and Negroes, shaking them down for money, and beating them. In such activities, the young men have the tacit approval of their parents who daily complain about how the neighborhood has run down since these minority groups have moved in. At Bathcellar's Billiard Parlor and Barber Shop, Studs hears from the older men lewd talk about sexual exploits and yearns for his sexual initiation. When he sees Weary Reilley (who has left his parents' home and now carries a rusty, empty .22-caliber pistol) go off with Iris, Studs grows jealous and even more eager.

A few days later, Studs' desires are satisfied when Iris entertains all of the boys at a "gang shag," all, that is, except Davey Cohen, whom she rejects because he is a Jew. Bitter and frustrated, Davey avenges himself on a hostile world by beating up both an Irish and a Jewish boy, each considerably younger than himself. After the session with Iris, the boys stand at the corner and rehearse their deeds. But as Lucy Scanlan passes by, Studs experiences a deep sense of guilt and contemplates with terror the possibilities of death and hell.

The last section of the novel opens in November as Weary, Studs, and Paulie—all playing hookey from high school—wander along the streets seeking some kind of interesting activity. Paulie has contracted a venereal disease, Davey Cohen has left Chicago hoping to find a world that will accept him, and Iris has been sent off to boarding school after Weary Reilley's mother has caught the two of them in sexual activity. At home Studs listens with ill-disguised resentment to his father's nagging insistence about a job, his mother's importuning him about the priesthood. Mr. Lonigan, however, confides to his wife that the children are coming along wonderfully well and that, as successful parents, they can indulge themselves more frequently in vacations. Alone at the window, Studs stares out upon the cold streets and "felt like he was a sad song."

Critical Opinion

Studs Lonigan is not, as James Farrell has pointed out, a tough or a gangster. Nor is he the product of the slums. In the first novel of the trilogy, at least, Studs displays many of the qualities of an average American boy—dreams of grandeur, a rebellious spirit, an essential decency. And his family, with its faith in church and home, work and duty, represents a characteristically American approach to life. Moreover, the Lonigans have the economic means and security to translate that approach into reality. What, then, goes wrong?

According to Farrell, Studs' downfall is caused by "spiritual poverty," the failure of church, family, school, and community to provide a significant direction for the boy and for his friends. Platitudes have taken the place of purpose, allowing social and moral decay to seep into and rot the vital substance of youth. Studs is not a villain, then, but a victim of the world he inhabits, and his story, Farrell has asserted, is "the story of an American destiny in our time."

Young Lonigan, like the other books in the trilogy, is compelling and affecting. It records disillusion, degeneration, and despair with an almost photographic accuracy and with meticulous attention to fine detail. Farrell has sought to emulate the compass of Balzac and the scientific detachment of Zola, the thundering power of Dreiser and the stylistic elegance of Joyce. Unfortunately, he achieves less than he aspires to. Farrell's prose style is almost featureless, his accumulation of details often repetitious to the point of ennui, and his sense of life's ceaseless boredom nearly suffocating. The naturalistic novel—of which Farrell has been the outstanding writer since Dreiser—often falls prey to these faults, and Farrell's novel sometimes reads more like a case history than a novel. Nevertheless, *Young Lonigan* and the two novels that follow it belong to the great tradition of American naturalistic writing, a tradition that sharply contrasts romantic dream and hideous reality.

The Author

Like Studs Lonigan, *James T. Farrell* was born, attended parochial school, and grew up on Chicago's South Side. But Farrell's career more closely resembles that of Danny O'Neill, about whom he has written several novels: *A World I Never Made* (1936), *No Star Is Lost* (1938), *Father and Son* (1940), *My Days of Anger* (1943), and *The Face of Time* (1953). After a successful career as an all-round boy athlete, Farrell attended the University of Chicago for three years without taking a degree. There, he studied writing and in one course wrote a short story called "Studs," published in *This Quarter*. Encouraged by two of his professors to expand the story, Farrell worked at it for the next three years while holding a variety of jobs that provided material for his expanding manuscript. "I worked on with this project," Farrell has written, "setting up as an ideal the strictest possible objectivity." What began as a short story in 1929 became at last a thousand-page trilogy completed in 1935, the three novels—*Young Lonigan* (1932), *The Young Manhood of Studs Lonigan* (1934), and *Judgment Day* (1935)—providing a panoramic study of Chicago life and a close analysis of the forces that destroy Studs by the time he is twenty-nine.

The trilogy won Farrell a considerable reputation. But despite the success of some of the Danny O'Neill novels, little of Farrell's prolific output since that time has added to his stature as a novelist. He has now written eighteen novels and several volumes of short stories and literary criticism. He has frequently expounded Marxist political as well as esthetic points of view.

tempted to tell "the truth about a certain group in American life." And the *Atlanta Journal* added that Caldwell's are passionately sincere novels whose "appeal is to humanity, to fairness and decency."

Other charges are not so easily countered. Critics agree that the characters of *God's Little Acre* are for the most part too broadly presented, often turning into comic grotesques. The situations are occasionally preposterous (for example, Jim Leslie's terminal visit to Ty Ty's household for the unconcealed purpose of ravishing Griselda). The climax of the novel (Will's heroic return to the mill and his murder by the mercenaries who have preceded him there), while melodramatically effective, is hardly convincing.

Obviously, *God's Little Acre* is an imperfect work. But so are a number of other significant American novels—*Uncle Tom's Cabin, The Grapes of Wrath, The 42nd Parallel,* to name only three. And like them, *God's Little Acre* describes in a new way, authentically and compassionately, a submerged part of America and the people who inhabit it. At first these people may arouse our laughter. But as one Southern critic observes, it is laughter that dissolves into pity even if the pity is mixed with revulsion.

Caldwell's dialogue is masterly—vivid, real, and racy. His plot, though marred by sensationalism and slapstick in particular episodes, is expertly and suspensefully contrived. And at least one character, Pluto Swint, promises to become a permanent part of the gallery of great fictional grotesques.

The Author

Few writers have had greater variety of experience than *Erskine Preston Caldwell.* Though born in Georgia, he claims the "entire South, from Virginia to Florida, from the Atlantic to the Mississippi," as his home. It was the duty of his father, a Presbyterian minister, secretary to his denomination, to live in each parish for a few months. Consequently Caldwell, until he was twenty, "rarely lived longer than six months in the same place." He attended primary school in Virginia, grammar school in Tennessee, and secondary school in Georgia—each for one year. The three years constituted his total early schooling, his mother supplying all his other formal education. In spite of his sporadic school attendance, Caldwell was admitted to Erskine College in South Carolina, the University of Virginia, and the University of Pennsylvania, but stayed in none for very long.

Caldwell has been by turns a poolroom attendant, a gun runner, a hack driver, a stagehand, a sodajerk, a cook, a waiter, a bodyguard, a lecture-tour manager, a variety-store clerk, a professional football player, a newspaperman, a script writer, an editor, and a war correspondent. He has frequently traveled across the United States, and has visited every country in South America and Europe at least once. He has been married four times.

Punctuating Caldwell's multitudinous activities are about forty published books, which have sold more than 25 million copies. He began to write seriously in 1928, when he abandoned newspaper work and settled in Maine. After five years the story, "Country Full of Swedes," which had made the rounds of the magazines, won the *Yale Review's* $1,000 Award for Fiction. From then on, Caldwell's graphic studies of the disinherited in America, the poor whites and Negroes of the South, especially, have made him one of America's best-selling authors. *Tobacco Road* (1932) was an enormously successful novel, and its dramatization established a new Broadway record for number of continuous performances. *God's Little Acre* (1933) sold even more widely. *Trouble in July* (1940), *Georgia Boy* (1943), and *Tragic Ground* (1944) have also enjoyed great popularity.

Appointment in Samarra

by

JOHN O'HARA (1905–)

Main Characters

Julian English—President of a Cadillac agency, aged thirty, handsome, charming, sensual, and compulsively driven to destroy everything he cherishes.

Caroline English—Julian's wife, a year older than he, pretty, sensitive, and deeply in love with her husband—less with the present reality than with the memory of their past and the improbable hope for their future.

Lute Fliegler—A salesman at Julian's agency, lower middle class in taste and manner, but endowed with candor, courage, and compassion.

Irma Fliegler—Lute's wife, mother of three, simple, unsophisticated, and not overly intelligent.

Ed Charney—Bootlegger and owner of the Stage Coach Inn. A devoted family man during holiday seasons, he prefers his mistress during the rest of the year.

Al Grecco—A young hoodlum and ex-boxer, jailbird, and errand boy for Ed Charney. Born Anthony Murascho, he gained his nickname from a lady sportswriter who decided that his physical beauty recalled the canvases of El Greco.

Harry Reilly—A former suitor of Caroline, part owner of Julian's agency, a loud low-brow, shrewd and dangerous.

253

Helene Holman—Ed Charney's mistress, nightclub singer, alcoholic, and nymphomaniac.

Dr. William English—Julian's father, a prosperous though incompetent surgeon. Proud, cold, and vindictive, he has tried to live down the shame of his father's suicide.

Mrs. Waldo Walker—Caroline's mother, a widow, an efficient committeewoman, but emotionally sterile and intellectually vapid.

The Story

The events leading to Julian English's "appointment in Samarra"—that is, his death—fill three days that begin just after midnight on December 25, 1930. During that time, Julian plods a liquor-sodden course across the caste lines that stratify Gibbsville's social system. A wealthy anthracite mining town of 25,000 in southern Pennsylvania, Gibbsville has suffered from the impact of union strikes and the advent of the oil burner. But even the stock market crash of 1929 has not seriously perturbed its wealthy citizens or shattered its lower middle class. The marginal group—the bootlegger and his hirelings—is thriving. Julian English still manages to sell Cadillacs, Lute Fliegler, his salesman, earns enough to stay out of the coal mines and the ranks of the proletariat. Ed Charney, the bootlegger, rides the crest of Prohibition.

The upper and middle classes of Gibbsville have much in common. They have faith in Herbert Hoover's conviction that the nation's economy has undergone a "strong technical reaction." They attend parties, get drunk, and make tentative passes at other men's wives. They belong to a variety of clubs, social and charitable. While they tolerate certain Catholics (especially those who can afford Cadillacs), they despise all Jews (whether or not they can afford Cadillacs). Within this tidy framework, the population of Gibbsville enjoys the advantages of democracy, and when the novel opens, rejoices after its fashion in the heightened pleasures of the Christmas season.

Julian English, who grew up on fashionable Lantenengo Street with his rich childhood friends, played with the sons of parents less affluent. The boys enjoyed a variety of con-

ventional and some less conventional games. While playing
Five-Finger Grab, Julian was arrested for stealing mer-
chandise. From then on, Julian's father has regarded him as
nothing more than a common thief.

Julian avoided World War I by staying at Lafayette College until he was graduated. He refused to study medicine,
as his father wished him to, or to join his father's fraternity.
After graduation he entered the garage and auto business.
Before his marriage to Caroline he had only one serious love
affair, with a beautiful, lower-class Polish girl named Mary.

When the novel opens, Julian has been married five years,
has no children, and has fallen considerably into debt, especially to Harry Reilly. His charm and grace, however, help
him maintain his status as one of the most popular members
of the exclusive Lantenengo Country Club.

Caroline English's past is more colorful than her husband's.
A well-bred Bryn Mawr graduate, she taught briefly among
the underprivileged, but soon concentrated on her essential
interest—men. Though she had known Julian from childhood, he was the last man she thought about seriously as a
lover. There was a wounded but dashing British officer, her
cousin, who first roused but refused to take advantage of her
youthful passion. Then there was Joe Montgomery, gentle,
wealthy, daring. (He took Caroline swimming at night, nearly
nude.) Caroline loved Joe but refused to give herself to him
until she returned from a European trip with her mother.
While Caroline lingered abroad, Joe wrote her, ending their
relationship.

In 1926, at the age of twenty-seven, Caroline had at her
disposal several men, including Harry Reilly and Julian. She
thought Harry "too lavish and considerate," Julian too much
a "habit." Her most likely prospect, Harvard-bred Ross Campbell, proved to be a stingy stuffed shirt. Caroline was beginning to believe that no man would ever meet her demands,
when she realized that she had loved Julian since childhood.
Swiftly, their love burst into passion, sustained itself, and led
them to marriage.

As the novel begins, the Englishes are attending a Christmas Eve party at the Lantenengo Country Club. Julian has
been listening disgustedly to Harry Reilly tell another of his
dirty stories in an Irish brogue and has been contemplating

the pleasure of throwing a drink (complete with ice cube) into Harry's "fat, cheap, gross Irish face." Julian savors the impulse, then acts on it. By Christmas morning, news of Julian's act has spread through Gibbsville, leaving a wake of speculation about the form of Harry's revenge. Furious with her husband, Caroline insists that he apologize to Reilly. She reminds him that he owes Reilly money and that Reilly, a prominent Catholic, can dissuade many other Catholics from buying Cadillacs. Julian consents but hints nastily that Caroline is as interested in Reilly as in himself. To prove otherwise, Caroline promises to be in their bed waiting to make love when Julian returns that afternoon from meeting Reilly.

Reilly refuses even to see Julian, and Mrs. Gorman, Reilly's sister, tells him that her brother, humiliated and enraged (the ice cube blackened his eye), has determined to "fix" Julian. Julian's concern about the threat diminishes a few minutes later when he returns to Caroline's arms. That evening, on their way to a dinner party, Caroline begs Julian to stay sober and promises him as a reward his favorite recreation—a lovemaking bout in their Cadillac. At the party, however, twitted by friends about the Reilly fracas, Julian grows sullen and drinks too much. When Reilly's priest, Father Creedon, confides to Julian in the men's room that he, too, dislikes Reilly, Julian's spirits revive and he goes to Caroline and asks her to join him now in their car. Aware that he is drunk, she refuses him. Antagonized, Julian begins to drink in earnest.

Later in the evening, Julian takes Caroline and several other friends to the Stage Coach Inn, Ed Charney's nightclub. Already there is Al Grecco, assigned by Ed to keep close watch on his mistress, Helene Holman, the club singer. At home for Christmas with his wife and children, Ed knows that Helene's alcoholic and amorous inclinations may lead her astray. Also present are Lute and Irma Fliegler, with a group of earthy friends who nag and bait one another while reaching under the table for their friends' wives.

Julian drifts to the Flieglers' table, then to the table where Al Grecco has been trying with difficulty to keep Helene in line. Al warns Julian, whom Ed likes and admires, about Ed's relationship with Helene, but Julian, stung by his wife's rebuff earlier in the evening, takes Helene to his car—where he promptly falls asleep. Al, Caroline, and others have seen what he has done and react with varying degrees of irritation.

The next morning, gossip about Julian's behavior is again rampant. Irma Fliegler teases him when they meet on the street, but Lute adopts a sterner tone in the office, pointing out that Julian has humiliated his wife and alienated Ed Charney, one of their most powerful business connections. Caroline, no longer able to tolerate Julian's behavior, turns to her mother but finds only platitudes of small comfort.

Alone in his office, having failed once more to win Harry Reilly's forgiveness and having discovered how deeply he is in debt, Julian briefly contemplates the possibility of suicide. Instead, he lunches at the country club and argues about his recent behavior with Froggy Ogden, a one-armed veteran whom Julian has long thought of as his best friend. To Julian's astonishment and chagrin, Froggy not only berates him (especially for his treatment of Caroline) but adds that he has always hated him. Froggy rises and offers to fight Julian. Though Julian refuses, other club members rush to their table thinking that Julian intends to hit a cripple. Suddenly Julian goes berserk, smashing the face of one intruder (a Polish lawyer and thus another potential Catholic customer), punching Froggy, and throwing bottles in all directions. Then Julian drives away, feeling strangely sleepy but not wanting to be awakened.

Julian meets Caroline in the street as she leaves her mother's house. Again they argue, agreeing only to cancel the party scheduled at their house for that evening. Julian returns to their home alone. Only one guest shows up—Miss Cartwright, a reporter checking the names of the invited guests. Julian makes an unsuccessful play for her. After she leaves, Julian gets very drunk and listens to jazz records. Half-aware of what he is doing, he goes to the garage outside his house, locks himself in his Cadillac, smashes the clock, and starts the engine.

The doctor who verifies Julian's death is his father. Because of the history of suicide in their family, Dr. English is eager to avoid a coroner's verdict. He knows, however, that the Jewish coroner—whom Dr. English deliberately did not invite to a local medical dinner—will allow no irregularities.

When Dr. English tells Caroline that he will try in every way to alter the verdict, she screams at him that Julian's death was as much his fault as anyone's and that the manner of death was Julian's choice and should be so recorded.

The novel ends with three brief, ironically juxtaposed scenes: Harry Reilly expresses astonishment that "a real gentleman" like Julian would kill himself; Julian's Polish friend, Mary, and Caroline's stuffy suitor, Ross Campbell, arrange a weekend rendezvous; and Lute and Irma Fliegler wonder what effect Julian's death will have upon their economic future.

Critical Opinion

The loosely structured plot of *Appointment in Samarra* centers, of course, on the catastrophe that befalls Julian English. But the novel's true force lies elsewhere. O'Hara never satisfies us about the reasons for Julian's compulsive self-destruction. His father's psychic cruelty and his own sensitivity are inadequate explanations for his own explosive and often sadistic behavior. Nor do we really understand what—other than sex—binds Julian and Caroline. Analysis in depth of human motives lies beyond O'Hara's skill.

O'Hara's power—and it is considerable—derives from other sources. Above all else, O'Hara is, as Edmund Wilson has written, "a social commentator; and in this field of social habit and manners . . . he has done work that is original and interesting." With his unerring ear for dialogue, keen eye for detail, and rich store of information about the minutiae of daily life, O'Hara captures the mood and movement of the American middle class in the Gibbsvilles throughout America. If he fails to discover the psychological motivation of his characters, he compensates in part by precisely locating their social drives.

For each of the classes he describes, O'Hara documents domestic and communal life: furniture, cars, songs, stories, and sprees, insulated egos, and deeply graven prejudices. With reportorial detachment and irony, O'Hara communicates his vision of a part of the American way. Because he cannot penetrate the deepest recesses of his character's hearts, he falls short of greatness. But in his delineation of surfaces, he has no master among observers of the twentieth-century American scene.

The Author

Son of an Irish physician, *John O'Hara* was born in Pottsville, Pennsylvania, and attended private schools in preparation for admission to Yale. But his father's death compelled him to give up the hope of college and undertake a variety of odd jobs, among them working as secretary to Heywood Broun, the well-known journalist. After newspaper and moviescript writing, O'Hara began to devote himself to fiction.

His first and best novel, *Appointment in Samarra,* which appeared in 1934, immediately won him a large and appreciative audience. Although he has published nine novels and as many volumes of short stories since then, his skill as a narrator and his insight as a keen critic of American middle-class mores remain substantially the same as in the first book. Nevertheless, several of his subsequent works deserve attention. *Butterfield 8* (1935) captures the sterile gaiety of the Jazz Age. *Pal Joey* (1940), originally a collection of stories from *The New Yorker,* later a musical comedy and a film, epitomizes the opportunism and cynicism of diverse Broadway types. O'Hara's most ambitious novels since *Appointment in Samarra* have been *A Rage to Live* (1949) and *Ten North Frederick* (1955). The first of these is a vigorous study of upper-class amours in a typically O'Hara-like Pennsylvania town; the second, another study of Gibbsville, ranges from the Civil War to the present as it analyzes the career of Joseph B. Chapin, an aspirant to the presidency of the United States. *Ten North Frederick* won for O'Hara the National Book Award.

The Late George Apley

by

JOHN P. MARQUAND (1893–1960)

Main Characters

George Apley—An upper-class Bostonian whose initial impulse to revolt has faded. He has lost touch with his son and daughter and feels that his world is careening toward destruction.

Horatio Willing—His very conservative Bostonian biographer, a good man but a little obtuse.

Thomas Apley—George's father, a pillar of Boston society, moral, dominating, very sure of what is right for George.

Elizabeth—George's mother, a tender, loving, but exceedingly possessive woman.

Mary Monahan—The "unsuitable" Irish girl with whom George falls in love.

Catharine Bosworth—George's wife, a Boston lady who is of George's own class and who exerts firm control over him.

John Apley—George's non-conformist son whom he loves but does not understand.

Eleanor Apley—George's daughter whose bohemian preferences puzzle and grieve him.

The Story

The story of George Apley, Bostonian, unfolds in the papers he has left behind—letters, memoranda, occasional essays. These are presented by an official biographer, the very conservative and slightly obtuse Horatio Willing who has been instructed by George Apley's son, John, to tell the truth, to make the proper Bostonian seem real.

George Apley was born into an old Bostonian family. Its fortunes were founded by Moses Apley, his grandfather, a ship's captain who got his wealth by shrewd trading during war and maintained it by relentless dealing. George's father, Thomas, though educated for the law at Harvard, went into the textile business and, with an acuteness equal to his father's, branched out in partnership with his brother William.

George's childhood was a happy one. He spent his summers at Hillcrest, the Apley home in Milton, where only the boredom of Sundays at the Unitarian church marred the idyllic weeks. The winters in Boston were less perfect, but at Mr. Hobson's school he formed the friendships that would endure for a lifetime. His mother, Elizabeth, a tender woman with literary leanings, taught him the manners that always distinguished him. His father, Thomas, a much more severe parent, planted the attitudes—toward money, toward class, and especially toward family—that controlled him all his life.

Harvard, of course, was the goal of all the Apleys. George distinguished himself there not by scholarship (he was always in the middle of his class) but by his talent for good fellowship and by his prowess as a boxer. The former brought him all sorts of honors, among them appointment to the board of the *Lampoon*, selection as one of the first ten of the D.K.E. Society, and ultimately, the chief accolade, election to the Club. His boxing skill enabled him to become the university titleholder for his weight.

For the Apleys, Boston was the hub of the universe, their class the peak of social evolution, their family the epitome of culture. Despite his youthful fondness for pranks, George never challenged the opinion of the Apleys and frequently won their guarded approbation. In his senior year, however, he fell headlong in love with a lovely Irish girl, Mary Monahan, and she loved him, too. When the senior Apley discovered the relationship, George, protesting, was shipped off to Europe as soon as final examinations were over. The tour through France and England, with stops at all the conventional places, was a dull ache to George, especially since he was accompanied by his Aunt Martha, Uncle Horatio, and Cousin Henrietta and regularly advised and cautioned in letters from home. Indeed, George felt hardly out of Boston at all. His companions carried Boston with them.

Returning home, George entered Harvard Law School, where he did well if not brilliantly, joined his father's Boston clubs and the boards of his father's several charities. One summer he worked for his Uncle William at the family mills in Apley Falls, proving (at least to his uncle's satisfaction) that he was not cut out to be a real businessman and that he ought instead to become an estate lawyer.

George gradually adjusted to Boston, not happily, perhaps, but tranquilly. His mother and father were particularly pleased when he asked Catharine Bosworth, a young lady of considerable will power, to marry him. Catharine belonged to his own class, came from the same background, and held the same prejudices. The families, of course, were intimately involved in the marriage. James Bosworth gave them a summer home at Mulberry Beach, and Thomas Apley a house on Gloucester Street in Boston. Catharine's parents clung to her and George's to him, but Catharine's more active cooperation with the Bosworths gave them the advantage.

The marriage was not an unhappy one, though George often thought longingly of Mary Monahan. He escaped regularly to his clubs, writing a paper that brought him a good deal of local fame—a history of a Boston Street, "Cow Corner," and the people connected with it. He found hunting and fishing trips more congenial than he had as a single man. Before long, a son was born to Catharine and George. Both the Bosworths and the Apleys insisted that the child bear the first name traditional to each family. Finally the child was christened "John," which was fortunately both a Bosworth and an Apley name. The daughter who shortly followed was called "Eleanor"—a Bosworth triumph.

George's sister, Amelia, another firm Boston lady, married well—that is, to a young man who had the right background and a large fortune. Soon after the marriage, Thomas Apley died quite suddenly, leaving a large fortune in trust for George as well as about two and a half million dollars to charities. One estate expenditure came as a surprise. A woman living in New York alleged that she had been the mistress of Thomas Apley and that he was the father of her twelve-year-old son. George Apley refused to credit the allegation, but to avoid scandal he settled the claim by payment of a lump sum.

For some years George's life passed uneventfully. He devoted himself to his philanthropic enterprises, to civic movements (especially the Save Boston Association which was dedicated to honest government and good morals), and to his camp at Pequod Island. He had purchased Pequod Island as a retreat for himself and his male companions. But soon the Apley women invaded it, and Amelia organized it ruthlessly. George formed a kind of sub-organization of male campers, but Pequod was never quite the same. He developed an interest in bird watching, and went on Sunday jaunts with an old friend, Clara Goodrich. The jaunts were beyond criticism, but they nevertheless were criticized by an old family friend. George, however, persisted and the bird watching ultimately became a serene part of his life.

During World War I, George waxed fiercely patriotic, resenting any lukewarm attitude toward the Allies and suspecting German espionage everywhere. His son, John, who had attended Groton unwillingly and then Harvard without passionate commitment to Boston ideals, seemed far less willing than George had been to conform to Apley ways. At first he pretended neutrality toward the war, but when trouble broke out on the Mexican border, he enlisted. When war was declared he was sent to France, fought at the front, and was wounded. Long after his recovery, he stayed on in France, despite George's impatience to see him again and apprentice him to his Boston duties.

When John did return to Boston and to Harvard Law School, he resisted the round of activities that engrossed his father. Upon graduation, John accepted a position in a New York law firm. George, who loved his son deeply, felt aggrieved. Other troubles came, too. His daughter, Eleanor, would not behave in the approved way of the women of her class. She did not direct her total energies toward marrying well. She occasionally took two cocktails before dinner and discussed Freud at the dinner table. She even turned down a thoroughly eligible suitor. George's worry grew. His world had changed and he could not adjust to it. More and more, he

264 *A Student's Guide to 50 American Novels*

complained about politicians, literature, manners. Often he sounded like an echo of his father. Nevertheless, to George's satisfaction, John married a woman of excellent background though she was a divorcée. George was thoroughly displeased, however, by Eleanor's choice: a penniless journalist, whom he suspected of marrying her for her money and position.

An almost disastrous adventure interrupted George's smooth professional progress in the early twenties. In pursuit of his reforming activities, he tried to bring charges against an astute Irish politician named O'Reilly. The latter got George to a hotel room, lured by the prospect of getting additional information for his case. When the door to the room shut, there was no informant. Instead, a nearly nude woman faced him. And the police were not long in arriving to arrest him. George was determined to fight the frame-up until he received a letter from his boyhood sweetheart, Mary Monahan, a relative of O'Reilly's. When George and Mary met again, she found it easy to persuade George to abandon the case. He was happy to do her the favor. Charges were dropped, and his reputation suffered scarcely a mark.

Not much else happened to George. The crash of 1929 affected his fortune not at all. He had seen it coming. Gallantly he came to the aid of friends who had been caught. He campaigned for Hoover. He made a trip to Rome, during which he discovered that he had a heart condition. Upon returning home, though still quarreling with the doctor's diagnosis, he set his affairs in meticulous order—even sending John a diagram of seating arrangements for his funeral service. In December, 1933, he died in his Boston Street House.

Critical Opinion

The Late George Apley is a delightful and dexterously written novel. The memoirist, Horatio Willing, who belongs to the same class and shares the same ideals as his subject, exposes himself thoroughly in the process of exploring George Apley's life and times. Both excessively proper Bostonians are conformists, a trifle pompous and more than a trifle smug. Yet George Apley earns our affection. He is lost in a world in which all the old markers have been destroyed. He has had engraved on his consciousness the watchwords "City, Class, and Family," and he learns sorrowfully that his own beloved children reject them. He has been rigidly molded, and can find no way out of the mold. Indeed, he finally sees it as a product of the highest art.

Then why do we come to like and appreciate George Apley? Because he tries always to do the right thing—as he conceives of right. What he does is often mistaken and misdirected, but he is motivated by an admirable code of decency and service.

Marquand's pervasive irony sometimes flattens Horatio Willing, makes him too obviously a type. Though, however, we see George Apley's similarities to other men of his place, time, and class, he never becomes a caricature. We always recognize him as an individual creation. And we mourn that someone so intelligent, so compassionate, so loving, should find no worthier outlet for his talents than protesting electric signs along Beacon Street or crusading against suggestive books and plays.

The novel, constructed largely as a series of flashbacks— through letters, reminiscences, diary entries and the like—is generally acknowledged to be Marquand's masterpiece: "the most experimental in form among Mr. Marquand's books," one critic says, "and quite the most brilliant." Some years after it won the Pulitzer Prize, *The Late George Apley* was converted into a successful play by Marquand in collaboration with George S. Kaufman, and later into an equally successful movie. But neither play nor movie manages to convey the tenderness and satire implicit in the novel, or the discreet biographer's reluctant disclosure of his hero's humanity, or the gallantry and misbegotten idealism that make men cooperate in their own defeat. *The Late George Apley* firmly established Marquand's reputation and is today still the most widely read of his novels.

The Author

John Phillips Marquand was born in Wilmington, Delaware. His family had their roots in Newburyport, Massachusetts, to which they returned when he was fourteen, and to which, despite excursions to New York and Tokyo, Marquand always returned, in his life and in his novels.

After Harvard, he became a reporter for the Boston *Transcript*. During World War I, he served as a lieutenant, first on the Mexican border and later in France. Home from the war, he returned to reporting, on the New York *Tribune* this time, but shifted to advertising. He soon abandoned that occupation to devote himself to writing. After a good deal of miscellaneous romantic fiction published in *The Ladies' Home Journal* and *The Saturday Evening Post*, some detective stories featuring an amiable Japanese secret-service agent, Mr. Moto, and one delightful biography of a New England eccentric, *Lord Timothy Dexter* (1925), Marquand wrote his first important work of fiction, *The Late George Apley* (1937), a story firmly grounded in his own background and experience. In it Marquand sounded his distinctive satirical note and established his fundamental themes: the decline of a family and the human waste entailed in the refusal to adjust to changing conditions. *Wickford Point* (1939) and *H. M. Pulham, Esquire* (1941) satirically yet compassionately portray the rigidities of the Boston Brahmin, and *So Little Time* (1943), *Repent in Haste* (1945), *B. F.'s Daughter* (1946), and *Point of No Return* are poignant studies in human terms of frustration and failure.

All of Marquand's later novels have been enormously successful, critically and financially. After *The Late George Apley* won the Pulitzer Prize, book clubs, magazines, and motion-picture companies competed for the right to purchase Marquand's novels, reviewers praised them, and the reading public bought them eagerly.

Though Marquand will probably not survive as an important name in the literature of the twentieth century, he is nevertheless a masterly writer. As Granville Hicks has observed, "He is a social novelist of great talent, and neither his slick past nor his successful present should blind us to that fact."

The Grapes of Wrath

by

JOHN STEINBECK (1902–)

Main Characters

Ma Joad—Matriarch of the Joad clan, a large woman, as ample in spirit as in body. She shoulders the responsibility of welding the family together in its time of despair.

Pa Joad—A hard-working, dogged man, earnestly trying to help, but spiritually tired.

Tom Joad—Loyal to family and friends, quiet, but capable of violence in the face of injustice.

Jim Casy—Tom's friend, an erstwhile itinerant preacher who has lost his "calling" but none of his fervor. For God he has substituted Man and set himself the task of preaching the gospel of human brotherhood.

Grampa Joad—A salty, cantankerous old man filled with zest for life as he remembers it—fighting Indians and tilling the soil.

Granma Joad—Testy and lecherous and, until she sinks into senility, almost as vibrant as her husband.

Rose of Sharon Joad—The pregnant young daughter (also called Rosasharn), yearning simply for a sensual, comfort-filled life.

Connie Rivers—Her husband who hates farming and wants to open a radio-repair shop.

Al Joad—Aged sixteen and lusty. A gifted auto mechanic who would prefer to be off on his own, he stays with the family because he admires Tom.

Ruthie and *Winfield Joad*—The youngest children, mischievous but deprived of the experience of normal childhood pleasures.

Noah Joad—Deformed and disfigured by a birth injury, he finds peace in solitude and in nature.

The Story

The spring rain was light in Oklahoma, enough to raise the corn but not enough to settle the dust that had already begun to sweep across the fields. By June the crops were dry, the land crusted, the air fogged with dust—and the sharecropping farmers had grown frightened. Thus, in the opening chapter, Steinbeck describes the setting against which his novel develops. In succeeding chapters, he alternates narrative and exposition. The events in the lives of the Joads hold the narrative center. Their drama is played out against a series of interchapters concerned with the socio-economic, political, and philosophical issues that have bred disaster. In the following summary, the story of the Joads occupies the foreground. The related material is interwoven wherever appropriate.

Just paroled from prison after serving four years of a seven-year sentence for homicide, Tom Joad hitches a ride home with an inquisitive truck driver. As Tom walks across the fields later, he picks up a turtle that has just been spun off the road by the wheels of a truck. The up-ended turtle, seeds of oat and barley embedded in its shell, has righted itself, dropping some of the seed onto the ground. Pocketed by Tom, the turtle carries within its shell other seeds to be planted elsewhere. This symbol of struggle and regeneration links Tom's arrival with his meeting Jim Casy, who remembers having baptized Tom years earlier. Jim confesses his loss of faith but vows to find a new way to help his fellow man.

Together the men discover the Joad farm, desolate and deserted. Like other sharecroppers, the Joads have been ousted, unable to meet payments on their land because it has dried up and failed to produce a paying crop. Forced by the economic squeeze to produce cotton, unable to rotate crops, the farmers have knowingly though unwillingly ruined the soil. Now the landowners—themselves pressured by Eastern money interests—refuse to share the crops. By displacing their tenants and using a single tractor, they need pay only a single wage and can take the entire crop. Thus, the farmers' homes must go, the land must be drained of its last resources and then sold to satisfy the bankers' demands. The frustrated and embittered farmers struggle hopelessly against an enemy they cannot even see.

Tom and Jim find the Joad family staying with an uncle near by and learn that they are scrimping to raise money to head toward California, where (they have learned from widely distributed handbills) work seems plentiful. The family decides to invite Casy along, making a total of thirteen jammed aboard a wheezing Hudson truck. To buy the truck, the Joads have sold nearly all their personal belongings as well as their farming implements. Almost half the paltry $200 they get for their worldly goods goes for the truck. At the last moment Grampa decides not to leave, arguing, "This country ain't no good, but it's my country." The family drugs the old man, loads him aboard, and the Joads head West.

Along Route 66, the truck groans toward the state line. Once Tom crosses it, he is violating his parole, but he knows that his family needs him and he chooses to be with them. Before they reach the line, however, Grampa suffers a stroke and dies. Lacking the money to hire an undertaker, the family digs a wayside grave. Casy performs the burial rite. A kindly couple, the Wilsons, driving a battered sedan, join the Joad caravan. On the road, gas-station and hamburger-stand owners incredulously gape at the bizarre, overladen truck. Occasionally a compassionate waitress underprices a loaf of bread or some candy for them. But as they move farther west, they are received with increasing suspicion and hostility.

In Texas, where the Wilsons' car breaks down, Pa and Tom urge Ma to drive on ahead in order not to lose time. Already worried about the possible break-up of the family (Rosasharn and Connie intend to settle in the city when they reach the Coast), Ma Joad adamantly refuses to budge: "All we got is the family unbroke," she argues, bolstering her reasoning by brandishing a jack handle. She compromises by agreeing to stop at a campsite just ahead until the car is repaired. From this point forward, her indomitable will sustains the family's courage and determination, even when increasingly ominous signs undermine her resolve. Thus, before they leave Texas, a returning migrant tells them how the work handbills deceive the farmers. Owners advertise for 800 workers. As many as 5,000 appear. Then the owners, confident that the 800 hungriest workers will labor for little, lower the hourly rate to the barest minimum.

The Joads press on—across New Mexico and Arizona, to the edge of the California desert. There, for the first time, they hear the word Okie, an epithet for an Oklahoman migrant that "means you're scum." At a river's edge, just before they enter the desert, Noah abandons the family. When they stop for a night, sheriffs threaten them with arrest, treat them like vermin. Ma refuses to be browbeaten and challenges one deputy with a skillet. Tom teases her, then tells her of Noah's departure. Saddened by this, by Granma's weakness and senility, and by Mrs. Wilson's illness, which prevents the Wilsons from continuing the journey, Ma still goads her brood on.

As they reach the end of the desert, the fertile valley extends before them. They gaze at it, awed and exultant. Ironically, at this moment Ma tells them that Granma died during the night's journey across the desert. Fearing they might be delayed if she spoke, Ma lay silently beside the dead woman all night. On the other side of the truck, Connie and Rosasharn made love. Despite everything, they are in California, land of plenty and poverty, of patriotism and terrorism, a land where Okies—the enemy invaders—breed fear and hate in the hearts of native Californians.

At a Hooverville camp, the Joads set up a tent and Ma tries to organize a household. But there is no work. Uncle John gets drunk, and Connie deserts his pregnant wife. When a deputy intrudes, threatens them all, and shoots a woman, Tom disarms him and Casy kicks the felled man unconscious. To save Tom from arrest and jail as a parole violator, Casy takes full blame and goes off with the police. The camp breaks up when it learns that American Legionnaires plan to burn it. As the Joads leave, Tom refuses to obey the deputies' order to head south. Defiantly, he drives north. Ma soothes him, assuring him that he will not lose his integrity: "They ain't gonna wipe us out. Why, we're the people—we go on."

At a Government-run camp, Weedpatch, things go more promisingly. Treated like human beings, protected from invading sheriffs, the migrant farmers govern themselves cooperatively, and even the children learn once more how to play. A humane but beleaguered employer hires Tom and warns him to beware of an invasion of the camp's Saturday-night dance by troublemakers. Quietly the campers plan their strategy. During the dance, as the toughs arrive, armed deputies wait outside the camp for sound of a riot—the only legal justification they have to enter. The riot call never sounds, for Tom and others spirit away each rowdy as he tries to stir up trouble and efficiently dump him over the camp fence. The dancers continue unmolested.

A month later the Joads have had a total of only five days of work, all of it Tom's. Ma insists that they move on lest Pa lose all his spirit and determination. Above all, she counts on Tom, her favorite, to maintain the level of decency she wishes for all her family. They move north to a peach farm and are hired to pick fruit at a nickel for each three-gallon bucket of unbruised fruit. By sundown, with the entire family working, the Joads have earned a dollar. To cap their disillusion, the prices set by the ranch store are so high that their dollar will not even buy them a decent meal.

That night Tom steals out of the camp past armed guards who tell him they are protecting the pickers against Communist agitators. At a tent in the fields, Tom finds Jim Casy, now a labor leader and strike organizer, trying to stop the wage-cutting methods used by ranch owners. As Tom and Jim talk, they hear voices near by and then stare into a flash light. Two men leap at Casy, one swinging a pickhandle that crushes Casy's skull. Tom wrests the club from the man and bashes in his head. Grazed by a blow, Tom escapes and manages to crawl back to the Joads' camp house. He tells his family what has happened and insists that he must leave. Ma begs him to stay for the sake of the family, especially as Rosasharn will soon have her child. Tom agrees to remain.

Next day the wage for peach picking drops to two and a

half cents, young Winfield collapses from hunger, and a posse searches for Tom. Nearly distraught, the Joads leave, hiding Tom between two mattresses. Continuing north, they come to a cotton camp and are assigned housing in a boxcar. Tom, his face still bruised, must hide in a culvert. During a childish fracas, Ruthie boasts to another youngster that her brother has killed a deputy. Ma realizes that she must now tell Tom to flee. When she goes to him, Tom tells her that he intends to carry on Jim Casy's mission, for he has become convinced of Casy's rightness: "a fella ain't got a soul of his own, but on'y a piece of a big one. . . ." Ma gives the reluctant Tom money, and they part stoically after Tom's assurance that he will return when things have settled.

At the camp, Pa Joad feels that command of his family has slipped from his grasp. Worse, he has ceased to care, despite Ma's assurance that what has happened simply proves that women are more flexible than men. For a brief time the cotton picking continues, but all work ceases when the torrential seasonal rains pour down on the land. Disease sets in among the workers. Stealing and begging replace dignity and pride. And the native Californians, now more hostile than ever, swear in new deputies to cow and beat the Okies. Only their wrath—the grapes that have matured during their terrible experience—keeps the downtrodden together.

In the final chapter of the novel, a counterpoint of life and death echoes the imagery of turtle and seed. As the men dig banks against the rising flood waters, Rosasharn delivers her child in the boxcar. It is born dead, "a blue shriveled little mummy." As the flood waters rise toward the floor of the car, Ma and Pa Joad remove Rosasharn to a dry barn. There they discover an elderly worker dying of starvation. Lying beside the ailing man, Rosasharn nurses him, "and her lips came together and smiled mysteriously."

Critical Opinion

In recent years critics have grown increasingly impatient with John Steinbeck. He has been called a "naïve mystic" and, worse, a "hausfrau sentimentalist." Yet a quarter of a century ago, when *The Grapes of Wrath* appeared, Steinbeck's work stirred intense reactions. Supporters called his novel "The *Uncle Tom's Cabin* of the Depression." Antagonists joined Lyle Boren, an Oklahoma Congressman, in attacking the novel as "a lie, a black, infernal creation of a twisted, distorted mind."

Today distance enables us to adopt a more judicious attitude. Few view the novel as a mere piece of left-wing propaganda despite the warning sounded by its title, a title Steinbeck chose "because it is in our own revolutionary tradition and because in reference to this book it has a large meaning." The novel does, however, urge the development of a communal spirit and affirms a sense of the mystical spirit of the group. Jim Casy possesses this instinctive sense of the surging force of mankind, and Ma Joad expresses it in her insistence upon the unity of the family. Tom Joad moves gradually toward awareness of this higher sanctity and, at the end of the novel, assumes the responsibility for pressing forward its ineffaceable truth.

Because of Steinbeck's interest in marine life, some critics have argued that he has reduced life to a series of animalistic patterns like those he had observed in the sea: survival of the fittest, rejection of alien elements by the established group. Certainly the migrant farmers of *The Grapes of Wrath* represent intruders who upset the balance. And in this, as in other Steinbeck novels, property, ownership, indeed the land itself —all upset the natural balance disastrously. But Steinbeck is a man of compassion, not a clinical precisionist. Like Jim Casy, he seems to say, "All things are holy," and to urge all men and women to love one another, to march forward together. His confidence in man triumphs over despair.

The style and structure of *The Grapes of Wrath* seem at times overwrought, the symbols transparent, and the episodes —especially the much-debated closing scene of Rosasharn nursing the starving man—often melodramatic. Nevertheless, at its best—which it often is—the novel nears the level of epic in its lyric sweep and agonized power. And in Ma Joad, Jim Casy, and Grampa, among others, Steinbeck has created a gallery of American portraits that body forth our American heritage of courage, compassion, and humor.

The Author

Born and raised in Salinas, California, son of a local politician and a schoolteacher, *John Steinbeck* worked on farms and in laboratories as a high-school student. At Stanford he registered only for courses that interested him, and remained there intermittently for six years without taking a degree. Determined to write, he set out for New York in 1925 and arrived there by way of the Panama Canal. The side trip provided him with material for his first published novel, *Cup of Gold* (1929), a tale about Henry Morgan, the pirate. During his two years in New York, he worked variously as reporter, chemist, and hod carrier.

Back in California, his first novel published, he married and began to work in earnest. His succeeding novels got favorable reviews but little money—even the best of them, *Tortilla Flat* and *In Dubious Battle*. With *Of Mice and Men* (1937), Steinbeck became a best-selling novelist. Two years later he published *The Grapes of Wrath*, his finest book, the outgrowth of a newspaper series about migrant workers he had published three years earlier in the San Francisco *News*.

During the war years, Steinbeck served overseas as a correspondent. Since *The Grapes of Wrath*, he has been enormously productive but has failed to maintain his earlier force. *Cannery Row* (1945) and *Sweet Thursday* (1954), for example, are gentle, sentimental tales based upon his recollections of Ed Ricketts, a marine ecologist. But they lack the point and purpose of *The Sea of Cortez*, a semi-scientific work he had written earlier with Ricketts. In 1962 Steinbeck won the Nobel Prize for Literature, largely for *The Grapes of Wrath*. Despite his fame, Steinbeck has remained shy, avoiding publicity, preferring to travel the length and breadth of the nation with his poodle (*Travels with Charley*, 1962), observing, reflecting, and recording.

The Ox-Bow Incident

by

WALTER VAN TILBURG CLARK (1909–)

Main Characters

Gil Carter—A good-natured cowhand, tough, ready to fight on little or no provocation.

Art Croft—His friend, the narrator of the episode, a more sensitive and perceptive man.

Jeff Farnley—A trigger-tempered, proud, vengeful cowboy.

Drew—A rancher whose cattle have reportedly been rustled.

Canby—A saloonkeeper, efficient, shrewd, and a little cynical.

Greene—The young excitable cowboy who reports Kinkaid's death.

Risley—The capable, level-headed sheriff.

Mapes—The deputy sheriff, brutal, stupid, touchy.

Smith—The town drunk, a vicious blowhard.

Bartlett—A rancher whose cattle have been stolen in the past and who is all-out to hang rustlers.

Moore—Drew's foreman, a firm, fair-minded man.

Winder—The perpetually angry stage-coach driver.

Gabe Hart—Winder's powerful, moronic, but gentle hostler.

Ma Grier—A huge, loud, easy-going woman, owner of the town's boardinghouse.

Major Tetley—The leader of the posse, cruel, poised, power-mad.

Gerald Tetley—His frightened, oversensitive son.

Amigo—Tetley's amiable Mexican cowhand.

Osgood—The town minister, pompous, timorous, ineffectual.

Tyler—The town judge, florid, eloquent, but as ineffectual as Osgood.

Sparks—A Negro handyman, simple, religious, good.

Davies—A storekeeper, idealistic, intense, but wholly powerless to stop the posse from acting.

Rose Mapen—Formerly Gil's girl friend, driven from the town by jealous women.

Swanson—Her poised, dangerous new husband.

Donald Martin—A courageous and honest rancher who, along with his Mexican cowhand and a feeble, half-insane old man, is accused of rustling Drew's cattle.

Kinkaid—Farnley's friend, the man supposedly shot by the rustlers.

The Story

After spring round-up in the year 1885, two cowhands, Gil Carter and Art Croft, come to the small Nevada town of Bridger's Wells. Gil is a powerfully built, proud, pugnacious but essentially good-hearted man. Art, the narrator, is slighter, more equable, and much more sensitive. Occasionally Gil feels the need for a fight, and now, after a poker game with Jeff Farnley, a trigger-tempered cowboy, he gets it. He knocks Farnley out and is similarly treated by the saloonkeeper, Canby, who breaks a bottle over his head. More violence seems to be in the offing, but the men in the saloon are distracted by a young fellow who furiously breaks in to report that cattle have been rustled from Drew, a local ranch owner, and that one of his hands, Kinkaid, has been killed.

The report is circumstantial but suspect. Greene, who retails it, has observed nothing firsthand: he was asked to ride for the sheriff and was told only that Kinkaid had been shot. Cattle rustlers have been active in the region, and the men are quickly inflamed. They decide not to wait for the sheriff, Risley, though nobody denies his effectiveness because they want immediate justice, not the slow and doubtful process of law.

The posse formed by the vigilantes and illegally sworn by Mapes, the brutal deputy sheriff, has some odd members:

Farnley, Kinkaid's buddy, bristling for revenge; Smith, a drunkard and blowhard; Bartlett, a rancher, who has had some of his cattle stolen and who is nearly as eager as Farnley to get the rustlers; Moore, Drew's foreman, a firm and fair-minded man; Winder, the stage-coach driver, perpetually angry and avid for action first, explanations later; Gabe Hart, his gentle, moronic, apelike hostler; Ma Grier, a huge, loud, easygoing woman, owner of a boardinghouse; Major Tetley, a former Confederate officer, cruel, perfectly poised, driven by an abnormal craving for power; Gerald, his son, sensitive, weak-willed, terrorized; and Amigo, his Mexican cowhand. Major Tetley at once emerges as the leader of the posse through his force of will and singleness of purpose.

Opposed to the vigilantes are an impotent few: Osgood, the minister, pompous, timorous, wholly out of touch with the hard-living cowboys and ranchers; Tyler, the judge, florid, eloquent, full of law but as empty of understanding as Osgood; Sparks, a Negro handyman, simple, religious, and good; and Davies, a storekeeper, deeply troubled, idealistic, passionately dedicated to the law which he regards as the conscience of society. He pits himself against the posse. But despite his eloquence and good sense, he fails to sway them from their purpose: to pursue the rustlers and to hang them.

The most likely stopping-place for the rustlers is the Ox-Bow, a little valley named for a creek in the middle that winds back on itself. The men riding in the bitter cold are diversely motivated: Farnley utterly set on killing the rustlers, Sparks hoping somehow to help them if they are caught, Tetley triumphant at having achieved command. Most, perhaps, stay with the posse simply because they are hemmed in by a few resolute men and because they are ashamed to desert. Art is troubled by the moral issue and Gerald Tetley despairs at his inability to oppose his father.

At the summit of a hill, where the wind bites most fiercely, the posse pauses in a clearing. Art makes Sparks borrow his coat—he is wearing only jeans and a thin shirt. The tension of the posse grows. Art lights a cigarette and is threatened by Winder, but the danger passes when Sparks notes that half a dozen men have lighted up. Suddenly they are startled into immobility. They hear horses and see the stagecoach crashing toward them. The driver, thinking the group he sees are bandits, whips the horses madly onward. The men pursue, trying to halt the stagecoach. Art, in the lead, is hit by the guard's bullet. Finally, Ma Grier raises her big voice and the driver pulls the stagecoach to a precarious halt. The passengers, two women and a man, descend. They are Rose Mapen, with whom Gil had an affair from which he has not recovered and who was driven from the town by jealous women; her new husband, Swanson, an elegant but clearly dangerous young man; and the latter's sister. Gil and Swanson exchange guarded words—Swanson with fluency and pointed politeness. Art's wound is bound up, and though he faints, he is determined to continue in pursuit of the rustlers.

After the stagecoach departs, the men go ahead with their mission despite the now relentlessly falling snow. At Ox-Bow they come upon their quarry, three men sleeping round a campfire: a swart Mexican, shrewd and alert; an old gray man, obviously feeble-minded; and their leader, a tall, thin, dark young fellow. When they are awakened, only the Mexican retains his alertness and bravado. The old man mumbles, seized with a vague dread. The young man, brave despite his chattering, asks what the charge is. Hearing that it is rustling and murder, he protests their innocence. Farnley is in an agony of impatience, but Tetley sternly quiets him in order to question the presumed criminal. The story he tells is hardly convincing. His name is Donald Martin; he is from Ohio and has recently purchased a ranch near Pike's Hole; he has bought fifty head of cattle from Harley Drew and is now driving them. But the ranch he says that he has bought is part of a larger ranch owned by someone else; and he has no bill of sale for the cattle, Drew allegedly having promised to mail it. Martin's protests do not impress the vigilantes. Davies tries vainly again to persuade the men to check on Martin's story. The Mexican tries to escape, but is shot in the leg. The old man blabs the charge that the Mexican committed the murder, but is put down by Martin. Davies promises to find someone to look out for Martin's wife and children and to see that Martin's final letter gets to her. Then, in the gray light of dawn, Major Tetley supervising, the three criminals are hanged. But young Tetley bungles the job his father assigns him; he fails to prod Martin's horse, and Martin, who has at the end exhibited his proud courage, is left dangling and has to be shot. The major strikes his son with the butt of a pistol and drops him where he stands.

The posse leaves the scene to return to town. On the way back they meet the sheriff, Tyler, Drew, Davies' clerk—and Kinkaid, the man reported dead. Judge Tyler denounces them as murderers, promises to try every man for murder. But Sheriff Risley refuses to recognize any of them, asking for volunteers for a legal posse. They all volunteer, but Risley passes up Mapes and Tetley and eight others.

In town, Art's wound is expertly treated by Canby. Art falls into a deep sleep. When he awakes, Davies is there. He is tortured by guilt, desperately wants someone to confess to, and Art seems to have the necessary sympathy and sensitivity. Davies accuses himself of the sin of omission—for not, apparently, exercising leadership equal to Tetley's. In agony of spirit, he insists that he lacked real courage. His self-castigation, though unquestionably sincere, is nevertheless tinged by a sort of pleasure, as Art acutely notes. Davies tells Art that young Tetley has hanged himself from a rafter upon returning home. The major seems unmoved. But Gil comes in and adds to the story: the major has killed himself.

Gil and Art come down to eat, contribute to the collection for Martin's family, and casually discuss Rose Mapen and her new husband. Gil wants to fight Swanson because his self-assured possession of Rose irritates him, but Gil knows that a fight with him would come to shooting. "I'll be glad to get out of here," he says. Art agrees.

Critical Opinion

The Ox-Bow Incident, Walter Van Tilburg Clark's first novel, may be read (and often has been) simply as a western. And on that level it is a remarkably satisfying story: the episodes are exciting, the action mounts steadily toward the climax, the characters are real, the style is hard and lean, the backgrounds are graphically drawn. However, Clifton Fadiman comments, "It bears about the same relation to an ordinary western that *The Maltese Falcon* does to a hack detective story."

The core of *The Ox-Bow Incident* is the lynching of three

alleged cattle rustlers in Nevada in 1885. But Mr. Clark gives the vigilantes and their victims faces, converts the "incident" into a significant study of mob cruelty and irrationality, dissects the separate motives of the members of the posse and shows how their motives reinforce one another. He does more, too, for as Frederic I. Carpenter points out, "The novel is the story of the tragic failure of an idea in action—the idea of law and justice. It can also be taken, if you will, as a parable on the tragedy of Western civilization."

There are faults in the novel, certainly. The reader would like to know a good deal more about several of the characters: massive, easygoing, loud "Ma" Jenny Grier, for example, or humane yet steel-purposed Sparks. But detailed analysis of all the characters might have impaired the force and drive of the story. As it stands, *The Ox-Bow Incident* is one of the two or three important westerns in contemporary American literature.

The Author

Born in Maine in 1909, *Walter Van Tilburg Clark* spent part of his childhood in Nyack, New York, and in 1917 moved with his family to Reno, Nevada. His life there supplied the background for his sensitive novel of adolescence, *The City of Trembling Leaves* (1945). He attended the University of Nevada, of which his father was president, getting his bachelor's degree in 1931 and his master's in 1932. After two more years of graduate study at the University of Vermont, he taught for ten years in the public schools of Cazenovia, a small town in upstate New York. Married in 1933, Clark is the father of two children. He has taught with distinction in several colleges, but his main efforts are now devoted to writing.

Though he has published both poetry and essays, Clark's special bent is for fiction. He has been represented with unusual frequency in the O. Henry Memorial Collections of short stories, and in 1945 he won the O. Henry Short Story Award for "The Wind and the Snow of Winter." *The Ox-Bow Incident* (1940) and *The Track of the Cat* (1949), the latter a stirring, symbol-laden tale of the pursuit of a mountain lion, have been made into superb movies.

Mr. Clark's novels and some of his stories are westerns—but with a difference. His uniqueness, one critic says, is in "the total 're-interpretation' of the traditional western stock-type characters and the subdued but penetrating insight into their motives, their human and universal passions." Moreover, the realistic settings, natural dialogue, and the taut, spare language put the stamp of authenticity on everything he writes.

The Heart Is a Lonely Hunter

by

CARSON MCCULLERS (1917–)

Main Characters

John Singer—A deaf-mute, thirty-two years old, with a deep
wisdom that makes people confide in him.

Antonapoulos—Singer's beloved deaf-mute companion, a
gross, unbalanced Greek.

Mick Kelly—A fourteen-year-old tomboy who idolizes Singer
and is bewitched by music.

Dr. Copeland—A Negro physician whose mission is to raise
the Negro people to freedom and a sense of purpose, and
who is bitterly disappointed at his children's failure to share
his vision.

Portia—Dr. Copeland's daughter, servant of the Kellys, a
good, loving, but unintellectual woman.

Jake Blount—A driven man, short, ugly, hammer-fisted, who
is maddened because people will not understand that a
better life is possible for them.

Biff Brannon—Proprietor of a restaurant, a lonely, impotent
man whose tenderness and love are never realized.

The Story

Singer, a deaf-mute about thirty-two years old, has been
living in a Southern town for ten years working as an en-

graver. Living with him is another deaf-mute, a Greek named
Antonapoulos. The latter is gross, greedy, cretinous, but Singer
adores him, attributing to him intelligence and sympathy that
he does not possess.

When Antonapoulos's odd behavior becomes intolerable and
he is sent to the state insane asylum 200 miles away, Singer is
distraught. He moves into a furnished room in a house run
by the Kellys, a large, impoverished family. He begins taking
his meals at the New York Café, a restaurant owned by Biff
Brannon, a lonely man filled with a tenderness that finds no
outlet. Biff's wife, Alice, treats him with contempt, especially
since he has become impotent.

Singer soon becomes, without his willing it or understanding
it, a magnet for four unfulfilled, spiritually restless people.
First there is Jake Blount, a five-foot, huge-fisted, raging wanderer who goes on periodic drunks. Jake is maddened by the
hopelessness of people, their refusal to learn what they can do
to improve their miserable lot. He goes from place to place in
the South, always unheeded or misunderstood. Singer seems to
him to comprehend and even to share the emotions that drive
him. On Sundays, when he is free from his job as a carnival
mechanic, Jake comes to Singer's room to talk tumultuously
of his experiences, his hopes, his ideals.

Mick Kelly, a gangling fourteen-year-old girl, is another who
finds in Singer a sensitive understanding of things she cannot
fully articulate. A bit rough, she is nevertheless a girl who
loves her little brothers until it hurts, and who has a passion
for music that leads her to sacrifice her lunches in order to take
lessons from a more fortunate girl who can play the piano.
Music is with her always—little tunes that go through her
head and that she tries, without technical knowledge, to put
down on paper. She comes to identify music and Singer, and
she worships the deaf-mute for his apparent compassion and,
she supposes, empathy.

Dr. Benedict Copeland, a tubercular Negro physician, also
feels that Singer shares his ideals. The doctor is filled with
suppressed fury at the brutality of white men and at the
ignominy of his race. He has always striven to invest his people
with a sense of mission—freedom to serve humanity as equals
and receive their due. He names his children Karl Marx, Ham-
ilton, William, and Portia, but they reject his ambitions for

them and remain content with their trivial round of pleasures. Only Singer, different from all other white men he has known, will respond to his impassioned statement of purpose which has alienated his wife whom he loved but who rejected him and drove his children from him.

Finally Biff Brannon, inquiring and skeptical, a searcher but not a devotee, comes often to see Singer. Restless, unceasingly interested in penetrating beneath the surface, feminine in spite of his hirsute masculine appearance, Biff is misinterpreted by Jake who cannot understand that Biff feels an affinity for him though not for his beliefs, and by Mick who distrusts him intuitively and feels that he harbors animosity toward her. Biff, in fact, likes freaks and children. He likes freaks, his wife once sharply informed him, because he is a bit of a freak himself. He has a secret fondness for perfume, which he dabs under his ears, and he keeps a complete file of newspapers dating back twenty years to World War I. He likes children, too, in an ambiguous fashion, varying from a tender parental longing for children of his own to a diffuse sexual longing for Mick.

Other people are drawn to Singer, imagining that he possesses a great silent wisdom. They ascribe superhuman qualities to him and construct a number of myths about him— always in their own image. He is variously said to be a Jew, a Turk, a union organizer, a wealthy man, a poor man. And Singer is supported by a myth of his own. He builds for himself the illusion that Antonapoulos—the poor, deranged Greek —is a godlike man. He writes letters to the illiterate Antonapoulos, then destroys them. Whenever he can, he visits Antonapoulos, bringing him expensive gifts and talking to him eagerly despite the Greek's unresponsiveness.

The four cling to Singer, wanting to love, wanting to be loved, and being continually disappointed. Jake is ravaged by his desire to communicate his message. He is scorned and repelled by everyone except Singer who appears to agree. Jake thinks he has discovered another comrade, a man who scrawls warnings to the rich and mighty of the earth. But he proves to be a half-crazed evangelist.

Dr. Copeland tries to draw nearer to his children, to enlist them for his true purpose. They, however, fear and resent him. Only Portia visits him, but neither can achieve any kind of spiritual union. With none of his race, in fact, does he experience it. At a family party he sits stiff and alien, refusing to eat or drink and leaving as early as he can. As judge of an essay contest for Negro high-school students on the subject of advancing the Negro race in society, he awards the prize by default to a wild composition full of racial hatred. The other students have really nothing to say. During the Christmas party following the award, Dr. Copeland speaks of his hopes for his people and preaches his version of Marx's gospel. But his belief that his meaning has been perceived and appreciated is momentary. His son Willie gets involved in a knifing, is sent to jail, and because he attempts to escape, is punished by being put in a freezing room for three days until his feet swell, develop gangrene, and have to be amputated. When Dr. Copeland attempts to approach the local judge, he is beaten as an uppity Negro and thrown into jail. After his release, Singer and Jake call on him. With Jake he gets into a fierce argument about what must be done to improve conditions for Negroes, becomes enraged, and is seized with a severe attack of tubercular coughing.

Mick, gangling and awkward, suffers more than than most adolescents. She tries to "belong," to be one of her high-school crowd. She throws a "prom" party that becomes a disaster when some neighborhood rowdies break it up. She struggles unsuccessfully to put down on paper the tunes that haunt her. She finds no suitable response to her emotional needs in her family. Her seven-year-old brother, torn by an ecstasy of love for a little girl, Biff's niece, and unable to express it otherwise, shoots her. Mick's impoverished family goes deeper in debt as they toil to pay the medical bills. Only one brief fulfillment comes to her—and that is marred. Harry, a Jewish boy, hires bicycles and they go on a swimming outing. They have a glorious time; but afterward the fourteen-year-old girl and the sixteen-year-old boy come together in a sexual encounter. Guilt-ridden, Harry flies home to take a job as mechanic in another city while Mick remains behind and endures. Finally she is subtly persuaded by her family to take a job in a five-and-ten-cent store.

Biff Brannon goes from disillusionment to disillusionment. He remains friendless. His aunt and her spoiled daughter exploit him. Jake rejects him. After a while he does not even have the satisfaction of illusion: he realizes that Singer has none of the qualities that the hopes and needs of people endow him with.

As for Singer himself, on one of his periodic visits to Antonapoulos, he is informed that his friend has died from nephritis. The world is henceforth blighted, hopeless. Singer shoots himself.

Singer's death arouses despair in his disciples. Dr. Copeland, perhaps fatally ill, goes off to the country farm of his father-in-law, convinced that his life has been a failure and is now at an end. Jake gets into a murderous fight at a carnival and leaves town, determined to continue spreading his futile doctrine of rebellion through the South. Mick, chained to her onerous job, no longer hears the music that once filled her being and looks forward to nothing at all. Biff fleetingly undergoes a kind of illumination, catching a glimpse of the human struggle, of men and women laboring and seeking love. But then he glimpses darkness and terror, too—the realization of aloneness. And he is suspended between the two, the radiance and the blackness.

Critical Opinion

The action of *The Heart Is a Lonely Hunter,* which Carson McCullers wrote when she was twenty-three, is contained within the winter of one year and the summer of the next. It is a tightly constructed and intensely concentrated novel. Yet remarkably, it presents a panorama of the "strangled South." As Ihab Hassen notes, "The novel finds a way of acknowledging the social realities of its time."

Its central theme is the inevitable isolation of each man. Each reaches out, lonely and longing, for communion with another human being. And each finds it is only an illusion—an illusion that must be ultimately shattered. Nevertheless, the illusion is what makes life livable.

The characters in the novel are realistically, sometimes ironically drawn—but always the quality of mercy mitigates the irony. Mick Kelly, who loves music and strives dimly for a kind of beauty, perhaps touches readers most poignantly. But the unexpressed tenderness of Biff Brannon, the futile rage of Jake Blount, the unfulfilled purpose of Dr. Copeland—these, too, evoke compassion. Richard Wright, an important Negro novelist, especially praises Mrs. McCullers for "the astonishing humanity that enables a white writer, the first time in Southern fiction, to handle Negro characters with as much ease and justice as those of her own race."

Singer, a deaf-mute, is the centripetal force of the novel. Toward him all of the characters gravitate to speak their deepest wants and to hear the saving words—and he can neither hear nor speak. Though *The Heart Is a Lonely Hunter* is set in the deep South during the early thirties, it is more than reportage, even spiritual reportage, dealing with a particular place and time. It is a parable on the human condition, men's fragile visions, their frustrated aims, their shut-in agonies, their necessary self-deceptions and, not least, their valorous endurance.

The Author

Carson McCullers was born in 1917 in Columbus, Georgia. Though her first ambition was to be a concert pianist, she began writing at fifteen and published her remarkable first novel, *The Heart Is a Lonely Hunter*, at twenty-three. When she was seventeen, she came to New York to study at the Juilliard School of Music. On her second day in the city, she lost her tuition money in the subway. She worked at a series of part-time jobs, going to school at night and writing in her scant spare time. In 1940, three years after her marriage to Reeves McCullers, she sold two of her stories to *Story* magazine and embarked on a full-time writing career. She has won several literary awards and two Guggenheim fellowships which have allowed her to live and work abroad where she has read widely, particularly the French novelists and poets. She lives in Nyack, New York.

Carson McCullers' novels explore the world of the lonely, the isolated, the misfits. Her dominant theme is the futile search for love and identity. Her most characteristic and important novels are *Reflections in a Golden Eye* (1941), a brilliant, grotesque study of the failure of love; *The Member of the Wedding* (1946), a foray into the adolescent world of its twelve-year-old heroine, which Miss McCullers turned into a first-rate play; *The Ballad of the Sad Café* (1951), dramatized in 1963 by Edward Albee, a mirror of the distortions of personality created by love bitterly mixed with pain.

Miss McCullers, it is true, works within a small compass and perhaps develops her central theme too often. "But within the small, lonely, lost world which she has created in her fiction," Stanley Kunitz observes, "she moves with sure and steady artistry. She is one of the most admired and imitated authors of her generation."

The Human Comedy

by

WILLIAM SAROYAN (1908–)

Main Characters

Katey Macauley—A widow of limited economic means, abundant faith in mankind, and endless resources of love. Her creed: "Nothing good ever ends. . . . And the world is full of people and full of wonderful life."

Homer—Her fourteen-year-old son, a schoolboy and a telegraph messenger.

Ulysses—Her youngest son, four years old. Like his namesake, he is an adventurer to whom the whole world represents an exciting voyage of discovery.

Marcus—Her eldest son, a soldier in World War II.

Bess—Her daughter, aged seventeen, sweet, understanding, gentle.

Mary Arena—Marcus' girl friend, the girl next door, seventeen, innocent and lovable.

Thomas Spangler—The genial, fatherly manager of the local telegraph office, onetime high-school low-hurdle champion whom Homer idolizes.

Mr. Grogan—An elderly, kindly drunkard and philosopher, once the world's fastest telegrapher, now perhaps the last of his kind and fearful of being replaced by machines.

Tobey George—Marcus' buddy in the Army, a homeless orphan.

Lionel Cabot—Ulysses' seven-year-old friend, a bungling but eager fellow traveler in the wonderful world of Ithaca, California.

Miss Hicks—Teacher of ancient history at Ithaca High, antiquated but wise, compassionate, and just.

The Story

As the novel opens, Ulysses Macauley watches in wonder as a gopher emerges from a hole and squints at him. A moment later he joyously gazes at a bird settling in a walnut tree. Even more exciting than the worlds of bird, beast, and tree, however, is the world of man and machines that comes into view as a freight train passes through Ithaca, California. All of the men aboard ignore Ulysses' happy waves except for a Negro who waves and cries out to him, "Going home, boy —going back where I belong!" Without comprehending just what the Negro means, Ulysses senses that the world is a funny, lonely, but wholly exciting place. What he fears most is having the people he knows best go away, for they seem not to come back. His father has never returned, and now he is worried that Marcus may not, either. When Homer tells of his plans for travel, Ulysses pleads with him not to leave and Homer assures him that he will not go for a long, long while.

At fourteen, Homer has taken on a job as messenger boy to help support his mother. Mr. Spangler and Mr. Grogan are astonished at his eagerness to prove that he is the best messenger boy they have ever had. He delivers messages and returns to the office with amazing speed. He and Mr. Grogan enjoy long discussions about the ways of the world, and Homer feels a deep urge to help Mr. Grogan keep the job he has always performed so commendably. Unfortunately Mr. Grogan often falls into drunken stupors and ignores the signals of the telegraph ticker. Mr. Grogan receives and Homer delivers to a Mexican woman a War Department message notifying her of the death of her son in combat. When Homer reads the note to the illiterate mother, she refuses at first to accept the truth, and then insists that Homer sit with her, eat candy, and even become her boy to take the place of Juan. When Homer returns home that night, he tells his mother of the events of the day and confesses to her that they have made him feel lonely, though why or for what he cannot say. She explains to him that he has reached the end of childhood, and that loneliness is a worldwide affliction. War, she tells her son, does not make loneliness; rather, it is man's loneliness that makes war.

Homer's immediate goal is to win the 220-yard low-hurdle race at Ithaca High. Rising early each morning, he exercises while the fascinated Ulysses watches, then practices leaping fences on his way to school. But Homer's ambitions encounter more opposition than he anticipates. For one thing, Coach Byfield, the bigoted, tyrannical athletic coach, has been training Hubert Ackley III, son of a wealthy townsman, to win the event. On the day of the race, a more formidable obstacle looms before Homer. Miss Micks, who teaches ancient history, keeps Homer and Hubert in after school because they have exchanged insults during the class hour. Homer's dislike of Hubert is based not only on that young man's snobbishness but also on his friendship with Helen Eliot, the prettiest girl in the class and also a snob but, in Homer's eyes, nonetheless adorable. Coach Byfield tries to get the principal to release Hubert, and when the principal refuses, lies to Miss Hicks that the principal has authorized Ackley to run. Annoyed at what she recognizes at once as a lie, Miss Hicks releases both boys and goes to the track meet to root for the best man.

Homer, arriving at the meet too late to change into track clothes, runs as he is—to the chagrin of both Hubert and Coach Byfield. For most of the race, Hubert and Homer run almost side by side, Homer a bit ahead despite Ackley's insistence that he slow down. Meanwhile Coach Byfield, furious at the way things have turned out, steps onto the track and makes Homer stumble. Ackley has the decency to wait until Homer is back on his feet, and then the race continues to a close finish with Ackley the winner by the narrowest of margins. Miss Hicks prevents Coach Byfield from punishing Homer for almost winning the race and even makes him apologize for a slurring remark he makes to Homer's Italian friend. Then she sends all the youngsters home, urging them to be cheerful about the future.

On his way home, Homer is called to rescue Ulysses from

an unexpected and unusual situation. During an afternoon of wandering about town, Ulysses has drifted into a sporting-goods store where the proprietor is demonstrating to a prospective customer a new and improved bear trap. It suspends the bear in mid-air, keeps turning him around, but does him no other physical harm. By some mischance, when the trap is sprung, Ulysses gets caught. Though somewhat puzzled, Ulysses seems more interested in the consternation of the onlookers than in his own plight. No one seems to know how to release the trap though several persons, including the local policeman, try. When Homer arrives, he takes charge of matters and sees to it that the trap is destroyed and the still curious but undisturbed Ulysses set free. A few minutes later Ulysses is amusing himself at Mr. Spangler's telegraph office where Homer has gone to catch up with the messages that have accumulated in his absence.

Homer has worked for three days at the telegraph office, and, as Mr. Spangler points out, has already matured considerably. That night Homer has a dream that marks just how far he has come toward manhood. Riding his bicycle down a street, Homer dreams that Coach Byfield tries to stop him. Homer manages to make the bicycle fly over Byfield's head and on upwards into the clouds. As he sails along he sees another cyclist, and they race along side by side until Homer suddenly realizes that the other cyclist is Death. The phantom rider moves swiftly toward Ithaca, and Homer tries desperately but unsuccessfully to stop him. Homer's sobs waken Ulysses who watches his brother's anguish, then goes to fetch their mother. She comes and gently reassures the boy. She takes the alarm clock from his room so that he may enjoy a long night's rest.

The next morning Homer tells his mother that delivering telegrams to people whose sons have been killed in the war caused his sad dreams and made him cry even though he knows that grown boys ought not to. Mrs. Macauley tells him that pity has led him to tears, and that pity for one's fellow man is essential to a humane spirit. ". . . out of pity comes balm which heals." She tells Homer, too, that his sobbing as he slept was but the echo of the world's grief. When Homer leaves, Mrs. Macauley sees—as she has innumerable times before—a vision of her dead husband,

Matthew, standing before her. He tells her that Marcus must join him in death, and quietly, as she turns to her daily chores, Mrs. Macauley says, "I know, Matthew."

Ulysses and his friend Lionel continue their excursions into the outside world, watching a funeral, visiting the library and examining carefully the pictures in books they marvel at despite their inability to read. Only once does terror invade Ulysses' happy world of innocence, and it reduces him to terrified sobs. As he watches a waxen-faced man made up as a robot to advertise a quack medicine in a store window, Ulysses senses death without consciously knowing the word, and he flees into the darkness, lost until a newsboy discovers him and brings him to Homer who comforts him.

Across the sea, en route to battle, Marcus Macauley and his friend, Tobey George, talk about the Macauley family, a source of pleasure and hope for the orphaned Tobey who laments the fact that he does not even have a clear national identity. Marcus assures him that he is an American and that that is all he need know about himself. After a brief silence, the two young men pray, Marcus for a home for all the homeless of the world, Tobey for the survival of Ithaca and all the people there whom he has learned to love through Marcus.

Letters arrive from Marcus for each member of the Macauley family. Homer brings his with him to the telegraph office where Mr. Grogan urges him to read it aloud. The letter tells Homer that he is "the best of the Macauleys" and must go on being so. Marcus bequeathes all his possessions to Homer and urges him to welcome Tobey when he arrives with Marcus after the war. Moved to tears by his brother's letter, Homer tells Mr. Grogan that if his brother dies in the war, he will spit at the world and hate it.

Six months later—after soldiers have begun to return to Ithaca and Ulysses has watched with his usual enthusiasm a host of new marvels—the inevitable tragedy befalls the Macauley family, As Homer and Ulysses walk through town, Homer sees a penny and tells Ulysses to pick it up for good luck. Across the street Homer sees Mr. Grogan alone in the telegraph office and stops by to see whether he needs any help. Mr. Grogan seems again to have fallen into a drunken stupor, and since the machine is clicking, Homer resorts to his usual water splashing to revive the old man, then goes out for coffee. When he returns, the old man has slumped across the machine, the incoming message only partly typed. Homer moves the old man, sees that he is dead, and then notices that the incomplete telegram is from the War Department, announcing the death of Marcus.

Mr. Spangler takes Homer away from the office and listens as the boy tells him that the hate he wishes to feel cannot emerge, but that he cannot find any direction for the love he wishes to feel. "Who's the enemy?" the boy asks the man, hoping to find a target for his pent-up anger. Mr. Spangler tells him that one cannot hate, but must carry on through the love he feels for those closest to him. A good man never dies, Mr. Spangler argues, and at the heart of a good man is love.

That same night Tobey George, limping from a war wound, arrives in Ithaca. He wanders about the town and comes upon Mr. Spangler and Homer pitching horseshoes. Homer feels he knows the youth but cannot be certain. Tobey walks on and comes to the Macauley house where Bess is astonished when he greets her by name and tells her he knows all of them. She senses that he has come to tell of Marcus' death, but instead he tells her that Marcus is not dead. Homer arrives and, now realizing who Tobey is, tells him that the telegram about Marcus' death arrived that afternoon. Tobey tells him to destroy the message because it is not true. Together they enter the house where Mrs. Macauley greets her son's friend who is now also her son.

Critical Opinion

From the outset, William Saroyan has rebelled against the formalities of literary craftsmanship. He boasts of writing swiftly and easily, and of paying little heed to such matters as plot construction, grammar, punctuation, and diction. His writing proves his assertion, and provides hostile critics with an easy target. But despite Saroyan's technical naïveté, his best writing has an undeniable appeal. However slap-dash the structure of *The Human Comedy*, however indifferent it is to the niceties of language and imagery, the novel manages to win the hearts of readers open to a simple, unabashedly sentimental approach to experience.

The Macauley family is perhaps too beautiful to be true, but in its gentle commitment to an unmaterialistic way of life and in its passionate dedication to the worth and dignity of all men, it argues for an approach to living that few readers can resist. Homer's approach to maturity is accomplished with poignancy and humor, and Ulysses' wide-eyed embrace of all experience enchants as it delights. He represents, if not the reality of childhood, at least our dream of what it might be if the world would only allow it to be so. Saroyan, then, tries to substitute a different kind of American dream, one of protracted innocence in which evil does not exist except to be absorbed and transmuted back into innocence. His is a primitive version of the possibilities available to modern man that will not withstand the critical scrutiny of historical evidence. But at his best Saroyan communicates his sense of a fantasy world of goodness with abundant good humor, tenderness, and an astringent insight into the limitations of the world most of us accept as real.

The Author

Son of an Armenian minister and vineyard worker who died very young, *William Saroyan* was born in Fresno, California, and attended public schools there until he was fifteen. During those years he worked as a newsboy and as a telegraph messenger, much like Homer in *The Human Comedy*. At sixteen, to help his family, he worked in his uncle's vineyards for a time, and then drifted into a series of jobs that were to contribute much to his later fiction. Though he read widely, he found much that was considered great literature was of little consequence to him. "In order to write the way the world wanted me to write," he said later, "I would have to work twice and three times as hard as I would writing the way I wished to write, so I decided to write the way I wished to write."

In 1934 the first of his short stories began to appear (he has since written more than 350 stories), and with the appearance of the first collection, *The Daring Young Man on*

the Flying Trapeze, in that same year, his fame was immediately established. His output from that time on has been
extraordinarily prolific. Among the most popular and most
admired of his works are *The Human Comedy,* two plays—
My Heart's in the Highlands (1939), a warmly affecting plea
for rent-free housing for poets, and *The Time of Your Life*
(1939), his best play, awarded the Pulitzer Prize (which
Saroyan rejected)—and *My Name Is Aram* (1940), a collection of stories about an Armenian family in the San
Joaquin Valley, supposedly narrated by one of the sons,
Aram Garoghlanian.

All the King's Men

by

ROBERT PENN WARREN (1905–)

Main Characters

Jack Burden—The narrator, aged thirty-five, onetime journalist, then aide to Willie Stark. An apprentice to life, he passes through phases of cynicism, defeatism, and escapism en route to maturity.

Willie Stark—The "Boss," Governor of a Southern state, a pragmatic despot who tries to shape men, affairs, and even nature to his will.

Anne Stanton—Jack's friend who becomes Willie's mistress; intelligent, sensitive, and idealistic.

Adam Stanton—Anne's brother, Jack's friend, and Willie's assassin; director of the State Hospital and an absolute idealist who refuses to believe that good can come from evil.

Judge Irwin—The "upright judge," a man of integrity, decency, compassion, and fallibility.

Sadie Burke—Willie's mistress (before Anne). Pock-marked, hot-tempered, and vile-mouthed, she is fiercely and jealously devoted to the "Boss," and ruthless when he crosses her.

Tiny Duffy—A fat, unprincipled wardheeler whom Willie makes Lieutenant-Governor.

Sugar-Boy—Willie's chauffeur and bodyguard, a dim-witted, stuttering Irishman, fanatically loyal to Stark.

Mrs. Burden—Jack's mother. Vain and shallow, she manages at least once in her life to love selflessly, wholly.

Ellis Burden—The "scholarly attorney," long since separated from his wife and now a religious fanatic.

Lucy Stark—Willie's wife, patient, loyal, and utterly alone.

Tom Stark—Willie's arrogant, irresponsible son.

The Story

Ostensibly, Jack Burden is narrating the story of Willie Stark and his career as Governor of a Southern state from 1936 until his assassination in 1939. But *All the King's Men* is also the story of Jack Burden, and he intersects the present with flashbacks that fill in his own boyhood, adolescence, and young manhood. Thus in the second chapter Jack recalls meeting Willie for the first time in 1922 when Stark, running for the post of county treasurer in Mason City, unsuccessfully tried to block local politicians from handing out a crooked school-building contract. As a young reporter assigned to cover Stark's campaign, Jack found Willie a teetotaling idealist inspired by his schoolteacher wife, Lucy, and hoping to keep local politics clean. Badly beaten in the election, Willie supported his family by peddling during the day, but at night he diligently studied law. When the jerry-built school collapsed, Willie became a local hero. But later he chose to ignore politics and pass his bar examination.

Soon after Willie sets up as a lawyer, a group of incumbent Democratic state politicians decide to use Willie's local popularity in order to split the primary support for the rival candidate for the governorship. Tiny Duffy is delegated to offer Willie the candidacy. Unaware that none of his supporters expects or wants him to win, Willie accepts. Again Jack is assigned to cover Stark's campaign. This time Willie irritates no one; he simply bores them. Speaking quietly and keeping to the facts, Willie loses audiences with painful ease. He has, Jack says, "galloping political anemia," an opinion voiced more boldly though less quotably by Sadie Burke who has been assigned to guide his candidacy to failure.

Just before the election, Sadie tells Willie the facts about his candidacy. Shocked and angry, he gets drunk and passes out. At a political rally next day, still half-drunk, he ignores his prepared speech and tells the astonished audience how he has been duped by Duffy and the machine. Willie withdraws from the campaign, throws his support to the opposition, and helps them win. Then Willie vanishes from the political scene. In 1930, when he does return, as Jack observes, "there wasn't any Democratic Party. There was just Willie . . . he had a meat axe in his hand and was screaming for blood." No longer the pure-hearted idealist but a shrewd opportunist, Willie lashes the electorate to a political frenzy and wins by a landslide. To remind himself forever that hacks are useful and despicable, he creates a post for Tiny Duffy—but Tiny is too grateful to recognize the irony.

During the campaign, when Jack's newspaper insists that he support Willie's opponent, he resigns and sinks into what he calls "The Great Sleep," a period of disengagement during which Jack refuses to acknowledge reality except as a succession of sensory impressions. Unlike his earlier experiences with The Great Sleep, this one is short-lived, for soon after Willie Stark becomes Governor, he hires Jack as his all-round aide, friend, consultant, and research specialist in digging political dirt.

When the novel opens in 1936, Governor Stark (who has already survived impeachment proceedings and won re-election) assigns Jack the most painful—and painstaking—dirt-digging job of his career: to search the past for something that will destroy the reputation of Judge Montague Irwin, the man who has, since Jack's childhood, been his idol. Irwin has, in fact, been a surrogate for Ellis Burden, Jack's legal father. But because Irwin refuses to support Stark's candidate for the Senate, Jack must find Irwin's Achilles' heel. And Jack finds it—though the search is long, intricate, and agonizing.

As he begins his research into what he calls "The Case of the Upright Judge," Jack remembers his last scholarly venture into the past, his unfinished doctoral dissertation in American history. For several years Jack sifted the journal and letters of Cass Mastern, the uncle of the "scholarly attorney," hoping to reconstruct a social portrait of the pre-Civil War era. The facts were relatively simple. Cass seduced Annabelle Trice, his best friend's wife. Her husband, aware of her infidelity, placed his wedding ring under her pillow, then committed suicide. Phebe, Annabelle's young Negro slave, discovered the ring and silently returned it to her. To silence Phebe, Annabelle took her downriver and sold her. Horrified when he learned this, Cass purchased Phebe himself and then gave her her freedom. Haunted by the episode, Cass sought atonement in death on the battlefield. In the past Jack could not understand the truth inherent in the tale. Not until he completes his research on Judge Stark does he realize the significance of the Cass Mastern episode: that all experience is interrelated, that good and evil are inextricably linked. In those early days, however, Jack walked out of his study, leaving his notes and his doctoral thesis behind, and entered into The Great Sleep.

Jack's research in the Irwin case is more intricate but more successful. His quest begins with a single word, "foulness," spoken by the "scholarly attorney" when Jack asks him about Irwin. From Adam Stanton he learns that long ago the judge was poor; from Anne Stanton, that his second marriage in 1914 brought wealth. Court records reveal that in 1907 Irwin borrowed more than $40,000 on his home mortgage, in 1910 repaid a small sum, but nothing more until 1914. When foreclosure proceedings were initiated, he suddenly paid his account in full. Irwin's wife, having squandered her wealth, could not have helped him.

Where, then, had the money come from? No, not from Irwin's piddling salary as attorney general under the distinguished and honorable Governor Stanton (father of Anne and Adam). But in 1915, the records show, Irwin resigned this post to become an executive in an electric power company at $20,000 a year. Jack's suspicions aroused, he searches stock-market records and learns that Irwin also owned 500 shares of stock. Next he scans the newspapers for a further lead, and strikes a lode in a story about the suicide of Mortimer Littlepaugh, Irwin's predecessor as counsel to the power company. Tracking down a possible survivor, Jack locates in Memphis the sister of the dead lawyer, a penny-pinching medium and fortuneteller whom he pays to give him the truth: Littlepaugh, discovering that his company had bribed Attorney General Irwin not to prosecute a conspiracy case, carried the evidence all the way to Governor Stanton who refused to listen to him. The company fired Littlepaugh and hired Irwin. In despair, Littlepaugh took his own life. But he left with his sister a letter giving the details of the swindle. Jack buys the letter from her. His seven-month search has disclosed the meaning of the word "foulness."

While Jack plays out his role as ferret, Willie makes plans for a state hospital and medical center to be the finest in the nation. He fends off Duffy and others who want to make a financial plum of the $6,000,000 building contract, insisting upon absolute assurance that all will be orderly, legitimate, perfect. To head the medical organization, Stark wants the capable and unqualifiedly honest Adam Stanton, and he sets Jack the task of enlisting his boyhood friend for the job. Again, it is a difficult assignment because Adam despises everything Willie represents. When Jack offers him the post, Adam categorically rejects it.

A few days later Anne sees Jack and demands that he make Adam accept the job. Jack suggests that one way may be to teach Adam a "history lesson" about good and evil, that is, to show him evidence of his own father's corruption in protecting Judge Irwin. Anne shows photostats of Littlepaugh's letter to Adam. Adam, damning his father and without further comment, accepts the hospital job. One question still puzzles Jack: How did Anne know that Stark wanted Adam for the job? Neither he nor Adam had told her. He learns the answer to this, too. Just a few days later Sadie Burke tells him in a jealous rage that Anne has become Willie Stark's mistress.

Shattered by this knowledge about the woman he has loved since childhood, Jack takes flight to the West, hoping to find refuge in sheer movement. But as he lies on a hotel bed in California, he relives their burgeoning love, its aspirations and frustrations, its failure ever to reach consummation because of Jack's confused sense of purity and morality (as wrong a sense, he realizes, as Cass Mastern's sense of sin). He recalls, too, his absurd and short-lived marriage to Lois Seager whose mechanized sexuality and crude banality drove him to his first experience with The Great Sleep. Jack thinks that the events of his life have no central relevance, that will and aspiration mean nothing—"for nothing was your fault or anybody's fault, for things are always as they are." A man with an uncontrollable tic and a lobotomized patient, now symbolize for Jack the absurdity of man's will before the force of what he calls The Great Twitch, the thoughtless, mechanical power that determines human behavior.

Once Jack returns East, the innumerable strands of his and Willie's life swiftly and tragically spin out their fates. To beat off his opponents, Willie reluctantly gives the hospital-building contract to Duffy's friend, Gummy Larson. But when his son, Tom, has his spine crushed in a football game, Willie's conscience compels him to withdraw the contract. The next day someone telephones Adam to tell about Anne's affair with Stark. Sickened by the belief that his sister's body has earned him his job, Adam approaches Willie on the steps of the Capitol and shoots him. Willie dies a few days later, protesting to Jack that things might have been different. Adam is shot to death by Sugar-Boy. Some weeks later Jack learns that it was Sadie Burke, infuriated by Willie's determination to return to his wife after their son's injury, who told Tiny Duffy and Gummy Larson about Anne and Willie, and it was Duffy's voice that Adam heard on the telephone.

Jack presents to Judge Irwin the damning evidence against him. Broken by the revelation of an event so remote he has nearly forgotten it, Judge Irwin tells Jack he still may block disclosure of the evidence by one further revelation. The next morning, "a bright, beautiful, silvery soprano scream" awakens Jack: It is his mother, who has just been told that Irwin has committed suicide. She tells Jack that he has killed his father. For the first time in his life, Jack realizes that his vapid, silly mother has been capable of love, ironically, for a man Jack, too, has loved and, in effect, killed.

That terrible scream wakens Jack from The Great Sleep and compels him to abandon the easy despair of The Great Twitch. That his mother could love, that Adam and Anne, Lucy and Willie could live despite their pre-ordained doom—all of this convinces Jack that man must act against his fate. As the novel ends, Jack and Anne, married, live in the house Irwin has willed him. Jack works to complete his study of Cass Mastern, after which he and Anne "shall go out of the house and go into the convulsion of the world. . . ."

Critical Opinion

When *All the King's Men* appeared in 1946, the obvious parallel between Willie Stark and the late Huey Long, Governor of Louisiana, aroused greater attention than the more significant merits of the novel. To those who insist that the novel is an apology for Long's life, Warren's own answer serves best: "There is really nothing to reply to this kind of innocent boneheadedness or gospel-bit hysteria."

Most critics since those first days of stormy dissension have recognized the novel for its more relevant qualities. They have seen that Willie Stark and Jack Burden are alike in their quest for self-knowledge and for the identity that enable a man to shape his destiny in a chaotic world. Willie's moral neutrality leads him at last to destruction, but so too does Adam's moral absolutism. Jack Burden alone comes to a maturity that permits survival. He experiences the extremes of idealism and despair but settles at last for a kind of pragmatic realism that opens the way to meaningful life.

The novel has tremendous narrative impact, even though its episodes occasionally border on the melodramatic. The prose style has energy and sweep, except when the contrast between Jack Burden's rhetorical asides to the reader and his hard-boiled, laconic dialogue tax the reader's credulity. Warren draws upon a rich fund of imagery and certain basic mythic patterns—the motifs of journey and return, birth and death, sin and repentance—to deepen the implications of his narrative. The abiding strength of *All the King's Men* remains in its characterizations, not only the masterly handling of Willie Stark, but also the shrewdly and vividly portrayed minor figures who cluster about him.

The Author

Novelist, poet, dramatist, biographer, critic, and teacher, *Robert Penn Warren* was born in Guthrie, Kentucky, attended Vanderbilt University as an undergraduate and Oxford as a Rhodes Scholar. A member of the *"Fugitive* group" of young Southern agrarian poets and critics dedicated to creating a

Southern literature more vital than sentimental, Warren wrote for their magazine, *The Fugitive*, and later helped found and edit the important journal *Southern Review*.

Winner of the Pulitzer Prize for *All the King's Men*, Warren has for the past twenty-five years taught English at several universities—Louisiana State (where he gathered material for his novel), Minnesota, and Yale. He collaborated with Cleanth Brooks on the important college text *Understanding Poetry* which has introduced students and teachers to the "new criticism."

From the outset, Warren's fiction has dealt with regional problems that touch universal themes. In *Night Riders* (1939), his first novel, an account of a historical struggle between Kentucky farmers and tobacco companies, Warren stresses Percy Munn's conflict as he tries to reconcile principle with reality. In *World Enough and Time* (1950), *The Cave* (1959), and *The Flood* (1964), Warren also draws on historical events, past and present, to highlight the complexities of man's fate.

The Naked and the Dead

by

NORMAN MAILER (1923–)

Main Characters

General Edward Cummings—Division commander, a Mid-westerner and a graduate of West Point, a fascist-minded despot, loather of men, a pseudo-intellectual, and a subtle homosexual.

Lt. Robert Hearn—The General's aide, Chicago-born and Harvard-educated, a sensitive but ineffectual dilettante who has played with love and radicalism without ever embracing either. To escape the emptiness of his mother-dominated life, he enlists just before Pearl Harbor.

Sgt. Sam Croft—A platoon leader, son of illiterate Texas parents, a hunter from his boyhood and as cold and ruthless toward men as he is toward animals. ("I hate everything which is not in myself.")

Red Valsen—Son of a Montana coal miner killed in a shaft explosion. At fourteen he is a miner; at nineteen, a vaga-bond drifting eastward through America's hobo jungles; at twenty-nine, a complete nihilist who, to keep moving and to avoid any lasting involvement with women or jobs, joins the Army.

Joey Goldstein—Son of poor Brooklyn candy-store keepers, a welder before his induction, settled in a gray but tolerable marriage, deeply sensitive to the anti-Semitism of his Army comrades.

Roy Gallagher—An ugly, acne-ravaged Boston Irishman, viciously anti-Semitic, and a minor bully-boy hoodlum in right-wing groups before being drafted.

Julio Martinez—A lithe young Mexican from Texas, shy, mannerly, and though frightened, a fine soldier. Nicknamed "Japbait."

Woodrow Wilson—Aged thirty, married and devoted to his wife and children, but nevertheless the most virile, free-booting lover in his Southern hillbilly environs. He amuses himself and his fellow soldiers with recollections of his amorous prowess.

William Brown—Formerly a salesman in Tulsa, Oklahoma, popular, middle-class in fortune and taste, blandly interested in his wife but more willing to repent the morning after than to forego whoring and drinking.

Polack Czienwicz—Product of a Chicago slum and a stern parochial education, a butcher, numbers runner and, when he is drafted, about to become a white slaver.

Roth—An intelligent, hypersensitive youth, wholly alien to his comrades in interests and sensibilities.

Steve Minetta—An Italian soldier from New York, terrified of the rigors of combat and willing to use any device to avoid battle.

Major Dalleson—Operations officer of the division, a dull-witted but persistent opportunist.

The Story

Aboard the troop convoy, the men variously occupy the hours before the assault craft will be lowered to land them on the Pacific island of Anopopei. Wilson, Gallagher, and Croft play poker, Red Valsen sneaks on deck at night and watches the shore line, Brown discusses the faithlessness of wives, and Martinez lies in his bunk tensely anticipating the violence of the morrow. Next morning, as the assault craft moves toward the shore, Croft senses that young Hennessey, who seems overly cautious and tense, will be the first to die. When his prediction is swiftly borne out, Croft experiences a surge of self-confidence. For Martinez, the boy's death merely frees him of the terror he suffers before battle begins.

The progress of General Cummings' task force inland from the beaches is slow and costly, but gradually the men infiltrate the Japanese positions. General Cummings expects that the campaign will consume time and men but satisfies himself that he has both in abundance and sets about establishing for himself quarters as luxurious as the jungle permits. At the officers' mess that afternoon, Cummings demands that a loud argument between Hearn and his fellow officers cease at once. Hearn had listened impatiently while several of his superiors discoursed ignorantly but vituperatively about labor unions. Finally Hearn interposes questions and comments that challenge the intelligence of his fellow officers. Just when the others seem ready to discipline him, Cummings intervenes, saving Hearn.

Later, in the general's tent, Hearn tries to answer Cummings' query about his behavior. Hearn's replies move Cummings to ridicule his aide as a foolish liberal hopelessly out of line in a century that belongs to the power-lusting reactionary. To prove his point, Cummings compels Hearn to snap to attention and salute him. Angry, humiliated, Hearn nevertheless grudgingly admires his commanding officer, partly because he shares the general's snobbery, partly because he takes pride in Cummings, singling him out as a fit intellectual companion. But above all, Hearn is fascinated by the riddle Cummings poses for him, the "shoddy motive" that he is certain he will ultimately discover, the hidden core that has always aroused Hearn's curiosity.

After a month of confused battle plans, the division has advanced almost twenty-five miles, seriously overextending supply and communication lines. For some time, Croft's platoon has served only in reconnaissance duty and has experienced no combat. Rain soaks the men's spirits as well as their bodies, typhoons rip up their tents, interrupting their card games and windy conversations. For Cummings, the storms represent a form of natural chaos he cannot tolerate in the orderly, disciplined world he hopes to control. Nevertheless, despite the disorganization of his forces by the storms, Cummings orders that no general retreat take place. He determines to risk an assault by the Japanese.

Anticipating an enemy attack that night, Cummings orders Croft's reconnaissance squad to the front in support of the forward lines. Croft anticipates the battle with eagerness, Valsen with absolute indifference, most of the others with varying degrees of fear and anticipation. A mile from the front, Croft receives orders to drag two anti-tank guns through the jungle mud to the front lines. The trail along which the men slog is only a few feet wide, their progress tortuously slow. At a bank, the gun dragged by Goldstein and two other soldiers slips from their grasp and tumbles down the embankment into a creek. Croft, calling Goldstein "Izzy," places the blame on him and accuses him of goldbricking. Goldstein was not solely responsible for the accident, but no one comes to his defense.

The next evening, lying at the edge of a river, the men hear the enemy calling across softly that they are coming to kill. Croft roars at them to come on, fires his machine gun, and attracts a volley of enemy fire. When the Japanese begin to charge, Croft enthusiastically mows them down like wheat stalks before a thresher. The sound of a wounded Jap near by irritates him, and he tosses a grenade to silence the dying man. But the slaughter leaves Croft still unsated. "One of these days I'm gonna really get me a Jap," he says as he watches the dead bodies drift downstream.

While the battle continues at the front, Cummings' electric refrigerator arrives at the bivouac with a supply of fresh meat to stock it. The general puts Hearn in charge of establishing an officers' recreation tent, and Hearn quickly discovers, while working with several incompetent enlisted men, that he shares some of the general's contempt for them and their transparent efforts to balk him in his assigned task. That night the general calls Hearn to his tent to play chess. Though Hearn is a competent player, he finds Cummings more than his match. Cummings uses the chess game to draw an analogy with human experience, "a concentration of life," he calls it. As in the game, Hearn feels that during the ensuing conversation about the worthlessness of all but supremely powerful men, he has been outmaneuvered and kept off balance by Cummings. Whenever he attempts a crude retort, Cummings responds by treating him as a subordinate. Something in the general's voice and manner, nevertheless, makes Hearn realize Cummings' intentions are sexual. He has, he now knows, found the "shoddy motive," and nothing Cummings tries will any longer disturb him.

At the front, Croft, Red, and Gallagher come upon four Japs and hurl a grenade at them. Valsen, sent by Croft to mop up the wounded, is attacked by a survivor when his gun jams. Croft disarms the Jap and sends Valsen on ahead. Croft makes Gallagher give the prisoner candy, allows him to smoke a cigarette and show pictures of his wife and family. As the prisoner relaxes against a tree at Croft's invitation and closes his eyes with a smile of pleasure on his face, Croft fires a bullet through his head. Gallagher looks on, horrified. A few hours later, the platoon is ordered to the rear where the men sit about listening to Croft recount the death of the prisoner. By the time they are all drunk, however, Croft's brief pleasure has disappeared and his hunger for blood surges within him again. Restless, the men set out to plunder a ravaged Japanese camp. Martinez recovers the gold teeth of one corpse. The others rampage among bodies and parts of bodies, sickened by the stench but driven by their desire to bring home some tangible evidence of their expedition. But a snake appears and they flee even after Red blasts its head off.

One day the chaplain brings Gallagher word that his wife has died in childbirth. Stunned, Gallagher can think only that a Jew must have been the doctor. Her letters bring Gallagher close to breakdown. Ironically, it is Roth, a Jew, who feels most deeply for Gallagher but cannot even talk to him or attempt to console him.

Little progress in the campaign rewards Cummings' ingenious plans. Stalled and unable to effect any significant advance, Cummings rages inwardly, conscious that he may lose his command, powerless to alter the course he thought he could control. The butt of his frustration becomes Hearn upon whom he imposes all sorts of petty and humiliating tasks that make his aide a laughingstock among the officers. In revenge, Hearn executes the maneuver he knows may cause his own destruction. After having the general's quarters spruced and the floor scrubbed absolutely clean, Hearn drops a match near the general's footlocker and grinds a cigarette butt into the middle of the floor.

Later, when the general calls him to his quarters, Hearn deliberately avoids the kind of tact he knows the general insists upon. To Cummings' query about the reason for the war, Hearn answers too pointedly, "It's a bad thing when millions of people are killed because one joker has to get some things out of his system." Cummings' theory is that the war is an expression of "power morality," that all men are moved toward omnipotence and those who cannot adjust to such a course must be crushed. To prove his point he demands that Hearn pick up a cigarette he throws at his feet. The men exchange stares, but Hearn picks up the butt and puts it into an ashtray. Hearn then asks for a transfer, but Cummings assigns him to Major Dalleson's section for further humiliation until he can conceive a more fitting resolution to the problem Hearn poses for him. Hearn, Cummings knows, represents the kind of rebellion his theories cannot survive.

Cummings' proposed solution seems demoniacally clever since it purports to rid him of Hearn and simultaneously to set in motion a plan to further the campaign. He places Hearn in charge of Croft's reconnaissance platoon and assigns the men to travel by assault boat to the farthest end of the island, there to land, march through the jungle to the rear of the Japanese lines and, by reconnaissance, determine the feasibility of a large-scale amphibious attack.

Hearn assumes command of the patrol, aware of Croft's competence and sure that the sergeant resents the presence of an officer. He is right on both counts but has no real measure of Croft's bitterness toward him. Most of the other men accept Hearn as a decent person, though Red Valsen resents him as he does any figure of authority. The men march wearily through the jungle, cutting a trail along the river until they come to a flat valley at the foot of tall, rugged Mount Anaka. Thus far, apart from physical exhaustion and Wilson's desperate case of diarrhea, the patrol has experienced neither incident nor accident. All of them know, however, that on the morrow, when they attempt to work their way through a narrow pass leading to the rear of the Japanese lines, they face the threat of a Japanese ambush.

Croft's instinct tells him to have the men climb Mount Anaka, but he keeps his counsel to himself for the moment, reluctantly ordering the men to enter the pass as Hearn has directed. Shortly after the patrol enters the pass, they are ambushed, but with the exception of Wilson, who is shot in the stomach, all scurry to safety. That night Croft, along with Red Valsen, Gallagher, Goldstein, and a Southerner named Ridges, worms his way through the tall grass and brings the wounded Wilson back to the encampment. The men improvise a litter and Hearn and Croft assign four men (including Brown, Goldstein, and Ridges) to try to carry Wilson back to the beachhead where they originally landed.

While the men are cutting the stretcher poles, Roth picks up a small crippled bird and gently cups it in his hand. The other men crowd about him, concerned and sympathetic. Annoyed by the interruption, Croft breaks into the circle and demands to see what Roth is holding. Taking the bird from Roth's hand, Croft is momentarily torn between compassion and his lust to kill. Possessed by the urge to destroy, he squeezes the bird to death, then hurls it into the valley. Instantly the men recoil in horror, then, led by Red, denounce Croft. Only Hearn's intrusion prevents a violent flare-up. But Hearn's insistence that Croft apologize to Roth deepens Croft's hostility toward his superior officer.

While the litter bearers begin their agonizing journey to the rear—Wilson's cries of pain tormenting them more than the burden of his heavy body—Croft sends Martinez out on a mission intended to lead to Hearn's destruction. Martinez' assignment, Croft tells him, is to determine whether a second Japanese bivouac lies beyond the one in the pass. If so, Croft wants Martinez to report only to him. Croft's hope is that if the enemy is present, Hearn, leading the patrol, will be the first killed. Martinez ventures forth, discovers a Jap sentry, kills him, then reports that the pass is cleared. Within a half-hour after the patrol enters the pass the next morning, Hearn is killed by a machine-gun bullet. Croft assumes command at once, telling the men that they will climb Mount Anaka and, after they descend on the other side, scout the Japanese rear.

Under Croft's orders, Martinez tells the men that Hearn, despite knowing that the pass was Jap-infested, insisted upon making the entry. But even the knowledge that the lieutenant was a fool fails to diminish the growing irritation the men feel toward Croft as he drives them brutally and relentlessly toward the crest of Mount Anaka. To Croft, climbing the mountain has become an obsession, almost a "human thing" he must conquer. When they reach a point less than a thousand feet from the top, the ledge along which they have been alternately walking and crawling narrows to less than a foot. Below, the mountain sheers off into a walled abyss. The only way to proceed, Croft recognizes, is to leap across the crevice to surer footing on the other side. The leap is only four feet, but because of the awkward terrain, the men, laden with full packs, must leap sideways and gain an immediate foothold. The alternative is death. All of the men except Roth make the leap successfully. Exhausted, frightened, bullied a few minutes earlier by Gallagher, Roth simply lacks the force to propel himself to safety. Bellowing in horror and disbelief, he hurtles to his death.

By the next morning, the already limp morale of Croft's platoon has crumbled. While Croft sleeps, the men determine that they will not go on, and ask Martinez, whom Croft most respects, to tell the platoon leader about their intention. By challenging Martinez' good sense, loyalty, and courage, Croft regains his support. A few minutes later, however, Valsen forces Martinez to reveal the truth about Hearn's death by frightening the superstitious young Mexican into believing that his knifing of the Japanese sentry has brought him nearer to his own death. As Martinez again wavers about defying Croft, Red announces that he has no intention of moving on. Croft threatens to shoot him, but Red suggests that Croft will have to shoot everyone. Unfortunately the other men are too awed by Croft to stand beside Red. With Croft's rifle pointed at his stomach, Red at last yields.

The climb continues for a few more hours, the last ounce of energy dwindling even in Croft. Just beyond the dense foliage through which he is leading the men, Croft sees sunlight and knows he is nearing the summit. At that instant, however, he stumbles and falls upon a hornets' nest. The insects swarm over the men, driving them frantically and aimlessly down the sides of the mountain they had so laboriously climbed. Silently and uneventfully, they retrace their steps through the jungle trail to the beachhead. The stretcher bearers are waiting, but Wilson has already died. On the assault boat returning them to their base, Croft looks at the unconquered mountain and experiences again the old hunger and with it the knowledge that he has failed and will never have another chance to learn just how far he might have gone.

When the men return, they learn that their expedition was wholly unnecessary. Cummings' clever schemes have amounted to nothing, for the enemy resistance has simply collapsed because their supplies are exhausted. To add to the absurdity, the Japanese defeat was achieved in a single day while General Cummings was away at headquarters. The conquering hero is the bumbling Major Dalleson, who (wholly unaware of what he was about) mounted a full-scale attack on the crumbling Japanese supply depot. All that remains is to mop up stray Japanese soldiers. The American patrols take few prisoners, shooting most of the wounded, and rifle-butting others to death. As the novel ends, Major Dalleson, contemplating his promotion, thinks of a brave new idea to further his career: a field map with an overlay of a pin-up girl so that trainees will attend more carefully to instruction.

Critical Opinion

In the early short story "A Calculus at Heaven," which provided the basis for *The Naked and the Dead*, Mailer wrote: "In America, men live, work, and die without the rudest conceptions of dignity." The blighted lives of the men involved in the campaign on Anopopei extend to a bitter conclusion the deep pessimism implicit in the short story. At first glance the reader may be misled into assuming that war alone has fashioned the dead end toward which all the events seem to lead. But by means of the technical device he calls the "time machine" (a technique for which he is indebted to John Dos Passos' *U.S.A.*), Mailer flashes back to the pre-war lives of his characters and reveals that their doom had already been spelled out before they entered the Army.

Racial and religious discrimination has foreshortened possibilities for Martinez, Goldstein, and Roth, and distorted truth for the bigoted Gallagher. Yet Gallagher, too, has been victimized by an economic environment which precluded open-mindedness. Beyond economic and social handicaps, nearly all of the characters have also suffered the tensions resulting from America's ambivalent sexual attitudes. Towering over and beyond these forces is the climactic struggle between the representatives of absolute power (Cummings and Croft) and those of liberalism (Hearn) or compassionate nihilism (Valsen). What is most terrifying about Mailer's resolution is that it is not a resolution at all. Good and evil cancel each other out. Hearn is killed, Valsen is faced down by Croft. Cummings' victory is hollow since it comes by accident rather than by plan. Croft suffers humiliation (ironically, a stinging defeat by hornets) at the hands of the natural forces he wants most to control. Mount Anaka thus becomes, as Mailer himself has indicated, "a consciously ambiguous symbol" suggesting the hopelessness of aspiration as well as the defeat of evil intention.

Not all readers agree that the novel ends in despair. Some prefer Mailer's interpretation of his own work, in which he argues that although he acknowledges the corruption and confusion of man, he tries in *The Naked and the Dead* to prove that "there are limits beyond which [man] cannot be pushed," and that despite the corruption, "there are yearnings for a better world."

Mailer's novel, whatever we may think about its philosophical orientation, is thoroughly absorbing throughout. Although the characters are more prototypical than real, the episodes in which they appear more often than not obscure the psychological limitations of type casting. The language is commonly harsh, the vulgate familiar to men at war, but because of its accuracy only the prudish will object to it. In all, *The Naked and the Dead*—the first novel of a young man of twenty-five—still remains the best war novel to emerge from World War II.

The Author

Brooklyn-bred, *Norman Mailer* set out to become an aeronautical engineer, but shifted to writing during his freshman year at Harvard. A year after graduation, Mailer entered the Army, served for two years in the Philippines and in Japan as clerk, cook, surveyor, and rifleman. Before he was out of the Army, he had won story-writing contests. One of his stories, "A Calculus at Heaven," contains the germ of *The Naked and the Dead*.

Mailer's success with his first novel, *The Naked and the*

Dead, was immediate and widespread. His reputation has not diminished since, though several of his experiences in public and private life have added notoriety rather than dignity to his stature. His second novel, *Barbary Shore* (1951), blasted by most critics, tells about a young man settled in a Brooklyn boardinghouse writing a novel about the war. Politics (chiefly left-wing) and neuroticism invade Mikey Lovett's privacy and distort his artistic purpose. Mailer's third novel, *The Deer Park* (1955), received mixed but essentially admiring notices for its satirical analysis of the debauchery and sterility of Hollywood life.

Since his first three novels, Mailer has completed no full-length novel, though he has published a novella, *The American Dream* (1964), and *Advertisements for Myself* (1959), a collection of stories and essays. Mailer's anti-Stalinist Marxism and his profound interest in existentialism find voice in the essays published in *Advertisements* and in the more recent *The Presidential Papers of Norman Mailer* (1964), a collection of articles he wrote about the late President Kennedy and about the problems Mailer regarded as central to a successful Administration. He has also published a volume of poems, *Deaths for the Ladies* (1962).

The Catcher in the Rye

by

J. D. SALINGER (1919–)

Main Characters

Holden Caulfield—A seventeen-year-old boy who believes
   that the world is dominated by "phonies," and is in frantic
   search of some refuge.
Ackley—A classmate at Pencey Prep, whom Holden finds re-
   pulsive.
Stradlater—Another classmate, a clean-looking young man
   whom Holden regards as a lecher.
Mr. Spencer—One of Holden's teachers, kind but ineffectual.
Phoebe Caulfield—Holden's younger sister, a sweet, innocent,
   very precocious girl, one of the few people Holden loves
   and admires.
Mr. Antolini—A former teacher of Holden's, a bright, sophisticated man whom Holden suspects of homosexual intentions
   toward him.

The Story

Holden Caulfield, a seventeen-year-old student at Pencey
Prep, writes this autobiographical account of his misadven-
tures in a world of "phonies." He sees them everywhere: the
headmaster who snoots people with the wrong accent while
kowtowing to those with the right moneyed-manner; the jazz

pianist who plays showy and false to please the crowd; and almost all professional actors, especially movie actors. Partly because of his hypersensitivity and his low threshold for boredom, he has just flunked out of Pencey—the third prep school he has attended. Among Holden's companions there is Ackley who constantly squeezes the pimples on his face, dislikes everybody he thinks at all superior to him, and doggedly pesters his classmates. But Ackley is perhaps preferable to Holden's roommate, Stradlater, a clean-looking, athletic young man whose goals seem to be conforming, avoiding work, and seducing young ladies.

Holden has a brief fight with Stradlater about a girl, Jane Gallagher, whom he likes and whom he suspects Stradlater of attempting to seduce. After the fight, Holden bids an uncomfortable farewell to an old teacher, Mr. Spencer, and leaves Pencey for New York.

Holden knows that his mother will be heartbroken and his father furious at his latest failures, but they won't have the news from Pencey for three days. Since he has plenty of money, he decides to check into a hotel and have as good a time as he can before confronting them. Though he is six feet two and a half and has grey hair, he does not look older than sixteen. When he descends to the Lavender Room of the rather sleazy hotel he has chosen, the waiter refuses to bring him whiskey. Disgruntled, he settles for a coke. Then he attempts to pick up a girl who is sitting with two friends—"witches," Holden calls them. He dances with each of them, buys them drinks, but is once again snubbed as a child.

Restless, he takes a cab to Ernie's, a Greenwich Village nightclub where anyone over six can get a drink. On the way he asks the driver one of the questions that has been plaguing him: Where do the ducks that swim in the Central Park lagoon go in winter? The driver isn't helpful. At Ernie's, while sipping Scotches, he is repelled by all the prep-school and college phonies who talk vacuously and applaud the music because they think it sophisticated. He meets an old flame of his big brother, D.B.—now in Hollywood writing scripts (selling himself, Holden believes) after producing a first-rate book of stories. She exerts her charm, but to no avail. She's a phony, too, hoping to work on D.B. at long distance through Holden.

Returning to the hotel, Holden is asked by the elevator man if he wants a girl to visit him in his room. Because he is depressed, he answers Yes without thinking. When the girl arrives, he is unable to carry the affair off. He pays her the five dollars agreed upon, but she insists he must give her ten. He refuses. A little later the prostitute returns, accompanied by the elevator man who punches Holden in the stomach, knocking him on the floor, while the prostitute extracts five more dollars from his wallet.

The next day Holden leaves the hotel, phones a girl friend named Sally (whom he likes only intermittently), and arranges a theater date for the afternoon. He checks his bags, has breakfast, and offers ten dollars that he can now ill afford to two nuns whom he meets, then wanders around Broadway. He really wants to phone Jane Gallagher or his sister Phoebe. Phoebe is a wonderful ten-year-old—wonderful as almost all children are in Holden's eyes (in contrast to adults). The theater date proves disastrous, first, because the Lunts are good but don't behave like people, and second, because Sally meets an Andover student who activates every phony fiber in her. They go skating afterward, and when she rejects Holden's suggestion that they go away to some cabin camp in the woods and escape the tedium and falsity of New York, he insults her. He is immediately sorry, but she won't accept his apologies.

Holden phones an older acquaintance—somebody who was at a prep school with him—and they meet at a swanky bar. Holden teases him, drinking heavily the while, until his former schoolmate goes off to an engagement. Drunk, Holden goes to the park to check on the ducks. It begins to rain. He has very little money left. He decides to sneak into his parents' home and see his sister Phoebe for whom he has been longing. Luckily for him, his parents aren't in, and he negotiates the passageway without awaking the maid. Phoebe is ecstatic at seeing him until she deduces that he's been kicked out of Pencey. She upbraids him, and his attempts to explain to her his exasperation about school are only partly successful. In spite of this, their meeting is filled with affection.

Their parents suddenly arrive. Before Holden hides, Phoebe attempts to convince him of the importance of school. He says he's going West. Phoebe quickly puts out the light just before her mother enters the room. She questions Phoebe, who conceals the fact that Holden is with her, even confessing to puffing a cigarette to explain the smell of cigarette smoke in the room. (Holden is a chain smoker.)

Holden sneaks out and goes to the home of a former English teacher, Mr. Antolini, whom he has phoned. Though it is now very early in the morning, he is greeted warmly, and he listens to Mr. Antolini's witty lecture as attentively as his sleepy mind will allow. Mr. Antolini tells Holden that education would be valuable for him because it would teach him the size mind he had and what it would fit. Holden agrees, yawning. Finally he is allowed to go to sleep on the sofa. He awakens suddenly to feel Mr. Antolini's hand stroking his head. He jumps up and despite Mr. Antolini's protests, scurries out of the apartment. He is convinced of Mr. Antolini's perverse intentions.

Holden spends the rest of the night in the Grand Central waiting room, snatching what sleep he can. Next morning he leaves a note at Phoebe's school asking her to meet him at the Metropolitan Museum of Art. At the school he is perturbed by the obscene scrawls on the walls. Phoebe arrives at the museum hugging a suitcase. She has determined to go with Holden on his projected journey West. Holden is moved, but he firmly declines her offer. She becomes angry, refusing to talk to him—though when he walks into Central Park past the zoo to the carousel, she follows him. He persuades her to ride the carousel. After some protests, she does. As she rides, it begins to rain. But Holden has made his decision. He will not run away. He will face whatever he must.

At the end Holden implies that he is writing the book from a sanitarium. His psychoanalyst keeps asking him if he is going to apply himself when he goes back to school in September. Holden thinks so, but he doesn't know. How can one know what one's going to do until one does it?

Critical Opinion

The Catcher in the Rye is Salinger's only published novel. (It may be that the stories about the Glass family will take the shape of a novel of sorts eventually.) Its hero, Holden Caulfield, is a modern version of Huck Finn, like him a moralist in spite of himself, racked by the frauds and shams and cruelties he sees everywhere about him. Huck, of course, comes through sound, and Holden may, too; but at our last glimpse of him he is still under treatment by a psychoanalyst.

The dominant objection to Salinger is that he is sentimental, that he holds a number of unrealistic attitudes about life and society, especially his notion that children are basically innocent and good and that they degenerate as they grow older. Salinger has confessed his fondness for children: "Some of my best friends are children. In fact, all my best friends are children. It's almost unbearable for me to realize that my book will be kept on a shelf out of their reach." (In Windsor, at the library nearest Salinger's home, it is.)

However, not Salinger's attitudes but Holden's are relevant to *The Catcher in the Rye*. And it is completely believable that Holden—an adolescent with nerve endings where he ought to have skin—might love the innocence he sees (or thinks he sees) in children but not in adults. The psychoanalyst Ernest Jones, though less than enthusiastic about the novel, says it reflects "what every sensitive sixteen-year-old since Rousseau has felt, and of course what each one of us is certain he has felt."

Even antagonistic critics agree that *The Catcher in the Rye* is a fascinating, witty story. Indeed, one may extract from their comments a small anthology in praise of Salinger. For example, George Steiner, a hostile critic who objects that the reputation of the book is inflated, admits that "Salinger has caught with uncanny precision the speech and thought—rhythms of the young." And Harvey Breit, discounting *The Catcher in the Rye* as a serious novel, nonetheless declares it "a brilliant tour de force, one that has sufficient power and cleverness to make the reader chuckle and—rare indeed—even laugh aloud."

The Author

Jerome David Salinger, for a decade now one of the favorite authors of American college undergraduates, was born in New York City. After attending public schools in Manhattan, a military academy in Pennsylvania, and three colleges (none of which conferred a degree upon him), he spent a year abroad. During the war he served with the Fourth Infantry Division as a staff sergeant, took part in five campaigns from D-Day to V-Day. He began writing at fifteen, published his first story at twenty-one, and since then has appeared in a number of magazines (as he says, "mostly—and most happily—in *The New Yorker*"). He lives with his second wife and their two children in Cornish, New Hampshire, in virtual seclusion.

Besides three volumes of short stories—*Nine Stories* (1953), *Franny and Zooey* (1961), and *Raise High The Roof Beam, Carpenters* (1963)—Salinger has published only one other work in book form, *The Catcher in the Rye*. His best stories concern the trials, aspirations, frustrations, and occasional successes of the nine members of the Glass family: an Irish mother and a Jewish father (former vaudeville performers), and their seven eccentric, charming, perceptive, and neurotic children.

Salinger's are delightful pieces, sometimes funny, sometimes touching, sometimes painful—but always gracefully constructed and admirably phrased. He has an extraordinary ear for dialogue. Readers are virtually unanimous in praise of the uncanny accuracy of his crisp, colloquial lines.

A few critics have called Salinger a "slick middle-brow writer," "a delayed adolescent," "a garrulous pseudo-mystic." A far greater number, however, have compared him to Mark Twain, have found his stories "original, first-rate, serious, and beautiful," and have termed him "a twentieth-century classic." The truth probably lies somewhere between. While Salinger is no Mark Twain, he is an interesting, intelligent, often perceptive writer, and a consummate craftsman.

Lie Down in Darkness

by

WILLIAM STYRON (1925—)

Main Characters

Milton Loftis—The head of the decaying Loftis family of Port Warwick, Virginia, who at forty-three has betrayed his aspirations and degenerated into a weak, guilt-ridden sensualist.

Helen Loftis—Milton's wife, possessive, bigoted, her heart "a nest of little hatreds," she yearns to rid herself of but cannot.

Peyton Loftis—Their intelligent, seductive daughter. She is a suicide at twenty-two, victim of her relationship to her family and to her Southern world.

Maudie Loftis—The youngest daughter (already dead when the novel opens), retarded and crippled, the center of her mother's life.

Dolly Bonner—Milton's mistress, flighty, sensuous, silly, but deeply in love with Milton.

Pookie Bonner—Dolly's husband, hearty, uncouth, well-intentioned.

Carey Carr—A failure as a poet, he turns minister without "having been able to attain a complete vision of God."

Adrienne Carr—Carey's sophisticated, skeptical, and rather cynical wife.

Dick Cartwright—Peyton's first lover, a carefree, unimaginative college boy.

Harry Miller—Peyton's husband, a New York artist, who tries ardently but unsuccessfully to save his wife.

La Ruth, Ella, Stonewall—The Negro family employed by the Loftises.

Daddy Faith—A Negro evangelist whose preaching about love unifies and inspires the local Negro community.

The Story

One morning in August, 1945, a small group gathers at the railway depot in Port Warwick, Virginia, a shipbuilding city near Richmond. An undertaker and his chauffeur work furiously to repair the broken radiator pipe of an empty hearse. Near by in a limousine sits the weeping Dolly Bonner who has joined her lover, Milton Loftis, to await the arrival of the body of his daughter, Peyton, from New York. Helen Loftis has coldly refused to accompany her husband, promising only to attend the funeral services with the Rev. Carey Carr.

In the present, the seven sections of the novel trace with brief notations the slow progress of the cortege from the depot to the cemetery. The past, however, holds the true center of dramatic interest. Thus in each chapter one or more of the major characters recalls those crucial events of the past years leading to the tragic climax.

By refusing to attend the funeral with her husband, Helen hopes to make him experience a lonely despair that will at last reveal to him what intense suffering can really be. She recalls how the death of her youngest child, Maudie, emptied her spirit but hardly affected Milton's. Now, with the death of Peyton, whom he loved with a passion beyond fatherliness, Helen prays that Milton, too, will suffer comparable agony. As he waits at the depot, Milton more than fulfills Helen's desire. Two memories invade his tormented consciousness: first, his father's urging him in adolescence never to let passion be his guide, advice he has abysmally failed to follow since his college days, and second, Peyton's last, despairing letter from New York with its hauntingly prophetic images of birds and falling. As these recollections of the past torture him,

Milton is obsessed by a desire to be reunited with his estranged wife.

Peyton's body arrives and is placed in the hearse, and the ride to the cemetery begins. Unwillingly seated beside the adoring Dolly, Milton recalls the beginning of their affair. A dozen years earlier, Dolly and her fat, balding husband, Pookie, along with their young son, Melvin, visit the Loftises' home one Sunday. Dolly boldly flirts with Milton and he freely studies her shapely legs. Alone for a brief moment, they admit their mutual affection but are interrupted by a shrill cry. La Ruth, the maid, has discovered the crippled Maudie tied and gagged by Peyton and Melvin. Helen grasps the sobbing child to her, slaps Peyton, and takes Maudie into the house. After the Bonners leave, Milton quiets Peyton and gently persuades her to apologize to Helen. Later, Peyton curls up beside him and he is filled with a strangely profound love for the child. Though he resents Helen for hitting Peyton, he hopes to make her understand his special love for his daughter and even his sensual need of Dolly.

As the cortege moves past the town dump, Dolly sadly realizes that Milton no longer loves her and that she will soon be utterly alone since Pookie has long since divorced her. She recalls the night in 1939 when Milton first made love to her at the country club. At this moment Milton and Helen also think back to that evening, the night of Peyton's sixteenth birthday party. Helen is jealous of Dolly, at once loving and despising Milton, resenting Peyton's youth, beauty, and, most of all, her love for her father and cool disdain for her mother. When Helen discovers that Peyton has been drinking party punch spiked with liquor, she demands that the girl return home. Milton intercedes in Peyton's behalf, and Helen, after denouncing him as a sinner and an atheist who has destroyed love, stalks off alone. Milton consoles himself by getting drunk and then, finding Dolly alone, leads her to the darkened golf museum room and distractedly makes love to her. On the lawn Peyton, saddened by the evening's cruelties, lies weeping in the embrace of a teen-age boy.

As Milton and Dolly sit in the cemetery-bound limousine waiting for the last of a long procession of Negroes to pass on their way to Daddy Faith's revival meeting, the Rev. Carey Carr drives to the Loftis home to pick up Helen and bring her

to the funeral. As he drives, he remembers when Helen first
came to him for spiritual advice just after Peyton's unhappy
birthday party. Helen tells him of her adoration for her father,
a strict, severe military man known as "Blood and Jesus
Peyton." From him, she insists, "I learned what's right and
what's wrong." And she recalls her happy years with Milton—
before he begins drinking and lusting. Carr remembers, too,
how Helen recounted with horror Peyton's easy display of her
physical charms, a sure sign, Helen believes, that she will sin
and be damned. Helen admits to Carr that she wants to stop
hating and he tries, with little success, to convince her that
God is love. Finally, he remembers hearing from several people about Helen's confronting Dolly in a local restaurant two
weeks after Peyton's party and loudly accusing her of having
carried on a six-year affair with Milton. Coolly, but as audibly
as Helen, Dolly replies that their love had first been con-
summated at Peyton's party but that the affair would continue
as long as Milton wanted her.

When Carr arrives at Helen's house, she is upstairs dressing.
La Ruth weeps and prays as she helps her. In a gesture of love
and compassion, La Ruth grasps Helen's hand and begs her to
take Milton back to fill her loneliness. Helen recoils at the
woman's touch and sharply rejects her advice. Helen descends
the steps and, as she leaves with Carr, says, "The end is upon
us."

In fact, Milton and Helen do not separate after Peyton's
party. For the sake of the children, they maintain a working
relationship, Milton tactfully keeping Dolly and his drinking
under cover. A brief crisis interrupts the peace when Peyton
returns from college for her Christmas holiday in 1941. She
and Helen clash bitterly, but Milton embraces Peyton and
begs her not to leave. During the next year, Peyton does not
return for her vacations and Milton's dreams are tormented
with her image.

In the fall of 1942, Helen takes Maudie to the university
hospital in Charlottesville for a check-up. One night while they
are away and Milton has returned from his rounds as an air-
raid warden (he has daydreamed of being a colonel in Libya)
determined to finish writing a letter to Peyton, he discovers
Dolly on the living room couch. Milton tries to talk to Dolly
about Peyton but she manifests only mild interest. They get

drunk together, and in a moment of bitter vengefulness, Milton leads Dolly to Helen's bed and makes love to her there. Ironically, after his passion, Milton dreams of Peyton. Milton and Dolly are interrupted by a call summoning Milton to the hospital where Maudie is dying.

At the hospital Helen pleads with Milton to stay with her and he agrees. Alone in the waiting room, Milton watches a blue kite flying like a bluebird in the distance, and he recalls his adolescent search for love, a romantic quest he has never abandoned. An old college classmate chances by to interrupt his reverie and insist that Milton join him for one drink at their old fraternity house. Remembering that Peyton's boy friend, Dick Cartwright, will probably be there with her, Milton goes along. Caught up in the wild pre-football-game party, Milton fails to see Peyton who, however, is there. He drifts into a restaurant and meets Pookie Bonner with his girl friend. Jealous of Pookie's wealth and insensibility which, Milton thinks, free him from responsibility and guilt, he patronizes and then insults Pookie. Drunkenly seeking Peyton, he wanders into the football stadium, sits beside a drunken woman for a while, then stumbles out of the arena into the street, careens along the roadway, and at last falls face down in a muddy culvert. There he is found by a Negro, and later, by Peyton and Dick. When he tells Peyton about Maudie, she reproves him. "I love you," she says, adding, "I just think you're a jerk." Milton's image of their perfect union has been shattered, but he recovers enough to go with her to the hospital.

There Helen tongue-lashes them, Milton as a sot, Peyton as a whore, both as utterly incapable of love. She tells how years earlier, Maudie, despite her illness, came closer to genuine love in a fleeting, momentary embrace with an ugly little man named Bennie who would stop in the fields to amuse her by juggling and making faces. Then Helen walks off. Peyton goes off with Dick, gets drunk, and sleeps with him, their relationship pathetically loveless. In the background the radio blares out news of the war.

At a filling station along the road to the cemetery, the limousines of Carey Carr and Milton meet. Milton tells Carr that he wants Helen back, that there must be something left for them. He reminds Carr that the year after Maudie's death was a reasonably happy one for him and Helen. He stopped

drinking and seeing Dolly and even controlled his guilty longing for his daughter. All went well until the day of Peyton's
wedding to Harry Miller.

Peyton's determination to get married in her home represents not sentiment, as she tells Milton the morning of the
wedding, but an effort to come to terms with her past, to
achieve a normalcy despite all the trauma: "Oh, I feel so sorry
for us all. If just she'd had a soul and you'd had some guts."
Milton tries to control his emotions during Carr's reading of
the wedding ceremony, but his hunger for Peyton obsesses
him. Meanwhile Helen behaves well, graciously, and amiably.
During the party, Milton begins to drink, kisses Peyton too
often and too strongly—all in full sight of Harry and Helen.
Peyton begs her father as they dance not to smother her.
Minutes later, Helen and Peyton argue violently in the bedroom. Peyton claws her mother's face and rushes out of the
house with Harry. Milton follows her to the lawn, clings to
her, then lets her leave. Then he telephones Dolly to tell her
that he and Helen are finished.

The final section of the novel—except for a brief prologue
and epilogue—rehearses Peyton's stream-of-consciousness as,
nude, she prepares to leap to her death from a window in
Harlem. In the prologue, Harry and a friend reclaim her body
from potter's field. Harry remembers their meeting at a Greenwich Village party in 1943, his fascination with her beauty,
intelligence, and psychic anguish. Though his friends warn him
that she will bring grief to both of them, he is certain that
together they will triumph. Peyton's stream-of-consciousness
proves how false his expectations are.

The failure of Peyton's marriage lies in the fact that she
needs Harry more than she loves him. Because Harry is fully
aware of this, Peyton irrationally punishes him for his insight
by taking lovers—Tony, the milkman, and Earl Sanders, one
of their artistic friends. Finally disgusted, Harry leaves,
pursued by the hysterical Peyton who begs him to give her
another chance—not, as she says, to let her drown. She brings
him a clock, explaining that they can lose themselves within
its fine mechanism, safe at last from the terror of time: "Not
out of vengeance have I accomplished all my sins," she tells
him, ". . . only in order to lie down in darkness and find, somewhere in the net of dreams, a new father, a new home." But

Harry rejects her. Peyton rides the subway to Harlem, enters a loft building, and climbs the stairs. In the ladies' room, she undresses, envisions flights of birds soaring free, and leaps from the window.

In the epilogue, Milton rushes to Helen in the anteroom of the funeral parlor, demanding that she return to him. When she refuses, he begins to choke her. Then suddenly, he stops and walks alone into the rain. Helen presses her head against the wall, murmuring "Nothing! Nothing! Nothing! Nothing!" Down the road, La Ruth, Ella, and Stonewall share with other Negroes the joyous frenzy of Daddy Faith's river baptism.

Critical Opinion

The title of Styron's novel derives from a passage in Sir Thomas Browne's seventeenth-century study of ancient urn burials. Like the people of old, Browne reminds us, it cannot be long before we lie down in darkness and have our light in ashes. Styron's novel is an analysis of the contemporary forces that cause a whole family to lie down in darkness or, more explicitly, to rot.

Thus no single character can be isolated as chief protagonist or victim. In a sense, it is a whole society wasting away. The raging hatreds that corrode the Loftis family bond are mirrored in the racial tensions and religious bigotry smoldering just below the surface. Moreover, both the society and the characters are ridden with guilt and strive to find forgiveness through love. The tragedy lies in the failure of love to bring them together. Only the Negroes, in a primitive way, discover a path to spiritual redemption.

Styron's narrative fragmentation underscores the fractured psyches of his characters. "The business of the progression of time seems to me one of the most difficult problems a novelist has to cope with," Styron has observed. In *Lie Down in Darkness* he achieves a masterly solution by recording varied points of view as they hover about, then plunge into the crucial episodes of the past. Moreover, his use of dreams, stream-of-consciousness, and, on occasion, omniscient narration, lend variety as well as density to his writing.

Some critics, though admiring Styron's skill, have protested against the novel's solemnity and despair, assigning it to "the dread-despair-and-decay camp of U.S. letters." Styron scorns this attitude, insisting that "new writers haven't cornered any market on faithlessness and despair, any more than Dostoevski or Marlowe or Sophocles did." Several critics share Styron's view. While admitting that Peyton's suicide on the day the atom bomb dropped on Hiroshima seems rather overdrawn, they argue that the novel truthfully and graphically analyzes certain tensions afflicting contemporary man and his society. *Lie Down in Darkness* is not a cheerful novel, but it is an honest one, its characters deeply and closely studied, its techniques imaginatively developed.

The Author

Born in Newport News, Virginia (the actual setting of *Lie Down in Darkness*), *William Styron* attended Duke University until World War II. After three years of service with the Marines, he returned to Duke to complete his education, especially to study writing with William Blackburn. Later he came to New York, writing at the New School under the tutelage of Hiram Haydn. Haydn advised and encouraged Styron during the writing of *Lie Down in Darkness*, his first novel. Published when Styron was twenty-five, it won wide acclaim and was awarded the Prix de Rome of the American Academy of Arts and Letters. While in Rome, Styron married. Today he lives with his wife and three children in Roxbury, Connecticut.

Recalled to Marine duty during the Korean War, Styron gathered material for his short novel, *The Long March*, published in 1952 as a magazine story and in 1956 as a book. Styron has written one other novel, *Set This House on Fire* (1960), a long, disappointing, rather static analysis of the conflict of wills between two men—Mason Flagg, a gifted but cruel American playboy, and Cass Kinsolving, an artist who panders to Flagg's whims in order to keep himself supplied with liquor.

Invisible Man

by

RALPH ELLISON (1914–)

Main Characters

The Narrator—A young Negro, unnamed and "invisible." His invisibility, however, is spiritual rather than physical, the result of his inability to discover the identity he desperately seeks. He is a man of fine intelligence, great sensibility, and courage.

Brother Jack—A one-eyed Brotherhood district leader, cold, ruthless, willing to sacrifice anyone to his cause.

Tod Clifton—A young Negro worker for the Brotherhood cause. Like the narrator, he is seeking his reason for being.

Ras, the Exhorter—A fanatical black-race-supremacy leader in Harlem.

Sybil—A white woman obsessed with fantasies of being raped by a Negro.

Lucius Brockway—A Negro boilerman at the Liberty Paint Company, violently anti-union and terrified of losing his job.

Mary Rambo—A gentle and sympathetic Negro landlady.

Dr. Bledsoe—President of the narrator's college in the South, a hard-headed opportunist who kowtows to important white men to win financial support for his institution.

The Rev. Homer A. Barbee—A blind preacher from Chicago, guest speaker at the college, who believes in the Negro's courage and endurance.

Mr. Norton—A white benefactor of the college, driven by a sense of personal as well as social guilt.

Jim Trueblood—A Negro farmer guilty of incest, but happily surprised by the social approbation the episode wins him among the white community.

The Story

"I am an invisible man," says the narrator in the opening sentence of the Prologue. Hiding in the abandoned basement of a white man's apartment building, the narrator has tapped electric wires to provide himself with more than a thousand lights—free—to illuminate his home and to make himself visible. The light really represents his quest for the truth about himself—his psychic identity. The novel tells how and why the narrator became "invisible," sought an underground refuge, and chose to remain there until, as he hopes, he can emerge into real rather than artificial light.

The narrator's earliest recollection is of a white stag "smoker" in the South in which, after the usual striptease, a group of Negro boys—including himself—entertain by boxing while blindfolded and by picking up coins from an electrified rug. At the close of the festivities, the narrator is made to deliver his recent commencement address. His reward is a scholarship to the state college for Negroes.

During his junior year at college, the narrator is assigned one day by Dr. Bledsoe to drive the visiting white benefactor, Mr. Norton, about the countryside. The sightseeing tour proves disastrous. First, the narrator unwisely allows Norton to meet an elderly Negro farmer, Jim Trueblood, who tells the horrified white man how, while abed with his wife and daughter, he mistakenly made love to his daughter. Ironically, though the local Negroes ostracize Trueblood, the white population is understanding and generous. Before Norton leaves—his agonized memories of his incestuous love for his own daughter stirred by the narrative—he gives Trueblood a hundred dollars. When the distraught Norton demands a drink, the narrator stops at the Golden Day, an inn and brothel where Negro inmates of a mental institution (most of them educated professional people whose advanced ideas qualify them for commitment) are brought for recreation under the supervision of a menacing attendant named Supercargo. One of the patients insists that Norton is his grandfather, and a prostitute genially strokes his forehead. Faint with terror and aghast when one patient, a former doctor, diagnoses him as an hysteric, Norton shrieks to be released. A brawl ensues and Norton's head is cut before the narrator gets him into the car.

For the trouble he has caused, the narrator is expelled. First, however, he listens to Dr. Bledsoe lecture him about the need to please white men and to acknowledge his own insignificance. "I had to be strong and purposeful to get where I am," Bledsoe says. "Yes, I had to act the nigger!" With that advice and a sealed letter of reference from Bledsoe, the narrator ventures North to search for identity beyond the black world that he had thought his.

Wherever the narrator displays his letter of reference, he is turned away. At last a homosexual whose father has turned the narrator away, tells him that the letter warns employers against hiring him. The homosexual offers the narrator employment as a valet or companion, is refused, and finally recommends that the narrator seek employment at the Liberty Paint Company. He is hired there to add the ingredients needed to make a special Government-contract paint known as Optic White and used specially on national monuments. To mix the paint, the narrator must add a specific number of drops of black until the black is dissolved and makes the white even more brilliant. Unfortunately, the narrator adds the wrong substance and allows the black to show.

He is given another chance to keep his job, but in a different department, as assistant to Lucius Brockway, an elderly Negro long employed in the boiler room, deep in the bowels of the factory. Brockway created the slogan "If It's Optic White, It's the Right White" and believes himself essential to the success of the company. In fact, his terror of being a Negro in a white company has made him a complete Uncle Tom, blindly loyal to the management, frantically suspicious of his fellow employees. When Brockway suspects the narrator of belonging to the union, he starts a violent fight and tricks the inexperienced narrator into overpressuring a boiler which explodes, nearly killing him. In the company hospital, the narrator is treated by electric shock that deprives him of memory and identity.

Released from the hospital, the narrator travels to Harlem

and, after a brief time in a "Y," rents a room from Mary Rambo who tries gently to orient the young man to his environment. Walking the streets of Harlem, he tries unsuccessfully to reassert his Negro identity by eating his favorite Negro food, baked yams. Later he tries to destroy the image of himself as Negro by smashing a cast-iron figurine of a Negro (used as a doorstop in his room) and tossing it away. But someone, thinking he has dropped the figure accidentally, follows him and returns it.

While his inward struggle continues, he is suddenly thrust into the violence of the outside world. Watching the eviction of an elderly Negro couple, he first holds off the bystanders who threaten the marshal, arguing that Negroes are "a law-abiding and a slow-to-anger people." Then, when the white marshal refuses to let the old people re-enter their apartment to pray, the narrator rouses the mob to action. They beat the marshal off and are carrying furniture back into the apartment when the police arrive. A handful of whites who have encouraged the Negroes during the fracas help the narrator escape from the police. One of them, Brother Jack, later invites the narrator to join his organization as a speaker for the underprivileged.

At the insistence of his new white friends, who have admired his skill in haranguing the mob, the narrator attends a party and enlists in the party of Brotherhood. Hired at a good salary, the narrator delivers his first address to a large group of Negroes assembled in a meeting hall. His subject—as in his eviction speech—is the dispossessed; his theme, "We'll be dispossessed no more." Despite the enthusiasm of the audience, Brother Jack and Hambro, the Brotherhood theoretician, condemn the narrator for his speech. They object to its emotional content, its evasion of principles. For the next four months, the narrator leaves the rostrum to study with Hambro the doctrines of scientific materialism. His lessons have a single purpose: to teach him to submerge his own deeply felt passion. "You will have freedom of action," he is told, "and you will be under strict discipline to the committee." Once more the narrator has stumbled into a blind alley from which he can emerge only as an invisible man.

In the arena of love, as in that of politics, the narrator discovers that he lacks identity. Sex-starved white women lust

after him as a stereotype of potency. One seduces him, and
another, Sybil, drunkenly demands that he rape her. When
she passes out, the narrator—who has not touched her—writes
in lipstick on her flesh, "Sybil, you were raped by Santa Claus.
Surprise."

One aim of the Brotherhood is to oppose the aggressive,
terroristic methods of Ras the Exhorter. Tod Clifton, youth
leader of the Brotherhood, takes the narrator along to help
disrupt a street meeting led by Ras. After a violent battle in
which they subdue Ras, Tod and the narrator listen to his
impassioned argument that the only possible cause they share
is the unity of blacks. Cooperation with white men is both
futile and treasonous. Tod retorts that this is emotion, not reason, and that what Ras asks is that the Negro plunge outside
the current of history.

Ironically, only a few weeks later, Tod (whose name in
German means "death") himself takes that plunge, fatally.
Disillusioned by party discipline, incapable of following Ras,
Tod symbolically destroys himself by peddling dancing Sambo
dolls in the street. When Tod punches a policeman who shoves
him, the policeman shoots him dead. Rejecting the party's
judgment of Tod as a traitor to their cause, the narrator delivers an eloquent funeral oration before a Harlem audience.
Ras, however, accuses the narrator of merely bandying words,
not avenging Tod's murder. No longer Ras the Exhorter but
Ras the Destroyer, the extremist leader incites the angry mob
to violence.

While the riot rages, the narrator has a series of strange encounters. A girl approaches him and addresses him as Rinehart, mistakenly thinking him her lover; a policeman calls
him by the same name, assuming him to be a local payoff
runner. Always using the name Rinehart, others mistake him
for a gambler, a bookie, and a minister. Stunned, the narrator
suddenly realizes that this total loss of identity—he is at once
all men and no man—has granted him absolute freedom from
responsibility to white or to black, to North or to South, to the
Brotherhood or to Ras. Denied existence and identity by the
external world, he can turn his gaze wholly inward and discover for himself who he believes himself to be.

When Ras, mounted on a horse and carrying a spear, tries
to have the mob apprehend and hang the narrator, the narrator

knows that he wants desperately to live. Hanging, he realizes, will not make him visible any more than assenting to the white man's will or rising in anger against the white man. He flees from the scene of danger and plunges into an open man-hole. In the underground world—where he opens his narrative—he continues to contemplate his place in the universe. Shorn of illusion, he is neither barren of hope nor empty of love. "There's a possibility," he says as the novel ends, "that even an invisible man has a socially responsible role to play."

Critical Opinion

The years since World War II have produced several outstanding novels by Negro writers, Richard Wright's *Native Son* and James Baldwin's *Go Tell It on the Mountain* among the very best. But Ellison's *Invisible Man*, many critics insist, cannot be classed simply as a novel by a Negro about Negroes. It is rather a novel about mankind written by a man of enormous skill and profound sensibility.

Ellison's vision has its sources in Dostoievski's insight into the "underground man," the alienated, isolated, neurotic child of disorder and chaos. But Ellison's expression of the theme is wholly American. Folk materials, evangelical fervor, and the language of jazz, especially the blues, endow the narrative with nervous, rhythmic energy. About the blues, for example, Ellison has written that it "is an impulse to keep the painful details and episodes of a brutal experience alive in one's aching consciousness . . . and to transcend it, not by consolation of philosophy, but by squeezing from it a near-tragic, near-comic lyricism." All of these techniques combine in *Invisible Man* to render what Ellison has called "the bright magic of the fairy tale."

The fairy tale he tells is grim and gothic, a nightmarish story of violence and guilt narrated by a haunted hero. Nevertheless, the very irrationality of the narrator's situation—whether in the illuminated basement or in the raging world above—breeds a sense of the comic as well as of the tragic. Deeply involved as he is in the drama of seeking his identity, the narrator maintains a certain ironic detachment. By refusing to recognize him as a man, both white and black races have cloaked him in invisibility. Thus garbed, he is utterly alone, but he can also see those about him and judge them for their failures. More important, he can begin to recognize himself and perhaps discover the selfhood he has never really known.

The novel is an existential work because the hero sloughs off all abstract notions about reality and attains a total freedom that demands choice and a course of action. In his underground habitat, the narrator must reevaluate everything afresh. Only then can he possibly venture forth confident of his own existence. Although the narrator is a Negro, experiencing the agony of blackness in a white society, he emerges symbolically as Everyman. His problem of self-discovery is a universal one affecting men of all races.

The Author

Ralph Ellison was born and educated in Oklahoma City, and later won a scholarship to Tuskegee Institute where he majored in music. In 1936 he came to New York City to study musical composition and sculpture. A friendship with Richard Wright, already famous as the author of *Native Son,* encouraged him to write. During the seven years he was writing *Invisible Man,* Ellison worked as photographer, jazz trumpeter, and waiter.

Invisible Man remains Ellison's only published novel, though one chapter of a second novel has appeared in *Partisan Review.* Meanwhile, since winning the National Book Award in 1952 for his first novel, he has published several short stories, critical and sociological essays, and reviews in *Horizon* and *The Saturday Review,* among other publications. In addition, he has lectured widely and taught courses in literature and creative writing at Bard College and, currently, at Rutgers University.

The Adventures of
Augie March

by

SAUL BELLOW (1915–)

Main Characters

Augie March—The picaresque hero, fiercely dedicated to a free-style pursuit of his fate. Sympathetically open-minded and insatiably curious, he refuses to commit himself to any of the creeds that shape human destiny.

Simon March—Augie's elder brother, intelligent but ruthless in his quest for wealth and power.

Georgie March—The youngest March, a gentle idiot, as happy in an institution as he was at home.

Mrs. March—Their mother, deserted by her husband, a kindly, well-meaning woman but passive and ineffectual.

Grandma Lausch—An aged Russian-Jewish boarder at the March home. Proud, Machiavellian, she influences the lives of the young March brothers.

William Einhorn—A total paralytic, but a man of enormous energy and gusto—economic, intellectual, and sexual; a major influence in Augie's youth.

Tillie Einhorn—His patient, devoted, and self-effacing wife.

Arthur Einhorn—The Einhorns' self-centered, self-indulgent, and wholly unproductive Harvard-educated son.

Mrs. Renling—A wealthy, motherly woman who vainly undertakes to adopt Augie and make him "successful."

Thea Fenchel—A rich, passionate, and lovely young woman who pursues men, eagles, and iguanas with equal determination.

Stella Chesney—A beautiful actress, a mildly compulsive liar, and the woman with whom Augie more or less settles down at last.

Mimi Villars—An intellectual waitress, tough and experienced, who is willing to suffer for the only cause she holds dear —love.

Hooker Frazer—Mimi's lover (succeeded by Arthur Einhorn), a brilliant political theorist and a Trotskyite.

Charlotte Magnus Einhorn—Simon March's wife, a shrewd complement to her husband.

Renee—Simon's attractive, predatory mistress.

Robey—An eccentric millionaire engaged in writing a history of happiness from the point of view of the rich.

Harold Mintouchian—A wealthy Armenian lawyer and businessman, worldly, cynical.

Hyman Basteshaw—A ship's carpenter, but also a gifted, if mad, scientist who insists he has discovered a method to create protoplasm.

Tom Gorman, Jimmy Klein, Sylvester—Boyhood friends of Augie's.

Padilla, Kayo Obermark, Clem Tambow—Friends of Augie's at the university.

Hilda Novinson, Sophie Geratis, Esther Fenchel—Onetime loves in Augie's life.

Wiley Moulton, Iggy, Oliver—Expatriate friends of Thea's in Mexico.

The Story

Narrator of his own inexhaustible experience, Augie March begins with his boyhood in Chicago. Poor and Jewish, Augie starts life economically and socially alienated, yet he is neither bitter nor vengeful, only eager to absorb the knowledge and experience he hopes will help him discover a "good enough fate" to live by.

"A man's character," Augie quotes from Heraclitus, "is his fate," and Augie learns at the outset that he must shape as well as be shaped by his encounters with life. Grandma Lausch, his first "teacher," sets for him and his brother Simon a single goal—to rise above the laboring class. But though she teaches Augie at the age of eight how to deceive municipal officials into issuing free eyeglasses for his mother, she cannot force Augie into the mold she envisions for him. Simon, determined to succeed, labors shrewdly and effectively, but Augie shows little inclination to accept the conventional notions of successful living. At school and at work, Simon easily outshines his younger brother. Moreover, when Simon cheats, he escapes unscathed; Augie is usually caught or outwitted. As a twelve-year-old elf, for example, working with Santa Claus, Augie and his fellow elf expropriate every tenth quarter the children pay to receive a surprise package. A store inventory quickly reveals the elfin duplicity, and Augie suffers humiliations and ostracism at home.

By the time Augie enters high school, his ties to his family have weakened. His beloved idiot brother, Georgie, has been institutionalized, and Grandma Lausch, her ambitions for her chosen family far short of fulfillment, has suffered a decline and accepted with her usual dignity a place in an old folks' home. In her stead, Augie finds as his new mentor William Einhorn, "the first superior man I knew." Hired as the paralyzed Einhorn's general factotum, Augie carries him about on his back, dresses him, runs his errands, and listens attentively to his searching comments about life. Einhorn, Augie realizes, refuses to be intimidated by his physical limitations. All life beckons him, and Einhorn reaches out in all directions to absorb and, if possible, to dominate. Augie admires his courage and genius but not his cheapness and occasional cruelty.

When the stock market crash of 1929 ruins Einhorn, Augie yields to the pleas of a local tough, Joe Gorman, to participate in a robbery. Although he eludes capture, Augie has been deeply shaken and sickened by the experience. When Einhorn, now managing one of his few remaining properties, a poolroom, hears of Augie's escapade, he berates him as a fool. He perceives, however, a reason for Augie's adventure outside the law. "You've got *opposition* in you," he observes. "You don't slide through everything."

Gratified by this astute insight into his character, Augie rewards Einhorn by rejecting his efforts to shape his life, even as he had fended off Grandma Lausch and Joe Gorman. Einhorn does not, however, disappear from Augie's expanding world. As a graduation present for Augie, Einhorn takes him to a brothel.

That fall Augie joins his brother Simon at the college, but again finds himself disinclined to accept the rigorous discipline of the academic community. Nor does he apply himself enthusiastically to the demands of his sales job in the basement of a department store. Fortunately, he is hired to sell luxury items in a suburban sporting-goods store. Leaving school to work for the Renlings, owners of the store, Augie is thrust into a millionaire's world. Moreover, Mrs. Renling, a middle-aged woman as forceful and energetic as Grandma Lausch, determines to make the attractive youth her protégé, paying his tuition for courses in advertising, enrolling him in a riding school, and taking him along as her companion at a health resort.

At the wealthy vacation spot, Augie sees the beautiful and fabulously wealthy Fenchel sisters, Esther and Thea, and after a brief inward struggle, decides that he has fallen in love with Esther. For days Augie follows her about at a distance, fantasying their love for one another, aspiring yet not daring to try to win her. When at last he musters courage to ask Esther for a date, she flatly refuses him. Augie promptly faints. Later, Thea tells him that she and Esther thought he was Mrs. Renling's gigolo. Disabused of that false notion, Thea goes on to tell Augie of her own love for him. She offers herself to the confused and embarrassed young man, who manages to flee.

Mrs. Renling, although annoyed at Augie's indifference, decides to adopt him. She tempts him with wealth and status, hinting that through these he may gain access to the enviable world of the Fenchel sisters. Uncertain, Augie seeks Einhorn's advice, but discovers that his erstwhile mentor is too involved with a new mistress to concern himself about Augie's problem. When Augie realizes that yielding to Mrs. Renling would necessitate surrendering his fate to another's will, he refuses the offer and departs.

After trying a variety of odd jobs, Augie encounters his

old tempter, Joe Gorman, now engaged in smuggling immigrants across the Canadian border. Halfheartedly Augie joins Joe, but takes flight when police trap them in the stolen car they have been using. Hours later, taking refuge in a crowd, Augie sees Joe in the custody of the police. For the next few weeks, Augie rides the rails and, after spending a night in jail as a suspect, hitchhikes back to Chicago.

During Augie's absence, Simon, desperately in love with Cissie Flexner, has tried in many ways to earn enough money to marry. He has sold the furniture from their apartment and moved their mother in with neighbors. He has borrowed money from Einhorn (on the pretext of sending it to Augie) and lost it in a crooked baseball pool. When, after all his effort, Cissie breaks their engagement and marries an older cousin of the Marches', Simon goes berserk and lands in jail—the same night that Augie, on the road, is imprisoned. When the brothers are reunited, Simon swears to Augie that henceforth he will fix upon success, not love. Within weeks after his statement of purpose, Simon wins Charlotte Magnus, chosen because her father owns a successful chain of coal-yards. Simon's rise is swift, but Augie senses in it a "consent to death." As Simon grows more opulent and more powerful, he also becomes more vicious and, as Augie constantly fears, suicidal—qualities hitherto alien to his personality, now apparent as a kind of self-imposed punishment for having sold his birthright of independence.

While Simon surges toward a success he is secretly ashamed of, Augie continues his quest for his personal destiny. As always, his approach veers from the conventional. From a young Mexican student, Padilla, Augie learns the art of shoplifting scholarly texts which are much in demand by college students. Though Augie proves adept, he irritates his accomplice by insisting upon reading the pilfered texts before he sells them. Although his income suffers, Augie's intellectual resources grow enormously.

At the rooming house where he lives and carries on his business, Augie befriends the mistress of Hooker Frazer, a political-science student who is one of his best, though non-paying, customers. Mimi Villars, Frazer's girl, is like Augie in her opposition to accepted norms. But whereas Augie is still seeking his fate, Mimi has already—to her endless pain

—found hers in love. Ironically, when Mimi becomes pregnant, Frazer (who already has a wife) disappears and it is Augie who sees her through an abortion.

Helping Mimi extricate herself from her predicament plunges Augie into one of his own. For several months Simon has been trying to force Augie to share the delights of marriage and wealth. He has involved Augie in a mildly amorous arrangement with Lucy Magnus, Charlotte's sister. Almost ready to drift into Simon's prearranged order for his life, Augie stops short. What halts his final step toward marriage is the report to Lucy and her family—communicated by a cousin—that Augie and a young woman were seen together leaving an abortionist's office. Lucy and Simon banish Augie. Augie comments, "I didn't mount the step of power. I could have done so from love, but not to get to the objective."

Once more Augie ventures forth in search of his fate, and soon embarks on the wildest of his many adventures. For a brief time he works as a labor organizer for the C.I.O. and takes his recreation with a Greek girl named Sophie Geratis. One evening his recreation is disturbed by a knock at his door. Thea Fenchel, his ardent pursuer of an earlier time, stands at the door. Conscious that Augie is not alone, Thea decently asks only that Augie call her at her hotel. The next day, after he has been beaten by a goon squad from an opposing union and decides that his fate does not include political or labor leadership, Augie hastens to Thea. They embrace passionately when they meet in the elevator, and in Thea's apartment their ardor continues unabated for the next three days.

En route to Mexico to obtain a divorce and to hunt iguana with a man-trained eagle, Thea urges Augie to join her. Deeply conscious of Thea's obsessive need to have her way, Augie knows, too, that he has never been so fully absorbed with or by another human being. In love, he accepts, and for a considerable time, as he says, "I followed her sense wherever it went." Once Thea has arranged the details of their trip (insisting that Augie take whatever cash he needs from the refrigerator where the bills lie mingled with salad leaves), the two set forth on their first enterprise to purchase and train an eagle.

With Thea as his tutor, Augie undertakes the physical task

of training the eagle, not, however, without wondering why training an eagle should seem to Thea an adventure even greater than their love.

They settle in Acatla at Thea's Mexican home, Casa Descuitada (Carefree House), and continue to train the eagle, now christened Caligula. Augie flinches as Caligula learns to kill and eat small lizards. Thea twits Augie for his sentimental objections, arguing that natural law cannot be altered for beasts or for men. Augie refuses to accept her creed and takes considerable pleasure in Caligula's fright when one of the lizards bites the eagle before dying. On the day of the supreme test, the hunting of the iguana, Caligula disproves Thea's assumption and demonstrates that even eagles can be "in opposition," and can seek an independent fate. Thus, though Caligula soars gracefully above the iguana and swoops murderously down for the kill, the violent resistance the iguana offers convinces Caligula that discretion is better than valor. As Thea shrieks in fury, Caligula flies back to Carefree House and safety. Augie's compassion and affection for the bird increase immeasurably.

Some days later Augie persuades Thea to give Caligula another chance. This time, with Caligula perched on his gauntlet and himself mounted on Old Bizcocho, Augie climbs high into the hills while Thea waits just below to stir iguana from their rocky hiding places. At the critical moment Augie spurs the horse downhill and releases Caligula. But the slope is too steep, the horse balks, throws Augie, then kicks him in the head. Caligula performs as before, sighting the iguana and soaring back to its perch in Carefree House. Disgusted with the bird's cowardice and Augie's horsemanship, Thea ships the bird to a zoo and confines Augie to the house. During Augie's confinement (which he welcomes as a refuge from hunting), Thea goes off daily to hunt rare snakes.

Conscious that they are drifting apart, Augie offers Thea marriage on the day her divorce becomes official. But she refuses, fearful of jeopardizing her inheritance. To restore their happiness, Thea argues, Augie must begin again to hunt with her and cease his bouts of drinking and gambling with the American expatriates of their community. Thea despises the "faulty humanity" Augie tolerates. They try to reconcile their differences, but a party given by Oliver, one of the

American colony, forces the issue. Leaving Thea to dance with a man she loathes, Augie walks into a garden with Stella Chesney, Oliver's mistress. Stella begs for Augie's help, telling him that her lover is about to be arrested by American agents and that she wants to escape. Stella offers herself to Augie if he will take her to Mexico City. Augie, however, volunteers only to take her to a nearby town where she can find transportation. As Augie tries to crank his ancient station wagon to begin the journey, Thea discovers the two of them and stalks off angrily. Augie and Stella drive off into the hills, where the car stalls on the edge of a precipice, compelling them to stay there for the night. Almost instinctively they make love. The next morning, with the aid of natives, Augie drives Stella to Cuernavaca, lends her money to make good her escape, and returns to Carefree House.

His reception by Thea is predictably hostile. She makes clear that their relationship is at an end. Her emotions, she insists, are stirred less by jealousy than by disappointment. Augie's quick humanitarian responses, she protests, leave him open to all people and thus prevent the absolute commitment to idealism she had hoped they might share. Augie's retort that his indulgence of her eccentricity about hunting deserves at least some reciprocal tolerance infuriates Thea and she leaves. Frustrated and miserable, Augie kicks open all of Thea's snake boxes and wrecks the house furnishings. When he calms down, he ponders the failure of his affair. He realizes that once more he has discovered that he cannot be shaped absolutely by another person, even one with whom he is deeply in love. Nevertheless, he believes that Thea's determination to triumph over nature represents a quality he must further explore if he is to achieve roundness and fullness as a personality. He determines to pursue her and beg her to renew their love. As he sets out, however, one of Thea's friends tells him that Thea already has another lover, one she entertained before Augie and during the time he was recuperating from his injury. Shattered but persistent, Augie goes to Thea, but she tells him she no longer feels anything toward him but indifference.

Despondent, Augie journeys back toward Chicago. En route he is briefly involved in a plot to save Trotsky from assassination. In Chicago he visits his brother Georgie and his mother, contemplating sadly what he regards as their imprisonment in mental and old-age institutions. Whatever else he may lack, Augie remains deeply proud of his freedom. When his mother asks him whether he is making a living, he replies, "I *am* living." Renewing his long-broken union with Simon, Augie feels deep pity for his brother, now a millionaire, a bully, and a lecherous brute. Augie denies to Simon that he feels superior because he has no money, but to himself Augie admits that money, though good to have, must follow the discovery of a fate significant enough to tolerate prosperity. And Augie has not yet discovered that fate.

As he visits his old friends—Mimi, Einhorn, Padilla, and others—he listens as each argues a cause for Augie's failure to have made his mark in the world. He has placed too much faith in the good, ignored the basic evil that dominates the universe, failed to adjust to reality, thought too abstractly. Acknowledging to himself the partial validity of each claim, Augie nevertheless refuses "to lead a disappointed life." It has not been at all bad, he observes, to have been "a runner after good things, servant of love, embarker on schemes, recruit of sublime ideas, and Good Time Charlie."

Augie, nevertheless, decides to find a career and returns to the university, taking courses to prepare for teaching. He envisages a school in some idyllic pastoral setting where children can learn and experience the joy of living. To support himself, he accepts a job assisting an eccentric millionaire, Robey, who has embarked on a history of happiness as the rich have experienced it. Plunged into histories of materialism, Augie discovers that he has no desire, as Robey has, to turn his complex knowledge to any single, directed purpose. "I don't want to prove a single thing," he tells himself, and adds that he has no compelling need "to beat life at its greatest complication and *meshuggah* power, so I want to start in lower down and simpler."

The outbreak of World War II disrupts Augie's determination to simplify his life. After an operation for a hernia suffered when he was unhorsed, he joins the merchant marine. While he is in training, Stella Chesney suddenly re-enters his life. They fall in love and plan to marry as soon as possible. In the happy weeks preceding their marriage, Augie meets and holds long discussions with Harold Mintouchian, the wealthy lover of one of Stella's friends. Mintouchian lectures Augie about love and reality, insisting that love, for example, is a form of adultery, an expression of the need for change, and that a variety of loves affirms the principle of reality that moves the universe. Although he recognizes once more the partial truth of Mintouchian's thesis, Augie (especially because he is in love) refuses to accept it. He observes, too, with ironic detachment, that Mintouchian, who is married, knows that his mistress is cheating him.

Two days after their wedding, Augie ships out and Stella leaves for Alaska to join a USO troupe. Off the Canary Islands, Augie's ship is torpedoed and he finds himself adrift in a lifeboat with Hyman Basteshaw, the ship's carpenter, a mad genius who has been fired from six universities for claiming to have discovered a technique for making protoplasm. A self-designated superman, Basteshaw rejects Augie's pleas that they use every means possible to locate a rescue ship. Basteshaw intends that they reach the Canary Islands, have themselves interned, and continue with experiments on protoplasm. Basteshaw fells Augie and binds him, but during the night Augie frees himself and secures the now-feverish madman. The next day they are rescued, briefly hospitalized, and soon afterward, Augie returns home.

After the war, Augie and Stella live abroad, chiefly in Paris, where she makes movies. Though he loves her, Augie learns that his wife has a compulsion to lie and that she has hidden from him her involvement with a previous lover, one more powerful and influential than her American refugee in Mexico. But Augie accepts these weaknesses in his determination to simplify his life and have a family. As the novel ends, Augie is on a business trip as an agent for Mintouchian. Traveling with him on her way to visit relatives is the Marches' maid Jacqueline, an ugly woman but consummately proud of her sex appeal. Observing her stubborn refusal to accept disappointment in life, Augie feels renewed in his faith in his own quest for a suitable fate. He thinks of himself as a "laughing creature, forever rising up," refusing to be cowed by nature or man, a kind of Columbus eternally exploring the unknown. "I may well be a flop at this line of endeavor," he thinks, but adds, "Columbus too thought he

was a flop, probably, when they sent him back in chains.
Which didn't prove there was no America."

Critical Opinion

In an interview shortly after publication of *The Adventures of
Augie March*, Saul Bellow pointed out that, a Chicagoan, like
his hero, he nevertheless composed not a single word of his
novel in that city. Most of it was written in Paris, but sections
were set down in Austria, Italy, Long Island, and New Jersey,
as well as in the Pennsylvania Station in New York and in
his publisher's office. What Bellow found significant in this
he has summed up thus: "I do not see what else we can do
than refuse to be condemned with a time or a place. We are
not born to be condemned but to live."

In theme and in style, *The Adventures of Augie March*
bears out the validity of Bellow's observation. Breaking from
the modern novel's concern with form and structure, Bellow's
has the shapeless, episodic structure of the picaresque novel,
a twentieth-century version of Henry Fielding's *Tom Jones*.
Out of the apparent chaos, however, emerges an order imposed by sheer exuberance for living, a vibrant affirmation of
the joy contained in infinite variety and ceaseless experimen-
tation.

But although Augie is above all else determined to remain
a free man, he is by no means indifferent to the claims of
the world about him. What he does, however, is to sift ideas
and experiences through his consciousness, impatiently rejecting whatever he believes to be temporary or irrelevant.
Lured by the temptations of body and mind, he refuses to be
trapped by either. Conscious of the alienation of man—
especially the Jew—he assumes the role of the opposition
but he rejects flight. If the family has been dissolved as a
cohesive unit in modern life, then man must search for other
means to come to terms with the world. In other words, no
matter how hostile the world or society, Bellow insists that
man remains. Those men who, like Simon, surrender to the
conventions accepted by the Establishment, face psychic
annihilation. Augie discovers the comic possibilities in man's
tragic condition and, at the end, sees himself as *homo ridens*,

man laughing. Experience suffered, enjoyed, but always felt to the utmost—this becomes the measure of affirmation in Bellow's version of modern society.

Apart from its complex philosophic implications, *The Adventures of Augie March* enthralls readers with its marvelous control of language, its seemingly endless range of narrative invention, and its brilliant array of unforgettable characters. Like Augie—who accepts all of these people regardless of their faults—the characters possess an animation and vivacity that quicken interest and never let it flag. In an age when the fashionable literary attitude seems to be one of despair, Saul Bellow has placed himself in opposition. Without sinking to the banal or the sentimental, he has expressed a resoundingly vigorous affirmation of life.

The Author

Youngest of four sons of Russian immigrants, *Saul Bellow* was born in Canada and moved to Chicago nine years later. Schooled in Chicago, which he regards as his cultural home, Bellow left the University of Chicago after two years and completed his course at Northwestern where he was graduated with honors in anthropology and sociology. A brief venture into graduate study proved abortive, and Bellow, just married, turned at once to the writing that has since preoccupied him. He has taught at several colleges, most recently the University of Chicago.

Bellow's first novel, *Dangling Man* (1944), deals with the anxiety of a young man awaiting his call to the Army. Critics found promise rather than fulfillment in this novel, but felt more hopeful about his second novel, *The Victim* (1947). At first glance an analysis of anti-Semitism, *The Victim* penetrates to far deeper levels, searching beyond the relationships between Jew and Gentile for ways in which man can translate alienation to reconciliation. With the appearance of *The Adventures of Augie March* in 1953, Bellow's reputation reached its height, and he won the National Book Award for distinguished fiction. In *Seize the Day* (1956), a short novel, Bellow again deals—less melodramatically but perhaps more poignantly than in *Augie March*—with man's need to recognize the absurdity of his world, yet to live in it as well as he can. *Henderson, the Rain King* (1959) pursues a similar theme but locates the action in Africa. Bellow's most recent novel, *Herzog* (1964), acclaimed by many critics as his finest novel thus far, deals with the spiritual crisis confronting Moses Herzog, a Canadian-born college professor whose second marriage has just collapsed. In 1964 Bellow's first play, *The Last Analysis,* was produced on Broadway.

The Assistant

by

BERNARD MALAMUD (1914–)

Main Characters

Morris Bober—A kindly, gentle, long-suffering Jewish grocery owner.

Ida Bober—His constantly complaining but wholly devoted wife.

Helen Bober—Their daughter who longs without fulfillment for love, education, and a better life.

Karp—The smug owner of a liquor store adjoining Morris' grocery.

Frank Alpine—The young man with an affinity for suffering who is Morris' assistant and (for a while) Helen's lover.

Ward Minogue—The hoodlum son of an honest policeman.

Nat Pearl—A law student, bright and ambitious, with whom Helen has had a brief affair but whom she rejects because she thinks his interest in her is merely sexual.

The Story

Morris Bober, sixty, a kind and gentle Jew to whom hard luck clings, owns a grocery store in a run-down section of Brooklyn. His wife, Ida, complains incessantly about their lot but devotedly helps him tend the store. Their daughter,

Helen, longs for college, for a larger and better life. But she works as a secretary, turning over most of her salary to her father to help him survive.

One night Karp, the owner of the flourishing liquor store next door, asks Morris to phone the police. Two men have been driving around the block and Karp suspects that they intend to break into his store. Karp closes the store and hurriedly drives off. The holdup men enter Morris' grocery instead. There is fifteen dollars in the register, but one of the men insists that Morris is hiding the rest. Though his companion tries to dissuade him, he hits Morris with his gun.

Morris, seriously injured, lies in bed for a week. During this time a tall, seedy, melancholy young man haunts the neighborhood. He is Frank Alpine, one of the two holdup men. Bad luck pursues Frank, too. He had been unwilling to take part in the robbery, but had been talked into it by Ward Minogue, the hoodlum son of an honest cop. He tried to dissuade Ward from striking Morris, and he gave the grocer a drink of water when Ward slapped him. Now, torn with guilt and obscurely attracted to his victim, he wants to atone for his part in the crime. When Morris recovers, Frank helps him carry cases of milk in the morning and cleans his store windows. He asks Morris for a job without wages—so that he can learn the business, he says. Morris, supported by Ida, refuses.

Then one night Morris finds Frank in his cellar which he has entered through a door that the grocer generally forgets to lock. Frank has been keeping alive by stealing milk and rolls from Morris. Over Ida's objections, Morris allows Frank to sleep on a couch for the night. Next morning, dragging in some milk boxes, Morris reopens the wound on his head and collapses. Frank takes over the store and manages it much more successfully than Morris. Ida, still suspicious, becomes almost reconciled to his remaining, even pressing five dollars of the meager profits on him despite his reluctance to take the money.

Troubled by conscience, Frank puts the seven and a half dollars that the robbery yielded him back into the store's register. He visits Ward, too, trying to recover the gun used in the robbery, but leaves without it. Ward accuses him of being after the "Jew girl." And in a way that Frank is yet unaware of, Ward is right. For Helen profoundly attracts Frank. He undresses her in fantasy, and once he secretly watches her as she undresses.

After Morris returns, Frank stays on. During the winter the two men exchange intimate conversations and come to like each other. Finally Frank gets to know Helen, too. He goes frequently to the library hoping to meet her there. One night they walk home together, confiding their ambitions to each other. She wants to go to college. He tells her he does, too.

Despite Helen's resistance, their relationship grows. She chooses books for Frank to read, listens to him sympathetically. At Christmas he gives her two expensive gifts. When she returns them, he throws them out. Quite by accident she sees them and rescues them from the rubbish. She finally accepts one of the gifts, and he promises to return the other to the store. Helen begins to respond seriously to Frank, even spurning dates with Nat Pearl, a law student with whom she had an affair but whom she has rejected. At last, acceding to Frank's urgings, she goes to his room where they kiss and neck. She refuses to sleep with him.

Ida has become increasingly suspicious of Helen's activities. She follows Helen one night and sees her kiss Frank. She pleads with her to stop seeing Frank, but Helen will not agree. Morris, though perturbed when Ida informs him that Helen has kissed Frank, refuses to fire Frank. Ida extracts a promise from Helen to go on a date with Nat. While she is with him, Morris catches Frank stealing—ringing up less money than he has taken in. While he has regularly pilfered in this fashion, he frequently has restored sums and he intends to repay the whole. Morris, despite his pain at discovering Frank's thefts, fires him. Disconsolate, Frank goes to meet Helen who has arranged to see him after her unsuccessful date with Nat.

At their meeting place Helen is accosted by Ward who attempts to rape her. Frank arrives in time to rout him, and Helen melts into his arms. But Frank, his desires long pent and heightened by the whiskey he has drunk, pulls her to the ground. She pleads, "Please not now, darling," but Frank takes her.

From this point on, Helen, disgusted with herself and with

men, will have nothing to do with Frank. One night Morris, by either design or accident, neglects to light the gas radiator and is saved by Frank from dying in the fumes. When Morris is taken to the hospital, Ida very reluctantly allows Frank to continue working at the store. A new grocery has opened around the corner and Morris' profits have shrunk disastrously. Frank gets a job as a counterman from 10 P.M. to 6 A.M. to supplement the store's earnings, snatching what sleep he can during the day. Helen, unaware of Frank's sacrifice, continues to snub him. And as soon as Morris is home from the hospital and able to tend the store again, he discharges Frank. Before that, however, Frank confesses that he was one of the holdup men, a fact that Morris has already deduced.

The grocery slides downhill rapidly. One day Morris is visited by an arsonist who offers, for a fee, to set fire to his store so that the grocer can collect the insurance. Morris declines, but that night he experiments, using a piece of celluloid in accordance with the directions he received. After setting the fire, though, he becomes terrified and smothers it —nearly burning himself in the process. Frank appears, having apparently been near the store, and saves Morris. But the grocer still will not take him back.

Another fire almost changes Morris' luck. Ward breaks into Karp's prosperous liquor store next door, gets drunk, and burns the store down—himself with it. Karp, Morris' longtime antagonist, offers to buy Morris' grocery and convert it into a liquor store. Morris and his family are delighted, but the change in luck proves illusory. On the last day of March, Morris, not wearing warm clothes, shovels snow away from the sidewalk fronting his store, catches pneumonia and dies. At his funeral, the rabbi lauds him for his endurance, his kindness, his probity—for his "Jewish heart."

Karp suffers a heart attack and backs out of his offer to buy the store. Once again Frank takes over, renting the store for more than it can possibly be worth. He works with Morris' dedication and slowly business picks up. Frank determines to send Helen to college. He approaches her, and while she is no longer furious with him, she abruptly turns down his offer. He insists that he owes her father a debt, confessing that he

was one of the robbers. Helen screams, denounces him, and
runs off.

Frank persists, nevertheless. He slaves in the store, denying
himself necessities to give Ida—and through her, Helen—
the money that will enable her to survive. He has become,
in fact, the poor, deprived, nearly hopeless man Morris was.
He has become, in effect, the man wedded to suffering—the
Jew. His affinity for pain convinces him. One day in April
he goes to the hospital to have himself circumcised. And
after Passover he becomes, literally, a Jew.

Critical Opinion

On its surface Bernard Malamud's *The Assistant* seems a
drab story, "a grocery-store idyl" bounded by pain on every
side. It is, nevertheless, "a lyrical marvel," has run through
dozens of printings, and is increasingly the subject of critical
comment.

One explanation for *The Assistant*'s vogue lies in its language. Malamud's ear for speech rhythms and nuances,
especially of the poor Jews who figure most largely in his
story, is nearly perfect. There is scarcely a line of dialogue
that does not ring true. It has, Ihab Hassan comments, "a
Hemingway clearness. . . , a kind of humility and courage,
but also a softness Hemingway never strove to communicate."

And the characters, too, convince through their authenticity.
Morris Bober, the gentle Jew, filled with suffering but retain-
ing pity and love; Helen, hemmed in by squalor and frustration, but still cleaving to her ideals; Frank Alpine, the man
with Bober's "talent for suffering," but enduring and even
hoping. These are people whom the reader is drawn to because of their essential humanity, which is, finally, more important than their condition.

The characters determine the novel's structure. It is taut
and pointed, every incident leading to Morris' death and
Frank's conversion. The dramatic effect, as Ben Siegel notes,
is enhanced by "implication, compression, and suggestion."
The Assistant is a short work, but powerful and major in its
effect and implications.

The Author

Bernard Malamud was born in Brooklyn, attended public schools there, then went to the City College of New York and later Columbia University where he received his master's degree. He has taught in several universities, mainly in the Pacific Northwest, and now lives in Vermont. He won the National Book Award for *The Magic Barrel* (1959) and was a Ford Foundation Fellow in 1959–61.

Malamud has written only three novels and two books of stories, yet he is generally ranked among the half-dozen best novelists in America. *The Natural* (1952) is a fantastic saga of a baseball player, "wild and nutty" but with mythic overtones. *The Assistant* (1957) is the moving record of Morris Bober, a Jew born to suffering, and his relations with his Italian assistant, Frank Alpine. *A New Life* (1961) tells, with mingled satire, indignation, and compassion, the story of S. Levin, "formerly a drunkard," who journeys from New York to teach in a college in the Pacific Northwest. The stories in his two collections, *The Magic Barrel* (1959) and *Idiots First* (1964), are alternately grotesque, poignant, bizarre, realistic—haunting fragments of experience.

Malamud's subjects are characteristically poor Jews, but the understanding penetration with which they are treated makes them representative of all mankind. Malamud's affirmation of the human spirit that transcends suffering and loneliness has been called "the humanism of the unfortunate."

Appendix

50 American Novels, arranged by date of publication

The Last of the Mohicans   1826
The Scarlet Letter   1850
Moby Dick   1851
The House of the Seven Gables   1851
Uncle Tom's Cabin   1851
The Adventures of Tom Sawyer   1876
The Adventures of Huckleberry Finn   1885
The Rise of Silas Lapham   1885
The Portrait of a Lady   1888
Looking Backward   1888
The Red Badge of Courage   1895
The Turn of the Screw   1898
Sister Carrie   1900
The Octopus   1901
The Call of the Wild   1903
Ethan Frome   1911
My Ántonia   1918
Winesburg, Ohio   1919
Jurgen   1919
Billy Budd—Foretopman   1924 (written between 1880 and 1890)
Babbitt   1925
An American Tragedy   1925
Arrowsmith   1925
The Great Gatsby   1925
The Sun Also Rises   1926
The Bridge of San Luis Rey   1927
Giants in the Earth   1927
A Farewell to Arms   1929
The Sound and the Fury   1929
Look Homeward, Angel   1929
The 42nd Parallel   1930
The Good Earth   1931
Light in August   1932

Mutiny on the Bounty   1932
Young Lonigan   1932
God's Little Acre   1933
Appointment in Samarra   1934
The Late George Apley   1937
The Grapes of Wrath   1939
The Heart Is a Lonely Hunter   1940
The Ox-Bow Incident   1940
The Human Comedy   1943
All the King's Men   1946
The Naked and the Dead   1948
The Catcher in the Rye   1951
Lie Down in Darkness   1951
The Old Man and the Sea   1952
Invisible Man   1952
The Adventures of Augie March   1953
The Assistant   1957

Bibliography

Books about the Novel

1. Aldridge, John W. (ed.). *Critiques and Essays on Modern Fiction, 1920–1951*. New York: The Ronald Press Company, 1952.

2. Bowen, Elizabeth. *Collected Impressions*. New York: Alfred A. Knopf, Inc., 1950.

3. Chase, Richard. *The American Novel and its Tradition*. New York: Anchor Books, Doubleday & Co., 1957.

4. Cowie, Alexander. *The Rise of the American Novel*. New York: American Book Co., 1951.

5. Fiedler, Leslie. *Love and Death in the American Novel*. New York: Meridian Books, Inc., The World Publishing Co., 1960.

6. Forster, E. M. *Aspects of the Novel*. New York: Harvest Books, Harcourt, Brace & World, 1956.

7. Goodman, Theodore. *The Technique of Fiction*. New York: Liveright Publishing Corp., 1955.

8. James, Henry. *The Future of the Novel: Essays in the Art of Fiction*, ed. Leon Edel. New York: Vintage Books, Random House, 1956.

9. Kazin, Alfred. *On Native Grounds: An Interpretation of Modern American Prose*. New York: Anchor Books (abridged edition), Doubleday & Co., 1956.

10. Lubbock, Percy. *The Craft of Fiction*. New York: Compass Books, The Viking Press, 1957.

11. Quinn, Arthur Hobson. *American Fiction: An Historical and Critical Survey*. New York: Appleton-Century-Crofts, 1936.

12. Trilling, Lionel. *The Liberal Imagination*. New York: Anchor Books, Doubleday & Co., 1953.

13. Van Doren, Carl. *The American Novel: 1780–1939*. New York: The Macmillan Company, 1940.

14. Wagenknecht, Edward. *Cavalcade of the American Novel*. New York: Holt, Rinehart and Winston, 1954.

Index

359